CHILTON'S

REPAIR & TUNE-UP GUIDE

FORD VANS
1961 to
1982

All ½, ¾ and 1 ton models:
E-100 • E-150 • E-200 • E-250 • E-300 • E-350

Vice President and General Manager JOHN P. KUSHNERICK
Managing Editor KERRY A. FREEMAN, S.A.E.
Senior Editor RICHARD J. RIVELE, S.A.E.
Editor RICHARD J. RIVELE, S.A.E.

CHILTON BOOK COMPANY
Radnor, Pennsylvania
19089

SAFETY NOTICE

Proper service and repair procedures are vital to the safe, reliable operation of all motor vehicles, as well as the personal safety of those performing repairs. This book outlines procedures for servicing and repairing vehicles using safe, effective methods. The procedures contain many NOTES, CAUTIONS and WARNINGS which should be followed along with standard safety procedures to eliminate the possibility of personal injury or improper service which could damage the vehicle or compromise its safety.

It is important to note that repair procedures and techniques, tools and parts for servicing motor vehicles, as well as the skill and experience of the individual performing the work vary widely. It is not possible to anticipate all of the conceivable ways or conditions under which vehicles may be serviced, or to provide cautions as to all of the possible hazards that may result. Standard and accepted safety precautions and equipment should be used when handling toxic or flammable fluids, and safety goggles or other protection should be used during cutting, grinding, chiseling, prying, or any other process that can cause material removal or projectiles.

Some procedures require the use of tools specially designed for a specific purpose. Before substituting another tool or procedure, you must be completely satisfied that neither your personal safety, nor the performance of the vehicle will be endangered.

Although information in this guide is based on industry sources and is as complete as possible at the time of publication, the possibility exists that the manufacturer made later changes which could not be included here. While striving for total accuracy, Chilton Book Company cannot assume responsibility for any errors, changes, or omissions that may occur in the compilation of this data.

PART NUMBERS

Part numbers listed in this reference are not recommendations by Chilton for any product by brand name. They are references that can be used with interchange manuals and aftermarket supplier catalogs to locate each brand supplier's discrete part number.

ACKNOWLEDGMENTS

The Chilton Book Company expresses its appreciation to the Ford Motor Company, Dearborn, Michigan for their generous assistance.

Copyright © 1982 by Chilton Book Company
All Rights Reserved
Published in Radnor, Pennsylvania, 19089 by Chilton Book Company

Manufactured in the United States of America
    4567890   109876543

Chilton's Repair & Tune-Up Guide: Ford Vans 1961–82
ISBN 0-8019-7171-3 pbk.
Library of Congress Catalog Card No. 81-70230

CONTENTS

Quick Reference Specifications For Your Vehicle

Fill in this chart with the most commonly used specifications for your vehicle. Specifications can be found in Chapters 1 through 3 or on the tune-up decal under the hood of the vehicle.

Tune-Up

Firing Order_____

Spark Plugs:

    Type_____

    Gap (in.)_____

Point Gap (in.)_____

Dwell Angle (°)_____

Ignition Timing (°)_____

    Vacuum (Connected/Disconnected)_____

Valve Clearance (in.)

    Intake_____   Exhaust_____

Capacities

Engine Oil (qts)

    With Filter Change_____

    Without Filter Change_____

Cooling System (qts)_____

Manual Transmission (pts)_____

    Type_____

Automatic Transmission (pts)_____

    Type_____

Front Differential (pts)_____

    Type_____

Rear Differential (pts)_____

    Type_____

Transfer Case (pts)_____

    Type_____

FREQUENTLY REPLACED PARTS

Use these spaces to record the part numbers of frequently replaced parts.

PCV VALVE

Manufacturer_____

Part No._____

OIL FILTER

Manufacturer_____

Part No._____

AIR FILTER

Manufacturer_____

Part No._____

General Information and Maintenance

HOW TO USE THIS BOOK

Chilton's Repair & Tune-Up Guide for the Ford Van is intended to teach you more about the inner workings of your van and save you money on its upkeep. The first two chapters will be used the most, since they contain maintenance and tune-up information and procedures. The following chapters concern themselves with the more complex systems of your van. Operating systems from engine through brakes are covered to the extent that we feel the average do-it-yourselfer should get involved. This book will not explain such things as rebuilding the differential for the simple reason that the expertise required and the investment in special tools make this task uneconomical. We will tell you how to change your own brake pads and shoes, replace points and plugs, and many more jobs that will save you money, give you personal satisfaction, and help you avoid problems.

A secondary purpose of this book is as a reference for owners who want to understand their van and/or their mechanics better. In this case, no tools at all are required.

Before removing any parts, read through the entire procedure. This will give you the overall view of what tools and supplies will be required.

The sections begin with a brief discussion of the system and what it involves, followed by adjustments, maintenance, removal and installation procedures, and repair or overhaul procedures. When repair is not considered feasible, we tell you how to remove the part and then how to install the new or rebuilt replacement. In this way, you at least save the labor costs. Backyard repair of such components as the alternator is just not practical.

Two basic mechanic's rules should be mentioned here. One, whenever the left side of the van or engine is referred to, it is meant to specify the driver's side of the van. Conversely, the right side of the van means the passenger's side. Secondly, most screws and bolts are removed by turning counterclockwise, and tightened by turning clockwise. Safety is always the most important rule. Constantly be aware of the dangers involved in working on an automobile and take the proper precautions. Use jackstands when working under a raised vehicle. Don't smoke or allow an exposed flame to come near the battery or any part of the fuel system. Always use the proper tool and use it correctly; bruised knuckles and skinned fingers aren't a mechanic's standard equipment. Always take your time and have patience; Once you have some experience, working on your van will become an enjoyable hobby.

TOOLS AND EQUIPMENT

It would be impossible to catalog each and every tool that you may need to perform all the operations included in this book. It would also not be wise for the amateur to rush out and buy an expensive set of tools on the theory that he may need one of them at some time. The best approach is to proceed slowly, gathering together a good quality set of those tools that are used most frequently. Don't be misled by the low cost of bargain tools. It is far better to spend a little more for quality, name brand tools. Forged wrenches, 10 or 12 point sockets and fine-tooth ratchets are by far preferable to their less expensive counterparts. As any good mechanic can tell you, there are few worse experiences than trying to work on a car or truck with bad tools. Your monetary savings will be far outweighed by frustration and mangled knuckles.

Begin accumulating those tools that are used most frequently; those associated with routine maintenance and tune-up. In addition to the normal assortment of screwdrivers and pliers, you should have the following tools for routine maintenance jobs:

1. SAE wrenches, sockets and combination open end/box end wrenches.
2. Jackstands—for support;
3. Oil filter wrench;
4. Oil filler spout or funnel;
5. Grease gun—for chassis lubrication;
6. Hydrometer—for checking the battery;
7. A low flat pan for draining oil;
8. Lots of rags for wiping up the inevitable mess.

In addition to the above items, there are several others that are not absolutely necessary, but are handy to have around. These include oil drying compound, a transmission funnel, and the usual supply of lubricants, antifreeze and fluids, although these can be purchased as needed. This is a basic list for routine maintenance, but only your personal needs can accurately determine your list of tools.

The second list of tools is for tune-ups. While the tools involved here are slightly more sophisticated, they need not be outrageously expensive. There are several inexpensive tach/dwell meters on the market that are every bit as good for the average mechanic as a $100.00 professional model. Just be sure that it goes to at least 1200–1500 rpm on the tach scale, and that it works on 4, 6, and 8 cylinder engines. A basic list of tune-up equipment could include:

1. Tach/dwell meter;
2. Spark plug wrench;
3. Timing light (preferably a DC light that works from the van's battery);
4. A set of flat feeler gauges;
5. A set of round wire spark plug gauges.

In addition to these basic tools, there are several other tools and gauges you may find useful. These include:

1. A compression gauge; The screw-in type is slower to use, but eliminates the possibility of a faulty reading due to escaping pressure.
2. A manifold vacuum gauge;
3. A test light;
4. An induction meter. This is used for determining whether or not there is current in a wire. These are handy for use if a wire is broken somewhere in a wiring harness. As a final note, you will probably find a torque wrench necessary for all but the most basic work. The beam type models are perfectly adequate, although the newer click type are more precise.

Special Tools

Normally, the use of special factory tools is avoided for repair procedures, since these are not readily available for the do-it-yourself mechanic. When it is possible to perform the job with more commonly available tools, it will be pointed out, but occassionally, a special tool was designed to perform a specific function and should be used. Before substituting another tool, you should be convinced that neither your safety nor the performance of the vehicle will be compromised.

Some special tools are available commercially from major tool manufacturers. Others for your Ford Van can be purchased from your dealer or from Owatonna Tool Co., Owatonna, Minnesota 55060.

SERVICING YOUR VEHICLE SAFELY

It is virtually impossible to anticipate all of the hazards involved with automotive maintenance and service but care and common sense will prevent most accidents.

The rules of safety for mechanics range from "don't smoke around gasoline," to "use the proper tool for the job." The trick to avoiding injuries is to develop safe work habits and take every possible precaution.

Do's

• Do keep a fire extinguisher and first aid kit within easy reach.

• Do wear safety glasses or goggles when cutting, drilling, grinding or prying. If you wear glasses for the sake of vision, then they should be made of hardened glass that can serve also as safety glasses, or wear safety goggles over your regular glasses.

• Do shield your eyes whenever you work around the battery. Batteries contain sulphuric acid; in case of contact with the eyes or skin, flush the area with water or a mixture of water and baking soda and get medical attention immediately.

• Do use safety stands for any under-car service. Jacks are for raising vehicles; safety stands are for making sure the vehicle stays raised until you want it to come down. Whenever the vehicle is raised, block the wheels remaining on the ground and set the parking brake.

• Do use adequate ventilation when working with any chemicals. Asbestos dust resulting from brake lining wear can cause cancer.

• Do disconnect the negative battery cable when working on the electrical system. The primary ignition system can contain up to 40,000 volts.

• Do follow manufacturer's directions whenever working with potentially hazardous materials. Both brake fluid and antifreeze are poisonous if taken internally.

• Do properly maintain your tools. Loose hammerheads, mushroomed punches and chisels, frayed or poorly grounded electrical cords, excessively worn screwdrivers, spread wrenches (open end), cracked sockets, slipping ratchets, or faulty droplight sockets can cause accidents.

• Do use the proper size and type of tool for the job being done.

• Do when possible, pull on a wrench handle rather than push on it, and adjust your stance to prevent a fall.

• Do be sure that adjustable wrenches are tightly adjusted on the nut or bolt and pulled so that the face is on the side of the fixed jaw.

• Do select a wrench or socket that fits the nut or bolt. The wrench or socket should sit straight, not cocked.

• Do strike squarely with a hammer to avoid glancing blows.

• Do set the parking brake and block the drive wheels if the work requires that the engine be running.

Don'ts

• Don't run an engine in a garage or anywhere else without proper ventilation— EVER! Carbon monoxide is poisonous; it is absorbed by the body 400 times faster than oxygen; it takes a long time to leave the human body and you can build up a deadly supply of it in your system by simply breathing in a little every day. You may not realize you are slowly poisoning yourself. Always use power vents, windows, fans or open the garage doors.

• Don't work around moving parts while wearing a necktie or other loose clothing. Short sleeves are much safer than long, loose sleeves. Hard-toed shoes with neoprene soles protect your toes and give a better grip on slippery surfaces. Jewelry such as watches, fancy belt buckles, beads or body adornment of any kind is not safe working around a van. Long hair should be hidden under a hat or cap.

• Don't use pockets for toolboxes. A fall or bump can drive a screwdriver deep into your body. Even a wiping cloth hanging from the back pocket can wrap around a spinning shaft or fan.

• Don't smoke when working around gasoline, cleaning solvent or other flammable material.

• Don't smoke when working around the battery. When the battery is being charged, it gives off explosive hydrogen gas.

• Don't use gasoline to wash your hands; there are excellent soaps available. Gasoline may contain lead, and lead can enter the body through a cut, accumulating in the body until you are very ill. Gasoline also removes all the natural oils from the skin so that bone dry hands will suck up oil and grease.

• Don't service the air conditioning system unless you are equipped with the necessary tools and training. The refrigerant, R-12, is extremely cold and when exposed to the air, will instantly freeze any surface it comes in contact with, including your eyes. Although the refrigerant is normally non-toxic, R-12 becomes a deadly poisonous gas in the presence of an open flame. One good whiff of the vapors from burning refrigerant can be fatal.

HISTORY

The Econoline series was introduced in 1961. Ford thus became the first American manufacturer to offer a van series as we now know it. The Econoline series included a pickup version, a closed van, a window van (with or without seating) and a Club Wagon series with two trim levels. The Club Wagons were given the Falcon designation.

Initial engine availability was limited to the 144 cid and 170 cid inline sixes. These were essentially the same engine.

One point of confusion concerning Ford van models is the exact date of the major styling change. All Ford vans through the 1967 model year have identical styling. All featured the mid-engine design and solid front axle. There was no 1968 model as such. The 1967 model run was extended into 1968 and the new-look, front engine, independent front suspension models were introduced in mid-1968 as 1969 models. In this book, 1967 models sold in 1968 will be referred to as

1968 models, in accordance with standard nomenclature.

In 1975 the styling was once again changed. The engine was moved much further forward giving greater interior room and an added margin of front end safety. Ford vans are now unique in offering a body-on-frame construction. This type of construction offers better handling, greater durability, and a quieter ride. A greater load carrying capability is also provided.

ROUTINE MAINTENANCE

Air Cleaner

Two types of air cleaners have been used: a replaceable paper type and an oil bath unit.

The procedure for cleaning an oil bath air cleaner and refilling the reservoir is as follows:

1. Unlock and open the engine compartment cover.

2. Remove the carburetor-to-air cleaner retaining wing nut. On a closed crankcase ventilation equipped engine, loosen the hose clamp at the air cleaner body and disconnect the hose. On the 240 and 300 six engine,

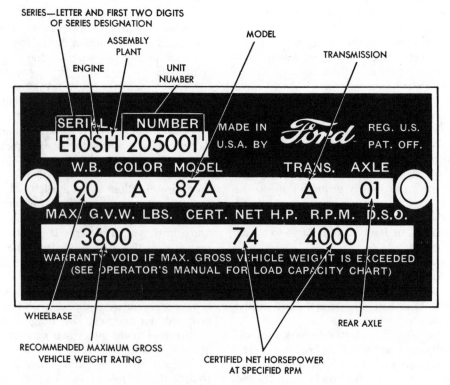

1961–62 Vehicle Identification Plate

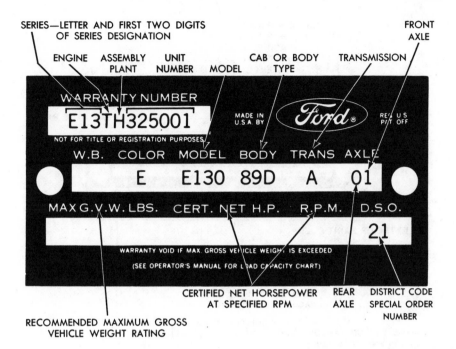

SERIES—LETTER AND FIRST TWO DIGITS
OF SERIES DESIGNATION

ENGINE   ASSEMBLY   UNIT   MODEL   CAB OR BODY   TRANSMISSION   FRONT
          PLANT   NUMBER   TYPE   AXLE

WARRANTY NUMBER   MADE IN   Ford   REG U S
E13TH325001   U.S.A BY   PAT OFF
NOT FOR TITLE OR REGISTRATION PURPOSES

W.B. COLOR MODEL BODY TRANS AXLE
E   E130   89D   A   01

MAX G.V.W. LBS.   CERT. NET H.P.   R.P.M.   D.S.O.
21

WARRANTY VOID IF MAX. GROSS VEHICLE WEIGHT IS EXCEEDED
(SEE OPERATOR'S MANUAL FOR LOAD CAPACITY CHART)

CERTIFIED NET HORSEPOWER   REAR   DISTRICT CODE
AT SPECIFIED RPM   AXLE   SPECIAL ORDER
                                    NUMBER

RECOMMENDED MAXIMUM GROSS
VEHICLE WEIGHT RATING

1963–65 Vehicle Identification Plate

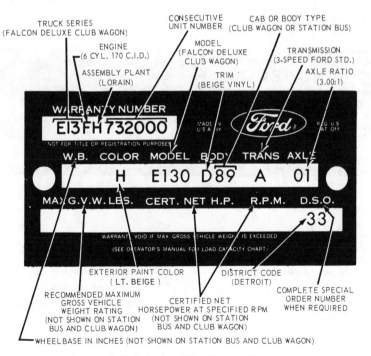

TRUCK SERIES   CONSECUTIVE   CAB OR BODY TYPE
(FALCON DELUXE CLUB WAGON) UNIT NUMBER   (CLUB WAGON OR STATION BUS)

                ENGINE   MODEL   TRANSMISSION
                (6 CYL. 170 C.I.D.) (FALCON DELUXE   (3-SPEED FORD STD.)
                                    CLUB WAGON)
           ASSEMBLY PLANT   AXLE RATIO
           (LORAIN)   TRIM   (3.00:1)
                                 (BEIGE VINYL)

WARRANTY NUMBER   MADE IN   Ford   REG U S
E13FH732000   U.S.A BY   PAT OFF
NOT FOR TITLE OR REGISTRATION PURPOSES

W.B. COLOR MODEL BODY TRANS AXLE
H   E130   D89   A   01

MAX G.V.W. LBS.   CERT. NET H.P.   R.P.M.   D.S.O.
33

WARRANTY VOID IF MAX GROSS VEHICLE WEIGHT IS EXCEEDED
(SEE OPERATOR'S MANUAL FOR LOAD CAPACITY CHART)

EXTERIOR PAINT COLOR   DISTRICT CODE
(LT. BEIGE)   (DETROIT)

RECOMMENDED MAXIMUM   COMPLETE SPECIAL
GROSS VEHICLE   CERTIFIED NET   ORDER NUMBER
WEIGHT RATING   HORSEPOWER AT SPECIFIED RPM WHEN REQUIRED
(NOT SHOWN ON STATION (NOT SHOWN ON STATION
BUS AND CLUB WAGON)   BUS AND CLUB WAGON)

WHEELBASE IN INCHES (NOT SHOWN ON STATION BUS AND CLUB WAGON)

1966 Vehicle Identification Plate

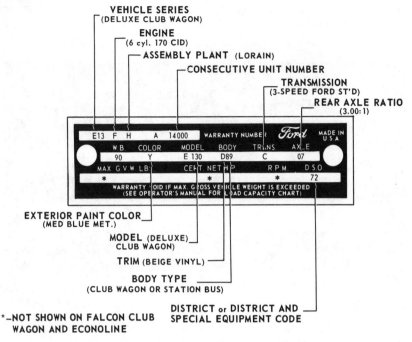

VEHICLE SERIES
(DELUXE CLUB WAGON)

ENGINE
(6 cyl. 170 CID)

ASSEMBLY PLANT (LORAIN)

CONSECUTIVE UNIT NUMBER

TRANSMISSION
(3-SPEED FORD ST'D)

REAR AXLE RATIO
(3.00:1)

EXTERIOR PAINT COLOR
(MED BLUE MET.)

MODEL (DELUXE)
CLUB WAGON)

TRIM (BEIGE VINYL)

BODY TYPE
(CLUB WAGON OR STATION BUS)

DISTRICT or DISTRICT AND
SPECIAL EQUIPMENT CODE

*–NOT SHOWN ON FALCON CLUB
WAGON AND ECONOLINE

1967–68 Vehicle Identification Plate

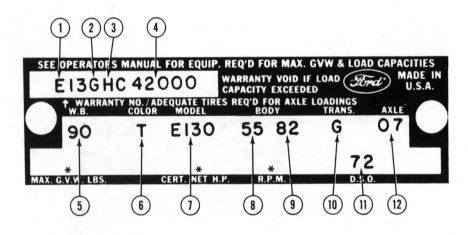

① VEHICLE SERIES CODE

② ENGINE CODE

③ ASSEMBLY PLANT CODE

④ CONSECUTIVE UNIT NUMBER

⑤ WHEELBASE (INCHES)

⑥ EXTERIOR PAINT COLOR CODE

⑦ MODEL CODE

⑧ TRIM CODE

⑨ BODY TYPE CODE

⑩ TRANSMISSION CODE

⑪ DISTRICT/SPEC. ORDER CODES

⑫ AXLE CODE

✱ NOT SHOWN FOR BRONCO OR CLUB WAGON

1969 Vehicle Identification Plate

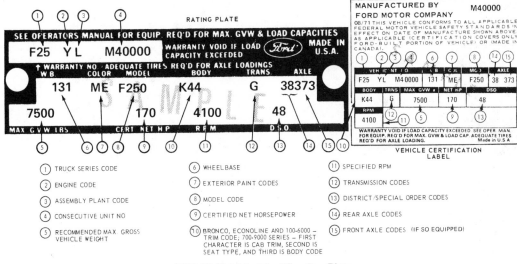

1970–72 Vehicle Identification Plate

1. TRUCK SERIES CODE
2. ENGINE CODE
3. ASSEMBLY PLANT CODE
4. CONSECUTIVE UNIT NO
5. RECOMMENDED MAX. GROSS VEHICLE WEIGHT
6. WHEELBASE
7. EXTERIOR PAINT CODES
8. MODEL CODE
9. CERTIFIED NET HORSEPOWER
10. BRONCO, ECONOLINE AND 100-6000 – TRIM CODE; 700-9000 SERIES – FIRST CHARACTER IS CAB TRIM, SECOND IS SEAT TYPE, AND THIRD IS BODY CODE
11. SPECIFIED RPM
12. TRANSMISSION CODES
13. DISTRICT/SPECIAL ORDER CODES
14. REAR AXLE CODES
15. FRONT AXLE CODES (IF SO EQUIPPED)

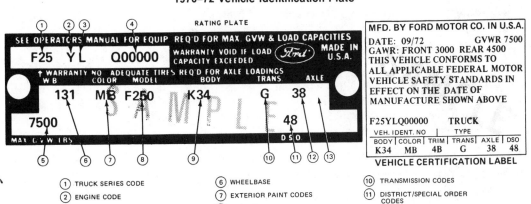

1973–77 Vehicle Identification Plate

1. TRUCK SERIES CODE
2. ENGINE CODE
3. ASSEMBLY PLANT CODE
4. CONSECUTIVE UNIT NO.
5. RECOMMENDED MAX. GROSS VEHICLE WEIGHT
6. WHEELBASE
7. EXTERIOR PAINT CODES
8. MODEL CODE
9. BRONCO, ECONOLINE AND 100-6000 – TRIM CODE; 700-9000 SERIES – FIRST CHARACTER IS CAB TRIM, SECOND IS SEAT TYPE, AND THIRD IS BODY CODE
10. TRANSMISSION CODES
11. DISTRICT/SPECIAL ORDER CODES
12. REAR AXLE CODES
13. FRONT AXLE CODES (IF SO EQUIPPED)

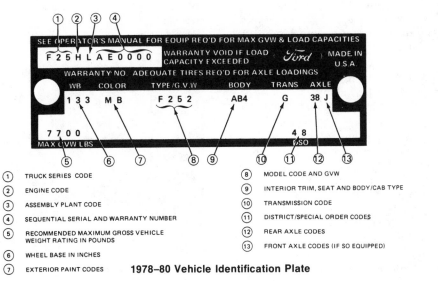

1. TRUCK SERIES CODE
2. ENGINE CODE
3. ASSEMBLY PLANT CODE
4. SEQUENTIAL SERIAL AND WARRANTY NUMBER
5. RECOMMENDED MAXIMUM GROSS VEHICLE WEIGHT RATING IN POUNDS
6. WHEEL BASE IN INCHES
7. EXTERIOR PAINT CODES
8. MODEL CODE AND GVW
9. INTERIOR TRIM, SEAT AND BODY/CAB TYPE
10. TRANSMISSION CODE
11. DISTRICT/SPECIAL ORDER CODES
12. REAR AXLE CODES
13. FRONT AXLE CODES (IF SO EQUIPPED)

1978–80 Vehicle Identification Plate

VIN Position Number	World Manufacturer Identifier			GVWR	Line, Series, Body Type			Engine Type	Check Digit	Model Year	Assy. Plant	Production Sequence Number				
	1	2	3	4	5	6	7	8	9	10	11	12	13	14	15	16	17
	First Section				Second Section							Third Section					
MPV VIN Bronco	1	F	M	E	U	1	5	G		B	L	A	0	0	0	0	1
Example Econoline Club Wagon	2	F	M	F	E	2	1	B		B	B	A	0	0	0	0	1

Positions 1-3 — World Manufacturer Identifier
Position 4 — GVWR
Positions 5, 6 & 7 — Line, Series, Body Type —
Position 8 — Engine Type
Position 9 — Check Digit
Position 10 — Model Year
Position 11 — Assembly Plant
Position 12 — Constant "A" until sequence number of 99,999 is reached, then index to a constant "B" and so on. Return to "A" at next model year.
Positions 13-17 — Sequence numbers begin at 00001

NOTE: All spaces provided for in the vehicle identification number must be occupied by one of the following ten numbers or twenty-three alphabetic letters.

Numbers: 1 2 3 4 5 6 7 8 9 0
Letters: A B C D E F G H J K L M N P R S T U V W X Y Z

1981–82 Vehicle Identification Label

remove the bolts securing the air cleaner body to the support brackets.

3. Remove the air cleaner assembly from the engine. Be careful not to spill the oil out of the air cleaner.

4. Remove the cover and drain the oil from the reservoir. Wash all of the air cleaner parts in a suitable cleaning solvent. Dry all of the parts with compressed air, or allow them to air dry.

5. Inspect the gasket between the oil reservoir chamber and the air cleaner body. Replace the gasket as necessary.

6. Saturate the filter element with clean engine oil.

7. Fill the oil reservoir to the full mark with engine oil. Use SAE 30 above 32° F and SAE 20 for lower temperatures.

8. Replace the air cleaner assembly on the carburetor and tighten the wing nut.

NOTE: *Check the air filter more often if the vehicle is operated under unusually dusty conditions and replace or clean it as necessary.*

The procedure for replacing the paper air cleaner element is as follows:

1. Unlock and open the engine compartment cover.

2. Remove the wing nut holding the air cleaner assembly to the top of the carburetor.

3. Disconnect the crankcase ventilation hose at the air cleaner and remove the entire air cleaner assembly from the carburetor.

4. Remove and discard the old filter element, and inspect the condition of the air cleaner mounting gasket. Replace the gasket as necessary.

5. Install the air cleaner body on the car-

buretor so that the word FRONT faces toward the front of the vehicle.

6. Place the new filter element in the air cleaner body and install the cover and tighten the wing nut. If the word TOP appears on the element, make sure that the side the word appears on is facing up when the element is in place.

7. Connect the crankcase ventilation hose to the air cleaner.

PCV Valve

Check the PCV valve to see if it is free and not gummed up, stuck or blocked. To check the valve, remove it from the engine and work the valve by sticking a screwdriver in the crankcase side of the valve. It should move. It is possible to clean the PCV valve by soaking it in a solvent and blowing it out with compressed air. This can restore the valve to some level of operating order. This

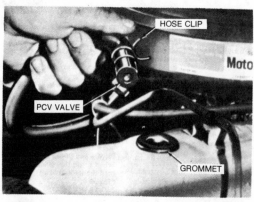

Removing the PCV valve from a 6 cylinder engine

COMPLETE VEHICLES

(UNITED STATES)

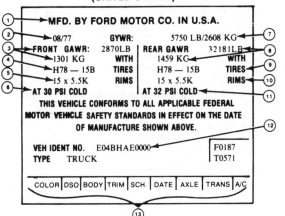

```
① ──► MFD. BY FORD MOTOR CO. IN U.S.A.
② ──► 08/77        GYWR:        5750 LB/2608 KG ◄── ⑦
③ ►FRONT GAWR:  2870LB | REAR GAWR    3218 1LB◄── ⑧
④ ──►1301 KG         WITH  | 1459 KG          WITH
⑤ ──►H78 — 15B    TIRES | H78 — 15B     TIRES ◄── ⑨
      15 x 5.5K        RIMS  | 15 x 5.5K      RIMS ◄── ⑩
⑥ ──►AT 30 PSI COLD       | AT 32 PSI COLD ◄── ⑪
      THIS VEHICLE CONFORMS TO ALL APPLICABLE FEDERAL
   MOTOR VEHICLE SAFETY STANDARDS IN EFFECT ON THE DATE
            OF MANUFACTURE SHOWN ABOVE.                 ◄── ⑫

   VEH IDENT NO.   E04BHAE0000 ◄──        | F0187
   TYPE      TRUCK                        | T0571

   COLOR|DSO|BODY|TRIM|SCH.|DATE|AXLE|TRANS|A/C
```
⑬

(CANADA)

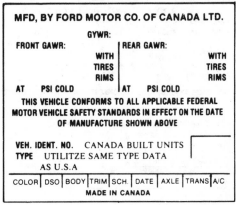

```
MFD, BY FORD MOTOR CO. OF CANADA LTD.
                 GYWR:
FRONT GAWR:              | REAR GAWR:
                   WITH  |              WITH
                   TIRES |              TIRES
                   RIMS  |              RIMS
AT    PSI COLD           | AT    PSI COLD
   THIS VEHICLE CONFORMS TO ALL APPLICABLE FEDERAL
MOTOR VEHICLE SAFETY STANDARDS IN EFFECT ON THE DATE
         OF MANUFACTURE SHOWN ABOVE

VEH. IDENT. NO.   CANADA BUILT UNITS
TYPE   UTILITZE SAME TYPE DATA
          AS U.S.A

COLOR|DSO|BODY|TRIM|SCH.|DATE|AXLE|TRANS|A/C
              MADE IN CANADA
```

1 Name of Manufacturer
2 Date of Manufacture
3 Front Gross Axle Weight Ratings in Pounds (LB) and Kilograms (KG)
4 Front Tire Size
5 Rim Size
6 Front Tire Cold PSI
7 Gross Vehicle Weight Rating in Pounds (LB) and Kilograms (KG)

8 Rear Gross Axle Weight Rating in Pounds (LB) and Kilograms (KG)
9 Rear Tire Size
10 Rim Size
11 Rear Tire Cold PSI
12 Vehicle Identification Number
13 Vehicle Data

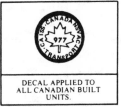

DECAL APPLIED TO
ALL CANADIAN BUILT
UNITS.

INCOMPLETE VEHICLES

THE INCOMPLETE VEHICLE LABEL IS ATTACHED TO A BOOKLET (INCOMPLETE VEHICLE MANUAL) AND SECURED TO A SUITABLE INTERIOR LOCATION FOR INFORMATION USE AT DESTINATION.

(UNITED STATES)

```
THIS INCOMPLETE VEHICLE MFD. BY
FORD MOTOR COMPANY
THE AMERICAN ROAD
DEARBORN, MICHIGAN 48121 ON: 08/77
VEH. IDENT. NO. E37HHAE0002
GVWR 1000 LB/4335 KG
```

FRONT GAWR	REAR GAWR	REAR REAR GAWR
4000 LB	6700 LB	LB
1814 KG	3039 KG	KG

FRONT	REAR
8.00 — 16.5E	8.00 — 16.5E
16.5 x 6.0	16.5 x 6.0
60	55

```
TIRES
RIMS
PSI COLD

MAY BE
COMPLETED AS: TRUCK BUS (NOT SCHOOL BUS)
```

(EXPORT)

```
THIS INCOMPLETE VEHICLE MFD. BY
FORD MOTOR COMPANY
THE AMERICAN ROAD
DEARBORN, MICHIGAN 48121 ON: 08/77
VEH. IDENT. NO.
GVWR
```

FRONT GAWR	REAR GAWR	REAR REAR GAWR

FRONT	REAR

```
TIRES
RIMS
PSI COLD

MAY BE           THIS VEHICLE MFD FOR EXPORT
COMPLETED AS:    ONLY ON DATE SHOWN ABOVE
```

NOTE — The same information is on all safety certification decal although the location of the information on the decal may be different.

1978–80 Vehicle Certification Plates

COMPLETE VEHICLES

(UNITED STATES)

MFD. BY FORD MOTOR CO. IN U.S.A.

DATE: 8/79   GVWR: 7650 LB/3470 KG

FRONT GAWR: 3050 LB   REAR GAWR: 5300 LB

1383 KG	WITH	2404 KG	WITH
F78-15B	TIRES	F78-15B	TIRES
15x5.5 K	RIMS	15x5.5 K	RIMS
AT 32 PSI COLD		AT 32 PSI COLD	

THIS VEHICLE CONFORMS TO ALL APPLICABLE FEDERAL MOTOR VEHICLE SAFETY STANDARDS IN EFFECT ON THE DATE OF MANUFACTURE SHOWN ABOVE

VEHICLE IDENTIFICATION NO.   1FTBF25G BLA00000

TYPE   TRUCK

EXTERIOR PAINT COLORS				DSO
WB	TYPE GVW	BODY	TRANS	AXLE

(CANADA)

MFD. BY FORD MOTOR CO. OF CANADA LTD.

DATE: GVWR:

FRONT GAWR: REAR GAWR:

	WITH		WITH
	TIRES		TIRES
	RIMS		RIMS
AT PSI COLD		AT PSI COLD	

THIS VEHICLE CONFORMS TO ALL APPLICABLE FEDERAL MOTOR VEHICLE SAFETY STANDARDS IN EFFECT ON THE DATE OF MANUFACTURE SHOWN ABOVE

VEH. IDENT. NO.   CANADA BUILT UNITS

TYPE   UTILIZE SAME TYPE DATA AS U.S.A.

EXTERIOR PAINT COLORS				DSO
WB	TYPE GVW	BODY	TRANS	AXLE

(QUEBEC)

FABR. AUX E-U PAR LA FORD MOTOR CO.

DATE: PNBV:

PNBE AVANT: PNBE ARRIERE:

AVEC

◄PNEUS►

◄JANTES►

A   LB/PO² A FROID   A   LB/PO² A FROID

CE VEHICULE EST CONFORME A TOUTES LES NORMES FEDERALES DE SECURITE DES V.A. EN VIGUEUR A LA DATE DE FABR. INIQUEE CI-DESSUS.

N° D'IDENT. DU VEHICULE

TYPE

FOR VEHICLES MFD IN U.S.A. FOR QUEBEC, CANADA.

FABR. PAR FORD DU CANADA LIMITEE

DATE: PNBV:

PNBE AVANT: PNBE ARRIERE:

AVEC

◄PNEUS►

◄JANTES►

A   LB/PO² A FROID   A   LB/PO² A FROID

CE VEHICULE EST CONFORME A TOUTES LES NORMES FEDERALES DE SECURITE DES V.A. EN VIGUEUR A LA DATE DE FABR. INIQUEE CI-DESSUS.

N° D'IDENT. DU VEHICULE

TYPE

COULEUR				4° COMM SPEC
EMPATT	TYPE/PSV	CARR	TRANSM	PONT

MADE IN CANADA

FOR VEHICLES MFD. IN CANADA FOR QUEBEC, CANADA.

INCOMPLETE VEHICLES

THE INCOMPLETE VEHICLE RATING DECAL IS INSTALLED ON THE DRIVER'S DOOR LOCK PILLAR IN PLACE OF THE SAFETY COMPLIANCE CERTIFICATION LABEL.

DECAL APPLIED TO ALL CANADIAN BUILT UNITS.

VEHICLE RATING DECAL

INCOMPLETE VEHICLE MANUFACTURED BY

GVWR: 3050 LB/1383 KG

VEHICLE IDENTIFICATION NUMBER   1FTBF25G BLA00000

EXTERIOR PAINT COLORS	2H				48	DSO
WB	TYPE-GVW	BODY	TRANS	AXLE		
133	F27C	AB4	G	38		1980

1981–82 Vehicle Certification Plates

Engine Codes

Engine	61	62	63	64	65	66	67	68	69	70	71	72	73	74	75	76	77	78	79	80	81	82
6—144	S	S	S	S																		
6—170	T	T	T	T	T	F	F	F	F	F												
6—200				S																		
6—240									A	A	A	A	A	A								
6—300															B	B	B	B	B	E	E	E
6—300LPG																					9	9
6—300HD																			K			
8—302									G	G	G	G	G	G					G	F	F	F
8—351W															H	H	H	H	H	G	G	G
8—400																				Z	Z	Z
8—460															A	A	A	A	A		L	L

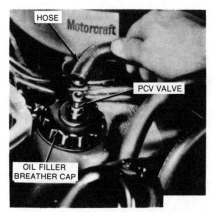

Removing the PCV valve from a V8 engine

should be used only as an emergency measure. Otherwise the valve should be replaced.

Evaporative Emission Canister

1. Inspect the canister for holes or damage caused by debris.

2. Inspect the hoses to the canister for holes, cracks or other damage.

3. Check the purge lines from the canister for proper installation.

4. Replace the canister and/or hoses if damaged.

Battery

The electrolyte level in the battery should be checked every few weeks. Remove the battery caps and check to see if the fluid level in the battery is up to the split rings in the bottom of the filler wells. If it is not, you can top it off with plain water unless you live in an area known to have hard water. If you do live in one of these areas, you should use distilled water. Fill the battery only to the split rings in the bottom of the filler wells. If you overfill the battery, the electrolyte will run out onto the pavement and you will be left with a battery full of plain water. Never light a match or use an open flame near the top of the battery, as the battery gives off *highly explosive* hydrogen gas.

Rear Axle Codes and Ratios

Read Ratios Across

Codes	61	62	63	64	65	66	67/68	69	70	71	72	73	74	75	76	77	78	79	80	81	82
01	3.50	3.50	3.50	3.50	3.50	3.50	3.50													2.75	2.75
02	4.00	4.00	4.00	4.00	4.00	4.00	4.00						3.00	3.00	3.00	3.00				3.00	3.00
03			3.80	4.11	4.11							4.11									
04			4.50	4.55	4.55							4.57								3.25	3.25
07						3.00	3.00													2.47	2.47
11						3.50	3.50					3.50	3.50	4.11							
12						4.11	4.11					3.70	3.70	3.70							
13						4.56	4.56													2.75	2.75
A7						3.00	3.00														
B1						3.50	3.50														
B2						4.11	4.11														
B3						4.57	4.57														
B5																				3.33	3.33
08								3.50	3.50	3.50	3.50	3.50	3.50	3.50	3.50	3.50					

Years

05	4.11	4.11	4.11	4.11	4.11	4.11	4.11
17	3.25	3.25	3.25	3.25	3.25	3.25	
09	3.70	3.70	3.70	3.70	3.70		
71	3.54	3.54	3.54	3.54	3.54		
72	3.73	3.73	3.73	3.73	3.73		
73	4.10	4.10	4.10	4.10			
G1	3.54	3.54	3.54				
G3	4.10	4.10	4.10	4.10			
06	4.57						
31	3.54						
33	3.73						
35	4.10						
36	4.56						
C1	3.54						
C2							
C3	3.73						
C5	4.10						

Rear Axle Codes and Ratios (cont.)

Read Ratios Across

	Years																				
Codes	*61*	*62*	*63*	*64*	*65*	*66*	*67/68*	*69*	*70*	*71*	*72*	*73*	*74*	*75*	*76*	*77*	*78*	*79*	*80*	*81*	*82*
B4												4.10	4.10	4.10	4.10	4.10					
C7												3.54								3.54	3.54
C8												3.73	3.73	3.73	3.73	3.73	3.73				
D7												4.10	4.10	4.10	4.10	4.10	4.10	4.10	4.10		
10												3.25	3.25								
18												3.50									
22												4.88									
14														3.00						3.00	3.00
15														3.25						3.25	3.25
16														3.50						3.50	3.50
17																				2.47	2.47
23												3.31	3.31	3.31	3.31	3.31	3.31	3.31	3.31		
24												4.10	4.10	4.10	4.10	4.10	4.10	4.10			
25												3.31								3.33	3.33

Code							
26	3.54	3.54					
32						3.00	3.00
37						3.54	3.54
38		3.73	3.73	3.73		3.73	3.73
41						3.54	3.54
42						3.73	3.73
43						4.10	4.10
B5	3.31	3.31					
D6	3.73		3.73	3.73		3.73	
H2	3.50		3.50	3.50	3.50	3.50	
H3	4.11		4.11		4.11	2.75	2.75
H4	3.25		3.25	3.25	3.25	3.00	3.00
H5			3.70	3.70		3.25	3.25
H7				3.00	3.00	2.47	2.47
H9	4.11			4.11		4.11	

Exhaust Manifold Heat Riser Valve

Check the thermostatic spring of the valve to make sure it is hooked on the stop pin. The spring stop is at the top of the valve housing when the valve is properly installed.

Make sure the spring holds the valve closed. Actuate the counterweight by hand to make sure it moves freely through approximately 90 degrees of rotation without binding.

The valve is closed when the engine is cold. However, a properly operating valve will open when very light finger pressure is applied to the counterweight. Rapidly accelerate the engine to make sure the valve momentarily opens. The valve is designed to open when the engine is at normal operating temperature and is operated at high rpm.

Lubricate and free the valve with non-flammable solvent if the valve is sluggish or stuck.

Cooling System

At least once every 2 years, the engine cooling system should be inspected, flushed, and refilled with fresh coolant. If the coolant is left in the system too long, it loses its ability to prevent rust and corrosion. If the coolant has too much water, it won't protect against freezing.

The pressure cap should be looked at for signs of age or deterioration. Fan belt and other drive belts should be inspected and adjusted to the proper tension.

Hose clamps should be tightened, and soft or cracked hoses replaced. Damp spots, or accumulations of rust or dye near hoses, water pump or other areas, indicate possible leakage, which must be corrected before filling the system with fresh coolant.

CHECK THE RADIATOR CAP

While you are checking the coolant level, check the radiator cap for a worn or cracked gasket. If the cap doesn't seal properly, fluid will be lost and the engine will overheat.

Worn caps should be replaced with a new one.

CLEAN RADIATOR OF DEBRIS

Periodically clean any debris—leaves, paper, insects, etc.—from the radiator fins. Pick the large pieces off by hand. The smaller pieces can be washed away with water pressure from a hose.

Carefully straighten any bent radiator fins with a pair of needle nose pliers. Be careful—the fins are very soft. Don't wiggle the fins back and forth too much. Straighten them once and try not to move them again.

DRAIN AND REFILL THE COOLING SYSTEM

Completely draining and refilling the cooling system every two years at least will remove accumulated rust, scale and other deposits. Coolant in late model vans is a 50-50 mixture of ethylene glycol and water for year round use. Use a good quality antifreeze with water pump lubricants, rust inhibitors and other corrosion inhibitors along with acid neutralizers.

1. Drain the existing antifreeze and coolant. Open the radiator and engine drain pet-

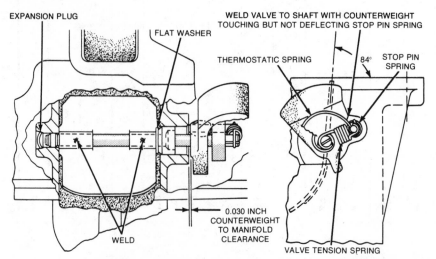

Heat riser valve plate position and counterweight clearance

cocks, or disconnect the bottom radiator hose, at the radiator outlet.

NOTE: *Before opening the radiator petcock, spray it with some penetrating lubricant.*

2. Close the petcock or re-connect the lower hose and fill the system with water.

3. Add a can of quality radiator flush.

4. Idle the engine until the upper radiator hose gets hot.

5. Drain the system again.

6. Repeat this process until the drained water is clear and free of scale.

7. Close all petcocks and connect all the hoses.

8. If equipped with a coolant recovery system, flush the reservoir with water and leave empty.

9. Determine the capacity of your cooling system (see capacities specifications). Add a 50/50 mix of quality antifreeze (ethylene glycol) and water to provide the desired protection.

10. Run the engine to operating temperature.

11. Stop the engine and check the coolant level.

12. Check the level of protection with an anti-freeze tester, replace the cap and check for leaks.

Air Conditioning

SAFETY PRECAUTIONS

There are two particular hazards associated with air conditioning systems and they both relate to the refrigerant gas.

First, the refrigerant gas is an extremely cold substance. When exposed to air, it will instantly freeze any surface it comes in contact with, including your eyes. The other hazard relates to fire. Although normally non-toxic, refrigerant gas becomes highly poisonous in the presence of an open flame. One good whiff of the vapor formed by burning refrigerant can be fatal. Keep all forms of fire (including cigarettes) well clear of the air-conditioning system.

Any repair work to an air conditioning system should be left to a professional. Do not, under any circumstances, attempt to loosen or tighten any fittings or perform any work other than that outlined here.

CHECKING FOR OIL LEAKS

Refrigerant leaks show up as oily areas on the various components because the compressor

oil is transported around the entire system along with the refrigerant. Look for oily spots on all the hoses and lines, and especially on the hose and tubing connections. If there are oily deposits, the system may have a leak, and you should have it checked by a qualified repairman.

NOTE: *A small area of oil on the front of the compressor is normal and no cause for alarm.*

KEEP THE CONDENSER CLEAR

Periodically inspect the front of the condenser for bent fins or foreign material (dirt, bugs, leaves, etc.) If any cooling fins are bent, straighten them carefully with needle-nosed pliers. You can remove any debris with a stiff bristle brush or hose.

OPERATE THE A/C SYSTEM PERIODICALLY

A lot of A/C problems can be avoided by simply running the air conditioner at least once a week, regardless of the season. Let the system run for at least 5 minutes a week (even in the winter), and you'll keep the internal parts lubricated as well as preventing the hoses from hardening.

REFRIGERANT LEVEL CHECK

There are two ways to check refrigerant level, depending on how your model is equipped.

With Sight Glass

The first order of business when checking the sight glass is to find the sight glass. It will either be in the head of the receiver/drier, or in one of the metal lines leading from the top of the receiver/drier. Once you've found it, wipe it clean and proceed as follows:

1. With the engine and the air conditioning system running, look for the flow of refrigerant through the sight glass. If the air conditioner is working properly, you'll be able to see a continuous flow of clear refrigerant through the sight glass, with perhaps an occasional bubble at very high temperatures.

2. Cycle the air conditioner on and off to make sure what you are seeing is clear refrigerant. Since the refrigerant is clear, it is possible to mistake a completely discharged system for one that is fully charged. Turn the system off and watch the sight glass. If there is refrigerant in the system, you'll see bubbles during the off cycle. If you observe no bubbles when the system is running, and the

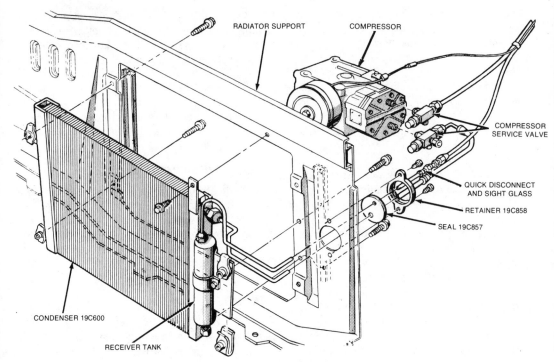

RADIATOR SUPPORT

COMPRESSOR

COMPRESSOR SERVICE VALVE

QUICK DISCONNECT AND SIGHT GLASS

RETAINER 19C858

SEAL 19C857

CONDENSER 19C600

RECEIVER TANK

Typical air conditioning installation

air flow from the unit in the car is delivering cold air, everything is OK.

3. If you observe bubbles in the sight glass while the system is operating, the system is low on refrigerant. Have it checked by a professional.

4. Oil streaks in the sight glass are an indication of trouble. Most of the time, if you see oil in the sight glass, it will appear as a series of streaks, although occasionally it may be a solid stream of oil. In either case, it means that part of the charge has been lost.

Without Sight Glass

On vehicles that are not equipped with sight glasses, it is necessary to feel the temperature difference in the inlet and outlet lines at the receiver/drier to gauge the refrigerant level. Use the following procedure:

1. Locate the receiver/drier. It will generally be up front near the condenser. It is shaped like a small fire extinguisher and will always have two lines connected to it. One line goes to the expansion valve and the other goes to the condenser.

2. With the engine and the air conditioner running, hold a line in each hand and gauge their relative temperatures. If they are both the same approximate temperature, the system is correctly charged.

3. If the line from the expansion valve to

the receiver/drier is a lot colder than the line from the receiver/drier to the condenser, then the system is overcharged. It should be noted that this is an extremely rare condition.

4. If the line that leads from the receiver/drier to the condenser is a lot colder than the other line, the system is undercharged.

5. If the system is undercharged or overcharged, have it checked by a professional air conditioning mechanic.

Windshield Wipers

Intense heat from the sun, snow and ice, road oils and the chemicals used in windshield washer solvents combine to deteriorate the rubber wiper refills. The refills should be replaced about twice a year or whenever the blades begin to streak or chatter.

WIPER REFILL REPLACEMENT

Normally, if the wipers are not cleaning the windshield properly, only the refill has to be replaced. The blade and arm usually require replacement only in the event of damage. It is not necessary (except on new Tridon refills) to remove the arm or the blade to replace the refill (rubber part), though you may have to position the arm higher on the glass. You can do this turning the ignition switch on and operating the wipers. When they are positioned where they are accessible, turn the ignition switch off.

There are several types of refills and your vehicle could have any kind, since aftermarket blades and arms may not use exactly the same refill as the original equipment.

Most Trico styles uses a release button that is pushed down to allow the refill to slide out of the yoke jaws. The new refill slides in and locks in place. Some Trico refills are removed by locating where the metal backing strip or the refill is wider. Insert a small screwdriver blade between the frame and metal backing strip. Press down to release the refill from the retaining tab.

The Anco style is unlocked at one end by squeezing 2 metal tabs, and the refill is slid out of the frame jaws. When the new refill is installed, the tabs will click into place, locking the refill.

The polycarbonate type is held in place by a locking lever that is pushed downward out of the groove in the arm to free the refill. When the new refill is installed, it will lock in place automatically.

The Tridon refill has a plastic backing strip with a notch about an inch from the end. Hold the blade (frame) on a hard surface so that the frame is tightly bowed. Grip the tip of the backing strip and pull up while twisting counterclockwise. The backing strip will snap out of the retaining tab. Do this for the remaining tabs until the refill is free of the arm. The length of these refills is molded into the end and they should be replaced with identical types.

No matter which type of refill you use, be sure that all of the frame claws engage the refill. Before operating the wipers, be sure that no part of the metal frame is contacting the windshield.

Fluid Level Checks

ENGINE OIL

Check the engine oil level every time you fill the gas tank. The oil level should be above the ADD mark and not above the FULL mark on the dipstick. Make sure that the dipstick is inserted into the crankcase as far as possible and that the vehicle is resting on level ground.

NOTE: *Don't check the level immediately after stopping the engine; wait a few minutes to let the oil drain back into the pan.*

TRANSMISSION
Manual

Before checking the lubricant level in the transmission, make sure that the vehicle is on level ground. Remove the fill plug from the right-side of the transmission. Remove the plug slowly when it starts to reach the end of the threads on the plug. Hold the plug up against the hole and move it away slowly. This is so as to minimize the loss of lubricant through the fill hole. The level of the lubricant should be up to the bottom of the fill hole. If lubricant is not present at the bottom of the fill hole, add SAE 90 or 80 transmission lube until it reaches the proper level. A suction gun or squeeze bottle is used to fill a manual transmission with lubricant.

Automatic Transmission

The fluid level in an automatic transmission is checked when the transmission is at operating temperatures. If the vehicle has been sitting and is cold, drive it at highway speeds for at least 20 minutes to warm the transmission.

1. With the transmission in Park, the engine running at idle speed, the foot brakes applied and the vehicle resting on level ground, move the transmission gear selector through each of the gear positions, including Reverse, allowing time for the transmission to engage. Return the shift selector to the Park position and apply the parking brake. Do not turn the engine off; leave it running at idle speed.

2. Clean all dirt from around the transmission dipstick cap and the end of the filler tube.

3. Pull the dipstick out of the tube, wipe it off with a clean cloth, and push it back into the tube all the way, making sure that it seats completely.

4. Pull the dipstick out of the tube again and read the level of the fluid on the stick. The level should be between the ADD mark and the FULL mark. If fluid must be added, add enough fluid through the tube to raise the level up to between the ADD and FULL

o oADD (x—)o DONT ADD IF BETWEEN ARROWS   CHECK WHEN HOT & IDLING IN PARK

Automatic transmission dipstick

marks. Do not overfill the transmission because this will cause foaming, loss of fluid through the vent, and malfunctioning of the transmission. Use type F transmission fluid (Ford Spec. ESW-M2C33-F) in all C4 and C6 transmissions through 1976. Use the new type fluid (Ford Spec. ESP-M2C138-CJ) in 1977 and later C6 transmissions. Use Dexron® II fluid in 1982 C5 transmissions.

BRAKE MASTER CYLINDER

The master cylinder is located under the floor pan on the right (driver's) side on 1961–1967 models. It is accessible by removing the attaching screws holding an access plate to the floor and removing the plate.

On 1969 and later model Ford vans, the brake master cylinder is located under the hood on the driver's side.

Before removing the master cylinder reservoir cap, make sure that the vehicle is resting on level ground and clean all dirt away from the top of the master cylinder. Pry off the retaining clip or unscrew the cap. The brake fluid level should be within ¼ in. of the top of the reservoir on both single and dual type master cylinders.

If the level of the brake fluid is less than half the volume of the reservoir, it is advised that you check the brake hydraulic system for leaks. Leaks most commonly occur at the wheel cylinder.

On 1969 and later models there is a rubber diaphragm in the top of the master cylinder cap. As the fluid level drops in the reservoir due to normal brake shoe wear or leakage, the diaphragm takes up the space. This is to prevent the loss of brake fluid out the vented cap and contamination by dirt. After filling the master cylinder to the proper level with brake fluid, but before replacing the cap, fold the rubber diaphragm up into the cap, then replace the cap on the reservoir and snap the retaining clip into place.

When replacing the screw-on cap on 1961–68 models, make sure that the gasket is in good condition and properly in place on the cap. If it is cracked or damaged in any way, it should be replaced.

COOLANT

The coolant level should be maintained at 2 in. below the bottom of the radiator filler neck when the engine is cold and 1 in. below the bottom of the filler neck when the engine is hot.

For best protection against freezing and overheating, maintain an approximate 50% water and 50% antifreeze mixture in the cooling system.

Avoid using water that is known to have a high alkaline content or is very hard, except in emergency cases. Drain and flush the cooling system as soon as possible after using such water.

CAUTION: *Cover the radiator cap with a thick cloth before removing it from a radiator in a vehicle that is hot. Turn the cap counterclockwise slowly until pressure can be heard escaping. Allow all pressure to escape from the radiator before completely removing the radiator cap.*

REAR AXLE

Clean the area around the fill plug before removing the plug. The lubricant level should be maintained to the bottom of the fill hole with the vehicle level. If lubricant does not appear at the hole when he plug is removed, additional lubricant should be added. Use hypoid gear lubricant SAE 80 or 90.

NOTE: *Limited-slip rear axles require that a special additive be used along with the hypoid lubricant. If it isn't used, the result will be noise and rough operation.*

STEERING GEAR

The steering gear is located under the floor, on the left-side at the end of the steering shaft.

The procedure for checking and adding lubricant to 1961–68 models is as follows:

1. Remove the floor mat and the steering gear access plate.
2. Remove the steering gear housing filler plug.
3. With a clean punch break the bubble which will be formed so that you can read the true lubricant level.
4. Slowly turn the steering wheel to the left stop. If the lubricant rises within the filler plug hole as the wheel turns, there is sufficient lubricant in the gear. Skip Steps 5 through 7 and proceed with Step 8. If the lubricant does not rise in the hole, perform the following Steps.
5. Turn the steering gear to the right stop in order to position the sector shaft teeth away from the filler plug hole.
6. Remove the cover-to-housing (top) retaining bolt.
7. Fill the gear through the filler plug hole until lubricant comes out of the cover bolt hole. Install the cover retaining bolt.

8. Install the filler plug, the steering gear access plate, and the floor mat.

The procedure for checking and adding lubricant to 1969–74 models is as follows:

1. Remove the steering gear housing filler plug.

2. With a clean punch or similar instrument, clean out or push the loose lubricant into the filler plug hole.

3. Turn the steering wheel to the left. Then turn the steering wheel slowly to the right until the linkage reaches the stop. Lubricant should rise in the filler plug hole. If lubricant does not rise in the filler plug hole, add to the supply.

The location of the steering gear does not allow any clearance for the removal of a cover bolt to create a vent. To prevent air from being trapped and forming pockets in the housing while lubricant is being added, it is suggested that a curved length of ¼ in. tubing be adapted to the end of the grease gun being used. This tube should be inserted into the filler hole and extend down toward the bottom of the housing cavity. By this method, the lower housing cavity will fill first and as lubricant is added, air will be expelled upward and out the fill hole.

To add lubricant, turn the steering wheel to the extreme left to position the ball nut away from the filler plug hole and fill the steering gear by the method described above until the lubricant rises in the filler plug hole.

NOTE: *The steering gear on 1975–82 models is permanently lubricated. No service is required unless solid grease (not an oily film) is escaping.*

POWER STEERING RESERVOIR

Position the vehicle on level ground. Run the engine until the fluid is at normal operating temperature. Turn the steering wheel all the way to the left and right several times. Position the wheels in the straight-ahead position, then shut off the engine. Check the fluid level on the dipstick which is attached to the reservoir cap. The level should be between the ADD and FULL marks on the dipstick, and at the FULL-HOT line on later models. Add fluid accordingly. Do not overfill. Use power steering fluid.

Wheel Bearings
PACKING AND ADJUSTMENT

Before handling the bearings there are a few things that you should remember to do and try to avoid.

DO the following:

1. Remove all outside dirt from the housing before exposing the bearing.

2. Treat a used bearing as gently as you would a new one.

3. Work with clean tools in clean surroundings.

4. Use clean, dry canvas gloves, or at least clean, dry hands.

5. Clean solvents and flushing fluids are a must.

6. Use clean paper when laying out the bearings to dry.

7. Protect disassembled bearings from rust and dirt. Cover them up.

8. Use clean rags to wipe bearings.

9. Keep the bearing in oil-proof paper when they are to be stored or are not in use.

10. Clean the inside of the housing before replacing the bearing.

Do NOT do the following:

1. Don't work in dirty surroundings.

2. Don't use dirty, chipped, or damaged tools.

3. Try not to work on wooden work benches or use wooden mallets.

4. Don't handle bearings with dirty or moist hands.

5. Do not use gasoline for cleaning; use a safe solvent.

6. Do not spin-dry bearings with compressed air. They will be damaged.

7. Do not spin unclean bearings.

8. Avoid using cotton waste or dirty cloths to wipe bearings.

9. Try not to scratch or nick bearing surfaces.

10. Do not allow the bearing to come in contact with dirt or rust at any time.

Front

To remove the wheel bearings from the front hubs:

1. Jack the van up until the wheel to be serviced is off the ground and can spin freely. It is easier to check all the bearings at the same time. If the equipment needed is available, raise the front end of the van so that both front wheels are off the ground. Use jackstands or suitable blocks to support the vehicle. Make sure that the van is completely stable before proceeding any further.

2. Remove the lug nuts and remove the wheel/tire assembly from the hub. It is possible to remove the hub assembly from the

spindle with the wheel/tire assembly still attached, but the added weight makes handling of the entire assembly a little clumsy which could result in possible damage to the bearings or spindle. Remove the caliper assembly on disc brakes. See Chapter 9 for details.

3. Remove the grease cap with a screwdriver or pliers.

Removing the grease cap

4. Remove the cotter pin and discard it. Cotter pins should never be reused.

5. Remove the nut lock, adjusting nut, and washer from the spindle.

6. Wiggle the hub so that the outer wheel bearing comes loose and can be removed. Remove the outer bearing.

7. Remove the hub from the spindle and place it on a work surface, supported by two blocks of wood under the brake drum.

NOTE: *If the drum brake hub will not come off easily, back off the brake shoe adjustment screw so that the shoes do not contact the brake drum.*

8. Place a block of wood or drift pin through the spindle hole and tap out the inner grease seal. Tap lightly so not to damage the bearing. When the seal falls out, so will the inner bearing. Discard the seal.

Perform the above procedures to all the wheels that are going to be serviced.

9. Place all of the bearings, nuts, nut locks, washers and grease caps in a container of solvent. Use a light soft brush to thoroughly clean each part. Make sure that every bit of dirt and grease is rinsed off, then place each cleaned part on an absorbent cloth or paper and allow them to dry completely.

10. Clean the inside of the hub, including the bearing races, and the spindle. Remove all traces of old lubricant from these components.

11. Inspect the bearings for pitting, flat spots, rust, and rough areas. Check the races in the hub and the spindle for the same defects and rub them clean with a cloth that has been soaked in solvent. If the races show hairline cracks or worn shiny areas, they must be replaced. The races are installed in the hub with a press fit and are removed by driving them out with a suitable punch or drift. Place the new races squarely onto the hub and place a block of wood over them. Drive the race into place with a hammer, striking the block of wood. Never hit the race with any metal object.

Replacement seals, bearings, and other required parts can be bought at an auto parts store. The old parts should be taken along to be compared with the replacement parts to ensure a perfect match.

12. Pack the wheel bearings with grease. There are special devices made for the spe-

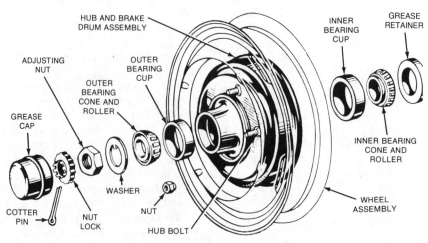

1961–74 front hub assembly

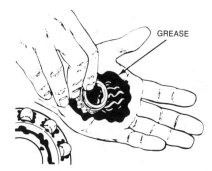

Packing the wheel bearings with grease by hand

cific purpose of greasing bearings, but if one is not available, pack the wheel bearings by hand. Put a large dab of grease in the palm of your hand and push the bearing through it with a sliding motion. The grease must be forced through the side of the bearing and in between each roller. Continue until the grease begins to ooze out the other side and through the gaps between the rollers; the bearing must be completely packed with grease.

NOTE: *Sodium based grease is not compatible with lithium based grease. Be careful not to mix the two types. The best way to prevent this is to completely clean all of the old grease from the hub and spindle before installing any new grease.*

13. Turn the hub assembly over so that the inner side faces up, making sure that the race and inner area are clean, and drop the inner wheel bearing into place. Using a hammer and a block of wood, tap the new grease seal in place. Never hit the seal with the hammer directly. Move the block of wood around the circumference until it is properly seated.

14. Slide the hub assembly onto the spindle and push it as far as it will go, making sure that it has completely covered the brake shoes. Keep the hub centered on the spindle to prevent damage to the grease seal and the spindle threads.

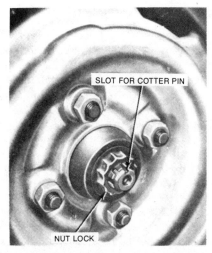

Nut lock installed so that a slot is aligned with cotter pin hole

15. Place the outer wheel bearing in place over the spindle. Press it in until it is snug. Place the washer on the spindle after the bearing. Screw on the spindle nut and turn it down until a slight binding is felt.

16. With a torque wrench, tighten the nut to 17–25 ft lbs to seat the bearings. Install the nut lock over the nut so that the cotter pin hole in the spindle is aligned with a slot in the nut lock. Back off the adjusting nut and the nut lock two slots of the nut lock and install the cotter pin.

17. Bend the longer of the two ends opposite the looped end out and over the end of the spindle. Trim both ends of the cotter pin just enough so that the grease cap will fit, leaving the bent end shaped over the end of the spindle.

18. Install the grease cap and the wheel/tire assembly. The wheel should rotate freely with no noise or noticeable endplay.

19. Adjust the brakes.

Installing the grease seal

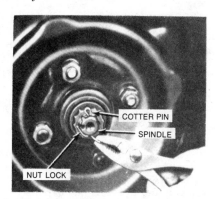

Bending the cotter pin

Rear

Only the heavy-duty full-floating rear axles require periodic wheel bearing maintenance service. These axles are the Dana (Spicer) 60, 61, and 70 models and can be identified by the large bearing hub protruding through the center of the wheel.

Rear wheel bearing service is not required on any of the semi-floating, lighter-duty, rear axles, unless the axle shafts or bearings are removed. See Chapter 7 for these procedures.

1. Set the parking brake and loosen the axle shaft bolts.

2. Raise the rear wheels off the floor and support the axle housing. Release the parking brake.

3. Remove the axle shaft bolts and lockwashers. If there are studs with tapered dowels instead of bolts, strike the axle shaft flange in the center to loosen them. Remove the axle shaft and gasket.

4. Pry out the locking wedge from inside the adjusting nut with a screwdriver on 1975 and later models.

5. Remove the locknut, locking washer, and wheel bearing adjusting nut. The locknut and locking washer are used only on models through 1974.

6. Support the wheel so that all load is taken off the bearings. Remove the outer bearing cone and pull the wheel, tire, and hub assembly straight out. One way this can be done is to rest the tire on a greased board.

7. Clean the axle housing spindle.

8. Use a brass drift to drive the inner bearing cone and seal out of the hub. Clean out the hub. If the bearing cups need replacement, drive them out with the brass drift. Make sure that the new cups are seated squarely by making sure that a .015 in. feeler gauge will not enter beneath the cup.

9. Clean and pack the bearings with grease as described for front wheel bearings. Place the inner bearing in the hub and carefully force in a new seal.

10. Tape the spindle threads to prevent damage. Slide the wheel, tire, and hub assembly straight on.

11. Remove the tape and install the outer wheel bearing and adjusting nut. Let the wheel and tire assembly rest on the bearings.

12. Rotate the wheel and tighten the adjusting nut to 50–80 ft lbs for models through 1974, and to 120–140 ft lbs for 1975–82.

13. On models through 1974, back the adjusting nut off ⅜ turn. Install a new locking washer coated with axle lube, smooth side out. Install the locknut and tighten it to 90–110 ft lbs.

14. On 1975–82 models, back the adjusting nut off ⅛ to ¼ turn.

15. The wheel assembly should rotate freely; end play should be .001–.010 in. measured with a dial indicator.

16. On 1975–82 models, position the locking wedge in the keyway slot. It must not be bottomed against the shoulder of the nut by about ¼ in. and must not be pressed into a previously cut groove in the nylon retainer.

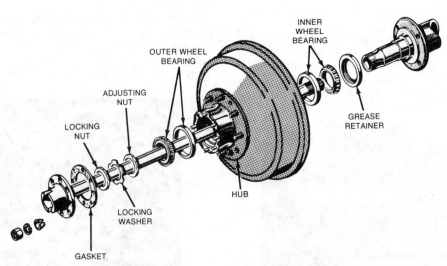

Full-floating rear axle bearings through 1974—this early model retains the axle shaft flange with stud nuts and tapered dowels instead of bolts

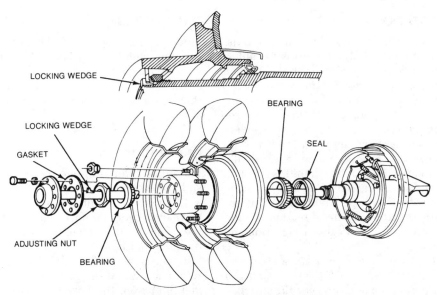

LOCKING WEDGE

LOCKING WEDGE

GASKET

ADJUSTING NUT

BEARING

BEARING

SEAL

1975–80 full-floating rear axle bearings

17. On models through 1974, bend two locking washer tabs in over the adjusting nut, and two tabs out over the locknut.

18. Replace the axle shaft with a new gasket and new lockwashers and retaining bolts, tightened to 40–50 ft lbs.

Tires

INFLATION PRESSURE

Tire inflation is the most ignored item of auto maintenance. Gasoline mileage can drop as much as .8% for every 1 pound per square inch (psi) of under inflation.

Two items should be a permanent fixture in every glove compartment; a tire pressure gauge and a tread depth gauge. Check the tire air pressure (including the spare) regularly with a pocket type gauge. Kicking the tires won't tell you a thing, and the gauge on the service station air hose is notoriously inaccurate.

The tire pressures recommended for your van are usually found on a plate on the driver's door or door pillar, or in the owner's manual. Ideally, inflation pressure should be checked when the tires are cool. When the air becomes heated it expands and the pressure increases. Every 10° rise (or drop) in temperature means a difference of 1 psi, which also explains why the tire appears to lose air on a very cold night. When it is impossible to check the tires "cold," allow for pressure build-up due to heat. If the "hot" pressure exceeds the "cold" pressure by more than 15 psi, reduce your speed, load or both. Otherwise internal heat is created in the tire. When the heat approaches the temperature at which the tire was cured, during manufacture, the tread can separate from the body.

CAUTION: *Never counteract excessive pressure build-up by bleeding off air pressure (letting some air out). This will only further raise the tire operating temperature.*

Before starting a long trip with lots of luggage, you can add about 2–4 psi to the tires to make them run cooler, but never exceed the maximum inflation pressure on the side of the tire.

TREAD DEPTH

All tires made since 1968 have 8 built-in tread wear indicator bars that show up as ½" wide smooth bands across the tire when 1/16" of tread remains. The appearance of tread wear indicators means that the tires should be replaced. In fact, many states have laws prohibiting the use of tires with less than 1/16" tread.

You can check your own tread depth with an inexpensive gauge or by using a Lincoln head penny. Slip the Lincoln penny into several tread grooves. If you can see the top of Lincoln's head in 2 adjacent grooves, the tires have less than 1/16" tread left and should be replaced. You can measure snow tires in the same manner by using the "tails" side of the Lincoln penny. If you can see the top of the Lincoln memorial, it's time to replace the snow tires.

TIRE ROTATION

Tire wear can be equalized by switching the position of the tires about every 6000 miles. Including a conventional spare in the rotation pattern can give up to 20% more tire life.

CAUTION: *Do not include the new "Space Saver®" or temporary spare tires in the rotation pattern.*

There are certain exceptions to tire rotation, however. Studded snow tires should not be rotated, and radials should be kept on the same side of the car (maintain the same direction of rotation). The belts on radial tires get set in a pattern. If the direction of rotation is reversed, it can cause rough ride and vibration.

NOTE: *When radials or studded snows are taken off the car, mark them, so you can maintain the same direction of rotation.*

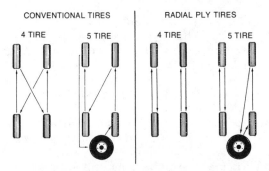

Tire rotation patterns—the radial tire pattern may also be used for bias or bias-belted tires

Recommended Lug Nut Torques

1961–82	5 lug		90 ft lbs.
1968–73	8 lug		135 ft lbs.
1974–82	8 lug	E-250	90 ft lbs.
		E-300, 350	135 ft lbs.
		E-300, 350 dual wheels	210 ft lbs.

8 LUG WHEEL

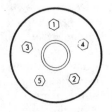

5 LUG WHEEL

Lug nut torque sequences

TIRE STORAGE

Store the tires at proper inflation pressures if they are mounted on wheels. All tires should be kept in a cool, dry place. If they are stored in the garage or basement, do not let them stand on a concrete floor; set them on strips of wood.

Fuel Filter

The inline filter is of one-piece construction and cannot be cleaned.

1. Unlock and remove the engine compartment cover. Remove the air cleaner.

2. Loosen the retaining clamp securing the fuel inlet hose to the fuel filter.

3. Unscrew the fuel filter from the carburetor and discard the gasket. Disconnect the fuel filter from the hose and discard the retaining clamp.

4. Install a new clamp on the inlet hose and connect the hose to the filter. Place a new gasket on the new fuel filter and screw the filter into the carburetor inlet port. Tighten the filter.

5. Position the fuel line hose clamp and tighten the clamp securely.

6. Start the engine and check for fuel leaks.

7. Install the air cleaner. Close and lock the engine compartment cover.

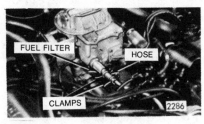

Replacing the fuel filter on a V8 engine. Replacement on a six is similar

PUSHING AND TOWING

To push start your vehicle, (manual transmission only) follow the procedures below:

Check to make sure that the bumpers of both vehicles are aligned so that neither will be damaged. Be sure that all electrical system components are turned off (headlights, heater blower, etc.). Turn on the ignition switch. Place the shift lever in Third gear and push in the clutch pedal. Have the driver of the other vehicle push your vehicle at a gentle but steadily increased rate of speed. At about 15 mph, signal the driver of the pushing vehicle to fall back, slightly depress the accelerator pedal, and release the clutch pedal slowly. The engine should start.

When you are doing the pushing, make sure that the two bumpers match so that you won't damage the vehicle you are to push. Another good idea is to put an old tire between the two vehicles.

Whenever you are towing another vehicle, make sure that the tow chain or rope is sufficiently long and strong, and that it is securely attached to both vehicles. Attach the chain at a point on the frame or as close to it as possible. Once again, go slowly and tell the other driver to do the same. Warn the other driver not to allow too much slack in the line when he gains traction or can move under his own power. Otherwise, he may run over the tow line and damage both vehicles.

If your vehicle has to be towed by a tow truck, it can be towed forward with the driveshaft connected no faster than 30 mph and no farther than 15 miles. Otherwise, disconnect the driveshaft and tie it up. If your vehicle has to be towed backward, make sure that the steering wheel is secured in the straight-ahead position.

JUMP STARTING

If the van is in a reasonably good state of tune and you haven't flooded the engine, but the battery is dead or dying, the van may be jump started by means of jumper cables. All you need is a willing assistant with a good 12-volt battery.

When using jumper cables to jump start a vehicle, a few precautions must be taken to avoid both charging system damage and damage to yourself should the battery explode. The old "positive to positive and negative to negative" jumper cable rule of thumb has been scrapped for a new revised procedure. Here it is. First, remove all the battery cell covers and cover the cell openings with a clean, dry cloth. Then, connect the positive cable of the assist battery to the positive pole of your battery and the negative cable of the assist battery to the engine block of your van. This will prevent the possibility of a spark from the negative assist cable igniting the highly explosive hydrogen and oxygen battery fumes. Once your van is started, allow the engine to return to idle speed before dis-

connecting the jumper cables. Don't cross the cables. Replace the cell covers and discard the cloth.

JACKING AND HOISTING

It is very important to be careful about running the engine on vehicles equipped with limited-slip differentials, while the vehicle is up on a jack. If the drive train is engaged, power is transmitted to the wheel with the best traction and the vehicle will drive itself off the jack.

Jack up the front of all 1961–68 models and 1974–82 E-250 and 350 models under the outer end of the axle. Jack up all other twin I-beam models under the axle radius arm within 3 in. of the sloped section. Jack up the rear of the van under the axle housing. Be sure to block the diagonally opposite wheel. Place jackstands under the vehicle at the points mentioned or directly under the frame when you are going to work under the vehicle.

When raising the vehicle on a hoist, position the front end adapters under the center

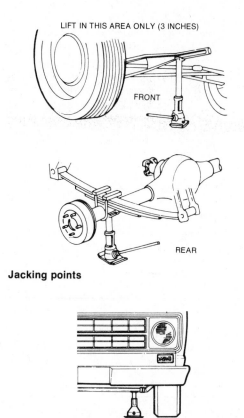

LIFT IN THIS AREA ONLY (3 INCHES)

FRONT

REAR

Jacking points

E-250, 300 front jacking point

of the lower suspension arm or the spring supports as rear to the wheels as practical. The rear hoist adapters should be placed under the spring mounting pads or the rear axle housing. Be careful not to touch the rear shock absorber mounting brackets.

LUBRICATION

See the Preventive Maintenance Chart for the recommended intervals for the operations in this section.

Fuel and Oil Recommendations

All engines through 1973 are designed to operate on regular grade leaded gasoline. 1974–77 models may use unleaded, low-lead, or regular gasoline. 1975 and later models with a catalytic converter must use unleaded fuel only. If your engine pings or knocks, use a higher octane fuel or retard the ignition timing of the engine, but not more than three degrees from the setting required for normal operation. This is only recommended for an emergency situation until you can get some higher octane fuel. A little knocking at low speeds is acceptable, but continued knock at high speeds is damaging to the engine.

Many factors help to determine the proper oil. The question of viscosity revolves around

Consistent Temperature (°F)	Multi-Viscosity Oil	Single Viscosity Oil
below + 32	5W-30	—
− 10 to + 90	10W-30, 10W-40, 10W-50, 15W-50, 20W-50	—
− 10 to + 32	—	10W *
+ 10 to + 60	—	20W-20
+ 32 to + 90	—	30
over + 60	—	40

* Use the next higher viscosity for sustained driving or speeds over 60 mph.

the anticipated ambient temperatures to be encountered. The recommended viscosities for various temperatures are listed here. They are broken down into multiviscosities and single viscosities. Multiviscosity oils are recommneded because of their wider range of acceptable temperatures and driving conditions. SE or SF rated oil must be used.

NOTE: *Always use detergent oil. Detergent oil does not clean or loosen deposits, it merely prevents or inhibits the formation of deposits.*

Lubricant Changes
ENGINE OIL

The oil should be changed more frequently if the vehicle is being operated in very dusty areas. Before draining the oil, make sure that the engine is at operating temperature. Hot oil will hold more impurities in suspension and will flow better, allowing the removal of more oil and dirt. To get the engine hot enough, drive the vehicle for 15 minutes at expressway speeds or the equivalent in city driving.

Drain the oil into a suitable receptacle. After the drain plug is loosened, unscrew the plug with your fingers, using a rag to shield your fingers from the heat. Push in on the plug as you unscrew it so that you can feel when all of the screw threads are out of the hole. You can then remove the plug quickly with the minimum amount of oil running down your arm and you will also have the plug in your hand and not in the bottom of a pan of hot oil. Be careful of the oil. If it is at operating temperatures, it is hot enough to burn you.

Oil Filter

The oil filter should be changed every time the oil is changed.

The oil filter is located on the left-side of all engines installed in Ford vans. To remove the filter after draining the oil, you may need an oil filter wrench since the filter may have been fitted too tightly and the heat from the engine may have made it even tighter. A filter wrench can be obtained at an auto parts store and is well worth the investment since it will save you a lot of grief.

NOTE: *To remove the oil filter with power steering and a V8 engine through 1974, it is necessary to have the wheels in the straight-ahead position. After unscrewing the filter, place it at a horizontal position*

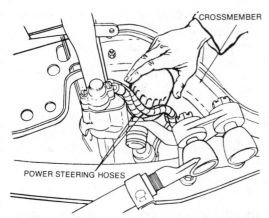

CROSSMEMBER

POWER STEERING HOSES

Removing the oil filter through 1974 with V8 and power steering

and allow the oil to drain. Next, slide the filter rearward to remove it from the vehicle. Some effort may be required to slide the oil filter between the engine crossmember and the power steering hoses. On 1973 and 1974 models, the front wheels must be in a full right turn position (against the stops) in order to remove the filter. Follow the procedure outlined above.

Loosen the filter with a filter wrench. With a rag wrapped around the filter, unscrew the filter from the boss on the side of the engine. Be careful of the hot oil that will run down the side of the filter. Make sure that you have a pan under the filter before you start to remove it from the engine; should some of the hot oil happen to get on you, you will have a place to dump the filter in a hurry. Wipe the base of the mounting boss with a clean, dry cloth. When you install the new filter, smear a small amount of oil on the gasket with your finger, just enough to coat the entire surface where it comes in contact with the mounting plate. When you tighten the filter, rotate it only a half-turn after it comes in contact with the mounting boss.

MANUAL TRANSMISSION

Remove the drain plug which is located at the bottom of the transmission. If there is no drain plug, remove the lower extension housing to case bolt. Allow all the lubricant to run out before replacing the plug. Refill the transmission with SAE 80 or 90 lubricant. See the "Capacities" chart.

If you are experiencing hard shifting and the weather is very cold, use a lighter viscosity lubricant in the transmission. If you don't

have a pressure gun to install the oil, use a suction gun.

AUTOMATIC TRANSMISSION

Aside from checking and adding fluid in order to maintain the proper level, there are no factory recommendations regarding the replacement of the automatic transmission fluid, except for severe service.

The transmission is filled at the factory with a high quality fluid that both transmits power and lubricates and will last a long time. In most cases, the need to change the fluid in the automatic transmission will never arise under normal use. But since this is a truck and possibly will be subjected to more severe operating conditions than a conventional vehicle, the fluid may have to be replaced. Also, an internal leak in the radiator could develop and contaminate the fluid, necessitating fluid replacement.

The extra load of operating the vehicle with a heavy load, towing a heavy trailer, etc., causes the transmission to create more heat due to increased friction. This extra heat is transferred to the transmission fluid and, if the fluid is allowed to become too hot, it will change its chemical composition or become scorched. When this occurs, valve bodies become clogged and the transmission doesn't operate as efficiently as it should. Serious damage to the transmission can result.

You can tell if the transmission fluid is scorched by noting a distinctive "burned" smell and discoloration. Scorched transmission fluid is dark brown or black as opposed to its normal bright, clear red color. Since transmission fluid "cooks" in stages, it may develop forms of sludge or varnish. Pull the dipstick out and place the end on a tissue or paper towel. Particles of sludge can be seen more easily this way. If any of the above conditions do exist, the transmission fluid should be completely drained, the filtering screens cleaned, the transmission inspected for possible damage and new fluid installed.

C4, C5

This transmission is used on all 1964–74 models and the 1975–81 E-100 and 150 sixes. The C5 is used on 1982 E-100 and 150 sixes.

1. Disconnect the fluid filler tube from the transmission pan to drain the fluid.

2. When the fluid has stopped draining from the transmission, remove and thoroughly clean the pan and the screen. Discard the pan gasket.

3. Place a new gasket on the pan and install the pan on the transmission.

4. Connect the filler tube to the pan and tighten the fitting securely.

5. Add three quarts of type F fluid to the C4 transmission or Dexron® II to the C5 through the dipstick tube.

6. Check the fluid level. With the transmission at room temperatures (70° F to 95° F) and the engine idling, the level should be between the middle and top holes on the dipstick. If the fluid level is below the middle hole, add enough fluid through the filler tube to raise the level to between the middle hole and the ADD mark. Please note that this check is only for when the transmission is at room temperatures. See the "Fluid Level Checks" Section for checking the transmission when it is at operating temperatures.

7. Replace the dipstick.

C6

This transmission is used on all 1975–82 models except the E-100 and 150 sixes.

1. Place a drain pan under the transmission. Loosen the pan bolts and pull one corner down to start the fluid draining. Remove and empty the pan.

2. When all the fluid has drained from the transmission, remove and clean the pan and screen. Make sure not to leave any solvent residue or lint from rags in the pan.

3. Install the pan with a new gasket and tighten the bolts in a criss-cross pattern.

4. Add three quarts of fluid through the dipstick tube. Use type F fluid for models through 1976; use the new type fluid (Ford Spec. ESP-M2C138-CJ) in 1977 and later C6 transmissions. The level should be at or below the ADD mark.

5. Check the fluid level as soon as the transmission reaches operating temperature for the first time. Make sure that the level is between ADD and FULL.

REAR AXLE

On axles with a rear differential cover, loosen the bolts to let the lubricant drain out. On axles without a rear differential cover, the lubricant will have to be removed with a suction gun through the filler opening. Use the suction gun or a service station filler hose to fill the housing with SAE 80 or 90 hypoid gear oil to the filler plug hole level.

NOTE: *Limited-slip rear axles require that a special additive be used along with the hypoid lubricant. If it isn't used, the result will be noise and rough operation.*

Chassis Greasing

The lubrication chart indicates where the grease fittings are located on Ford vans and other level checks that should be made at the time of a chassis grease job.

Preventive Maintenance Schedule

Interval	Item	Service
1961–71		
Every 6 months or 6,000 miles	Chassis fittings	lubricate
	Crankcase	change oil & filter
	Differential	check level
	Tires	rotate
	Transmission, automatic	adjust bands, check level
	Transmission, manual	check level
	Air cleaner, oil bath	clean & fill SAE 30
	Brake master cylinder	check level
	Cooling system	change coolant, inspect
	Drive belts	inspect & adjust
	Manifold heat riser	check
	Oil filler cap	clean
	Power steering	check level
	Spark plugs	change
	Points, condenser, rotor	change
	Fuel mixture	check & adjust
	Ignition wiring	inspect

Preventive Maintenance Schedule (cont.)

Interval	Item	Service
1961–71		
Every 12 months or 12,000 miles	Free-running hubs	clean and repack
	Intake manifold, 8 cylinder	torque bolts
	Thermactor	inspect hoses & belts
	PCV system	replace valve
	Choke linkage	inspect & adjust
Every 24 months or 24,000 miles	Brakes, drum type	inspect
	Front wheel bearings	clean & repack
	Rear wheel bearings, E-250, 350	clean and repack
	Transmission, manual	change lubricant
	Air cleaner paper element	change
	Distributor shaft or wick	oil with 10W
	Fuel filter	replace
	PCV filter, 1971	replace
	Speedometer and parking brake cables	lubricate
	Steering gear, manual	check level
	Transmission and clutch linkage	lubricate
1972–73		
Every 4 months or 4,000 miles	Brakes	inspect
	Crankcase	change oil & filter
	Differential	check level
	Chassis fittings	lubricate
	Tires	rotate
	Transmission, automatic	adjust bands, check level
	Transmission, manual	check level
	Air cleaner, oil bath	clean and refill
	Brake master cylinder	check level
	Cooling system	inspect, change coolant
	Manifold heat riser	inspect
	Oil filler cap, 1972	clean
	PCV filter	replace
	Power steering reservoir	check level
	Spark plugs, leaded fuel	replace
	TRS or throttle solenoid fuse	check
Every 12 months or 12,000 miles	Air cleaner paper element	replace
	Breather cap, 1973	clean
	Distributor points, condenser, rotor	replace
	Drive belts	check and adjust
	EGR system, 1973	clean and inspect
	Fuel filter	replace
	Fuel vapor system	inspect
	Idle speed and mixture	check and adjust
	Ignition coil, 1972 E-100	check for corrosion
	Ignition timing & dwell	check and adjust
	Intake manifold, 8 cylinder	torque
	Spark control system, E-100	inspect
	Spark delay valve	replace

Preventive Maintenance Schedule (cont.)

Interval	Item	Service
1972–73		
Every 12 months or 12,000 miles	Spark plugs, unleaded fuel	replace
	Thermostatic air cleaner	inspect
	Throttle and choke linkage	inspect
Every 24 months or 24,000 miles	Differential, E-250, 350	change lubricant
	Front wheel bearings	clean and repack
	Rear wheel bearings, E-250, 350	clean and repack
	Transmission, manual	change lubricant
	Distributor cap	replace
	Distributor shaft or wick	oil with 10W
1974		
Every 4 months or 4,000 miles	Crankcase	change oil & filter
	Air cleaner oil bath	clean and refill
	Idle speed	adjust
	Manifold heat riser	inspect
Every 6 months or 6,000 miles	Brakes	inspect
	Differential	check level
	Chassis fittings	lubricate
	Transmission, automatic	adjust bands, check level
	Transmission, manual	check level
	Cooling system	change coolant
	Drive belts	check and adjust
	Fuel filter	replace
	Idle speed and mixture	adjust
	PCV filter	replace
	Power steering	check level
	Throttle and choke linkage	inspect
	Ignition timing	adjust
Every 12 months or 12,000 miles	Air cleaner paper element	replace
	Breather cap	clean
	Brake master cylinder	check level
	Distributor points, condenser, rotor	replace
	EGR system	clean and inspect
	Intake manifold, 8 cylinder	torque
	PCV valve	replace
	Spark plugs, leaded fuel	replace
	Thermactor system	inspect
	Thermostatic air cleaner	inspect
Every 18 months or 18,000 miles	Distributor cap	replace
	Spark plugs, unleaded fuel	replace
Every 24 months or 24,000 miles	Front wheel bearings	clean and repack
	Rear wheel bearings, E-250, 350	clean and repack

Preventive Maintenance Schedule (cont.)

Interval	Item	Service
1975–76		
Every 5 months or 5,000 miles	Brakes	inspect
	Crankcase	change oil & filter
	Differential	check level
	Chassis fittings	lubricate
	Transmission, automatic	adjust bands, check level
	Transmission, manual	check level
	Air cleaner oil bath	clean and refill
	Power steering	check level
	Idle speed	adjust
	Throttle kickdown exc E-100	check
	Throttle solenoid-off speed	check
Every 6 months	Cooling system	inspect, change coolant
Every 15 months or 15,000 miles	Brake master cylinder	check level
	Parking brake linkage	oil with 10W
	Air cleaner element	replace
	Air cleaner temperature valve	check
	Choke system	inspect
	Distributor cap and rotor	inspect
	Distributor wick	oil with 10W
	Drive belts	check & adjust
	EGR system	clean and inspect
	Fuel filter	replace
	Ignition timing	adjust
	Intake manifold, 302 V8	torque
	Manifold heat riser	inspect
	PCV system	inspect
	Spark plugs	replace
	Spark plug wires	inspect
	Thermactor system	inspect
Every 20 months or 20,000 miles	Front wheel bearings	clean and repack
	Rear wheel bearings, Dana axle	clean and repack
Every 25 months or 25,000 miles	Differential, Dana	change lubricant
	Transmission, 4-speed	change lubricant
Every 30 months or 30,000 miles	Air cleaner crankcase filter	replace
	EEC canister	inspect
	Fuel vapor system	inspect
	PCV valve	replace
1977–82 E-100 Only		
Every 6 months	Cooling system	change coolant

Preventive Maintenance Schedule (cont.)

Interval	Item	Service
1977–82 E-100 Only		
Every 7 months or 7,500 miles	Crankcase	change oil and filter
	Drive belts	check and adjust
	Idle speed and TSP-off speed	adjust
	Ignition timing	check and adjust
	Chassis fittings	lubricate
	Clutch linkage	inspect and oil
	Transmission, automatic	adjust bands, check level
Every 15 months or 15,000 miles	Exhaust system heat shields	inspect
Every 22 months or 22,500 miles	Spark plugs	replace
	Exhaust control valve, 300cid	inspect
	PCV valve	replace
	Idle mixture	adjust
	Choke system	inspect
	Thermactor delay valve	inspect
Every 30 months or 30,000 miles	Air cleaner element	replace
	Air cleaner crankcase filter	replace
	Air cleaner temperature control valve	check
	Fuel vapor system	inspect
	Front wheel bearings	clean and repack
	Brakes	inspect
	Brake master cylinder	check level
1977–82 E-150, 250, 350		
Every 6 months or 6,000 miles	Crankcase	change oil & filter
	Cooling system	change coolant
	Idle speed and TSP-off speed	adjust
	Ignition timing	adjust
	Decel throttle control system	check
	Chassis fittings	lubricate
	Clutch linkage	inspect and oil
	Exhaust system heat shields	inspect
	Transmission, automatic	adjust bands, check level
Every 15 months or 15,000 miles	Spark plugs	replace
	Exhaust control valve	check & lubricate
	Drive belts	check and adjust
	Air cleaner temperature control	check
	Choke system	check
	Thermactor system	check
	Crankcase breather cap	clean
	EGR system	clean and inspect
	PCV system	clean and inspect

Preventive Maintenance Schedule (cont.)

Interval	Item	Service
	1977–82 E 150, 250, 350	
Every 30 months or 30,000 miles	PCV valve	replace
	Air cleaner element	replace
	Air cleaner crankcase filter	replace
	Fuel vapor system	inspect
	Brake master cylinder	check
	Brakes	inspect
	Front wheel bearings	clean and repack
	Rear wheel bearings, Dana axles	clean and repack

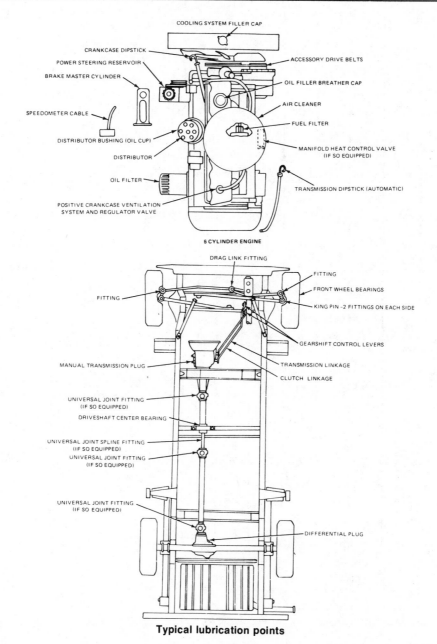

Typical lubrication points

Capacities

Year	Engine Displacement Cu In.	ENGINE CRANKCASE (qts)		TRANSMISSION (pts)			Drive Axle° (pts)	Gasoline Tank (gals)	Cooling System (qts)		
		With Filter	Without Filter	Manual 3-spd	Manual 4-spd	Automatic ■			W/AC	W/O AC	W/Extra Cooling
1961	all	4.5	3.5	2.5	—	—	2.0	14	—	12.3	—
1962	all	4.5	3.5	2.5	—	—	2.0	14	—	12.3	—
1963	all	4.5	3.5	3.0	—	—	2.0	14	—	10.5	—
1964	all	4.5	3.5	3.0	4.8	15.0	2.5①	14	—	9.5	—
1965	all	4.5②	3.5③	3.0	—	15.0	2.5①	14	—	9.5	—
1966	all	4.5②	3.5③	3.5	—	④	2.5①	14	—	⑤	—
1967–68	all	4.5②	3.5③	3.5	—	⑥	2.5①	14	—	⑤	—
1969	170	4.5	3.5	3.5	—	—	⑦	15	—	10.0	—
	240	5.0	4.0	3.5	—	20.5	⑦	15	—	12.0	16.3
	302	5.0	4.0	3.5	—	20.5	⑦	15	—	16.3	—
1970	170	4.5	3.5	3.5	—	20.5	5.0	24⑨	—	9.12	—
	240	5.0	4.0	3.5	—	20.5	6.0	24⑨	16.6	14.4	14.4
	302	5.0	4.0	3.5	—	20.5	6.0	24⑨	17.5	15.2	17.5

Year	Engine										
1971	240	5.0	4.0	3.5	—	20.5	[7]	21	16.7	14.4	16.7
	302	5.0	4.0	3.5	—	20.5	[7]	21	17.5	15.2	17.5
1972	240	5.0	4.0	3.5	—	20.5	[7]	21	—	14.1	16.2
	302	5.0	4.0	3.5	—	20.5	[7]	21	17.0	15.2	17.0
1973	240	5.0	4.0	3.5	—	20.5	[7]	20[10]	—	14.1	16.2
	300	5.0	4.0	3.5	—	20.5	[7]	20[10]	16.3	14.5	16.3
	302	6.0	5.0	3.5	—	20.5	[7]	20[10]	17.5	15.3	17.5
1974	240	5.0	4.0	3.5	—	20.5	[7]	20[11]	—	14.1	16.2
	300	5.0	4.0	3.5	—	20.5	[7]	20[11]	16.3	14.5	16.3
	302	6.0	5.0	3.5	—	20.5	[7]	20[11]	17.5	15.3	17.5
1975	300	6.0	5.0	3.5	—	20.5[12]	[7]	[13]	—	14.5[14]	—
	351W	6.0	5.0	3.5	—	20.5[12]	[7]	[13]	24.0	20.0	24.0
	460	6.0	5.0	—	—	20.5[12]	[7]	[13]	28.0	28.0	—
1976	300	6.0	5.0	3.5	—	20.0	[15]	[13]	—	14.5	—
	351W	6.0	5.0	3.5	—	20.0[12]	[15]	[13]	24.0	20.0	24.0
	460	6.0	5.0	—	—	20.0[12]	[15]	[13]	28.0	28.0	—

Capacities (cont.)

Year	Engine Displacement Cu In.	ENGINE CRANKCASE (qts)		TRANSMISSION (pts)			Drive Axle° (pts)	Gasoline Tank (gals)	Cooling System (qts)		
		With Filter	Without Filter	Manual 3-spd	4-spd	Automatic ■			W/AC	W/O AC	W/Extra Cooling
1977	300	6.0	5.0	3.5	—	20.0	⑯	⑬	—	14.5	—
	351W	6.0	5.0	3.5	—	20.0⑫	⑯	⑬	20.0	17.0	20.0
	460	6.0	5.0	—	—	20.0⑫	⑯	⑬	28.0	28.0	—
1978	300	6.0	5.0	3.5	5.0	20.5	⑯	⑬	—	14.5	—
	351W	6.0	5.0	—	—	20.0⑫	⑯	⑬	20.0	17.0	20.0
	460	6.0	5.0	—	—	20.0⑫	⑯	⑬	28.0	28.0	—
1979–82	300	6.0	5.0	3.5	5.0	20.0	17	18	20.0	15.0	—
	302	6.0	5.0	3.5	5.0	20.0	17	18	17.5	15.0⑲	17.5

1979–82 (cont.)	351W	460
	6.0	6.0
	5.0	5.0
	—	—
	—	—
	23.5	23.5
	17	17
	18	18
	20.0	28.0
	20.0	20.0
	—	—

① Optional 2700 lb axle: 5.0
② 240 cid: 5.0
③ 240 cid: 4.0
④ 170 cid: 15.6
   240 cid: 17.8
⑤ 170 cid: 10.0
   240 cid: 12.0
⑥ 170 cid: 16.0
   240 cid: 21.0
⑦ Ford axles: 5.0
   Dana axles: 6.0
⑧ not used
⑨ With fuel evaporative emission controls: 21.0
⑩ E-300: 23.0
⑪ E-300 van and camper special, except California: 23.0
⑫ C-6: 24.5
⑬ E-100 van and club wagon with evaporative emission controls: 18.0
   E-150: 18.0
⑭ All others: 22.1
   Optional auxiliary: 18.0
   With auto trans.: 16.6
⑮ Ford axles: 6.5
   Dana axles: 6.0
⑯ Ford axles: 6.5
   Dana model 61-1: 5.0
   Dana model 70: 5.5
⑰ Ford axles: 6.5
   Dana model 61-1: 6.0
   Dana model 70: 7.0
⑱ E-100, 150 with 124 inch wheel base: 18.0
   All others: 22.1
   Optional auxiliary: 18.0 except E-350 cutaway chassis: 40.0
⑲ With auto trans.: 17.5
* For limited slip units, add 1 oz of limited slip additive
■ Includes torque converter

Tune-Up

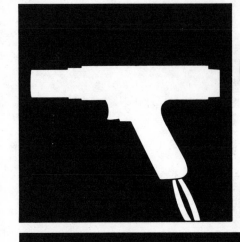

TUNE-UP PROCEDURES

Spark Plugs

A typical spark plug consists of a metal shell surrounding a ceramic insulator. A metal electrode extends downward through the center of the insulator and protrudes a small distance. Located at the end of the plug and attached to the side of the outer metal shell is the side electrode. The side electrode bends in at a 90° angle so that its tip is even with, and parallel to, the tip of the center electrode. The distance between these two electrodes (measured in thousandths of an inch) is called the spark plug gap. The spark plug in no way produces a spark but merely provides a gap across which the current can arc. The coil produces anywhere from 20,000 to 40,000 volts which travels to the distributor where it is distributed through the spark plug wires to the spark plugs. The current passes along the center electrode and jumps the gap to the side electrode, and, in so doing, ignites the air/fuel mixture in the combustion chamber.

SPARK PLUG HEAT RANGE

Spark plug heat range is the ability of the plug to dissipate heat. The longer the insulator (or the farther it extends into the engine), the hotter the plug will operate; the shorter the insulator the cooler it will operate. A plug that absorbs little heat and remains too cool will quickly accumulate deposits of oil and carbon since it is not hot enough to burn them off. This leads to plug fouling and consequently to misfiring. A plug that absorbs too much heat will have no deposits, but, due to the excessive heat, the electrodes will burn away quickly and in some instances, preignition may result. Preignition takes place when plug tips get so hot that they glow sufficiently to ignite the fuel/air mixture before the actual spark occurs. This early ignition will usually cause a pinging during low speeds and heavy loads.

The general rule of thumb for choosing the correct heat range when picking a spark plug is: if most of your driving is long distance, high speed travel, use a colder plug; if most of your driving is stop and go, use a hotter plug. Original equipment plugs are compromise plugs, but most people never have occasion to change their plugs from the factory-recommended heat range.

REPLACING SPARK PLUGS

A set of spark plugs usually requires replacement before about 10,000 miles on vans with conventional ignition systems and after about 20,000 to 30,000 miles on vans with electronic ignition, depending on your style of driving. In normal operation, plug gap increases about 0.001 in. for every 1,000–2,500 miles. As the gap increases, the plug's voltage requirement also increases. It requires a greater voltage to jump the wider gap and about two to three times as much voltage to fire a plug at high speeds than at idle.

When you're removing spark plugs, you should work on one at a time. Don't start by removing the plug wires all at once, because unless you number them, they may become mixed up. Take a minute before you begin and number the wires with tape. The best location for numbering is near where the wires come out of the cap.

1. Twist the spark plug boot and remove the boot and wire from the plug. Do not pull on the wire itself as this will ruin the wire.

2. If possible, use a brush or rag to clean the area around the spark plug. Make sure that all the dirt is removed so that none will enter the cylinder after the plug is removed.

3. Remove the spark plug using the proper size socket. Turn the socket counterclockwise to remove the plug. Be sure to hold the socket straight on the plug to avoid breaking the plug, or rounding off the hex on the plug.

4. Once the plug is out, check it against the plugs shown in this section to determine engine condition. This is crucial since plug readings are vital signs of engine condition.

5. Use a round wire feeler gauge to check the plug gap. The correct size gauge should pass through the electrode gap with a slight drag. If you're in doubt, try one size smaller and one larger. The smaller gauge should go through easily while the larger one shouldn't go through at all. If the gap is incorrect, use the electrode bending tool on the end of the gauge to adjust the gap. When adjusting the gap, always bend the side electrode. The center electrode is non-adjustable.

6. Squirt a drop of penetrating oil on the threads of the new plug and install it. Don't oil the threads too heavily. Turn the plug in clockwise by hand until is it snug.

7. When the plug is finger tight, tighten it with a wrench.

8. Install the plug boot firmly over the plug. Proceed to the next plug.

CHECKING AND REPLACING SPARK PLUG CABLES

Visually inspect the spark plug cables for burns, cuts, or breaks in the insulation. Check the spark plug boots and the nipples on the distributor cap and coil. Replace any damaged wiring. If no physical damage is obvious, the wires can be checked with an ohmmeter for excessive resistance.

When installing a new set of spark plug cables, replace the cables one at a time so there will be no mixup. Start by replacing the longest cable first. Install the boot firmly over the spark plug. Route the wire exactly the same as the original. Insert the nipple firmly into the tower on the distributor cap. Repeat the process for each cable.

Spark Plug Wires—Dura Spark System

The secondary wires used with the DURA SPARK II and III system are 8 mm to contain the higher output voltage. There are two types of wires used in the system and some engines will have both types. It is important to properly identify the type of wire used for each cylinder before replacements are made.

Both types are blue in color and have silicone jacketing. The insulation material underneath the jacketing may be EPDM or another silicone layer separated by glass braid. The cable incorporating EPDM is used where engine temperatures are cooler and are identified with the letters "SE" with black printing. The silicone jacket silicone insulation type is used where high engine temperatures are present and is identified with the letters "SS" with white printing.

The cables are also marked with the cylinder number, model year and date of cable manufacture (quarter and year). Service replacement wires will not have cylinder numbers, or manufacture date.

NOTE: *On any vehicle equipped with a catalytic converter, never allow the engine to run for more than 30 seconds with a spark plug wire disconnected. Use an oscilloscope for testing and diagnosis. Do not puncture wires or use adapters that can cause misfiring. Unburned fuel in the cylinders will ignite in the converter as it is exhausted and damage the converter.*

REMOVAL

When removing spark plug wires, use great care. Grasp and twist the insulator back and forth on the spark plug to free the insulator. Do not pull on the wire directly as it may become separated from the connector inside the insulator.

Tune-Up Specifications

When analyzing compression test results, look for uniformity among cylinders, rather than specific pressures.

Year	Engine Displace (Cu In.)	SPARK PLUGS		DISTRIBUTOR		IGNITION TIMING (deg)		Intake Valve Opens (deg)	Fuel Pump Pressure (psi)	Idle Speed (rpm) MT/AT ●	VALVE CLEAR (in.)	
		Type	Gap (in.)	Point Dwell (deg)	Point Gap (in.)	MT	AT				In	Ex
1961	144	BF-82	.034	35-38	.025	6B	—	9B	3.5-5.5	550	.018	.018
	170	BF-82	.034	35-38	.025	6B	—	9B	3.5-5.5	550	.018	.018
1962	144	BF-82	.034	35-38	.025	6B	—	9B	3.5-5.5	550	.018	.018
	170	BF-82	.034	35-38	.025	6B	—	9B	3.5-5.5	550	.018	.018
1963	144	BF-82	.035	35-38	.025	4B	—	9B	3.5-5.5	550	.018	.018
	170	BF-82	.035	35-38	.025	4B	—	9B	3.5-5.5	550	.018	.018
1964	144	BF-82	.035	35-38	.025	4B	—	9B	3.5-5.5	600	.018	.018
	170	BF-82	.035	35-38	.025	4B	8B	9B	3.5-5.5	600/575	.018	.018
1965	170	BF-82	.035	35-38	.025	4B	8B	9B	4-6	600/525	.018	.018
	200	BF-82	.035	35-38	.025	6B	10B	9B	4-6	600/525	Hyd.	Hyd.
	240	BF-82	.035	35-38	.025	6B	8B	12B	4-6	525/525	Hyd.	Hyd.
1966	170	BF-82	.035	37-42	.025	4B①	8B①	9B	4-6	②	.018	.018
	240	BTF-42	.035	37-42	.025	6B①	10B①	12B	4-6	③	Hyd.	Hyd.

Year	Cu. In.	Spark Plug	Gap	Dwell	Point Gap					Idle		
1967–68	170	BF-82	.035	37–42	.025	6B[1]	10B[1]	9B	4–6	[1]	.018	.018
	240	BTF-42	.035	37–42	.025	6B[1]	10B[1]	12B	4–6	[5]	Hyd.	Hyd.
1969	170	BF-82	.034	35–40	.027	6B	—	15B	4–6	700	.018	.018
	240	BTF-42	.034	35–40[6]	.027	6B[8]	10B[7]	12B	4–6	[5]	Hyd.	Hyd.
	302	BTF-31	.030	24–29[7]	.021	6B	6B	16B	4–6	625/550	Hyd.	Hyd.
1970	170	BF-82	.034	35–40	.027	6B	—	15B	4–6	775	.018	.018
	240	BTF-42	.034	35–40	.027	6B	6B	12B	4–6	[9]	Hyd.	Hyd.
	302	BTF-31	.030	24–29[11]	.021[11]	6B	6B	16B	4–6	[12]	Hyd.	Hyd.
1971	240	BTF-42[13]	.034[11]	35–40[15]	.027[16]	6B	6B	12B	4–6	[12]	Hyd.	Hyd.
	302	BTF-31	.030	24–29[11]	.021[11]	6B	6B	16B	4–6	[12]	Hyd.	Hyd.
1972	240	BTF-42[13]	.034[11]	35–40[15]	.027[16]	6B	6B	12B	4–6	[17]	Hyd.	Hyd.
	302	BTF-31	.030	24–29[11]	.021[11]	6B	6B	16B	4.5–6.5	[12]	Hyd.	Hyd.
1973	240	BRF-42	.034	33–39	.027	6B	6B	12B	4–6	[17]	Hyd.	Hyd.
	300	BRF-42[14]	.034	33–39	.027	6B	6B	12B	4–6	[17]	Hyd.	Hyd.
	302	BRF-42	.034	24–30	.017	6B	6B	16B	4.5–6.5	[12]	Hyd.	Hyd.
1974	240	BRF-42	.034	Electronic		6B	6B	12B	4–6	850/650	Hyd.	Hyd.

Tune-Up Specifications (cont.)

When analyzing compression test results, look for uniformity among cylinders, rather than specific pressures.

Year	Engine Displace (Cu In.)	SPARK PLUGS		DISTRIBUTOR		IGNITION TIMING (deg)		Intake Valve Opens (deg)	Fuel Pump Pressure (psi)	Idle Speed (rpm) MT/AT ●	VALVE CLEAR (in.)	
		Type	Gap (in.)	Point Dwell (deg)	Point Gap (in.)	MT	AT				In	Ex
1974 (cont.)	300	BRF-42 [18]	.034	Electronic		10B [21]	10B	12B	4-6	700/550 [19]	Hyd.	Hyd.
	302	BRF-42	.044 [20]	Electronic		6B	6B	16B	4.5-6.5	900/650	Hyd.	Hyd.
1975	300	BTRF-42	.044	Electronic		12B	12B	12B	4-6	700/550	Hyd.	Hyd.
	351W	ARF-42	.044	Electronic		14B	14B	16B	5-7	900/650	Hyd.	Hyd.
	460	ARF-42	.044	Electronic		—	12B	8B	5-7	—/650	Hyd.	Hyd.
1976	300	BTRF-42	.044	Electronic		12B	12B [21]	12B	4-6	700/550	Hyd.	Hyd.
	351W	ARF-32 [22]	.044	Electronic		8B	8B [23]	16B	5-7	650/650	Hyd.	Hyd.
	460	ARF-42	.044	Electronic		—	12B	8B	5-7	—/650	Hyd.	Hyd.
1977	300	BSF-42	.044	Electronic		10B [25]	10B [25]	12B	4-6	600/600 [26]	Hyd.	Hyd.
	351W	ASF-34 [24]	.044	Electronic		8B [27]	8B [27]	16B	5-7	650/550 [28]	Hyd.	Hyd.
	460	ASF-42	.044	Electronic		—	12B	8B	5-7	—/650	Hyd.	Hyd.
1978	300	BSF-42	.054 [29]	Electronic		[30]	[30]	12B	4-6	[30]	Hyd.	Hyd.
	351W	ASF-42	.044	Electronic		—	[30]	16B	5-7	[30]	Hyd.	Hyd.

Year	Engine	Spark Plugs	Gap	Distributor						Valve	
1979	460	ASF-42	.044	Electronic	—	[30]	8B	5–7	[30]	Hyd.	Hyd.
	300	BSF-42	.044	Electronic	[30]	[30]	12B	4–6	[30]	Hyd.	Hyd.
	302	ASF-42	.044	Electronic	[30]	[30]	16B	5–7	[30]	Hyd.	Hyd.
	351W	ASF-42	.044	Electronic	—	[30]	16B	5–7	[30]	Hyd.	Hyd.
	460	ASF-42	.044	Electronic	—	[30]	8B	5–7	[30]	Hyd.	Hyd.
1980–82	300	BSF-42	.044	Electronic	[30]	[30]	12B	4–6	[30]	Hyd.	Hyd.
	302	ASF-42	.044	Electronic	[30]	[30]	16B	5–7	[30]	Hyd.	Hyd.
	351W	ASF-42	.044	Electronic	[30]	[30]	16B	5–7	[30]	Hyd.	Hyd.
	400	ASF-42	.044	Electronic	[30]	[30]	16B	5–7	[30]	Hyd.	Hyd.
	460	ASF-42	.044	Electronic	[30]	[30]	8B	5–7	[30]	Hyd.	Hyd.

Part numbers in this chart are not recommendations by Chilton for any product by brand name.

① With Thermactor: TDC
② Without Thermactor: MT 600, AT 525
    With Thermactor: MT 650, AT 575
③ Without Thermactor: MT 525, AT 525
    With Thermactor: MT 650, AT 575
④ Without Thermactor: MT 575, AT 500
    With Thermactor: MT 700, AT 550
⑤ Without Thermactor: MT 525, AT 500
    With Thermactor: MT 600, AT 500
⑥ Without Thermactor: 37–42
⑦ With Thermactor: 26–31
⑧ With Emission Controls: 6B
⑨ E-300 Van: MT 600, AT 550
    E-100, 200, 300 Bus: MT 850 solenoid on; 500 solenoid off
    AT 575 solenoid on; 500 solenoid off
⑩ E-100: 26–31
⑪ E-300: .017
⑫ MT 800 solenoid on; 500 solenoid off
    AT 600 solenoid on; 500 solenoid off
⑬ E-300 van: BTF-31
⑭ E-300 van: .030
⑮ E-300 van: 37–42
⑯ E-300 van: .025
⑰ E-300 van: MT 600, AT 500
    E-100, 200, 300 Bus: MT 850 solenoid on; 500 solenoid off
    AT 600 solenoid on; 500 solenoid off
⑱ E-300 van: BRF-31
⑲ E-300 van: MT 600, AT 550. NOTE: AT not available in Calif.
⑳ Calif.: .054
㉑ Calif.: 6B
㉒ E-100: ARF-42
㉓ Calif.: 12B
㉔ E-100: ASF-42
㉕ E-100: 6B
㉖ E-100: MT 700, AT 550
㉗ E-100 High Altitude: 12B
    E-100 Calif.: MT 8B, AT 14B
    All other E-100: see underhood sticker
㉘ E-100 High Altitude: 550
    E-100 Calif.: MT 900, AT 700
    E-100 49 states: MT 800, AT 650
㉙ Calif., and all E-100: .044
㉚ See underhood sticker
● AT in Drive; brake on

INSTALLATION

1. Install each wire in or on the proper terminal of the distributor cap. Be sure the terminal connector inside the insulator is fully seated. The No. 1 terminal is identified on the cap. On six-cylinder engines, install the wires in a clockwise direction.

On 8 cylinder engines, cylinders are numbered from front to rear; right bank 1-2-3-4, left bank 5-6-7-8. On 8-cylinder engines install the wires in a counterclockwise direction in the firing order (1-5-4-2-6-3-7-8) starting at the No. 1 terminal for 4.9L (302 CID) V-8, 7.5L (460 CID) V-8 engines. On 5.8L (351 CID) W V-8, and 6.6L (400 CID) V-8 the firing order is 1-3-7-2-6-5-4-8.

2. On 8-cylinder engines, remove the brackets from the old spark plug wire set and install them on the new set in the same relative position. Install the wires in the brackets on the valve rocker arm covers. Connect the wires to the proper spark plugs. Install the coil high tension lead.

The wires in the left bank bracket must be positioned in the bracket in a special order to avoid cylinder cross-fire. Be sure to position the wires in the bracket in the order from front to rear.

Whenever a DURA SPARK II high tension wire is removed for any reason from a spark plug, coil or distributor terminal housing, silicone grease must be applied to the boot before it is reconnected. Using a small clean tool, coat the entire interior surface of the boot with Ford silicone grease D7AZ 19A331-A or equivalent.

Firing Orders

To avoid confusion, replace spark plug wires one at a time.

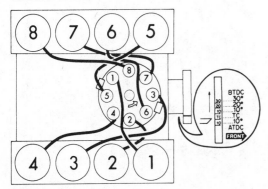

302 V8 through 1974
firing order: 1-5-4-2-6-3-7-8
distributor rotation: counterclockwise

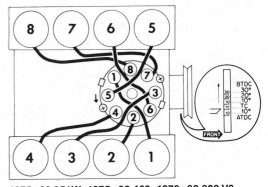

1975–80 351W, 1975–82 460, 1979–82 302 V8
firing order: 1-5-4-2-6-3-7-8
distributor rotation: counterclockwise
NOTE: Squares are the positions of latches on 1975–76 models; circles are the positions of latches on 1977–82 models

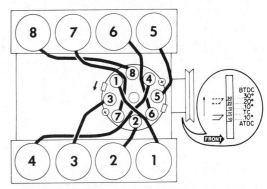

1980–82 400 and 1981–82 351W V8
firing order: 1-3-7-2-6-5-4-8
distributor rotation: counterclockwise

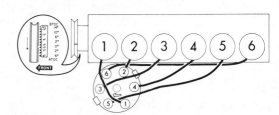

144, 170, 200 6-cylinder
firing order: 1-5-3-6-2-4
distributor rotation: clockwise

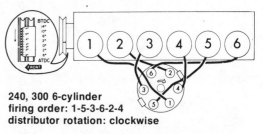

240, 300 6-cylinder
firing order: 1-5-3-6-2-4
distributor rotation: clockwise

Breaker Points

NOTE: *None of the discussion on breaker points applies to the solid-state, or elec-*

tronic, ignition system on some 1974 and all 1975 and later models.

The points function as a circuit breaker for the primary circuit of the ignition system. The ignition coil must boost the 12 volts of electrical pressure supplied by the battery to as much as 25,000 volts in order to fire the spark plugs. To do this, the coil depends on the points and the condenser to make a clean break in the primary circuit.

The coil has both primary and secondary circuits. When the ignition is turned on, the battery supplies voltage through the coil and on to the points. The points are connected to ground, completing the primary circuit. As the current passes through the coil, a magnetic field is created in the iron center core of the coil. As the cam in the distributor turns, the points open and the primary circuit is interrupted. The magnetic field in the primary circuit of the coil collapses and cuts through the secondary circuit windings around the iron core. Because of the scientific phenomenon called "electromagnetic induction," the battery voltage is at this point increased to a level sufficient to fire the spark plugs.

When the points open, the electrical charge in the primary circuit jumps the gap created between the two open contacts of the points. If this electrical charge were not transferred elsewhere, the metal contacts of the points would melt and the gap between the points would start to change rapidly. If this gap is not maintained, the points will not break the primary circuit. If the primary circuit is not broken, the secondary circuit will not have enough voltage to fire the spark plugs.

The function of the condenser is to absorb excessive voltage from the points when they open and thus prevent the points from becoming pitted or burned.

There are two ways to check the breaker point gap: It can be done with a feeler gauge or a dwell meter. Either way you set the points, you are basically adjusting the amount of time that the points remain open. The time is measured in degrees of distributor rotation. When you measure the gap between the breaker points with a feeler gauge, you are setting the maximum amount the points will open when the rubbing block on the points is on a high point of the distributor cam. When you adjust the points with a dwell meter, you are adjusting the number of degrees that the points will remain closed before they start to open as a high point of

the distributor cam approaches the rubbing block of the points.

When you replace a set of points, always replace the condenser at the same time.

When you change the point gap or dwell, you will also have changed the ignition timing. So, if the point gap or dwell is changed, the ignition timing must be adjusted also. Changing the ignition timing, however, does not affect the dwell of the breaker points.

REPLACEMENT OF THE BREAKER POINTS AND CONDENSER

1. Remove the coil high-tension wire from top of the distributor cap. Remove the distributor cap from the distributor and place it out of the way. Remove the rotor from the distributor shaft.

2. Loosen the screw which holds the condenser lead to the body of the breaker points and remove the condenser lead from the points.

3. Remove the screw which holds and grounds the condenser to the distributor body. Remove the condenser from the distributor and discard it.

4. Remove the points assembly attaching screws and adjustment lockscrews. A screwdriver with a holding mechanism will come in handy here so that you don't drop a screw into the distributor and have to remove the entire distributor to retrieve it.

5. Remove the points by lifting them straight up and off the locating dowel on the plate. Wipe off the cam and apply new cam lubricant. Discard the old set of points.

6. Slip the new set of points onto the locating dowel and install the screws that hold the asembly onto the plate. Do not tighten them all the way.

7. Attach the new condenser to the plate with the ground screw.

8. Attach the condenser lead to the points at the proper place.

9. Apply a small amount of cam lubricant to the shaft where the rubbing block of the points touches.

ADJUSTMENT OF THE BREAKER POINTS WITH A FEELER GAUGE

1. If the contact points of the assembly are not parallel, bend the stationary contact so that they make contact across the entire surface of the contacts. Bend only the stationary bracket part of the point assembly; not the moveable contact.

2. Turn the engine until the rubbing block

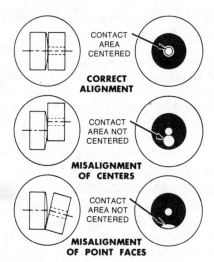

CONTACT
AREA
CENTERED

**CORRECT
ALIGNMENT**

CONTACT
AREA NOT
CENTERED

**MISALIGNMENT
OF CENTERS**

CONTACT
AREA NOT
CENTERED

**MISALIGNMENT
OF POINT FACES**

Alignment of the breaker point contacts

of the points is on one of the high points of the distributor cam. You can do this by either turning the ignition switch to the start position and releasing it quickly ("bumping" the engine) or by using a wrench on the bolt which holds the crankshaft pulley to the crankshaft.

3. Place the correct size feeler gauge between the contacts. Make sure that it is parallel with the contact surfaces.

4. With your free hand, insert a screwdriver into the notch provided for adjustment or into the eccentric adjusting screw, then twist the screwdriver to either increase or decrease the gap to the proper setting.

5. Tighten the adjustment lockscrew and recheck the contact gap to make sure that it didn't change when the lockscrew was tightened.

6. Replace the rotor and distributor cap, and the high-tension wire that connects the top of the distributor and the coil. Make sure that the rotor is firmly seated all the way onto the distributor shaft and that the tab of the rotor is aligned with the notch in the shaft. Align the tab in the base of the distributor cap with the notch in the distributor body. Make sure that the cap is firmly seated on the distributor and that the retainer clips are in place. Make sure that the end of the high-tension wire is firmly placed in the top of the distributor and the coil.

ADJUSTMENT OF THE BREAKER POINTS WITH A DWELL METER

1. Adjust the points with a feeler gauge as described above.

2. Connect the dwell meter to the ignition circuit according to the manufacturer's instructions. One lead of the meter is connected to a ground and the other lead is to be connected to the distributor post on the coil. An adapter is usually provided for this purpose.

3. If the dwell meter has a set line on it, adjust the meter to zero the indicator.

4. Start the engine.

NOTE: *Be careful when working on any vehicle while the engine is running. Make sure that the transmission is in Neutral or Park and that the parking brake is applied. Keep hands, clothing, tools, and the wires of the test instruments clear of the rotating fan blades.*

5. Observe the reading on the dwell meter. If the reading is within the specified range, turn off the engine and remove the dwell meter.

6. If the reading is above the specified range, the breaker point gap is too small. If the reading is below the specified range, the gap is too large. In either case, the engine must be stopped and the gap adjusted in the manner previously covered. After making the adjustment, start the engine and check the reading on the dwell meter. When the correct reading is obtained, disconnect the dwell meter.

7. Check the adjustment of the ignition timing.

Ignition Timing

Ignition timing is the measurement, in degrees of crankshaft rotation, of the point at which the spark plugs fire in each of the cylinders. It is measured in degrees before or after Top Dead Center (TDC) of the compression stroke. Ignition timing is controlled by turning the distributor body in the engine.

Ideally, the air/fuel mixture in the cylinder will be ignited by the spark plug just as the piston passes TDC of the compression stroke. If this happens, the piston will be beginning the power stroke just as the compressed and ignited air/fuel mixture starts to expand. The expansion of the air/fuel mixture then forces the piston down on the power stroke and turns the crankshaft.

Because it takes a fraction of a second for the spark plug to ignite the mixture in the cylinder, the spark plug must fire a little before the piston reaches TDC. Otherwise, the mixture will not be completely ignited as the piston passes TDC and the full power of the explosion will not be used by the engine.

The timing measurement is given in degrees of crankshaft rotation before the piston reaches TDC (BTDC). If the setting for the ignition timing is 5° BTDC, each spark plug must fire 5° before each piston reaches TDC. This only holds true, however, when the engine is at idle speed.

As the engine speed increases, the pistons go faster. The spark plugs have to ignite the fuel even sooner if it is to be completely ignited when the piston reaches TDC. To do this, the distributor has a means to advance the timing of the spark as the engine speed increases. This is accomplished by centrifugal weights within the distributor and a vacuum diaphragm mounted on the side of the distributor. It is necessary to disconnect the vacuum lines from the diaphragm when the ignition timing is being set.

If the ignition is set too far advanced (BTDC), the ignition and expansion of the fuel in the cylinder will occur too soon and tend to force the piston down while it is still traveling up. This causes engine ping. If the ignition spark is set too far retarded after TDC (ATDC), the piston will have already passed TDC and started on its way down when the fuel is ignited. This will cause the piston to be forced down for only a portion of its travel. This will result in poor engine performance and lack of power.

The timing is best checked with a timing light. This device is connected in series with the No. 1 spark plug. The current that fires the spark plug also causes the timing light to flash.

There is a notch on the crankshaft pulley on all engines, except the 302 and 351W V8. A scale of degrees of crankshaft rotation is attached to the engine block in such a position that the notch will pass close by the scale. On the 302 and 351W V8 engines, the scale is located on the crankshaft pulley and a pointer is attached to the engine block so that the scale will pass close by. When the engine is running, the timing light is aimed at the mark on the crankshaft pulley and the scale.

IGNITION TIMING ADJUSTMENT

1. Locate the timing marks on the crankshaft pulley and the front of the engine. On some sixes, the marks are on the flywheel.

2. Clean the timing marks so that you can see them.

3. Mark the timing marks with a piece of chalk or with paint. Color the mark on the scale that will indicate the correct timing when it is aligned with the mark on the pulley or the pointer. It is also helpful to mark the notch in the pulley or the tip of the pointer with a small dab of color.

4. Attach a tachometer to the engine.

5. Attach a timing light according to the manufacturer's instructions. If the timing light has three wires, one is attached to the No. 1 spark plug with an adapter. The other wires are connected to the battery. The red wire goes to the positive side of the battery and the black wire is connected to the negative terminal of the battery.

6. Disconnect the vacuum line to the distributor at the distributor and plug the vacuum line. A golf tee does a fine job.

7. Check to make sure that all of the wires clear the fan and then start the engine.

8. Adjust the idle to the correct setting.

9. Aim the timing light at the timing marks. If the marks that you put on the flywheel or pulley and the engine are aligned when the light flashes, the timing is correct.

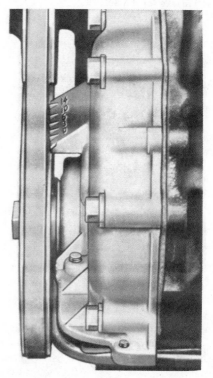

Typical timing marks: 1961–67 6-cylinder

Timing marks for 1968 and later sixes

Timing marks for the 302 V8

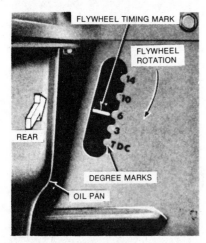

Timing marks for some sixes

Turn off the engine and remove the tachometer and the timing light. If the marks are not in alignment, proceed with the following steps.

10. Turn off the engine.

Typically pulley-mounted timing marks for V8, except 302

11. Loosen the distrubutor lockbolt just enough so that the distributor can be turned with a little effort.

12. Start the engine. Keep the wires of the timing light clear of the fan.

13. With the timing light aimed at the pulley and the marks on the engine, turn the distributor in the direction of rotor rotation to retard the spark, and in the opposite direction of rotor rotation to advance the spark. Align the marks on the pulley and the engine with the the flashes of the timing light.

14. When the marks are aligned, tighten the distributor lockbolt and recheck the timing with the timing light to make sure that the distributor did not move when you tightened the lockbolt.

15. Turn off the engine and remove the timing light.

Valve Lash

Valve adjustment determines how far the valves enter the cylinder and how long they stay open and closed.

If the valve clearance is too large, part of the lift of the camshaft will be used in removing the excessive clearance. Consequently, the valve will not be opening as far as it should. This condition has two effects: the valve train components will emit a tapping sound as they take up the excessive clearance and the engine will perform poorly because the valves don't open fully and allow the proper amount of gases to flow into and out of the engine.

If the valve clearance is too small, the intake valve and the exhaust valves will open too far and they will not fully seat on the cylinder head when they close. When a valve seats itself on the cylinder head, it does two things: it seals the combustion chamber so that none of the gases in the cylinder escape and it cools itself by transferring some of the heat it absorbs from the combustion in the cylinder to the cylinder head and to the engine's cooling system. If the valve clearance is too small, the engine will run poorly because of the gases escaping from the combustion chamber. The valves will also become overheated and will warp, since they cannot transfer heat unless they are touching the valve seat in the cylinder head.

NOTE: *While all valve adjustments must be made as accurately as possible, it is better to have the valve adjustment slightly loose than slightly tight as a burned valve may result from overly tight adjustments.*

ADJUSTMENT

144, 160 6 Cyl. (Solid Lifters)

1. Start the engine and let it run until it has reached operating temperature.

2. Remove the valve cover and gasket.

3. With the engine idling, adjust the valve lash using a step-type feeler gauge. This type of feeler gauge is sometimes more commonly known as a "go-no go" type feeler gauge. The proper clearance is reached when the smaller step on the gauge blade will pass through the gap while the larger step on the same blade will not pass through the gap.

Pass the proper size gauge blade between the valve stem and the rocker arm. If the clearance is correct, move on to the next valve. If the clearance is in need of adjustment, turn the adjusting screw on the opposite end of the rocker arm with a wrench until the proper clearance is reached. Turn the screw clockwise to decrease the clearance and counterclockwise to increase the clearance. Use this procedure for all of the valves.

4. After all of the valves have been adjusted, replace the valve cover gasket and cover. If the gasket is made of rubber, and is not torn, squashed or otherwise damaged it can be used again. If the gasket is cork, it is advised that the gasket be replaced.

5. Tighten the valve cover retaining bolts to 3–5 ft lbs.

Checking the valve clearance on either the 240, 300 six or the 302 V8

302 Cu In. V8

Some early models of the 302 cu in. V8 are equipped with adjustable rockers whereas the later models are equipped with positive stop type rocker mounting studs. Positive stop equipped rockers are adjusted by turning the adjusting nut down until it stops. You can identify a positive stop mounting stud by determining whether or not the shank portion of the stud that is exposed just above the cylinder head is the same diameter as the threaded portion at the top of the stud, to which the rocker arm retaining nut attaches. If the shank portion is larger than the threaded area, it is a positive stop mounting stud. Use the procedure given below for adjusting the valve lash on positive stop type mounting stud equipped vehicles.

There are two different procedures for adjusting the valves on the V8 engines. One is a preferred procedure and one is an alternate

Adjusting the valve clearance on either the 240, 300 six or the 302 V8

procedure. The preferred procedure is recommended, but the alternate procedure may be used.

NOTE: *These procedures are not tune-up procedures, but rebuild procedures to be performed only after valve train reassembly.*

PREFERRED PROCEDURE THROUGH 1969

1. Position the piston(s) on TDC of the compression stroke, using the timing mark on the crankshaft pulley as a reference for starting with the No. 1 cylinder. You can tell if a piston is coming up on its compression stroke by removing the spark plug of the cylinder you are working on and placing your thumb over the hole while the engine is cranked over. Air will try to force its way past your thumb when the piston comes upon the compression stroke. Make sure that the high-tension coil wire leading to the distributor is removed before cranking the engine. Remove the valve covers.

2. Starting with No. 1 cylinder, and the piston in the position as mentioned above, apply pressure to slowly bleed down the valve lifter until the plunger is completely bottomed.

3. While holding the valve lifter in the fully collapsed position, check the available clearance between the rocker arm and the valve stem tip. Use a feeler gauge.

4. If the clearance is not within the specified amount, rotate the rocker arm stud nut clockwise to decrease the clearance and counterclockwise to increase the clearance. Normally, one turn of the rocker arm stud nut will vary the clearance by 0.066 in. Check the break-away torque of each stud nut with a torque wrench, turning it counterclockwise. It should be anywhere from 4.5 to 15 ft lbs. Replace the nut and/or the stud as necessary.

5. When both valves for the No. 1 cylinder have been adjusted, proceed on to the other valves, following the firing order sequence 1–5–4–2–6–3–7–8.

6. Replace the valve covers and gaskets.

ALTERNATE PROCEDURE THROUGH 1969

Follow Step 1 of the preferred procedure given above, but instead of collapsing the lifter as in Step 2, loosen the rocker retaining nut until there is endplay present in the pushrod; then tighten the nut to remove all pushrod-to-rocker arm clearance. When the pushrod-to-rocker arm clearance has been

eliminated, tighten the stud nut an additional ¾ turn to place the lifter plunger in the desired operating range.

Repeat this procedure for all of the cylinders, using the firing order sequence as a guide. It takes ¼ turn of the crankshaft to bring the next piston in the firing order sequence up to TDC at the end of its compression stroke.

POSITIVE STOP TYPE MOUNTING STUD FROM 1970

1. Crank the engine until No. 1 cylinder is at TDC of the compression stroke and the timing pointer is aligned with the TDC mark on the crankshaft damper.

2. Scribe a mark on the damper at this point. This is mark A.

3. Scribe three additional marks on the damper; one at 90° from TDC (mark B), one at 180° (mark C), and the other one at 270° of rotation from TDC (¾ turn from TDC). The mark at 270° is mark D.

4. With the timing pointer aligned with Mark A on the damper, tighten the following valves until the nuts contact the rocker shoulder, then torque them to 18–20 ft lbs: No. 1, intake and exhaust.

5. Rotate the crankshaft 90° to mark B and tighten the following valves: No. 5 intake and exhaust.

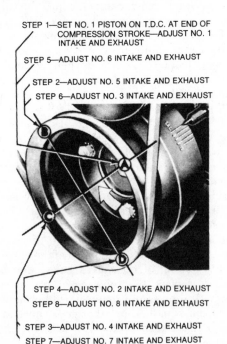

STEP 1—SET NO. 1 PISTON ON T.D.C. AT END OF COMPRESSION STROKE—ADJUST NO. 1 INTAKE AND EXHAUST

STEP 5—ADJUST NO. 6 INTAKE AND EXHAUST

STEP 2—ADJUST NO. 5 INTAKE AND EXHAUST

STEP 6—ADJUST NO. 3 INTAKE AND EXHAUST

STEP 4—ADJUST NO. 2 INTAKE AND EXHAUST

STEP 8—ADJUST NO. 8 INTAKE AND EXHAUST

STEP 3—ADJUST NO. 4 INTAKE AND EXHAUST

STEP 7—ADJUST NO. 7 INTAKE AND EXHAUST

Placement of marks on the crankshaft pulley for adjusting the valves on a 302 V8

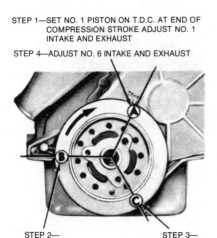

STEP 1—SET NO. 1 PISTON ON T.D.C. AT END OF COMPRESSION STROKE ADJUST NO. 1 INTAKE AND EXHAUST

STEP 4—ADJUST NO. 6 INTAKE AND EXHAUST

STEP 2—
ADJUST NO. 5
INTAKE AND
EXHAUST

STEP 3—
ADJUST NO. 3
INTAKE AND
EXHAUST

STEP 5—
ADJUST NO. 2
INTAKE AND
EXHAUST

STEP 6—
ADJUST NO. 4
INTAKE AND
EXHAUST

Placement of marks on the crankshaft pulley for adjusting the valves on a 240, 300 six

6. Rotate the crankshaft 90° to align mark C with the timing pointer and tighten the following valves: No. 4 intake and exhaust.

7. Rotate the crankshaft another 90° to mark D and adjust valves No. 2 intake and exhaust.

8. Continue in this manner (turning the crankshaft ¼ turn at a time) until all of the valves are adjusted in the firing order; 1–5–4–2–6–3–7–8.

Engines With Hydraulic Lifters

These engines require no periodic adjustments to the valve train.

Idle Speed and Mixture Adjustments

This section contains only tune-up adjustment procedures for carburetors. Descriptions, adjustments and overhaul procedures for carburetors can be found in the "Fuel System" Section (Chapter 4) of this book.

When the engine in your van is running, the air/fuel mixture from the carburetor is being drawn into the engine by a partial vacuum created by the downward movement of the pistons on the intake stroke. The amount of air/fuel mixture that enters the engine is controlled by the throttle plate(s) in the bottom of the carburetor. When the engine is not running, the throttle plates are closed, completely blocking off the air/fuel passage(s) at the bottom of the carburetor. The throttle plates are connected by the throttle linkage to the accelerator pedal in the passenger compartment. When you depress the pedal, you open the throttle plates in the carburetor to admit more air/fuel mixture to the engine.

The idle adjusting screw contacts a lever (throttle lever) on the outside of the carburetor. When the screw is turned, it opens or closes the throttle plates of the carburetor, raising or lowering the idle speed of the engine. This screw is called the curb idle adjusting screw.

IDLE SPEED ADJUSTMENT

1. Start the engine and run it until it reaches operating temperature.

2. If it hasn't already been done, check and adjust the ignition timing. After you have set the timing, turn off the engine.

3. Attach a tachometer to the engine.

4. Turn the headlights on high beam through 1973, or as specified on the underhood specifications sticker for later models.

5. On vans with manual transmissions, engage the parking brake and place the transmission in Neutral; vehicles equipped with automatic transmission, engage the parking brake, and place the gear selector in Drive. Block the wheels.

6. Make sure that the choke plate is in the fully open position.

7. Adjust the engine curb idle rpm to the proper specifications. The tachometer reading must be taken with the carburetor air cleaner in place. If it is impossible to make the adjustment with the air cleaner in position, remove it and make the adjustment. Then replace the air cleaner and check the tachometer for the proper rpm reading.

On carburetors equipped with a solenoid throttle positioner, loosen the jam nut on the solenoid at the bracket and rotate the solenoid in or out to obtain the specified curb idle rpm. Some late models have an adjusting screw. Disconnect the solenoid lead wire at the connector, set the automatic transmission in Neutral then adjust the carburetor throttle stop screw to obtain the lower specified speed or 500 rpm. Connect the solenoid lead wire and open the throttle slightly by hand. The solenoid plunger will follow the throttle lever and remain in the fully extended position as long as the ignition is on and the solenoid energized.

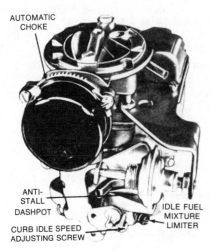

AUTOMATIC
CHOKE

ANTI-
STALL
DASHPOT

CURB IDLE SPEED
ADJUSTING SCREW

IDLE FUEL
MIXTURE
LIMITER

Carter Model YF 1-bbl carburetor adjustments

ADJUST HERE
TO OBTAIN
RPM
SPECIFIED

LEAD WIRE

SOLENOID

ADJUST HERE
TO SPECIFIED
CURB IDLE

Carter Model YF 1-bbl carburetor equipped with a solenoid

IDLE MIXTURE ADJUSTMENT

NOTE: *The factory recommended procedure for adjusting the idle mixture on 1975–82 models requires the addition of an artificial mixture enrichment substance (propane) to the air intake. This requires special tools not generally available. The following procedure is specifically recommended by the factory only for models through 1974.*

In 1969, limiter caps were installed on the idle mixture screws to prevent incorrect adjustment. A satisfactory adjustment should be obtainable within the range of the limiter caps.

The idle mixture screws are adjusted by turning them in and out until the fastest and smoothest idle is obtained. On models not equipped with limiter caps, start the adjustment procedure with the adjustment screw

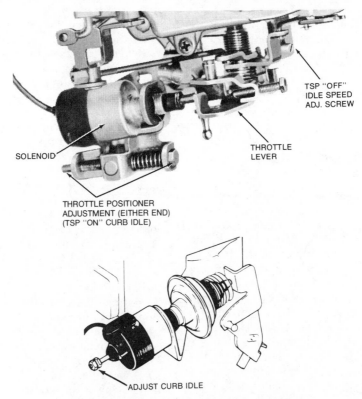

TSP "OFF"
IDLE SPEED
ADJ. SCREW

THROTTLE
LEVER

SOLENOID

THROTTLE POSITIONER
ADJUSTMENT (EITHER END)
(TSP "ON" CURB IDLE)

ADJUST CURB IDLE

Adjustment for two types of throttle solenoids

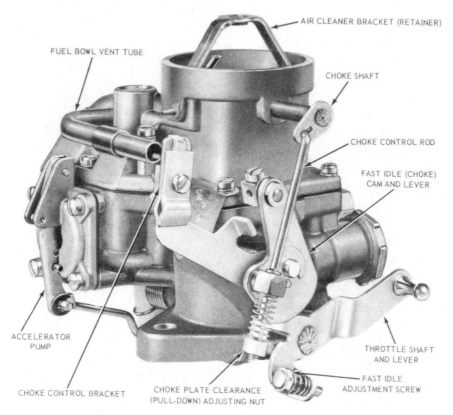

Ford Model 1100 1-bbl carburetor used on the 170 six

AIR CLEANER BRACKET (RETAINER)

FUEL BOWL VENT TUBE

CHOKE SHAFT

CHOKE CONTROL ROD

FAST IDLE (CHOKE) CAM AND LEVER

ACCELERATOR PUMP

THROTTLE SHAFT AND LEVER

FAST IDLE ADJUSTMENT SCREW

CHOKE CONTROL BRACKET

CHOKE PLATE CLEARANCE (PULL-DOWN) ADJUSTING NUT

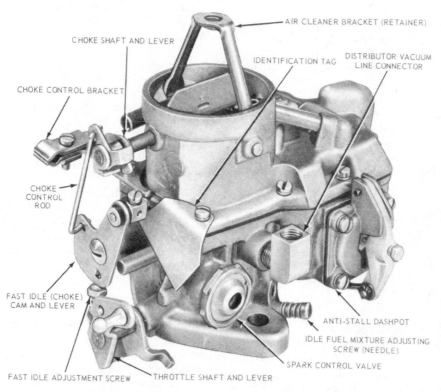

Ford Model 1100 1-bbl carburetor used on the 240 six

AIR CLEANER BRACKET (RETAINER)

CHOKE SHAFT AND LEVER

IDENTIFICATION TAG

DISTRIBUTOR VACUUM LINE CONNECTOR

CHOKE CONTROL BRACKET

CHOKE CONTROL ROD

FAST IDLE (CHOKE) CAM AND LEVER

ANTI-STALL DASHPOT

IDLE FUEL MIXTURE ADJUSTING SCREW (NEEDLE)

SPARK CONTROL VALVE

FAST IDLE ADJUSTMENT SCREW

THROTTLE SHAFT AND LEVER

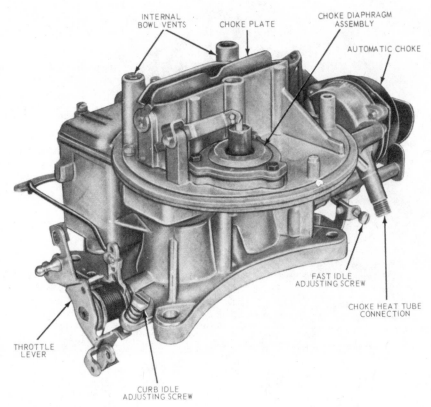

INTERNAL
BOWL VENTS

CHOKE PLATE

CHOKE DIAPHRAGM
ASSEMBLY

AUTOMATIC CHOKE

FAST IDLE
ADJUSTING SCREW

CHOKE HEAT TUBE
CONNECTION

THROTTLE
LEVER

CURB IDLE
ADJUSTING SCREW

Autolite Model 2100 2-bbl carburetor—view shows the curb idle adjustment screws

seated LIGHTLY. Then turn the screw out 1 to 1½ turns as a starting point.

NOTE: *Always favor a slightly rich mixture over a slightly lean mixture.*

If a satisfactory idle cannot be obtained within the range of the limiter caps, it is possible to remove the caps to obtain a better idle. This should be done only as a last resort.

NOTE: *The exhaust must be checked with an exhaust gas analyzer if the limiter caps are removed and the carburetor adjusted without them.*

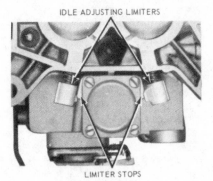

IDLE ADJUSTING LIMITERS

LIMITER STOPS

Autolite Model 2100 2-bbl carburetor—bottom view showing the idle mixture screws with limiter caps

Check the following as being possible causes for not obtaining a satisfactory idle before removing the limiter caps:

1. Vacuum leaks
2. Ignition system wiring continuity
3. Spark plugs
4. Distributor breaker points dwell
5. Ignition timing
6. Fuel level and fuel bowl vent
7. Crankcase ventilation system
8. Engine compression

Remove the plastic limiter caps by cutting them with a pair of side cutter pliers and a knife. After the cut is made, pry the limiter apart and remove it. Adjust the carburetor to the best idle and maximum engine rpm.

There are service limiter caps available for replacement of the factory caps. They are installed by pushing them straight on with either your thumb or a ⅜ in. drive socket wrench extension. Position the caps so that they are in the maximum counterclockwise positions, up against the stop of the carburetor body. This places the adjusting screw in the maximum allowable outward, or rich mixture, setting.

Engine and Engine Rebuilding

3

ENGINE ELECTRICAL

Ignition System

Two types of ignition systems are used in the Ford van. A conventional system using breaker points and condenser is used on 1961 through 1973, and some 1974 models. A breakerless (solid state) ignition system using an armature and magnetic pickup coil assembly in the distributor and a solid state amplifer module located inline between the coil and distributor is installed in some 1974 and all 1975 and later models as standard equipment.

Both systems employ a distributor which is driven by the camshaft at one half crankshaft rpm, a high voltage rotor, distributor cap and spark plug wiring, and an oil-filled conventional type coil.

The two systems differ in the manner in which they convert electrical primary voltage

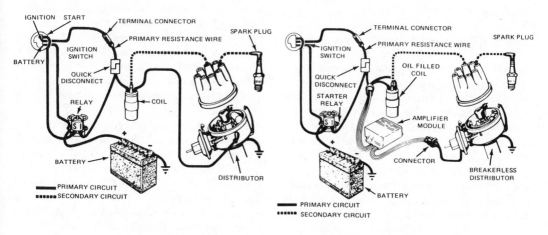

CONVENTIONAL   BREAKERLESS

Typical ignition systems

(12 volt) from the battery into secondary voltage (20,000 volts or greater) to fire the spark plugs. In the conventional ignition system, the breaker points open and close as the movable breaker arm rides the rotating distributor cam eccentric, thereby opening and closing the current to the ignition coil. When the points open, they interrupt the flow of primary current to the coil, causing a collapse of the magnetic field in the coil and creating a high tension spark which is used to fire the spark plugs. In the breakerless system, a distributor shaft-mounted armature rotates past a magnetic pickup coil assembly causing fluctuations in the magnetic field generated by the pickup coil. These fluctuations in turn, cause the amplifier module to turn the ignition coil current off and on, creating the high tension spark to fire the spark plugs. The amplifier module electronically controls the dwell, which is controlled mechanically in a conventional system by the duration which the points remain closed.

Both the conventional and breakerless ignition systems are equipped with dual advance distributors. The vacuum advance unit governs ignition timing according to engine load, while the centrifugal advance unit governs ignition timing according to engine rpm. Centrifugal advance is controlled by spring-mounted weights contained in the distributor, located under the breaker point mounting plate on conventional systems and under the fixed base plate on breakerless systems. As engine speed increases, centrifugal force moves the weights outward from the distributor shaft advancing the position of the distributor cam (conventional) or armature (breakerless), thereby advancing the ignition timing. Vacuum advance is controlled by a vacuum diaphragm which is mounted on the side of the distributor and attached to the breaker point mounting plate (conventional) or the magnetic pickup coil assembly (breakerless) via the vacuum advance link. Under light acceleration, the engine is operating under a low-load condition, causing the carburetor vacuum to act on the distributor vacuum diaphragm, moving the breaker point mounting plate (conventional) or pickup coil assembly (breakerless) opposite the direction of distributor shaft rotation, thereby advancing the ignition timing.

The distributors on many models incorporate a vacuum retard mechanism. The retard mechanism is contained in the rear part of the vacuum diaphragm chamber. When the engine is operating under high-vacuum conditions (deceleration or idle), intake manifold vacuum is applied to the retard mechanism. The retard mechanism moves the breaker point mounting plate (conventional) or pickup coil assembly (breakerless) in the direction of distributor rotation, thereby retarding the ignition timing. Ignition retard, under these conditions, reduces exhaust emissions of hydrocarbons, although it does reduce engine efficiency somewhat.

Ford Motor Company Solid-State Ignition

BASIC OPERATING PRINCIPLES

In mid 1974, Ford Motor Company introduced in selected models its new Solid-State Ignition System. In 1975, it became standard equipment in all vans in the Ford lineup. This system was designed primarily to provide a hotter spark necessary to fire the leaner fuel/air mixtures required by today's emission control standards.

The Ford Solid-State Ignition is a pulse-triggered, transistor controlled breakerless ignition system. With the ignition switch "on," the primary circuit is on and the ignition coil is energized. When the armature spokes approach the magnetic pick-up coil assembly, they induce a voltage which tells the amplifier to turn the coil primary current off. A timing circuit in the amplifier module will turn the current on again after the coil field has collapsed. When the current is on, it flows from the battery through the ignition switch, the primary windings of the ignition coil, and through the amplifier module circuits to ground. When the current is off, the magnetic field built up in the ignition coil is allowed to collapse, inducing a high voltage into the secondary windings of the coil. High voltage is produced each time the field is thus built up and collapsed.

Although the systems are basically the same, Ford refers to their solid-state ignition in several different ways. 1974–76 systems are referred to simply as Breakerless systems. In 1977, Ford named their ignition system Dura-Spark I and Dura-Spark II. Dura-Spark II is the version used in all states except California. Dura-Spark I is the system used in California V8's only. Basically, the only difference between the two is that the coil charging currents are higher in the California cars. This is necessary to fire the leaner fuel/air mixtures required by California's stricter emission laws. The difference in coils alters some of the test values. Beginning in 1981 Ford named their system Dura-Spark III, a more sophisticated version of earlier systems.

Ford has used several different types of wiring harness on their solid-state ignition systems, due to internal circuitry changes in the electronic module. Wire continuity and color have not been changed, but the arrangement of the terminals in the connectors is different for each year. Schematics of the different years are included here, but keep in mind that the wiring in all diagrams has been simplified and as a result, the routing of your wiring may not match the wiring in the diagram. However, the wire colors and terminal connections are the same.

Wire color-coding is critical to servicing the Ford Solid-State Ignition. Battery current reaches the electronic module through either the *white* or *red* wire, depending on whether the engine is cranking or running. When the engine is cranking, battery current is flowing through the *white* wire. When the engine is running, battery current flows through the *red* wire. All distributor signals flow through the *orange* and *purple* wires. The *green* wire carries primary current from the coil to the module. The *black* wire is a ground between the distributor and the module. Up until 1975, a *blue* wire provides transient voltage protection. In 1976, the *blue* wire was dropped when a zener diode was added to the module. The *orange* and *purple* wires which run from the stator to the module must *always* be connected to the same color wire at the module. If these connections are crossed, polarity will be reversed and the system will be thrown out of phase. Some replacement wiring harnesses were sold with the wiring crossed, which complicates the problem considerably. As previously noted, the *black* wire is the ground wire. The screw which grounds the black wire also, of course, grounds the entire primary circuit. If this screw is loose, dirty, or corroded, a seemingly incomprehensible ignition problem will develop. Several other cautions should be noted here. Keep in mind that on vehicles equipped with catalytic converters, any test that requires removal of a spark plug wire while the engine is running should be kept to a thirty second maximum. Any longer than this may damage the conver-

ter. In the event you are testing spark plug wires, do not pierce them. Test the wires at their terminals only.

BASIC TROUBLESHOOTING

Except Electronic Engine Control (EEC) Systems

NOTE: *Troubleshooting procedures are not given for the EEC systems because of their great complexity.*

Before troubleshooting the Dura Spark I system, a ballast resistor must be hooked in series with the ignition coil, or the coil and module could be damaged.

PRELIMINARY CHECKS

1. Check the battery's state of charge and connections.

2. Inspect all wires and connections for breaks, cuts, abrasions, or burn spots. Repair as necessary.

3. Unplug all connectors one at a time and inspect for corroded or burned contacts. Repair and plug connectors back together. DO NOT remove the Lubriplate® compound in the connectors.

4. Check for loose or damaged spark plug or coil wires. A wire resistance check is given at the end of this section. If the boots or nipples are removed on 8mm ignition wires, reline the inside of each with new silicone dielectric compound (Motorcraft WA 10).

SPECIAL TOOLS

To perform the following tests, two special tools are needed; the ignition test jumper shown in the illustration and a modified spark plug. Use the illustration to assemble the ignition test jumper. The test jumper must be used when performing the following tests. The modified spark plug (1977 and later) is basically a spark plug with the side electrode removed. Ford makes a special tool called a Spark Tester for this purpose, which besides not having a side electrode is equipped with a spring clip so that it can be grounded to engine metal. It is recommended that the Spark Tester be used as there is less chance of being shocked.

RUN MODE SPARK TEST

NOTE: *The wire colors given here are the main colors of the wires, not the dots or hashmarks.*

Step 1

1. Remove the distributor cap and rotor from the distributor.

2. With the ignition off, turn the engine over by hand until one of the teeth on the distributor armature aligns with the magnet in the pick-up coil.

3. Remove the coil wire from the distributor cap. On 1977 and later models, install the modified spark plug (see Special Tools, above) in the coil wire terminal and using heavy gloves and insulated pliers, hold the spark plug shell against the engine block. On 1975–76 models, using heavy gloves and insulated pliers, hold the coil wire terminal ¼ inch from the engine block or head.

4. Turn the ignition to RUN (not START) and tap the distributor body with a screwdriver handle. There should be a spark at the modified spark plug or at the coil wire terminal.

5. If a good spark is evident, the primary circuit is OK: perform Start Mode Spark Test. If there is no spark, proceed to Step 2.

Step 2

1. Unplug the module connector(s) which contain(s) the green and black module leads.

2. In the harness side of the connector(s), connect the special test jumper (see Special Tools, above) between the leads which connect to the green and black leads of the module pig tails. Use paper clips on connector socket holes to make contact. Do not allow clips to ground.

3. Turn the ignition switch to RUN (not START) and close the test jumper switch. Leave closed for about 1 second, then open. Repeat several times. There should be a spark each time the switch is opened. On Dura Spark I systems, close the test switch for 10 seconds on the first cycle. After that, 1 second is adequate.

4. If there is no spark, the problem is probably in the primary circuit through the ignition switch, the coil, the green lead or the black lead, or the ground connection in the distributor: perform Step 3. If there is a spark, the primary circuit wiring and coil are probably OK. The problem is probably in the distributor pick-up, the module red wire, or the module: perform Step 6.

Step 3

1. Disconnect the test jumper lead from the black lead and connect it to a good ground.

Turn the test jumper switch on and off several times as in Step 2.

2. If there is no spark, the problem is probably in the green lead, the coil, or the coil feed circuit: perform Step 5.

3. If there is spark, the problem is probably in the black lead or the distributor ground connection: perform Step 4.

Step 4

1. Connect on ohmmeter between the black lead and ground. With the meter on its lowest scale, there should be no measureable resistance in the circuit. If there is resistance, check the distributor ground connection and the black lead from the module. Repair as necessary, remove the ohmmeter, plug in all connections and repeat step 1.

If there is no resistance, the primary ground wiring is OK: perform Step 6.

Step 5

1. Disconnect the test jumper from the green lead and ground and connect it between the TACH-TEST terminal of the coil and a good ground on the engine.

2. With the ignition switch in the RUN position, turn the jumper switch on. Hold it on for about 1 second then turn it off as in Step 2. Repeat several times. There should be a spark each time the switch is turned off. If there is no spark, the problem is probably in the primary circuit running through the ignition switch to the coil BAT terminal, or in the coil itself. Check coil resistance (test given later in this section), and check the coil for internal shorts or opens. Check the coil feed circuit for opens, shorts or high resistance. Repair as necessary, reconnect all connectors and repeat Step 1. If there is spark, the coil and its feed circuit are OK. The problem could be in the green lead between the coil and the module. Check for open or short, repair as necessary, reconnect all connectors and repeat Step 1.

Step 6

To perform this step, a voltmeter which is not combined with a dwell meter is needed. The slight needle oscillations (½ V) you'll be looking for may not be detectable on the combined voltmeter/dwell meter unit.

1. Connect a voltmeter between the orange and purple leads on the harness side of the module connectors.

CAUTION: *On catalytic converter equipped cars, disconnect the air supply line between the Thermactor by-pass valve and the manifold before cranking the engine with the ignition off. This will prevent damage to the catalytic converter. After testing, run the engine for at least 3 minutes before reconnecting the by-pass valve, to clear excess fuel from the exhaust system.*

2. Set the voltmeter on its lowest scale and crank the engine. The meter needle should oscillate slightly (about ½ volt). If the meter does not oscillate, check the circuit through the magnetic pick-up in the distributor for open, shorts, shorts to ground and resistance. Resistance between the orange and purple leads should be 400–1000 ohms, and between each lead and ground should be more than 70,000 ohms. Repair as necessary, reconnect all connectors and repeat Step 1.

If the meter oscillates, the problem is probably in the power feed to the module (red wire) or in the module itself: proceed to Step 7.

Step 7

1. Remove all meters and jumpers and plug in all connectors.

2. Turn the ignition switch to the RUN position and measure voltage between the battery positive terminal and engine ground. It should be 12 volts.

3. Next, measure voltage between the red lead of the module and engine ground. To make this measurement, it will be necessary to pierce the red wire with a straight pin and connect the voltmeter to the straight pin and to ground. DO NOT ALLOW THE STRAIGHT PIN TO GROUND ITSELF.

4. The two readings should be within one volt of each other. If not within one volt, the problem is in the power feed to the red lead. Check for shorts, open, or high resistance and correct as necessary. After repairs, repeat Step 1.

If the readings are within one volt, the problem is probably in the module. Replace with a good module and repeat Step 1. If this corrects the problem, reconnect the old module and repeat Step 1. If problem returns, permanently install the new module.

START MODE SPARK TEST

NOTE: *The wire colors given here are the main colors of the wires, not the dots or hashmarks.*

1. Remove the coil wire from the distributor cap. On 1977 and later models, install the modified spark plug mentioned under "Special Tool", above, in the coil wire and ground it to engine metal either by its spring clip (Spark Tester) or by holding the spark plug shell against the engine block with insulated pliers. On 1976 and earlier models, hold the coil wire terminal ¼ in. from the engine block or head with insulated pliers.

NOTE: *See "CAUTION" under Step 6 of "Run Mode Spark Test", above.*

2. Have an assistant crank the engine using the ignition switch and check for spark. If there is good spark, the problem is probably in the distributor cap, rotor, ignition cables or spark plugs. If there is no spark, proceed to Step 3.

3. Measure the battery voltage. Next, measure the voltage at the white wire of the module while cranking the engine. To make this measurement, it will be necessary to pierce the white wire with a straight pin and connect the voltmeter to the straight pin and to ground. DO NOT ALLOW THE STRAIGHT PIN TO GROUND ITSELF. The battery voltage and the voltage at the white wire should be within 1 volt of each other. If the readings are not within 1 volt of each other. If the readings are not within 1 volt of each other, check and repair the feed through the ignition switch to the white wire. Recheck for spark (Step 1). If the readings are within 1 volt of each other, or if there is still no spark after power feed to white wire is repaired, proceed to Step 4.

4. Measure the coil BAT terminal voltage while cranking the engine. The reading should be within 1 volt of battery voltage. If the readings are not within 1 volt of each other, check and repair the feed through the ignition switch to the coil. If the readings are within 1 volt of each other, the problem is probably in the ignition module. Substitute another module and repeat test for spark (Step 1).

TROUBLESHOOTING DURA SPARK I

The above troubleshooting procedures may be used on Dura Spark I systems with a few variations. The Dura Spark I module has internal connections which shut off the primary circuit in the run mode when the engine stalls. To perform the above troubleshooting procedures, it is necessary to bypass these connections. However, with these connections by-passed, the current flow in the primary becomes so great that it will damage both the ignition coil and module unless a ballast resistor is installed in series with the primary circuit at the BAT terminal of the ignition coil. Such a resistor is available from Ford (Motorcraft part number DY-36). A 1.3 ohm, 100 watt wire-wound power resistor can also be used.

To install the resistor, proceed as follows.
NOTE: *The resistor will become very hot during testing.*

1. Release the BAT terminal lead from the coil by inserting a paper clip through the hole in the rear of the horseshoe coil connector and manipulating it against the locking tab in the connector until the lead comes free.

2. Insert a paper clip in the BAT terminal of the connector on the coil. Using jumper leads, connect the ballast resistor as shown.

3. Using a straight pin, pierce both the red and white leads of the module to short these two together. This will by-pass the internal connections of the module which turn off the ignition circuit when the engine is not running.
CAUTION: *Pierce the wires only AFTER the ballast resistor is in place or you could damage the ignition coil and module.*

4. With the ballast resistor and by-pass in place, proceed with the troubleshooting procedures above.

IGNITION COIL TEST

The ignition coil must be diagnosed separately from the rest of the ignition system.

1. Primary resistance must be 0.5–1.5 ohms for Dura Spark I through 1977, and 0.71–0.77 ohms 1978 and later. It must measure 1.0–2.0 ohms for Dura Spark II through 1977 and the 1975–76 system. For 1978 and later Dura Spark II, it must be 1.13–1.23 ohms.

2. Secondary resistance must be 7,000–13,000 ohms through 1977. 1978 and later Dura Spark I systems must read 7350–8250 ohms, while the 1978 and later Dura Spark II figure is 7700–9300 ohms.

3. If resistance tests are alright, but the coil is still suspected, test the coil on a coil tester by following the test equipment manufacturer's instructions for a standard coil. If the reading differs from the original test, check for a defective harness.

RESISTANCE WIRE TEST

Replace the resistance wire if it doesn't show a resistance of 1.0–2.0 ohms for the 1975–76 system, 0.7–1.7 for Dura Spark II through

1977, and 1.05–1.15 ohms 1978 and later. The resistance wire isn't used on Dura Spark I.

SPARK PLUG WIRE RESISTANCE

Resistance on these wires must not exceed 5,000 ohms per inch. To properly measure this, remove the wires from the plugs, and remove the distributor cap. Measure the resistance through the distributor cap at that end. Do not pierce any ignition wire for any reason. Measure only from the two ends.
NOTE: *Silicone grease must be reapplied to the spark plug wires whenever they are removed.*

When removing the wires from the spark plugs, a special tool such as the one pictured should be used. Do not pull on the wires. Grasp and twist the boot to remove the wire.

Whenever the high tension wires are removed from the plugs, coil, or distributor, silicone grease must be applied to the boot before reconnection. Use a clean small screwdriver blade to coat the entire interior surface with Ford silicone grease D7AZ-19A331-A, Dow Corning #111, or General Electric G-627.

ADJUSTMENTS

The air gap between the armature and magnetic pick-up coil in the distributor is not adjustable, nor are there any adjustments for the amplifier module. Inoperative components are simply replaced. Any attempt to connect components outside the vehicle may result in component failure.

MODULE IDENTIFICATION

The identity of the ignition module and of the ignition system itself (Dura Spark I, II, etc.) can be discovered by examining the color of the sealing block on the module.

COLOR	SYSTEM
• Red	Dura Spark I
• Blue	Dura Spark II
• Yellow	Dura Spark II with Dual Mode (except 1981)
• White	Dura Spark II with Cranking Retard
• Brown	Dura Spark III and other EEC controlled systems
• Yellow	Universal Ignition Module (1981)
• Green	Early Solid State Ignition

COMPONENT REPLACEMENT
Magnetic Pick-up Assembly Removal and Installation

NOTE: *If the engine is equipped with EEC, see the Emission Control Systems Unit Repair Section for information on rotor alignment and identification.*

1. Remove the distributor cap and rotor and disconnect the distributor harness plug.

NOTE: *To remove the two-piece Dura Spark distributor cap, take off the top portion, then the rotor, then the bottom adaptor.*

2. Using a small gear puller or two screwdrivers, lift or pry the armature from the advance plate sleeve. Remove the roll pin.

3. Remove the large wire retaining clip from the base plate annular groove.

4. Remove the snap-ring which secures the vacuum advance link to the pick-up assembly.

5. Remove the magnetic pick-up assembly ground screw and lift the assembly from the distributor.

6. Lift the vacuum advance arm off the post on the pick-up assembly and move it out against the distributor housing.

7. Place the new pick-up assembly in position over the fixed base plate and slide the wiring in position through the slot in the side of the distributor housing.

8. Install the fine wire snap-ring securing the pick-up assembly to the fixed base plate.

9. Position the vacuum advance arm over the post on the pick-up assembly and install the snap-ring.

10. Install the grounding screw through the tab on the wiring harness and into the fixed base plate.

11. Install the armature on the advance plate sleeve making sure that the roll pin is engaged in the matching slots.

12. Install the distributor rotor cap.

13. Connect the distributor wiring plug to the vehicle harness.

Distributor
REMOVAL AND INSTALLATION

1. Remove the air cleaner assembly, taking note of the hose locations.

2. On models equipped with a conventional ignition system, disconnected the primary wire at the coil. On models equipped with breakerless ignition, disconnect the distributor wiring connector from the vehicle wiring harness.

3. Noting the position of the vacuum line(s) on the distributor diaphragm, disconnect the lines at the diaphragm. Unsnap the two distributor cap retaining clamps and remove the cap. Position the cap and ignition wires to one side.

NOTE: *If it is necessary to disconnect ignition wires from the cap to get enough room to remove the distributor, make sure to label every wire and the cap for easy and accurate reinstallation.*

4. Using chalk or paint, carefully mark the position of the distributor rotor in relation to the distributor housing and mark the position of the distributor housing in relation to the engine block. When this is done, you should have a line on the distributor housing directly in line with the tip of the rotor and another line on the engine block directly in line with the mark on the distributor housing. This is very important because the distributor must be reinstalled in the exact same location from which it was removed, if correct ignition timing is to be maintained.

5. Remove the distributor hold-down bolt and clamp. Remove the distributor from the engine. Make sure that the oil pump (intermediate) driveshaft does not come out with the distributor. If it does, remove it from the distributor shaft, coat its lower end with heavy grease, and reinsert it, making sure that it fully engages the oil pump drive.

NOTE: *Do not disturb the engine while the distributor is removed. If you turn the engine over with the distributor removed, you will have to retime the engine.*

6a. If the engine was cranked (disturbed) with the distributor removed, it will now be necessary to retime the engine. If the distributor has been installed incorrectly and the engine will not start, remove the distributor from the engine and start over again. Hold the distributor close to the engine and install the cap on the distributor in its normal position. Locate the No. 1 spark plug tower on the distributor cap. Scribe a mark on the body of the distributor directly below the No. 1 spark plug wire tower on the distributor cap. Remove the distributor cap from the distributor and move the distributor and cap to one side. Remove the No. 1 spark plug and crank the engine over until the No. 1 cylinder is on its compression stroke. To accomplish this, place a wrench on the lower engine pulley and turn the engine slowly in a clockwise or counterclockwise (V8) direction until the TDC mark on the crankshaft

1975 Test Sequence

	Test Voltage Between	*Should Be*	*If Not, Conduct*
Key On	Socket #4 and Engine Ground	Battery Voltage ± 0.1 Volt	Module Bias Test
	Socket #1 and Engine Ground	Battery Voltage ± 0.1 Volt	Battery Source Test
Cranking	Socket #5 and Engine Ground	8 to 12 volts	Cranking Test
	Jumper #1 to #8 Read #6	more than 6 volts	Starting Circuit Test
	Pin #7 and Pin #8	½ volt minimum AC or any DC volt wiggle	Distributor Hardware Test
	Test Voltage Between	*Should Be*	*If Not, Conduct*
Key Off	Socket #7 and #3 Socket #8 and Engine Ground Socket #7 and Engine Ground Socket #3 and Engine Ground	400 to 800 ohms 0 ohms more than 70,000 ohms	Magnetic Pick-up (Stator) Test
	Socket #4 and Coil Tower Socket #1 and Pin #6	7000 to 13000 ohms 1.0 to 2.0 ohms	Coil Test
	Socket #1 and Engine Ground	more than 4.0 ohms	Short Test
	Socket #4 and Pin #6	1.0 to 2.0 ohms	Resistance Wire Test

1975 Electronic ignition wiring schematic

1976 Test Sequence

	Test Voltage Between	Should Be	If Not, Conduct
Key On	Socket #4 and Engine Ground	Battery Voltage ± 0.1 Volt	Battery Source Test
	Socket #1 and Engine Ground	Battery Voltage ± 0.1 Volt	Battery Source Test
Cranking	Socket #5 and Engine Ground	8 to 12 volts	Check Supply Circuit (starting) through Ignition Switch
	Jumper #1 to #8 Read #6	more than 6 volts	Starting Circuit Test
	Pin #3 and Pin #8	$\frac{1}{2}$ volt minimum AC or any DC volt wiggle	Distributor Hardware Test
	Test Voltage Between	*Should Be*	*If Not, Conduct*
Key Off	Socket #8 and #3 Socket #7 and Engine Ground Socket #8 and Engine Ground Socket #3 and Engine Ground	400 to 800 ohms 0 ohms more than 70,000 ohms more than 70,000 ohms	Magnetic Pick-up (Stator) Test
	Socket #4 and Coil Tower	7000 to 13,000 ohms	Coil Test
	Socket #1 and Engine Ground	more than 4.0 ohms	Short Test

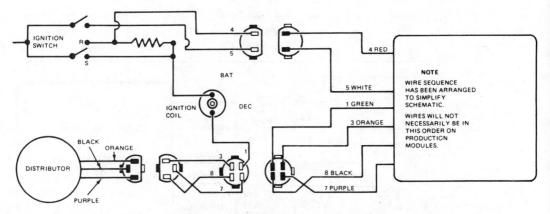

1976 Electronic ignition wiring schematic

1977–82 Test Sequence

	Test Voltage Between	Should Be	If Not, Conduct
Key On	Socket #4 and Engine Ground	Battery Voltage ± 0.1 Volt	Module Bias Test
	Socket #1 and Engine Ground	Battery Voltage ± 0.1 Volt	Battery Source Test
Cranking	Socket #5 and Engine Ground	8 to 12 volts	Cranking Test
	Jumper #1 to #8—Read Coil "Bat" Term & Engine Ground	more than 6 volts	Starting Circuit Test
	Sockets #7 and #3	½ volt minimum wiggle	Distributor Hardware Test

	Test Voltage Between	Should Be	If Not, Conduct
Key Off	Sockets #7 and #3	400 to 800 ohms	Magnetic Pick-up (Stator) Test
	Socket #8 and Engine Ground	0 ohms	
	Socket #7 and Engine Ground	more than 70,000 ohms	
	Socket #3 and Engine Ground	more than 70,000 ohms	
	Socket #4 and Coil Tower	7000 to 13,000 ohms	Coil Test
	Socket #1 and Coil "Bat" Term	1.0 to 2.0 ohms Breakerless & Dura-Spark II	
		0.5 to 1.5 ohms Dura-Spark I	
	Socket #1 and Engine Ground	more than 4.0 ohms	Short Test
	Socket #4 and Coil "Bat" Term (Except Dura-Spark I)	1.0 to 2.0 ohms Breakerless	Resistance Wire Test
		0.7 to 1.7 ohms Dura Spark II	

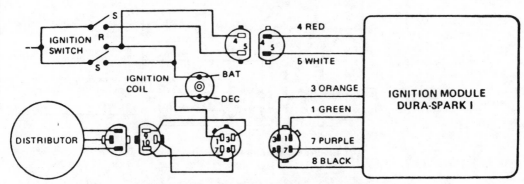

1977–82 Dura-Spark basic wiring schematic

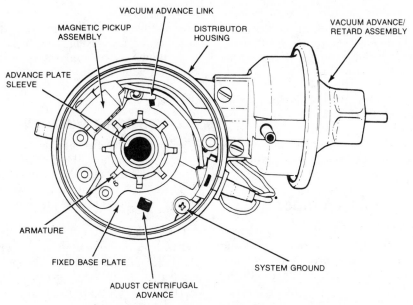

V8 breakerless distributor; cap and rotor removed

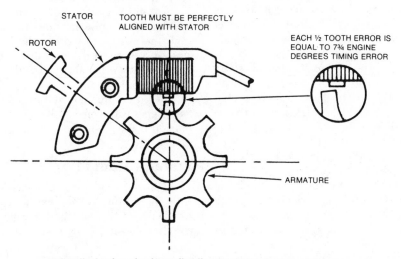

8-cylinder breakerless distributor static timing position

damper aligns with the timing pointer. If you place your finger in the No. 1 spark plug hole, you will feel air escaping as the piston rises in the combustion chamber. On conventional ignition systems, the rotor must be at the No. 1 firing position to install the distributor. On breakerless ignition systems, one of the armature segments must be aligned with the stator as shown in the accompanying illustration to install the distributor. Make sure that the oil pump intermediate shaft properly engages the distributor shaft. It may be necessary to crank the engine with the starter, after the distributor drive gear is partially engaged, in order to engage the oil pump intermediate shaft. In-

stall, but do not tighten the retaining clamp and bolt. Rotate the distributor to advance the timing to a point where the armature tooth is aligned properly (breakerless ignition) or to a point where the points are just starting to open (conventional ignition). Tighten the clamp.

6b. If the engine was not cranked (disturbed) when the distributor was removed, position the distributor in the block with the rotor aligned with the mark previously scribed on the distributor body and the marks on the distributor body and cylinder block in alignment. Install the distributor hold-down bolt and clamp fingertight.

7. Install the distributor cap and wires.

8. On models equipped with conventional ignition, connect the primary wire at the coil. On models equipped with breakerless ignition, connect the distributor wiring connector to the wiring harness.

9. Install the Thermactor air pump mounting bolt, if removed, and adjust the air pump drive belt tension, if necessary, as outlined in Chapter 1.

10. Install the air cleaner, if removed.

11. Check the ignition timing as outlined in Chapter 2.

Alternator and Generator

ALTERNATOR PRECAUTIONS

To prevent damage to the alternator and regulator, the following precautionary measures must be taken when working with the electrical system.

1. Never reverse battery connections. Always check the battery polarity visually. This should be done before any connections are made to be sure that all of the connections correspond to the battery ground polarity of the van.

2. Booster batteries for starting must be connected properly. Make sure that the positive cable of the booster battery is connected to the positive terminal of the battery that is getting the boost. The same applies to the negative cables.

3. Disconnect the battery cables before using a fast charger; the charger has a tendency to force current through the diodes in the opposite direction for which they were designed. This burns out the diodes.

4. Never use a fast charger as a booster for starting the vehicle.

5. Never disconnect the voltage regulator while the engine is running.

6. Do not ground the alternator output terminal.

7. Do not operate the alternator on an open circuit with the field energized.

8. Do not attempt to polarize an alternator.

REMOVAL AND INSTALLATION

1. Open the hood and disconnect the battery ground cable.

2. From under the vehicle, remove the adjusting arm bolt.

3. Remove the generator or alternator through-bolt. Remove the drive belt from the pulley and lower the generator or alternator.

4. Label all of the heads to the alternator so that you can install them correctly and disconnect the leads from the alternator.

5. Remove the generator or alternator from the vehicle.

6. To install, reverse the above procedure.

BELT TENSION ADJUSTMENT

The fan belt drives the generator or alternator and water pump. If the belt is too loose, it will slip and the alternator will not be able to produce its rated current. Also, the water pump will not operate efficiently and the engine could overheat.

Check the tension of the fan belt by pushing your thumb down on the longest span of the belt, midway between the pulleys. Belt deflection should be approximately ½ in.

To adjust belt tension, proceed as follows:

1. Loosen the alternator mounting bolt and the adjusting arm bolts.

2. Apply pressure on the alternator front housing only, moving the alternator away from the engine to tighten the belt. Do not apply pressure to the rear of the cast aluminum housing of an alternator; damage to the housing could result.

3. Tighten the alternator mounting bolt and the adjusting arm bolts when the correct tension is reached.

Voltage Regulator

The voltage regulator is a device which controls the output of the generator or alternator. Without this voltage limiting function of the regulator, the excessive output of the

CHARGE INDICATOR
LIGHT TERMINAL

FIELD COIL TERMINAL
FIELD RELAY TERMINAL
BATTERY TERMINAL FOR
FIELD SUPPLY VOLTAGE

Autolite (Motorcraft) sealed electro-mechanical voltage regulator for 1969 and later models

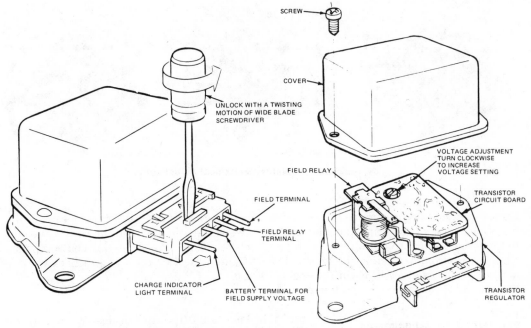

SCREW

COVER

UNLOCK WITH A TWISTING
MOTION OF WIDE BLADE
SCREWDRIVER

VOLTAGE ADJUSTMENT
TURN CLOCKWISE
TO INCREASE
VOLTAGE SETTING

FIELD RELAY

TRANSISTOR
CIRCUIT BOARD

FIELD TERMINAL

FIELD RELAY
TERMINAL

CHARGE INDICATOR
LIGHT TERMINAL

BATTERY TERMINAL FOR
FIELD SUPPLY VOLTAGE

TRANSISTOR
REGULATOR

Autolite (Motorcraft) transistorized voltage regulator adjustment

generator or alternator could burn out components of the electrical system. In addition, the regulator compensates for seasonal changes in temperature as it affects voltage output.

Three different types of adjustable, mechanical voltage regulators have been used: an Autolite unit used on 1961–64 models with DC generators; another Autolite unit on alternator-equipped 1963–67 models; and a Leece-Neville regulator used with all special order 1963–67 Leece-Neville alternators.

A nonadjustable electromechanical Autolite (Motorcraft) regulator, and an adjustable Motorcraft transistorized unit have also been used. The electromechanical unit has been used in conjunction with most 1968 and later Autolite (Motorcraft) alternators. The transistorized unit is installed in some 1974 and later models equipped with electronic ignition. The transistorized regulator is identical in appearance to the electromechanical unit, except where the sealed electromechanical unit has rivets holding down the regulator cover, the transistorized regulator has screws.

REMOVAL AND INSTALLATION

1. Remove the battery ground cable. On models with the regulator mounted behind the battery, it is necessary to remove the battery hold-down, and to move the battery.

2. Remove the regulator mounting screws.

3. Disconnect the regulator from the wiring harness.

4. Connect the new regulator to the wiring harness.

5. Mount the regulator to the regulator mounting plate. The radio suppression condenser mounts under one mounting screw; the ground lead under the other mounting screw. Tighten the mounting screws.

6. If the battery was moved to gain access to the regulator, position the battery and install the hold-down. Connect the battery ground cable, and test the system for proper voltage regulation.

MECHANICAL REGULATOR ADJUSTMENTS

Autolite Alternator Regulator

1963–67

Erratic operation of the regulator, indicated by erratic movement of the voltmeter pointer during a voltage limiter test, may be caused by dirty or pitted regulator contacts. Vehicle ammeter pointer waver at certain critical engine speeds and electrical loads, is normal. Use a very fine abrasive paper such as silicon carbide, 400 grade, to clean the field relay and the voltage limiter contacts. Wear off the sharp edges of the abrasive by rubbing it

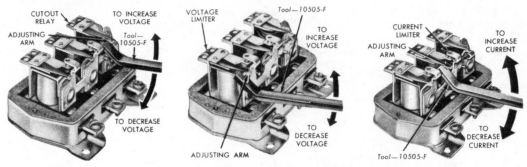

DC generator regulator mechanical adjustments

against another piece of abrasive paper. Fold the abrasive paper over and pull the paper through the contacts to clean them. Keep all oil or grease from contacting the points. Do not use compressed air to clean the regulator. When adjusting the gap spacing use only hospital-clean feeler gauges.

Regulator Gap Adjustments

VOLTAGE LIMITER

The difference between the upper stage and lower stage regulation (0.3 V), is determined by the voltage limiter contact and core gaps. Make the gap adjustment with the regulator removed from the van.

Bend the lower contact bracket to obtain 0.017–0.022-in. gap at the lower contacts with the upper contacts closed. Maintain the contacts in alignment.

Adjust the core gap with the upper contacts closed. Loosen the center lockscrew ¼ turn. Use a screwdriver blade in the adjustment slot under the lockscrew. Adjust the core gap for 0.049–0.056-in. clearance between the armature and the core at the edge of the core closest to the contact points. Tighten the lockscrew and recheck the core gap.

FIELD RELAY

Place a 0.010–0.018 in. feeler gauge on top of the coil core closest to the contact points. Hold the armature down on the gauge. Do not push down on the contact spring arm. Bend the contact post arm until the bottom contact just touches the upper contact.

Regulator Voltage Limiter Adjustments

Final adjustment of the regulator must be made with the regulator at normal operating temperature.

The field relay closing voltage is adjusted by bending the relay frame. To increase the closing voltage, bend the armature frame down. To decrease the closing voltage, bend the frame up.

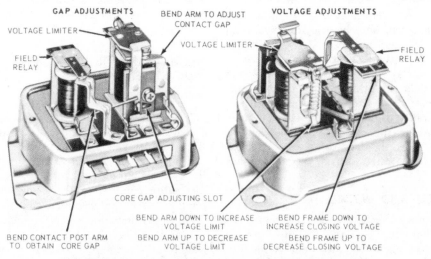

1963–67 Autolite alternator regulator mechanical adjustments

The voltage limiter is adjusted by bending the voltage limiter spring arm. To increase the voltage setting, bend the adjusting arm downward. To decrease the voltage setting, bend the adjusting arm upward.

Before setting the voltage and before making a final voltage test, the alternator speed must be reduced to zero and the ignition switch opened momentarily, to cycle the regulator.

Leece-Neville Alternator Regulator

1963–67

1. Run the engine for 10–15 minutes to allow the regulator to reach operating temperature. Connect a voltmeter across the battery posts. Turn off all electrical equipment. Check the voltage at the battery. It should be 13.9–14.1 volts.

2. The voltage control adjustment (voltage limiter) is adjusted at the component closest to the F terminal. Remove the regulator cover. Voltage may be increased by raising the spring tension and decreased by lowering the spring tension. To adjust the spring tension, move the lower spring mounting tab.

NOTE: *Voltage will drop about ½ volt*

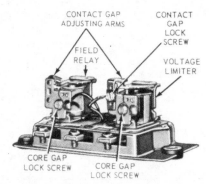

Leece-Neville alternator regulator gap adjustments

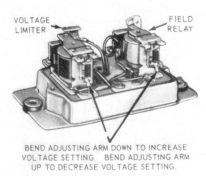

Leece-Neville alternator regulator voltage adjustments

when the regulator cover is installed and should be compensated for in the adjustment.

3. After making the adjustment, cycle the regulator by stopping and starting the engine. This will indicate if the adjustment is stable. If the voltage reading has changed, follow Steps 1 and 2 until the correct voltage is obtained.

Starter Motor
REMOVAL

1. Disconnect the positive battery terminal.

2. Raise the vehicle and disconnect the starter cable at the starter terminal. With the 460 V8, turn the front wheels all the way to the right and unbolt the steering idler arm bracket from the frame.

3. Remove all of the starter attaching bolts that attach the starter to the bellhousing.

4. Remove the starter from the engine.

5. Install the starter in the reverse order of removal.

STARTER DRIVE REPLACEMENT, EXCEPT 460 V8

1. Remove the cover of the starter drive's plunger lever arm, and the brush cover band. Remove the through-bolts, starter drive gear housing, and the return spring of the driver gear's actuating lever.

2. Remove the pivot pin which retains the starter gear plunger lever and remove the lever.

3. Remove the stop-ring retainer. Remove and discard the stop-ring which holds the drive gear to the armature shaft and then remove the drive gear assembly.

To install the drive gear assembly:

4. Lightly Lubriplate® the armature shaft splines and install the starter drive gear assembly on the shaft. Install a new stop-ring and stop-ring retainer.

5. Position the starter drive gear plunger lever to the frame and starter drive assembly.

6. Install the pivot pin.

7. Position the drive plunger lever return spring and the drive gear housing to the frame, then install and tighten the through-bolts. Be sure that the stop-ring retainer is properly seated in the drive housing.

8. Position the starter drive plunger lever cover and the brush cover band on the starter. Tighten the brush cover band retaining screw.

Alternator and Regulator Specifications

Year	Part No. or Manufacturer	Field Current @ 12 v	Output (amps)	Part No. or Manufacturer	Air Gap (in.)	Point Gap (in.)	Volts to Close	Air Gap (in.)	Point Gap (in.)	Volts @ 75°
	Alternator				Field Relay			Regulator		
					Regulator					
1961–63	C2DF-10000-B *	1.2–1.8	25	Ford	NA	NA	12.4–13.2	NA	NA	14.6–15.4
1964	Ford Gen. *	1.0–1.5	30	Ford	NA	NA	12.4–13.2	NA	NA	14.6–15.4
	Ford Alt.	2.4–2.6	42	Ford	.025	.018	2.5	.048	.012	13.6–14.2
1965	Autolite	2.8–3.3	45	Autolite	.017	—	2.5	.052	.020	14.1–14.7
1966–67	Autolite	2.5	38	Autolite	.014	—	2.5–4	.052	.020	14.1–14.9
	Autolite	2.9	45	Autolite	.014	—	2.5–4	.052	.020	14.1–14.9
	Autolite	2.9	55	Autolite	.014	—	2.5–4	.052	.020	14.1–14.9
1969–75	Autolite	2.4	38	Autolite	—	—	2.0–4.2	—	—	13.5–15.3
	Autolite	2.9	42	Autolite	—	—	2.0–4.2	—	—	13.5–15.3
	Autolite	2.9	55	Autolite	—	—	2.0–4.2	—	—	13.5–15.3
1976–80	Autolite	2.9	40	Autolite	—	—	—	—	—	—
	Autolite	2.9	60	Autolite	—	—	—	—	—	—
1981–82	Autolite	4.0	40	Autolite	—	—	—	—	—	—
	Autolite	4.0	60	Autolite	—	—	—	—	—	—
	Autolite	4.0	60	Autolite	—	—	—	—	—	—
	Autolite	4.0	100	Autolite	—	—	—	—	—	—

* Generator
NA: Not applicable

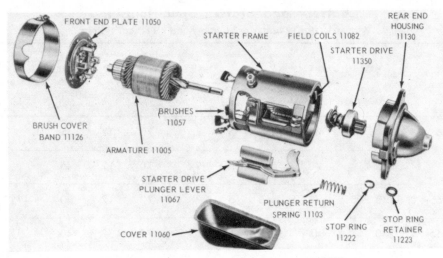

FRONT END PLATE 11050 STARTER FRAME FIELD COILS 11082 REAR END HOUSING 11130 STARTER DRIVE 11350 BRUSHES 11057 BRUSH COVER BAND 11126 ARMATURE 11005 STARTER DRIVE PLUNGER LEVER 11067 PLUNGER RETURN SPRING 11103 STOP RING 11222 STOP RING RETAINER 11223 COVER 11060

An exploded view of the starter (except 460 V8)

STARTER RELAY REPLACEMENT

The starter relay is mounted on the inside of the left wheel well. To replace it, disconnect the positive battery cable from the battery, disconnect all of the electrical leads from the relay and remove the relay from the fender well. Replace in the reverse order of removal.

Battery

REMOVAL AND INSTALLATION

1. Loosen the nuts which secure the cable ends to the battery terminals. Lift the battery cables from the terminals with a twisting motion.

2. If there is a battery cable puller available, make use of it.

3. Remove the hold-down nuts from the battery hold-down bracket and remove the bracket and the battery. Lift the battery straight up and out of the vehicle, being sure to keep the battery level to avoid spilling the battery acid.

4. Before installing the battery in the vehicle, make sure that the battery terminals are clean and free from corrosion. Use a battery terminal cleaner on the terminals and on the inside of the battery cable ends. If a cleaner is not available, use coarse grade sandpaper to remove the corrosion. A mixture of baking soda and water poured over the terminals and cable ends will help remove and neutralize any acid buildup. Before installing the cables onto the terminals, cut a piece of felt cloth, or something similar into a circle about 3 in. across. Cut a hole in the middle about the size of the battery terminals at their base. Push the cloth pieces over the terminals so that they lay flat on the top of the battery. Soak the pieces of cloth with oil. This will keep the formation of oxidized acid to a minimum. Place the battery in the vehicle. Install the cables onto the terminals. Tighten the nuts on the cable ends. Smear a light coating of grease on the cable ends and tops of the terminals. This will further prevent the buildup of oxidized acid on the terminals and the cable ends. Install and tighten the nuts of the battery hold-down bracket.

ENGINE MECHANICAL

Design

SIX CYLINDER ENGINES

The 144, 170, 200, 240 and 300 cu in. 6 cylinder engines installed in Ford vans are of an inline, overhead valve design.

The cylinder head carries the intake and exhaust valve assemblies and mechanism. Water passages in the cylinder head help keep the valves cool.

The distributor, located on the left-side of the engine, is gear-driven from the camshaft and also drives the oil pump through an intermediate shaft.

The 144 and 170 engine crankshafts have four main bearings with end thrust taken by the no. 3 bearing. The 200 cu. in. engine was offered in 1965 as an option in custom club

Battery and Starter Specifications

All trucks use 12 volt, negative ground electrical systems

| Year | Model | Battery Amp Hour Capacity | Starter | | | | | | Brush Spring Tension (oz) | Min Brush Length (in.) |
| | | | Lock Test | | | No Load Test | | | | |
			Amps	Volts	Torque (ft/lbs)	Amps	Volts			
1961–64	144	40	450	5	8	70	12		45	$5/16$
	170	40	500	5	9.6	70	12		45	$5/16$
1965–70	170, 200	45	460	5	9	70	12		40	$1/4$
1965–74	240	45	670	5	15.5	70	12		40	$1/4$
1973–77	300	45	670	5	15.5	70	12		40	$1/4$
1978–82	300	55	not recommended			80	12		80	$1/2$
1969–74	302	45	670	5	15.5	70	12		40	$1/4$
1979–82	302	55	not recommended			80	12		80	$1/2$
1975–82	351W	55	not recommended			80	12		80	$1/2$
1975–82	460	55	not recommended			80	12		80	$1/2$
1980–82	400	55	not recommended			80	12		80	$1/2$

wagon models. It is of the same design as the 144 and 170 cu in. engines, except that it has a seven main bearing crankshaft and a slightly higher compression ratio. The 240 and 300 have seven main bearings with thrust taken on no. 5.

The camshaft is mounted on 4 bearings and is driven by a sprocket and chain connection with the crankshaft in the 144 and 170; the 240 and 300 sixes use gears to drive the camshaft. An integral eccentric on the camshaft operates the fuel pump. The valve tappets are of the hydraulic type with solid type tappets installed in 144 and early 170 cu in. engines.

The engines are pressure lubricated by a rotor-type oil pump equipped with a pressure relief valve. Oil reaches the rocker arm shaft on the 170 through the No. 6 valve rocker arm shaft support at the rear of the engine.

V8

The V8 engines are of the standard, two-bank, V-design with the banks of cylinders opposed to each other at a 90° angle.

The crankshaft is supported by 5 main bearings, with crankshaft end thrust controlled by the flanged No. 3 bearing.

The camshaft, which is located in the center of the V-design of the engine, is mounted on 5 bearings and is driven by a sprocket and chain which are connected to a sprocket on the crankshaft. An eccentric bolted to the front of the camshaft operates the fuel pump. A gear on the front of the camshaft drives the distributor, which in turn drives the oil pump through an intermediate shaft. The oil pump is located in the left front of the oil pan.

All of the V8s are equipped with hydraulic valve lifters.

General Engine Specifications

Year	Engine Displacement Cu In. (cc)	Carburetor Type	Horsepower (@ rpm)	Torque @ rpm (ft lbs)	Bore x Stroke (in.)	Compression Ratio	Oil Pressure @ rpm (psi)
1961	144 (2360)	1-bbl	85 @ 4200	134 @ 2000	3.50 x 2.50	8.7 : 1	35–55
	170 (2786)	1-bbl	101 @ 4400	156 @ 2400	3.50 x 2.94	8.7 : 1	35–55
1962	144 (2360)	1-bbl	85 @ 4200	134 @ 2000	3.50 x 2.50	8.7 : 1	35–55
	170 (2786)	1-bbl	101 @ 4400	156 @ 2400	3.50 x 2.94	8.7 : 1	35–55
1963	144 (2360)	1-bbl	85 @ 4200	134 @ 2000	3.50 x 2.50	8.7 : 1	35–55
	170 (2786)	1-bbl	101 @ 4400	156 @ 2400	3.50 x 2.94	8.7 : 1	35–55
1964	144 (2360)	1-bbl	85 @ 4200	134 @ 2000	3.50 x 2.50	8.4 : 1	35–55
	170 (2786)	1-bbl	101 @ 4400	156 @ 2400	3.50 x 2.94	8.4 : 1	35–55
1965	170 (2786)	1-bbl	105 @ 4400	158 @ 2400	3.50 x 2.94	9.1 : 1	35–55
	200 (3278)	1-bbl	120 @ 4400	190 @ 2400	3.68 x 3.126	9.2 : 1	35–55
	240 (3934)	1-bbl	150 @ 4000	234 @ 2200	4.00 x 3.18	9.2 : 1	35–60
1966	170 (2786)	1-bbl	105 @ 4400	158 @ 2400	3.50 x 2.94	9.1 : 1	35–55
	240 (3934)	1-bbl	150 @ 4000	234 @ 2200	4.00 x 3.18	9.2 : 1	35–60
1967–68	170 (2786)	1-bbl	105 @ 4400	158 @ 2400	3.50 x 2.94	9.1 : 1	35–55
	240 (3934)	1-bbl	150 @ 4000	234 @ 2200	4.00 x 3.18	9.2 : 1	35–55

General Engine Specifications (cont.)

Year	Engine Displacement Cu In. (cc)	Carburetor Type	Horsepower (@ rpm)	Torque @ rpm (ft lbs)	Bore x Stroke (in.)	Compression Ratio	Oil Pressure @ rpm (psi)
1969	170 (2786)	1-bbl	100 @ 4000	156 @ 2200	3.50 x 2.94	8.7 : 1	35–55
	240 (3934)	1-bbl	150 @ 4000	234 @ 2200	4.00 x 3.18	9.2 : 1	35–60
	302 (4950)	2-bbl	205 @ 4600	300 @ 2600	4.00 x 3.00	8.6 : 1	35–60
1970	170 (2786)	1-bbl	100 @ 4000	156 @ 2200	3.50 x 2.94	8.7 : 1	35–55
	240 (3934)	1-bbl	150 @ 4000	234 @ 2200	4.00 x 3.18	9.2 : 1	35–60
	302 (4950)	2-bbl	205 @ 4600	300 @ 2600	4.00 x 3.00	8.6 : 1	35–60
1971	240 (3934)	1-bbl	140 @ 4000	230 @ 2200	4.00 x 3.18	8.9 : 1	35–60
	302 (4950)	2-bbl	205 @ 4600	300 @ 2600	4.00 x 3.00	8.6 : 1	35–60
1972	240 (3934)	1-bbl	140 @ 4000	230 @ 2200	4.00 x 3.18	8.5 : 1	35–60
	302 (4950)	2-bbl	200 @ 4600	285 @ 2600	4.00 x 3.00	8.2 : 1	35–60
1973	240 (3934)	1-bbl	140 @ 4000	230 @ 2200	4.00 x 3.18	8.5 : 1	40–60
	300 (4917)	1-bbl	168 @ 3800	250 @ 1600	4.00 x 3.98	8.4 : 1	40–60
	302 (4950)	2-bbl	200 @ 4600	285 @ 2600	4.00 x 3.00	8.2 : 1	40–60
1974	240 (3934)	1-bbl	140 @ 4000	230 @ 2200	4.00 x 3.18	8.5 : 1	40–60
	300 (4917)	1-bbl	168 @ 3800	250 @ 1600	4.00 x 3.98	8.4 : 1	40–60

General Engine Specifications (cont.)

Year	Engine Displacement Cu In. (cc)	Carburetor Type	Horsepower (@ rpm)	Torque @ rpm (ft lbs)	Bore x Stroke (in.)	Compression Ratio	Oil Pressure @ rpm (psi)
1974	302 (4950)	2-bbl	200 @ 4600	285 @ 2600	4.00 x 3.00	8.2 : 1	40–60
1975	300 (4917)	1-bbl	120 @ 3400	229 @ 1400	4.00 x 3.98	8.0 : 1	40–60
	351W (5753)	2-bbl	150 @ 3400	290 @ 1800	4.00 x 3.50	8.3 : 1	40–60
	460 (7539)	4-bbl	245 @ 4000	380 @ 2600	4.36 x 3.85	8.0 : 1	40–60
1976	300 (3934)	1-bbl	120 @ 3400①	229 @ 1400②	4.00 x 3.98	8.0 : 1③	40–60
	351W (5753)	2-bbl	147 @ 3400④	276 @ 1800⑤	4.00 x 3.50	8.3 : 1	40–60
	460 (7539)	4-bbl	237 @ 4000⑥	365 @ 2600⑦	4.36 x 3.85	8.0 : 1	40–60
1977	300 (3934)	1-bbl	120 @ 3400①	229 @ 1400②	4.00 x 3.98	8.0 : 1③	40–60
	351W (5753)	2-bbl	147 @ 3400④	276 @ 1800⑤	4.00 x 3.50	8.3 : 1	40–60
	460 (7539)	4-bbl	237 @ 4000⑥	365 @ 2600⑦	4.36 x 3.85	8.0 : 1	40–60
1978	300 (3934)	1-bbl	132 @ 3600	241 @ 1800	4.00 x 3.98	8.0 : 1③	40–60
	351W (5753)	2-bbl	147 @ 3400④	276 @ 1800⑤	4.00 x 3.50	8.3 : 1	40–60
	460 (7539)	4-bbl	237 @ 4000⑥	365 @ 2600⑦	4.36 x 3.85	8.0 : 1	40–60
1979	300 (3934)	1-bbl	⑧	⑨	4.00 x 3.98	⑩	40–60
	302 (4950)	2-bbl	⑪	⑫	4.00 x 3.00	8.4 : 1	40–60

General Engine Specifications (cont.)

Year	Engine Displacement Cu In. (cc)	Carburetor Type	Horsepower (@ rpm)	Torque @ rpm (ft. lbs.)	Bore x Stroke (in.)	Compression Ratio	Oil Pressure @ rpm (psi)
1979 (cont.)	351W (5753)	2-bbl	⑬	⑭	4.00 x 3.50	8.3 : 1	40–60
	460 (7539)	4-bbl	⑮	⑯	4.36 x 3.85	8.0 : 1	40–60
1980–82	300 (3934)	1-bbl	115 @ 3200	241 @ 1200	4.00 x 3.98	⑩	40–60
	302 (4950)	2-bbl	138 @ 3600	242 @ 1800	4.00 x 3.98	8.4 : 1	40–60
	351W (5753)	2-bbl	142 @ 3200	251 @ 2400	4.00 x 3.50	8.3 : 1	40–60
	400 (6600)	2-bbl	153 @ 3500	296 @ 1600	4.00 x 4.00	8.0 : 1	55–75
	460 (7539)	4-bbl	212 @ 4000	339 @ 2400	4.36 x 3.85	8.0 : 1	55–75

① E-100 49 states: 122 @ 3200
E-100 Calif.: 123 @ 3200
② E-100 49 states: 252 @ 1600
E-100 Calif.: 253 @ 1600
③ E-100 8.9 : 1
④ E-100 49 states: 141 @ 3200
E-100 Calif.: Man Trans., 152 @ 3200
Auto Trans., 143 @ 3200
⑤ Engines subject to noise legislation: 275 @ 1800
E-100 49 states: 286 @ 1400
E-100 Calif., with Man Trans.: 286 @ 2000
with Auto Trans.: 287 @ 1600
⑥ Engines subject to noise legislation: 230 @ 4000
⑦ Engines subject to noise legislation: 359 @ 2600
⑧ E-100 exc Calif.; all E-150: 117 @ 3000
E-250 Manual trans.: 114 @ 3000
E-250 Automatic trans.: 116 @ 3200
E-350: 114 @ 3000
⑨ E-100, 150: 243 @ 1600
E-250 Manual trans.: 234 @ 1600
E-250 Automatic trans.: 247 @ 1000
E-350: 247 @ 1000
⑩ E-100, 150, 250: 8.9 : 1
E-350: 8.0 : 1
⑪ E-100, 150 exc Calif.: 135 @ 3400
E-100 Calif.: 129 @ 3200
E-150 Calif.: 137 @ 3400

E-250: 136 @ 3400
⑫ E-100, 150 exc Calif.: 243 @ 2000
E-100 Calif.: 238 @ 2400
E-150 Calif.: 245 @ 2000
E-250: 235 @ 2400
⑬ E-100: 135 @ 2800
E-150 Manual trans.: 130 @ 3000
E-150 Automatic trans, except Calif.:
135 @ 2800
E-150 Automatic trans, Calif.: 139 @ 3200
E-250 Manual trans.: 130 @ 3000
E-250 Automatic trans.: 126 @ 2800
E-350: 143 @ 3200
⑭ E-100: 274 @ 1400
E-150 Manual trans, except Calif.:
267 @ 1800
E-150 Automatic trans, except Calif.:
274 @ 1400
E-150 Automatic trans, Calif.: 269 @ 1200
E-250 Manual trans, 267 @ 1800
E-250 Automatic trans, 270 @ 1400
E-350: 272 @ 2000
⑮ E-250: 214 @ 3600
E-350: 217 @ 4000
⑯ E-250: 362 @ 1800
E-350: 358 @ 2600

Piston and Ring Specifications

All measurements given in inches

Year	Engine	Piston to Bore Clearance	RING SIDE CLEARANCE			RING GAP		
			Top Compression	Bottom Compression	Oil Control	Top Compression	Bottom Compression	Oil Control
1961–63	144, 170	.0018–.0036	.0019–.0036	.0024–.0040	snug	.0100–.0200	.0100–.0200	.015–.055
1964	144, 170	.0018–.0036	.0019–.0036	.0024–.0040	snug	.0100–.0310	0.100–.0310	.015–.066
1965	170	.0021–.0027	.0009–.0026	.0020–.0040	snug	.0100–.0200	.0100–.0200	.015–.055
1966	170	.0014–.0020	.0009–.0026	.0020–.0040	snug	.0100–.0200	.0100–.0200	.015–.055
1967–70	170	.0014–.0020	.0019–.0036	.0020–.0040	snug	.0100–.0200	.0100–.0200	.015–.055
1965	200	.0020–.0026	.0019–.0036	.0020–.0040	snug	.0100–.0200	.0100–.0200	.015–.055
1965–71	240	.0014–.0022	.0019–.0036	.0020–.0040	snug	.0100–.0200	.0100–.0200	.015–.055
1972–74	240	.0014–.0022	.0024–.0041	.0025–.0045	snug	.0100–.0200	.0100–.0200	.015–.055
1973–76	300	.0014–.0022	.0024–.0041	.0025–.0045	snug	.0100–.0200	.0100–.0200	.015–.055
1977	300	.0014–.0022	.0019–.0036	.0020–.0040	snug	.0100–.0200	.0100–.0200	.010–.035
1978	300	.0002–.0004①	.0019–.0036	.0020–.0040	snug	.0100–.0200	.0100–.0200	.015–.055
1979–82	300	.0014–.0022	.0019–.0036	.0020–.0040	snug	.0100–.0200	.0100–.0200	.010–.035
1969–72	302	.0018–.0026	.0019–.0036	.0020–.0040	snug	.0100–.0200	.0100–.0200	.015–.069

Piston and Ring Specifications (cont.)
All measurements given in inches

Year	Engine	Piston to Bore Clearance	RING SIDE CLEARANCE			RING GAP		
			Top Compression	Bottom Compression	Oil Control	Top Compression	Bottom Compression	Oil Control
1973–74	302	.0018–.0026	.0020–.0040	.0020–.0040	snug	.0100–.0200	.0100–.0200	.015–.055
1979–82	302	.0018–.0026	.0019–.0036	.0020–.0040	snug	.0100–.0200	.0100–.0200	.015–.035
1975–76	351W	.0018–.0026	.0020–.0040	.0020–.0040	snug	.0100–.0200	.0100–.0200	.015–.055
1977	351W	.0022–.0030	.0019–.0036	.0020–.0040	snug	.0100–.0200	.0100–.0200	.010–.035
1978	351W	.0022–.0030	.0019–.0036	.0020–.0040	snug	.0100–.0200	.0100–.0200	.015–.055
1979–82	351W	.0022–.0030	.0019–.0036	.0020–.0040	snug	.0100–.0200	.0100–.0200	.015–.035
1980–82	400	.0014–.0022	.0019–.0036	.0025–.0045	snug	.0100–.0200	.0100–.0200	.015–.035
1975–76	460	.0022–.0030	.0020–.0040	.0020–.0040	snug	.0100–.0200	.0100–.0200	.015–.055
1977	460	.0014–.0022	.0025–.0045	.0025–.0045	snug	.0100–.0200	.0100–.0200	.010–.030
1978	460	.0022–.0030	.0025–.0045	.0025–.0045	snug	.0100–.0200	.0100–.0200	.010–.030
1979–82	460	.0022–.0030	.0019–.0036	.0020–.0040	snug	.0100–.0200	.0100–.0200	.010–.035

① Over 6,000 lb GVW: .0003–.0005

Crankshaft and Connecting Rod Specifications
All measurements are given in inches

Year	Engine Displacement Cu In.	CRANKSHAFT			CONNECTING ROD		
		Main Brg Journal Dia	Main Brg Oil Clearance	Shaft End-Play	Journal Diameter	Oil Clearance	Side Clearance
1961–63	144	①	.0007–.0025	.004–.008	②	.0008–.0023	.004–.008
1964	144	①	.0007–.0026	.004–.008	②	.0006–.0026	.004–.008
1961–63	170	①	.0007–.0025	.004–.008	②	.0008–.0023	.004–.008
1964–65	170	①	.0007–.0026	.004–.008	②	.0006–.0026	.004–.008
1966–69	170	2.2482–2.2490	.0005–.0015	.004–.008	2.1232–2.1240	.0008–.0015	.0035–.0105
1970	170	2.2482–2.2490	.0010–.0015	.004–.008	2.1232–2.1240	.0010–.0015	.0035–.0105
1965	200	2.2486–2.2490	.0007–.0026	.004–.008	2.1232–2.1240	.0006–.0026	.0035–.0105
1965	240	③	.0006–.0024	.004–.008	④	.0006–.0022	.0060–.0130
1966–69	240	2.3982–2.3990	.0005–.0015	.004–.008	2.1228–2.1236	.0008–.0015	.0060–.0130
1970–72	240	2.3982–2.3990	.0010–.0015	.004–.008	2.1228–2.1236	.0010–.0015	.0060–.0130
1973–74	240	2.3982–2.3990	.0005–.0015	.004–.008	2.1228–2.1236	.0008–.0015	.0060–.0130
1973	300	2.3982–2.3990	.0009–.0015	.004–.008	2.1228–2.1236	⑤	.0060–.0130
1974	300	2.3982–2.3990	.0009–.0015	.004–.008	2.1228–2.1236	⑥	.0060–.0130
1975–82	300	2.3982–2.3990	.0008–.0015	.004–.008	2.1228–2.1236	.0008–.0015	.0060–.0130
1969	302	2.2482–2.2490	.0005–.0015	.004–.008	2.1228–2.1236	.0008–.0015	.0100–.0200

Crankshaft and Connecting Rod Specifications (cont.)

All measurements are given in inches

Year	Engine Displacement Cu In.	CRANKSHAFT			CONNECTING ROD		
		Main Brg Journal Dia	Main Brg Oil Clearance	Shaft End-Play	Journal Diameter	Oil Clearance	Side Clearance
1970–72	302	2.2482–2.2490	.0010–.0015	.004–.008	2.1228–2.1236	.0010–.0015	.0100–.0200
1973–74 79–82	302	2.2482–2.2490	.0005–.0015⑦	.004–.008	2.1228–2.1236	.0008–.0015	.0100–.0200
1975–76	351W	2.9994–3.0002	.0008–.0015⑧	.004–.008	2.3103–2.3111	.0008–.0015	.0100–.0200
1977–82	351W	2.9994–3.0002	.0008–.0015	.004–.008	2.3103–2.3111	.0008–.0015	.0100–.0200
1980–82	400	2.9994–3.0002	.0008–.0015	.004–.008	2.3103–2.3111	.0008–.0015	.0100–.0200
1975–76	460	2.9994–3.0002	.0008–.0026⑨	.004–.008	2.4992–2.5000	.0008–.0015	.0100–.0200
1977–82	460	2.9994–3.0002	.0008–.0015	.004–.008	2.4992–2.5000	.0008–.0015	.0100–.0200

① Coded red: 2.2486—2.2490
   Coded blue: 2.2482–2.2486
② Coded red: 2.1236–2.1240
   Coded blue: 2.1232–2.1236
③ Coded red: 2.3986–2.3990
   Coded blue: 2.3982–2.3986
④ Coded red: 2.1232–2.1236
   Coded blue: 2.1228–2.1232

⑤ Light duty: .0008–.0015
   Heavy duty: .0009–.0027
⑥ Light duty: .0008–.0015
   Heavy duty: .0009–.0015
⑦ #1: .0001–.0015
⑧ #1: .0005–.0015
⑨ #1: .0008–.0015

Torque Specifications

All readings in ft lbs

Year	Engine Displacement Cu In. (cc)	Cylinder Head Bolts	Rod Bearing Bolts	Main Bearing Bolts	Crankshaft Pulley Bolt	Flywheel-to-Crankshaft Bolts	MANIFOLDS	
							Intake	Exhaust
1961–64	144, 170	65–70	19–24	60–70	45–55	75–85	—	13–18
1965	170, 200	70–75	19–24	60–70	85–100	75–85	—	13–18
1966–70	170	70–75	19–24	60–70	85–100	75–85	—	13–18
1965–66	240	70–75	40–45	60–70	130–145	75–85	20–25	20–25

Torque Specifications (cont.)

All readings in ft lbs

Year	Engine Displacement Cu In. (cc)	Cylinder Head Bolts	Rod Bearing Bolts	Main Bearing Bolts	Crankshaft Pulley Bolt	Flywheel-to-Crankshaft Bolts	MANIFOLDS	
							Intake	Exhaust
1967–74	240	70–75	40–45	60–70	130–150	75–85	23–28	23–28
1973–76	300	70–75	40–45	60–70	130–150	75–85	23–28	23–28
1977–82	300	70–85	40–45	60–70	130–150	75–85	22–32	28–33
1969	302	65–72	19–24	60–70	70–90	75–85	20–22	15–20
1970	302	65–72	19–24	60–70	70–90	75–85	23–25	12–16
1971–74	302	65–72	19–24	60–70	100–130	75–85	23–25	12–16
1979–82	302	65–72	19–24	60–70	70–90	75–85	23–25	18–24
1975–76	351W	65–70	19–24	60–70	70–90	75–85	23–25	18–24
1977–82	351W	105–112	40–45	95–105	70–90	75–85	23–25	18–24
1980–82	400	95–105	40–45	35–45	70–90	75–85	*	18–24
1975–82	460	130–140	40–45	95–105	70–90	75–85	22–32	28–33

* $3/8$": 22–32
  $5/16$": 17–25

Valve Specifications

Year	Engine Displacement Cu In. (cc)	Seat Angle (deg)	Face Angle (deg)	Spring Test Pressure (lbs @ in.)	Spring Installed Height (in.)	STEM TO GUIDE CLEARANCE (in.)		STEM DIAMETER (in.)	
						Intake	Exhaust	Intake	Exhaust
1961–64	144	45	44	117 @ 1.222	1.585	.00165	.00245	.31035	.30935
1961–70	170	45	44	117 @ 1.222	1.585	.00165	.00245	.31035	.30935
1965	200	45	44	150 @ 1.222	1.590	.00165	.00245	.31035	.30935
1965–66	240	45	44	①	1.700	.00185	.00185	.34195	.34195
1967–72	240	45	44	197 @ 1.300	1.700	.00185	.00185	.34195	.34195

Valve Specifications (cont.)

Year	Engine Displacement Cu In. (cc)	Seat Angle (deg)	Face Angle (deg)	Spring Test Pressure (lbs @ in.)	Spring Installed Height (in.)	STEM TO GUIDE CLEARANCE (in.)		STEM DIAMETER (in.)	
						Intake	Exhaust	Intake	Exhaust
1973–74	240	45	44	②	③	.00185	.00185	.34195	.34195
1973–82	300	45	44	②	③	.00185	.00185	.34195	.34195
1969–71	302	45	44	180 @ 1.230	1.660	.00185	.00185	.34195	.34195
1972	302	45	44	180 @ 1.230	1.660	.00185	.00235	.34195	.34145
1973–74	302	45	44	200 @ 1.310	1.690	.00185	.00235	.34195	.34145
1979–82	302	45	44	④	⑤	.00185	.00235	.34195	.34145
1975–76	351W	45	44	200 @ 1.340	1.790	.00185	.00235	.34195	.34145
1977–82	351W	45	44	⑥	⑦	.00185	.00235	.34195	.34145 ⑧
1980–82	400	45	44	80 @ 1.820 ⑨	1.875	.00185	.00235	.3423	.3418 ⑩
1975–76	460	45	44	252 @ 1.330	1.810	.00185	.00185	.34195	.34195
1977–82	460	45	44	229 @ 1.330	1.810	.00185	.00185	.34195	.34195

① Intake: 190 @ 1.325
   Exhaust: 197 @ 1.300
② Intake: 190 @ 1.300
   1982 Intake: 197 @ 1.30
   Exhaust: 192 @ 1.180
③ Intake: 1.700

Exhaust: 1.690
1982 Exhaust: 1.58
④ Intake: 202 @ 1.360
   Exhaust: 200 @ 1.200
⑤ Intake: 1.780
   Exhaust: 1.600

⑥ Intake: 200 @ 1.340
   Exhaust: 200 @ 1.200
⑦ Intake: 1.790
   Exhaust: 1.800
⑧ 1982: .3420
⑨ 1982: 229 @ 1.39
⑩ 1982: .3420

Engine Removal and Installation

144, 170 AND 200 SIX-CYLINDER

1. Drain the cooling system.
2. Remove the engine cover.
3. Remove the right-hand seat.
4. Raise the vehicle on a hoist.
5. Disconnect the driveshaft at the transmission flange. Remove the midship bearing support-to-chassis and position the driveshaft out of the way.
6. Disconnect the speedometer cable and housing at the transmission.
7. Disconnect the transmission shift rods at the transmission shift levers.
8. Disconnect the clutch retracting spring. Remove the equalizer bracket at the chassis side rail and remove the clutch equalizer arm and clutch linkage from the cylinder block. Position the assembly out of the way.
9. Position an engine support bar to the chassis and the engine to support the rear of the engine.
10. Remove the bolt and nut attaching the rear engine support to the crossmember to the chassis and remove the crossmember.
11. Position a transmission jack under the transmission and secure it.
12. Remove the bolts attaching the transmission to the clutch housing and remove the transmission.

13. Disconnect the muffler inlet pipe at the exhaust manifold.

14. Disconnect the ground wire at the cylinder block.

15. Disconnect the ground wire at the starter retaining bolt.

16. Drain the crankcase.

17. Remove the oil filter.

18. Remove the nuts attaching the engine supports to the chassis.

19. Lower the vehicle.

20. Disconnect the battery.

21. Disconnect the radiator upper hose at the radiator.

22. Disconnect the radiator lower hose at the radiator and drain the radiator.

23. Remove the radiator.

24. Remove the fan assembly and the spacer.

25. Disconnect the heater hose at the water pump.

26. Remove the air cleaner assembly.

27. Disconnect the tank-to-pump fuel line at the fuel pump and plug the line.

28. Disconnect the accelerator cable at the carburetor.

29. Disconnect the choke cable, remove it from the mounting bracket and position it out of the way.

30. Remove the accelerator cable mounting bracket from the carburetor and the cylinder head.

31. Disconnect the heater hose at the cylinder head.

32. Disconnect the oil filler pipe at the rocker arm cover and remove the oil filler pipe.

33. Remove the oil dipstick and tube from the cylinder block.

34. Disconnect the engine wire loom and position it out of the way (temp., oil, coil).

35. Disconnect the starter cable at the starter.

36. Remove the alternator from the mounting and adjusting brackets and position the alternator out of the way.

37. Position an engine lifting device to the engine and attach it to a crane boom and lift the engine out of the vehicle through the right front door.

To install:

1. Install the engine into the engine compartment through the right front door and allow it to rest on the front engine supports and the engine support bar at the rear of the engine.

2. Raise the vehicle on a hoist.

3. Install the engine support insulator attaching nuts to the chassis mounts.

4. Position the transmission to the clutch housing and install the attaching bolts.

5. Raise the transmission and position the crossmember to the chassis and the rear engine support. Install the bolts and nut attaching the crossmember to the transmission and chassis.

6. Remove the transmission jack and the engine support bar.

7. Position the equalizer arm to the cylinder block mount, position the linkage to the bearing fork, install the equalizer arm mounting bracket retracting spring.

8. Connect the shift rods at the transmission.

9. Connect the speedometer cable at the transmission.

10. Position the driveshaft to the transmission flange and install the "U" bolts and nuts. Position the midship bearing support to the chassis and install the attaching bolts.

11. Connect the muffler inlet pipe at the exhaust manifold and tighten the retaining clamp at the cylinder block.

12. Connect the ground wire to the starter.

13. Lower the vehicle.

14. Unplug and connect the fuel line from the tank to the fuel pump at the pump. Connect the fuel line from the fuel pump to the carburetor at the filter.

15. Position the engine wire loom in the retainers and connect at the respective locations (i.e., coil, oil, temp).

16. Position the alternator to the mounting brackets and install the attaching bolts.

17. Connect the alternator and battery ground wires.

18. Connect the starter cable at the starter.

19. Install the dipstick and tube to the cylinder block and support bracket.

20. Connect the heater hose at the cylinder head.

21. Install the accelerator cable mounting bracket to the cylinder head.

22. Connect the accelerator cable to the carburetor and mounting bracket and the retracting spring.

23. Connect the choke cable to the carburetor, if applicable.

24. Connect the oil filler pipe to the rocker arm cover.

25. Connect the heater hose at the water pump.

26. Position the alternator drive belt to the pulley and the water pump pulley to the water pump shaft.

27. Install the fan and spacer to the water pump shaft.

28. Adjust the alternator drive belt tension and tighten the attaching bolts.

29. Position the radiator to the radiator support and install the retaining bolts.

30. Connect the radiator upper and lower hoses.

31. Clean the oil filter mating surface and install the oil filter.

32. Fill the crankcase with oil.

33. Fill the cooling system.

34. Connect the battery.

35. Start the engine and check for leaks.

36. Adjust the carburetor idle speed and mixture as necessary.

37. Install the air cleaner assembly.

38. Install the right-hand seat and the engine cover.

240 AND 300 SIX-CYLINDER THROUGH 1972

1. Drain the cooling system and the crankcase. Remove the engine cover and remove the air cleaner assembly.

2. Disconnect the battery positive cable. Disconnect the heater hose from the water pump and the coolant outlet housing. Disconnect the flexible fuel line from the fuel pump.

3. Remove the radiator.

4. Remove the cooling fan, water pump pulley and the fan drive belt.

5. Disconnect the accelerator cable and the choke cable at the carburetor. Remove the cable retracting spring.

6. On a vehicle with power brakes, disconnect the vacuum line at the intake manifold.

7. On a vehicle with an automatic transmission, disconnect the transmission kickdown rod at the bellcrank assembly.

8. Disconnect the exhaust manifold from the muffler inlet pipe. Disconnect the body ground strap and the battery ground cable at the engine.

9. Disconnect the engine wiring harness at the ignition coil, coolant temperature sending unit and the oil pressure sending unit. Position the harness out of the way.

10. Remove the alternator mounting bolts and position the alternator out of the way, leaving the wires attached.

11. On a vehicle with power steering, remove the power steering pump from the mounting brackets and position it right-side up and to one side, leaving the lines attached.

12. Raise the vehicle. Remove the starter and the automatic transmission filler tube bracket, if applicable. Remove the engine rear plate upper right bolt.

On a vehicle with a manual tramsmission, remove all the flywheel housing lower attaching bolts. Disconnect the clutch retracting spring. On a vehicle with an automatic transmission, remove the converter housing access cover assembly. Remove the flywheel-to-converter nuts; then secure the converter assembly in the housing. Remove the transmission oil cooler lines from the retaining clip at the engine. Remove the converter housing-to-engine lower attaching bolts.

13. Remove the engine from the support insulator bolt.

14. Lower the vehicle and position a transmission jack under the transmission to support it. Remove the remaining flywheel or converter housing-to-engine bolts.

15. Attach the engine lifting device and raise the engine slightly. Carefully pull the engine from the transmission. Lift the engine out of the vehicle.

NOTE: *The 240–300 six is removed from the vehicle in the same manner as the 170 six, through the right-side door; consequently, the seat will have to be removed from the right-side if it hasn't already been done. The driver's seat should also be removed to afford the maximum amount of room for working.*

To install the engine:

1. Place a new gasket on the muffler inlet pipe.

2. Lower the engine carefully into the vehicle. Make sure that the studs on the exhaust manifold are aligned with the holes in the muffler inlet pipe and the dowels in the block engage the holes in the flywheel or converter housing.

On a vehicle with an automatic transmission, start the converter pilot into the crankshaft. Remove the retainer securing the converter in the housing.

On a vehicle with a manual transmission, start the transmission main drive gear into the clutch disc. It may be necessary to adjust the position of the transmission with relation to the engine if the transmission input shaft will not enter the clutch disc. If the engine hangs up after the shaft enters, turn the crankshaft slowly with the transmission in gear until the shaft splines mesh with the clutch disc.

3. Install the converter or flywheel housing upper attaching bolts. Remove the jack supporting the transmission.

4. Lower the engine until it rests on the engine support and remove the lifting device.

5. Install the front support bolt and nut. Install the bracket for the automatic transmission oil cooler lines.

6. Install the remaining converter or flywheel housing attaching bolts. Connect the clutch return spring.

7. Install the starter and connect the starter cable. Attach the automatic transmission oil cooler lines in the bracket at the engine block.

8. Install the exhaust manifold to the muffler inlet pipe lockwashers and nuts.

9. Connect the engine ground strap and the battery ground cable.

10. On a vehicle with an automatic transmission, connect the kick-down rod to the bellcrank assembly on the intake manifold.

11. Connect the accelerator linkage to the carburetor and install the retracting spring. Connect the choke cable to the carburetor and hand throttle, if so equipped.

12. On a vehicle with power brakes, connect the brake vacuum line to the intake manifold.

13. Connect the coil primary wire, oil pressure and coolant temperature sending unit wires, flexible fuel line, heater hoses, and the battery positive cable.

14. Install the alternator on the mounting bracket. On a vehicle with power steering, install the power steering pump on the mounting bracket.

15. Install the water pump pulley, spacer, cooling fan and drive belt. Adjust all the belt tensions and tighten the accessories' mounting bolts.

16. Install the radiator. Connect the radiator lower hose to the water pump and the radiator upper hose to the coolant outlet housing. On a vehicle with an automatic transmission, connect the oil cooler lines to the radiator.

17. Install and adjust the hood, if it was removed.

18. Fill the cooling system. Fill the crankcase. Operate the engine at a fast idle and check for leaks.

19. Adjust the carburetor idle speed and mixture. On a vehicle with manual transmission, adjust the clutch pedal free-play. On a vehicle with an automatic transmission, adjust the transmission control linkage. Check the fluid level in the automatic transmission and add as necessary.

20. Install the carburetor air cleaner.

1974–75 240 AND 300 SIX-CYLINDER

1. Disconnect the battery and drain the cooling system. Remove the engine cover and the right hand seat. Remove the grille and bumper.

2. Remove the hood lock support bracket, right and left headlight doors, and grille.

3. Disconnect all hoses and lines to the radiator, and remove the battery deflector. Remove the radiator.

4. Disconnect:

   A. The heater hoses, at the engine.

   B. Temperature, oil, and ignition wires.

   C. Starter solenoid, neutral safety switch, and back-up light wiring.

5. Remove the engine oil dipstick and oil filler tube. Remove hoses connecting the rocker cover and air filter. Remove the air cleaner and brackets.

6. Disconnect the choke and accelerator cables at the carburetor. Disconnect the auxiliary heater hose at the front heater. Disconnect the hoses at the right front of the engine, and position them out of the way.

7. Disconnect the fuel pump discharge line at the pump. Disconnect the alternator, and remove it from the brackets.

8. Disconnect the ground wires at the block, and the muffler inlet pipe at the manifold. Disconnect the modulator line at the intake manifold.

9. Put the vehicle on a hoist. Drain the crankcase and remove the oil filter.

10. Disconnect the starter wiring, and remove the starter.

11. Position an engine support bar to the chassis and engine, and adjust it.

12. On manual transmission vehicles:

   A. Disconnect the driveshaft, and remove it. Install a plug in the transmission extension housing.

   B. Disconnect the speedometer cable and housing, and secure the assembly out of the way.

   C. Remove the nut and bolt holding the

rear support to the crossmember. Raise the transmission, remove the mounting bolts, and remove the cross-member.

D. Remove the clutch equalizer arm bolts from the engine. Disconnect the retracting spring, and move the assembly away.

E. Remove the bolts connecting transmission and clutch, and remove the transmission.

13. On automatic transmission vehicles:

A. Remove the bolts connecting the adapter plate and inspection cover to the torque converter.

B. Unbolt and remove the transmission dipstick tube. Drain the transmission.

C. Remove the nuts attaching the converter to the flex plate. Disconnect the fluid cooler and modulator lines at the transmission.

D. Disconnect the driveshaft at the companion flange.

E. Disconnect the speedometer cable and housing from the transmission. Disconnect the shift rod at the lever on the transmission. Jack the transmission up slightly.

F. Remove the nuts and bolts attaching the rear engine mount bracket to the crossmember. Remove the side support bolts, and remove the crossmember.

G. Secure the transmission to the jack with a safety chain, remove the remaining bolts attaching the transmission to the cylinder block, and remove the transmission from the vehicle.

14. Remove the nuts which attach the engine front support insulator, remove the bellcrank bolt from the block, and position it out of the way.

15. Lower the vehicle, and remove the fan spacer, and water pump pulley. Lift the engine from the vehicle with a lifting hook. Remove the clutch housing on vehicles with manual transmission.

16. Install the clutch housing on manual transmission vehicles. Hoist the engine into the vehicle, and allow it to rest on the front supports and support tool.

17. Raise the vehicle on a hoist.

18. On manual transmission:

A. Raise the transmission and position it behind the clutch housing. Install the mounting bolts.

B. Raise the transmission slightly further, position the crossmember to the chassis and rear support, and install the at-

taching bolts. Torque crossmember to body bolts to 20–30 ft-lbs.

C. Remove the jack and engine support tool. Connect the shift linkage and the speedometer cable housing.

D. Install and connect the drive shaft.

19. Install the engine front support insulator bolts, and torque to 45–55 ft-lbs.

20. Install the transmission bellcrank.

21. On automatic transmission equipped vehicles:

A. Position the transmission against the block and install the mounting bolts. Torque to 23–33 ft-lbs.

B. Position the crossmember to the rear mount bracket and frame side members. Install the attaching nuts and bolts, and torque to 20–30 ft-lbs.

C. Remove the transmission safety chain, and remove the jack. Remove the engine support bar.

D. Install the converter to the flex plate. Connect the vacuum and oil cooler lines to the transmission.

E. Install the dipstick and tube into the transmission oil pan. Install the tube and vacuum line bracket attaching bolt to the block.

F. Connect the driveshaft to the transmission companion flange. Connect the speedometer cable and housing to the transmission. Connect the shift rods to the transmission levers.

G. Install the adapter plate and inspection cover.

22. Install the starter. Connect the muffler inlet pipe at the manifold.

23. Install the clutch equalizer arm bracket (on manual transmission models). Install the attaching bolts, and connect the retractor spring.

24. Lower the vehicle to the floor, install the remaining automatic transmission mounting bolts.

25. Install the starter ground wire and remaining starter attaching bolt. Connect the starter cable at the starter.

26. Install the water pump pulley, spacer, and fan assembly.

27. Install the alternator onto its mounting brackets, and install and tension the V-belt.

28. Connect the alternator wiring and back-up light and neutral safety switch leads.

29. Connect the alternator and battery ground wires to the block.

30. Connect the transmission modulator line to the manifold.

31. Connect the fuel line from the tank to the fuel pump.

32. Connect the choke and accelerator cables to the carburetor. Install the dipstick tube, and bolt it to the cylinder head.

33. Connect remaining neutral safety switch and back-up light wires. Position the wiring harness, and connect the coil, oil, and temperature leads.

34. Connect the auxiliary heater hoses. Connect the oil filler tube to the rocker arm cover and install the retaining clamp. Install the filler tube bracket to the dash panel.

35. Install the radiator and battery deflector. Connect the radiator hoses and oil cooler lines.

36. Install the grille, head light and hood lock bracket.

37. Fill the crankcase and cooling system. Fill the automatic transmission.

38. Connect the positive battery cable, and operate the engine to check for leaks. Adjust idle speed and mixture, and automatic transmission linkage.

39. Install the air cleaner and brackets, engine front cover, and right front seat, grille and bumper.

1975–82 300 SIX-CYLINDER

1. Take off the engine cover, drain the coolant, remove the air cleaner, and disconnect the battery.

2. Remove the bumper, grille, and gravel deflector.

3. Detach the upper radiator hose at the engine. Remove the alternator splash shield and detach the lower hose at the radiator. Remove the radiator and shroud, if any.

4. Disconnect the engine heater hoses and the alternator wires. Remove the power steering pump and support.

5. Disconnect and plug the fuel line at the pump.

6. Detach from the engine: distributor and gauge sending unit wires, brake booster hose, accelerator cable and bracket.

7. Disconnect the automatic transmission kickdown linkage at the bellcrank.

8. Remove the exhaust manifold heat deflector and unbolt the pipe from the manifold.

9. Disconnect the automatic transmission vacuum line from the intake manifold and from the junction. Remove the transmission dipstick tube support bolt at the intake manifold.

10. Remove the upper engine to transmission bolts.

11. Remove the starter. Remove the flywheel inspection cover. Remove the four automatic transmission torque converter nuts, then remove the front engine support nuts. Take off the oil filter.

12. Remove the rest of the transmission to engine fasteners, then lift the engine out from the engine compartment with a floor crane.

13. To replace the engine, lower it into place and start the mounting bolts. Install the upper transmission bolts, the converter nuts, and the lower transmission bolts. Tighten the mounting bolts. Replace all the items removed in the previous steps.

1969–72 302 V8

1. Remove the engine cover.

2. Remove the right front seat. Also remove the driver's seat if more room to work is desired.

3. Drain the cooling system.

4. Remove the air cleaner and intake duct assembly, including the crankcase ventilation hose.

5. Disconnect the battery and alternator ground cables at the cylinder block.

6. Remove the oil filler tube at the dash panel and disconnect it at the rocker arm cover.

7. Disconnect the radiator upper and lower hoses at the radiator and the automatic transmission oil cooler lines, if so equipped.

8. Disconnect the radiator attaching bolts and remove the radiator.

9. Disconnect the heater hoses at the engine and position them out of the way.

10. Remove the fan, spacer, pulley, and the drive belt.

11. Disconnect the accelerator linkage at the accelerator shaft on the left cylinder head. Disconnect the automatic transmission kick-down rod at the carburetor and the vacuum line at the intake manifold, if so equipped.

12. Disconnect the engine wire harness from the left rocker arm cover and position it out of the way.

13. Remove the upper nut attaching the right exhaust manifolds to the muffler inlet pipe.

14. Raise the vehicle on a hoist.

15. Drain the crankcase and remove the oil filter.

16. Disconnect the fuel link (tank-to-pump) at the fuel pump.

17. Disconnect the oil dipstick tube bracket from the exhaust manifold and oil pan.

18. On manual transmissions, remove the bolts attaching the equalizer arm bracket to the cylinder block and the clutch housing. This includes the clutch linkage connection and the retracting springs. Remove the bracket.

19. Disconnect the starter cable at the starter and remove the starter.

20. On a vehicle with a manual transmission, disconnect the driveshaft at the rear axle and remove the driveshaft. Install a plug in the end of the transmission. On vehicles with automatic transmissions, disconnect the driveshaft at the companion flange.

21. Disconnect the speedometer cable and the transmission linkage at the transmission.

22. Position a transmission jack under the transmission. Raise the transmission and remove the bolts attaching the crossmember to the chassis. Lower the transmission slightly and remove the bolt and nut attaching the engine rear support to the crossmember. Remove the crossmember.

23. Remove the bolts attaching the manual transmission to the clutch housing and remove the transmission.

24. On a vehicle with an automatic transmission, remove the lower front cover from the converter housing. Remove the transmission dipstick tube and drain the transmission. Install a plug in the transmission oil pan. Remove the nuts attaching the transmission converter to the flywheel. Disconnect the oil cooler lines and the vacuum lines at the transmission. Remove the remaining bolts fastening the transmission to the engine and remove the transmission.

25. Position an engine support bar under the engine to steady it.

26. Disconnect the muffler inlet pipes at the exhaust manifolds.

27. Remove the engine front support attaching nuts and washers.

28. Remove the bellcrank bolt from the side of the cylinder block and position the bellcrank assembly out of the way.

29. Lower the vehicle.

30. Remove the bolts attaching the alternator to the cylinder block and the water pump and position it out of the way.

31. Remove the carburetor air horn stud and disconnect the fuel line (pump-to-carburetor) at the fuel pump.

32. Install an engine lifting device and remove the engine through the right-side door.

To install the 302 V8 engine:

1. Lift the engine into place through the right-side door.

2. Connect the fuel line (pump-to-carburetor) at the fuel pump.

3. Position the alternator and adjusting arm to the cylinder block and water pump housing. Install and tighten the attaching bolts.

4. Lift the engine and position it to the chassis and supporting bar.

5. Raise the vehicle on a hoist.

6. Install the engine front support attaching nuts and washers.

7. On a vehicle with an automatic transmission, position the bellcrank assembly to the cylinder block and install the attaching bolt. Position the transmission to the engine and install the attaching bolts.

8. On a vehicle with a manual transmission, position the transmission to the clutch housing and install the attaching bolts.

9. Remove the engine support bar.

10. Position the engine rear support crossmember to the chassis and install the attaching bolts. Position the transmission with the engine rear support attached to the crossmember. Install and tighten the bolt and nut. Remove the jack.

11. On a vehicle with an automatic transmission, install and tighten the converter-to-flywheel attaching nuts. Connect the oil cooler and vacuum lines at the transmission. Install the transmission dipstick tube in the pan. Install the dipstick tube and vacuum line retaining bracket bolt to the cylinder block.

12. Connect the transmission shift linkages and the speedometer cable.

13. On a vehicle with an automatic transmission, connect the driveshaft to the transmission companion flange. On a vehicle with a manual transmission, remove the plug from the transmission and install the driveshaft into the transmission. Connect the rear end of the driveshaft at the rear axle.

14. Install the starter and connect the cable to the starter.

15. Install the muffler inlet pipe attaching bolts and nuts (except the upper nut on the right-side exhaust manifold).

16. On a manual transmission, install the

bolts connecting the equalizer arm bracket to the cylinder block and clutch housing. This includes connecting the clutch linkage and retracting spring.

17. Install the oil filter.

18. Install the oil dipstick tube bracket to the oil pan and the exhaust manifold.

19. Connect the fuel line (tank-to-pump) at the fuel pump.

20. Lower the vehicle.

21. Install the upper nut attaching the right exhaust manifold to the muffler inlet pipe.

22. Connect the engine wire harness at the left rocker arm cover. Connect the battery and the alternator ground cables at the cylinder block.

23. Connect the automatic transmission vacuum line at the intake manifold and the transmission kick-down rod at the carburetor, if so equipped. Connect the accelerator linkage to accelerator shaft on the left-side cylinder head.

24. Install the drive belt, pulley, spacer and fan, then tighten the belt tension.

25. Connect the heater hoses at the engine.

26. Position the radiator and install the attaching bolts. Connect the radiator upper and lower hoses and the automatic transmission cooler lines, if so equipped.

27. Install the oil filler tube.

28. Install the air cleaner and intake duct assembly, including the crankcase ventilation hose.

29. Fill and bleed the cooling system.

30. Fill the crankcase and the automatic transmission, if so equipped.

31. Install the engine cover and the right front seat.

32. Operate the engine at a fast idle and check for leaks.

351W, 400, 460 V8 AND 1979–82 302 V8

1. Take off the engine cover, drain the coolant, remove the air cleaner, and disconnect the battery. Remove the bumper, grille, and gravel deflector. Remove the upper grille support bracket, hood lock support, and air conditioning condenser upper mounting brackets.

2. With air conditioning, the system must be discharged to remove the condenser. Do not attempt to do this yourself, unless you are trained in air conditioning. Disconnect the lines at the compressor.

3. Remove the accelerator cable bracket and the heater hoses. Detach the radiator hoses and the automatic transmission cooler lines, if any. Remove the fan shroud, fan, and radiator.

4. Pivot the alternator in and detach the wires.

5. Remove the air cleaner, duct and valve, exhaust manifold shroud, and flex tube.

6. Disconnect the automatic transmission shift rod.

7. Disconnect the fuel and choke lines, detach the vacuum lines, and remove the carburetor and spacer.

8. Remove the oil filter. Detach the exhaust pipe from the manifold. Unbolt the automatic transmission tube bracket from the cylinder head. Remove the starter.

9. Remove the engine mount bolts. With automatic, remove the converter inspection cover and unbolt the converter from the flex plate.

10. Unbolt the engine ground cable and support the transmission.

11. Remove the power steering front bracket. Detach only one vacuum line at the rear of the intake manifold. Disconnect the engine wiring loom. Remove the speed control servo from the manifold. Detach the compressor clutch wire.

12. Install a lifting bracket to the intake manifold and attach a floor crane. Remove the transmission to engine bolts, making sure the transmission is supported. Remove the engine.

13. To install the engine, align the converter to the flex plate and the engine dowels to the transmission. With manual transmission, start the transmission shaft into the clutch disc. You may have to turn the crankshaft slowly with the transmission in gear. Install the transmission bolts, then the mounting bolts. Replace all the items removed in the previous steps.

Cylinder Head

REMOVAL AND INSTALLATION

Six Cylinder

1. Drain the cooling system. Remove the air cleaner. Remove the oil filler tube. Disconnect the battery cable at the cylinder head.

2. Disconnect the muffler inlet pipe at the exhaust manifold. Pull the muffler inlet pipe down. Remove the gasket.

3. Disconnect the accelerator rod re-

Cylinder head tightening sequence for the 144, 170, 200 six-cylinder

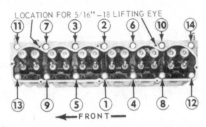

Cylinder head bolt tightening sequence for the 240, 300 six-cylinder

tracting spring. Disconnect the choke control cable if applicable and the accelerator rod at the carburetor.

4. Disconnect the transmission kickdown rod. Disconnect the accelerator linkage at the bellcrank assembly.

5. Disconnect the fuel inlet line at the fuel filter hose, and the distributor vacuum line at the carburetor. Disconnect other vacuum lines as necessary for accessibility and identify them for proper connection.

6. Remove the radiator upper hose at the coolant outlet housing.

7. Disconnect the distributor vacuum line at the distributor. Disconnect the carburetor fuel inlet line at the fuel pump. Remove the lines as an assembly.

8. Disconnect the spark plug wires at the spark plugs and the temperature sending unit wire at the sending unit.

9. Grasp the crankcase vent hose near the regulator valve and pull the regulator valve out of the grommet in the valve rocker arm cover. Disconnect the crankcase vent hose at the hose fitting in the intake manifold spacer and remove the vent hose and regulator valve.

10. Disconnect the carburetor air vent tube and remove the valve rocker arm cover.

11. Remove the valve rocker arm shaft assembly on the 144, 170 and 200; on the 240 and 300 loosen the rocker arm stud nuts and move the rocker arms aside. Remove the pushrods in sequence so that they can be identified and reinstalled in their original positions.

12. Remove the cylinder head bolts and remove the cylinder head. Do not pry be-

tween the cylinder head and the block as the gasket surfaces may be damaged. Two $5/16$ in. lifting eyes may be installed on the right side of the 240 and 300 head.

To install the cylinder head:

1. Clean the head and block gasket surfaces. If the cylinder head was removed for a gasket change, check the flatness of the cylinder head and block.

2. Apply sealer to both sides of the new 144, 170, 200 cylinder head gasket. Position the gasket on the cylinder block.

3. Install a new gasket on the flange of the muffler inlet pipe.

4. Lift the cylinder head above the cylinder block and lower it into position using two head bolts installed through the head as guides.

5. Coat the threads of the No. 1 and 6 bolts for the right-side of the 144, 170, 200 cylinder head with a small amount of water-resistant sealer. Oil the threads of the remaining bolts. Install, but do not tighten; two bolts at the opposite ends of the head to hold the head and gasket in position.

6. The cylinder head bolts are tightened in 3 progressive steps. Torque them (in the proper sequence) to the specified torque.

7. Apply Lubriplate® to both ends of the pushrods and install them in their original positions.

8. Install the valve rocker shaft assembly.

9. Adjust the valves on the 144 and 170. See Chapter 2.

10. Install the muffler inlet pipe lockwashers and attaching nuts.

11. Connect the radiator upper hose at the coolant outlet housing.

12. Position the distributor vacuum line and the carburetor fuel inlet line on the engine. Connect the fuel line at the fuel filter hose and install a new clamp. Install the distributor vacuum line at the carburetor. Connect the accelerator linkage at the bellcrank assembly. Connect the transmision kickdown rod.

13. Connect the accelerator rod retracting spring. Connect the choke control cable (if applicable) and the accelerator rod at the carburetor.

14. Connect the distributor vacuum line at the distributor. Connect the carburetor fuel inlet line at the fuel pump. Connect all the vacuum lines using their previous identification for proper connection.

15. Connect the temperature sending unit wire at the sending unit. Connect the spark

plug wires. Connect the battery cable at the cylinder head.

16. Fill the cooling system.

17. Install the valve rocker cover. Connect the carburetor air vent tube.

18. Connect the crankcase vent hose at the carburetor spacer fitting. Insert the regulator valve with the vent hose attached, into the valve rocker arm cover grommet. Install the air cleaner, start the engine and check for leaks.

302 and 351W V8

1. Remove the intake manifold and the carburetor as an assembly.

2. Remove the rocker arm cover(s).

3. If the right cylinder head is to be removed, loosen the alternator adjusting arm bolt and remove the alternator mounting bracket bolt and spacer. Swing the alternator down and out of the way. Remove the ignition coil and the air cleaner inlet duct from the right cylinder head assembly.

If the left cylinder head is being removed, remove the bolts fastening the accelerator shaft assembly at the front of the cylinder head.

4. Disconnect the exhaust manifold(s) from the muffler inlet pipe(s).

5. Loosen the rocker arm stud nuts so that the rocker arms can be rotated to the side. Remove the pushrods and identify them so that they can be reinstalled in their original positions.

6. Remove the cylinder head bolts and lift the cylinder head from the block.

To install the cylinder head(s):

1. Clean the cylinder head, intake manifold, and the valve cover and head gasket surfaces.

2. A specially treated composition head gasket is used. Do not apply sealer to a composition gasket. Position the new gasket over the locating dowels on the cylinder block. Then, position the cylinder head on the block and install the attaching bolts.

3. The cylinder head bolts are tightened

in 3 progressive steps. Tighten all the bolts in the proper sequence to 50 ft lbs, 60 ft lbs, and finally to 70 ft lbs of torque.

4. Clean the pushrods. Blow out the oil passage in the rods with compressed air. Check the pushrods for straightness. Never try to straighten a pushrod; always replace it.

5. Apply Lubriplate to the ends of the pushrods and install them in their original positions.

6. Apply Lubriplate ® to the rocker arms and their fulcrum seats and install the rocker arms. Adjust the 302 valves as detailed in Chapter 2.

7. Position a new gasket(s) on the muffler inlet pipe(s) as necessary. Connect the exhaust manifold(s) at the muffler inlet pipe(s).

8. If the right cylinder head was removed, install the alternator, ignition coil and air cleaner duct on the right cylinder head. Adjust the drive belt.

If the left cylinder head was removed, install the accelerator shaft assembly at the front of the cylinder head.

9. Clean the valve rocker arm cover and the cylinder head gasket surfaces. Place the new gaskets in the covers, making sure that the tabs of the gasket engage the notches provided in the cover.

10. Install the intake manifold and related parts.

400 V8

1. Remove the intake manifolds and the carburetor as an assembly.

2. Remove the rocker arm cover(s).

3. If the right cylinder head is to be removed, loosen the alternator adjusting arm bolt and remove the alternator mounting bracket bolt and spacer. Swing the alternator down and out of the way. Remove the air cleaner inlet duct from the right cylinder head assembly. Remove the ground strap at the rear of the head.

If the left cylinder head is being removed, remove the bolts fastening the accelerator shaft assembly at the front of the cylinder head. On vehicles equipped with air conditioning, the system must be discharged and the compressor removed. The procedure is best left to an air conditioning specialist. Persons not familiar with A/C systems can be easily injured when working on the systems.

4. Disconnect the exhaust manifold(s) from the muffler inlet pipe(s).

5. Loosen the rocker arm stud nuts so that the rocker arms can be rotated to the side.

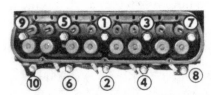

Cylinder head bolt tightening sequence for all V8s

Remove the pushrods and identify them so that they can be reinstalled in their original positions.

6. Remove the cylinder head bolts and lift the cylinder head from the block.

To install the cylinder head(s):

1. Clean the cylinder head, intake manifold, and the valve cover and head gasket surfaces.

2. A specially treated composition head gasket is used. Do not apply sealer to a composition gasket. Position the new gasket over the locating dowels on the cylinder block. Then, position the cylinder head on the block and install the attaching bolts.

3. The cylinder head bolts are tightened in 3 progressive steps. Tighten all the bolts in the proper sequence to 60 ft lbs, and finally to 70, 80 then 95–105 ft lbs.

4. Clean the pushrods. Blow out the oil passage in the rods with compressed air. Check the pushrods for straightness. Never try to straighten a pushrod; always replace it.

5. Apply Lubriplate® to the ends of the pushrods and install them in their original positions.

6. Apply Lubriplate® to the rocker arms and their fulcrum seats and install the rocker arms. Adjust the valves.

7. Position a new gasket(s) on the muffler inlet pipe(s) as necessary. Connect the exhaust manifold(s) at the muffler inlet pipe(s).

8. If the right cylinder head was removed, install the alternator, ignition coil and air cleaner duct on the right cylinder head. Adjust the drive belt.

If the left cylinder head was removed, install the accelerator shaft assembly at the front of the cylinder head.

9. Clean the valve rocker arm cover and the cylinder head gasket surfaces. Place the new gaskets in the covers, making sure that the tabs of the gasket engage the notches provided in the cover. Install the compressor, evacuate, charge and leak test the system. Let an expert do this.

10. Install the intake manifold and related parts.

460 V8

1. Remove the intake manifold and carburetor as an assembly.

2. Disconnect the exhaust pipe from the exhaust manifold.

3. Loosen the air conditioning compressor drive belt, if so equipped.

4. Loosen the alternator attaching bolts and remove the bolt attaching the alternator bracket to the right cylinder head.

5. Disconnect the air conditioning compressor from the engine and move it aside, out of the way. Do not discharge the air conditioning system.

6. Remove the bolts securing the power steering reservoir bracket to the left cylinder head. Position the reservoir and bracket out of the way.

7. Remove the valve rocker arm covers. Remove the rocker arm bolts, rocker arms, oil deflectors, fulcrums and pushrods in sequence so that they can be reinstalled in their original positions.

8. Remove the cylinder head bolts and lift the head and exhaust manifold off the engine. If necessary, pry at the forward corners of the cylinder head against the casting bosses provided on the cylinder block. Do not damage the gasket mating surfaces of the cylinder head and block by prying against them.

9. Remove all gasket material from the cylinder head and block. Clean all gasket material from the mating surfaces of the intake manifold. If the exhaust manifold was removed, clean the mating surfaces of the cylinder head exhaust port areas and install the exhaust manifold.

10. Position the two long cylinder head bolts in the two rear lower bolt holes of the left cylinder head. Place a long cylinder head bolt in the rear lower bolt hole of the right cylinder head. Use rubber bands to keep the bolts in position until the cylinder heads are installed on the cylinder block.

11. Position new cylinder head gaskets on the cylinder block dowels. Do not apply sealer to the gaskets, heads, or block.

12. Place the cylinder heads on the block, guiding the exhaust pipe connections. Install the remaining cylinder head bolts. The longer bolts go in the lower row of holes.

13. Tighten all the cylinder head attaching bolts in the proper sequence in three stages: 75 ft lbs, 105 ft lbs, and finally, to 135 ft lbs. When this procedure is used, it is not necessary to retorque the heads after extended use.

14. Connect the exhaust pipes to the exhaust manifolds.

15. Install the intake manifold and carburetor assembly. Tighten the intake manifold attaching bolts in the proper sequence to 25–30 ft lbs.

16. Install the air conditioning compressor to the engine.

17. Install the power steering reservoir to the engine.

18. Apply oil-resistant sealer to one side of the new valve cover gaskets and lay the cemented side in place in the valve covers. Install the covers.

19. Install the alternator to the right cylinder head and adjust the alternator drive belt tension.

20. Adjust the air conditioning compressor drive belt tension.

21. Fill the radiator with coolant.

22. Start the engine and check for leaks.

Rocker Arm Shaft Assembly

REMOVAL AND INSTALLATION

144, 170, 200 Six-Cylinder

1. Remove the air cleaner.

2. Remove the rocker arm cover and discard the gasket.

3. Remove the rocker shaft assembly by removing the bolts in alternating sequence starting from the ends and working toward the middle.

4. Remove the pin and spring washer from each end of the shaft.

5. Slide the rocker arms, springs and supports from the shaft. Some of the supports may stick. Loosen them with a penetrant such as Liquid Wrench® or CRC®. NEVER HAMMER ON THEM! Keep the parts in order for reference upon installation.

6. If it is necessary to remove the plugs from the ends of the shaft, pierce one plug and use a thin steel rod through the hole to knock out the opposite plug. In turn, knock out the pierced plug. The plugs will have to be replaced.

7. Inspect all parts and replace any cracked or damaged pieces.

8. Lubricate all parts with clean engine oil. Coat the two ends of each rocker arm with Lubriplate® or the equivalent.

9. Using a blunt piece of wood, install new plugs in either end of the shaft.

10. Install all parts in reverse order of removal.

CAUTION: *During reassembly, make absolutely certain that the drilled holes in the shaft face downward.*

11. On engine with hydraulic lifters, position #1 piston at TDC (use the timing mark). Then turn the crankshaft 60° in clockwise rotation as viewed from the front. Install the

pushrods and position the shaft assembly on the head, contacting the rocker arms with the pushrods. Tighten the shaft bolts, two turns at a time in sequence from the center to the ends. Torque the bolts to 30–35 ft lb.

12. On engines with mechanical lifters, install the pushrods and install the rocker shaft assembly contacting the rocker arms with the pushrods. Tighten the shaft bolts two turns at a time in sequence from the center to the ends. Adjust the valves as described under "Valve Lash Adjustment" in Chapter 2. Install the valve cover and run the engine to normal operating temperatures. Remove the cover and, with the engine running, adjust the valves as described under "Valve Lash Adjustment" in Chapter 2.

13. Install all parts in reverse order of removal. Use a new valve cover gasket coated on both sides with non-hardening sealer. Torque the bolts to 3–5 ft lb, wait two minutes then retorque.

Rocker Arm Stud

REMOVAL AND INSTALLATION

240, 300, 302, 351W

If it is necessary to remove a rocker arm stud, Tool T79T-6527-A is available. A 0.006 inch oversize reamer T62F-6A527-B3 and a 0.015 inch oversize reamer T62F-6A527-B5 are available. For 0.010 inch oversize studs, use reamer T66P-6A527-B. To press in replacement studs, use stud replacer T65P-6A527-A or T69P-6049-D for 5.0L (302 CID) V-8 and 5.8L (351 CID)-W-V-8 and T79T-6527-B for 4.9L (300 CID) I-6.

Rocker arm studs that are broken or have damaged threads may be replaced with standard studs. Loose studs in the head may be replaced with 0.006, 0.010 or 0.015 inch oversize studs which are available for service.

Standard and oversize studs can be identified by measuring the stud diameter within 1⅛ inch from the pilot end of the stud. The stud diameters are:

- 0.006 oversize . . . 0.3774-0.7781
- 0.010 oversize . . . 0.3814-0.3821
- 0.015 oversize . . . 0.3864-0.3871

When going from a standard size rocker arm stud to a 0.010 or 0.015 inch oversize stud, always use the 0.006 inch oversize reamer before finish reaming with the 0.010 or 0.015 inch oversize reamer.

1. Position the sleeve of the rocker arm stud remover over the stud so that ¼ inch of the stud length is engaged. Using a deep

socket, turn the outside forcing nut until it bottoms on the stud boss and pulls the stud from the boss.

If the rocker arm stud was broken off flush with the stud boss, use an easy-out to remove the broken stud following the instructions of the tool manufacturer.

2. If a loose rocker arm stud is being replaced, ream the stud bore using the proper reamer (or reamers in sequence) for the selected oversize stud.

CAUTION: *Make sure the metal particles do not enter the valve area.*

3. Coat the end of the stud with Lubriplate or its equivalent. Align the stud with the stud bore; then, tap the sliding driver until it bottoms. When the driver contacts the stud boss, the stud is installed to its correct height.

Rocker Arm

REMOVAL AND INSTALLATION

400 and 460 V8

1. Remove the air cleaner and intake duct assembly.

If a right cylinder head rocker arm is to be removed, remove the crankcase ventilation PCV valve from the valve rocker arm cover.

2. Disconnect the spark plug wires from the spark plugs. Remove the wires from the bracket on the valve rocker arm cover(s) and position the wires out of the way.

3. Remove the valve rocker arm cover(s).

4. Remove the valve rocker arm bolt, oil deflector, fulcrum seat and rocker arm.

5. Apply Lubriplate or equivalent to the top of the valve stems, the rocker arm and fulcrum seats.

6. Position the No. 1 piston on TDC at the end of the compression stroke, and install the rocker arm, fulcrum seat, oil deflector and bolt on the following valves:

- No. 1 Intake No. 1 Exhaust
- No. 7 Intake No. 5 Exhaust
- No. 8 Intake No. 4 Exhaust

Position the crankshaft 180 degrees clockwise and install the rocker arm, fulcrum seat, oil deflector and bolt on the following valves:

- No. 4 Intake No. 2 Exhaust
- No. 5 Intake No. 6 Exhaust

Position the crankshaft 180 degrees clockwise and install the rocker arm, fulcrum seat, oil deflector and bolt on the following valves:

- No. 2 Intake No. 3 Exhaust
- No. 3 Intake No. 7 Exhaust
- No. 6 Intake No. 8 Exhaust

NOTE: *Be sure that the fulcrum seat base is inserted in its slot on the cylinder head before tightening the fulcrum bolts.*

Tighten the fulcrum bolt to 18–25 ft lb. Adjust the valve clearance following the procedures under valve lash adjustment.

7. Clean the valve rocker arm cover(s) and the cylinder head gasket surface(s). Position the gasket in the cover, making sure that the gasket tangs are secured in the notches in the cover.

8. Position the cover(s) on the cylinder head(s). Make sure the gasket seats evenly all around the head. Install the bolts. The cover is tightened in two steps. Tighten the bolts to 5–6 ft lb. Two minutes later, tighten the bolts to the same specifications.

If the right cover was removed, install PCV valve.

Install the air cleaner and intake duct assembly.

9. Install the spark plug wires in the bracket on the valve rocker arm cover(s). Connect the spark plug wires.

10. Start the engine and check for leaks.

Intake Manifold

REMOVAL AND INSTALLATION

Six-Cylinder

See the exhaust manifold removal and installation procedure.

302 and 351W V8

1. Drain cooling system.

2. Remove air cleaner and intake duct assembly, including crankcase ventilation hose.

3. Disconnect accelerator rod, choke cable and automatic transmission kickdown rod (if applicable) at the carburetor. Remove the accelerator retracting spring, where so equipped.

4. Disconnect high tension lead and wires from the coil.

5. Remove spark plug wire from plugs and harness brackets, then remove distributor cap and spark plug wire assembly.

6. Disconnect fuel inlet line at carburetor.

7. Disconnect distributor vacuum hoses and remove distributor.

8. Remove heater hose, radiator hose and water temperature sending unit wire from manifold.

9. Remove water pump bypass hose from coolant outlet housing.

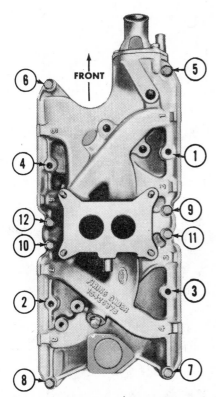

302 and 351W intake manifold tightening sequence

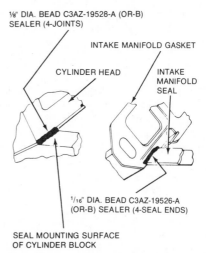

⅛" DIA. BEAD C3AZ-19528-A (OR-B) SEALER (4-JOINTS)

INTAKE MANIFOLD GASKET

CYLINDER HEAD

INTAKE MANIFOLD SEAL

$^1/_{16}$" DIA. BEAD C3AZ-19526-A (OR-B) SEALER (4-SEAL ENDS)

SEAL MOUNTING SURFACE OF CYLINDER BLOCK

RTV sealer installation, 302, 351W, 460 intake manifold

10. Disconnect crankcase ventilation hose from valve rocker cover.

11. Remove intake manifold and carburetor as an assembly, prying manifold from cylinder head if necessary. Throw away gaskets and bolt sealing washers.

12. When disassembling, identify all vacuum hoses before disconnecting them. Remove coolant outlet housing and gasket. Remove ignition coil and engine identification tag, temperature sending unit, carburetor, spacer, gasket, vacuum fitting, accelerator retracting spring bracket and choke cable bracket.

13. To install, first assemble manifold/carburetor unit by installing all components removed in Step 12, making sure vacuum lines are positioned correctly.

14. Clean all mating surfaces, using a suitable solvent to remove all oil. Apply a ⅛ in. bead of silicone-rubber RTV sealant at the points shown in the accompanying diagram.

CAUTION: *Do not apply sealer to the waffle portions of the seals as the sealer will rupture the end seal material.*

15. Position new seals on the block and press the seal locating extensions into the holes in the mating surfaces. Apply a $^1/_{16}$ in.

bead of sealer to the outer end of each manifold seal for the full length of the seal (4 places). As before, do not apply sealer to the waffle portion of the end seals.

NOTE: *This sealer sets in about 15 minutes, depending on brand, so work quickly but carefully. DO NOT DROP ANY SEALER INTO THE MANIFOLD CAVITY. IT WILL FORM AND SET AND PLUG THE OIL GALLERY.*

16. Carefully position manifold, making sure that gaskets and seals do not shift. Install bolts and new bolt seal washers, tightening in the sequence illustrated to the specified torque. *Retighten after engine has been operated until warmed up.*

17. Install water bypass hose to coolant outlet housing, radiator upper hose and heater hose.

18. Install distributor as described in "Distributor Removal and Installation." Install distributor cap and spark plug wires, positioning wires in harness brackets on valve rocker covers.

19. Connect crankcase ventilation hose, high tension lead and coil wires, accelerator rod and retracting spring, choke cable and automatic transmission kickdown rod (if applicable).

20. Fill and bleed cooling system.

21. Adjust ignition timing.

22. Connect vacuum hoses at distributor.

23. Operate engine until warmed up, checking for leaks.

24. Retorque manifold bolts.

25. Adjust transmission throttle linkage, if so equipped.

26. Install air cleaner and intake duct assembly including closed crankcase ventilation hose.

400 V8

1. Drain the cooling system, remove the air cleaner and the intake duct assembly.

2. Disconnect the accelerator rod from the carburetor and remove the accelerator retracting spring. Disconnect the automatic transmission kick-down rod at the carburetor, if so equipped.

3. Disconnect the high-tension lead and all other wires from the ignition coil.

4. Disconnect the spark plug wires from the spark plugs by grasping the rubber boots and twisting and pulling at the same time. Remove the wires from the brackets on the rocker covers. Remove the distributor cap and spark plug wire assembly.

5. Remove the carburetor fuel inlet line and the distributor vacuum line from the carburetor.

6. Remove the distributor lockbolt and remove the distributor and vacuum line. See "Distributor Removal and Installation."

7. Disconnect the upper radiator hose from the coolant outlet housing and the water temperature sending unit wire at the sending unit. Remove the heater hose from the intake manifold.

8. Loosen the clamp on the water pump bypass hose at the coolant outlet housing and slide the hose off the outlet housing.

9. Disconnect the PCV hose at the rocker cover.

10. If the engine is equipped with the Thermactor exhaust emission control system, remove the air pump to cylinder head air hose at the air pump and position it out of the way. Also remove the air hose at the backfire suppressor valve. Remove the air hose bracket from the valve rocker arm cover and position the air hose out of the way.

11. Remove the intake manifold and carburetor as an assembly. It may be necessary to pry the intake manifold from the cylinder head. Remove all traces of the intake manifold-to-cylinder head gaskets and the two end seals from both the manifold and the other mating surfaces of the engine.

Installation is as follows:

1. Clean the mating surfaces of the intake manifold, cylinder heads and block with lacquer thinner or similar solvent. Apply a ⅛ in. bead of silicone-rubber RTV sealant at the points shown in the accompanying diagram.

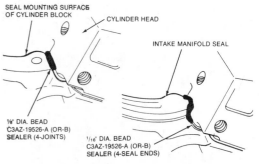

SEAL MOUNTING SURFACE OF CYLINDER BLOCK
CYLINDER HEAD
INTAKE MANIFOLD SEAL
⅛" DIA. BEAD C3AZ-19526-A (OR-B) SEALER (4-JOINTS)
1/16" DIA. BEAD C3AZ-19526-A (OR-B) SEALER (4-SEAL ENDS)

RTV sealer installation, 400 intake manifold

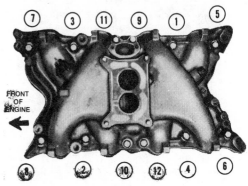

400 V8 intake manifold torque sequence

CAUTION: *Do not apply sealer to the waffle portions of the seals as the sealer will rupture the end seal material.*

2. Position new seals on the block and press the seal locating extensions into the holes in the mating surfaces.

3. Apply a 1/16 in. bead of sealer to the outer end of each manifold seal for the full length of the seal (4 places). As before, do not apply sealer to the waffle portion of the end seals.

NOTE: *This sealer sets in about 15 minutes, depending on brand, so work quickly but carefully. DO NOT DROP ANY SEALER INTO THE MANIFOLD CAVITY. IT WILL FORM AND SET AND PLUG THE OIL GALLERY.*

4. Position the manifold gasket onto the block and heads with the alignment notches under the dowels in the heads. Be sure gasket holes align with head holes.

5. Install the manifold and related equipment in reverse order of removal.

460 V8

1. Drain the cooling system and remove the air cleaner assembly.

2. Disconnect the upper radiator hose at the engine.

3. Disconnect the heater hoses at the intake manifold and the water pump. Position them out of the way. Loosen the water pump by-pass hose clamp at the intake manifold.

4. Disconnect the PCV valve and hose at the right valve cover. Disconnect all of the vacuum lines at the rear of the intake manifold and tag them for proper reinstallation.

5. Disconnect the wires at the spark plugs, and remove the wires from the brackets on the valve covers. Disconnect the high-tension wire from the coil and remove the distributor cap and wires as an assembly.

6. Disconnect all of the distributor vacuum lines at the carburetor and vacuum control valve and tag them for proper installation. Remove the distributor and vacuum lines as an assembly.

7. Disconnect the accelerator linkage at the carburetor. Remove the speed control linkage bracket, if so equipped, from the manifold and carburetor.

8. Remove the bolts holding the accelerator linkage bellcrank and position the linkage and return springs out of the way.

9. Disconnect the fuel line at the carburetor.

10. Disconnect the wiring harness at the coil battery terminal, engine temperature sending unit, oil pressure sending unit, and other connections as necessary. Disconnect the wiring harness from the clips at the left valve cover and position the harness out of the way.

11. Remove the coil and bracket assembly.

12. Remove the intake manifold attaching bolts and lift the manifold and carburetor from the engine as an assembly. It may be necessary to pry the manifold away from the cylinder heads. Do not damage the gasket sealing surfaces.

13. Install the intake manifold in the reverse order of removal.

14. Clean the mating surfaces of the intake manifold, cylinder heads and block with laquer thinner or similar solvent. Apply a 1/8 in. bead of silicone-rubber RTV sealant at the points shown in the accompanying diagram.

CAUTION: *Do not apply sealer to the waffle portions of the seals as the sealer will rupture the end seal material.*

15. Position new seals on the block and press the seal locating extensions into the holes in the mating surfaces.

16. Apply a $1/16$ in. bead of sealer to the outer end of each manifold seal for the full length of the seal (4 places). As before, do not apply sealer to the waffle portion of the end seals.

NOTE: *This sealer sets in about 15 minutes, depending on brand, so work quickly but carefully. DO NOT DROP ANY SEALER INTO THE MANIFOLD CAVITY. IT WILL FORM AND SET AND PLUG THE OIL GALLERY.*

When the manifold is placed on top of the engine run your fingers around the end seal areas to make sure that the end seals have not shifted. If they have, remove the manifold and reposition the seals. Tighten the intake manifold bolts in two stages in the proper sequence. After the engine has been started and has reached normal operating temperature, retorque the intake manifold bolts.

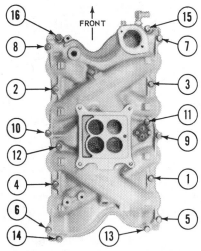

460 V8 intake manifold bolt torque sequence

Exhaust Manifold

REMOVAL AND INSTALLATION

144, 170, 200 Six-Cylinder

1. Raise the vehicle on a hoist and remove the air cleaner hot air duct.

2. Disconnect the muffler inlet pipe from the exhaust manifold.

3. Remove the attaching bolts and the exhaust manifold.

4. Clean the mating surfaces of the exhaust manifold and the cylinder head.

5. Apply graphite grease to the mating surface of the exhaust manifold.

6. Position the exhaust manifold on the cylinder head and install the attaching bolts and tab washers. Working from the center to the ends, torque the bolts to 18 ft lbs. Lock

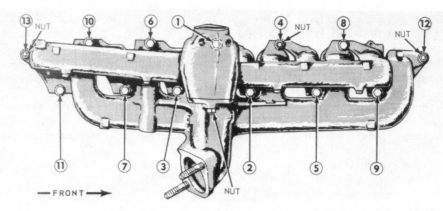

The 240, 300 six-cylinder intake and exhaust manifold torque sequence for the attaching bolts

the bolts by bending one tab of the washer over a flat on the bolt.

7. Place a new gasket on the muffler inlet pipe and install the pipe to the exhaust manifold. Install the air claner hot air duct and lower the vehicle.

240 and 300 Six-Cylinder

1. Remove the air cleaner. Disconnect the choke cable at the carburetor. Disconnect the accelerator cable or rod at the carburetor. Remove the accelerator retracting spring.

2. On a vehicle with automatic transmission, remove the kick-down rod retracting spring. Remove the accelerator rod bellcrank assembly.

3. Disconnect the fuel inlet line and the distributor vacuum line from the carburetor.

4. Disconnect the muffler inlet pipe from the exhaust manifold.

5. Disconnect the power brake vacuum line, if so equipped.

6. Remove the bolts and nuts attaching the manifolds to the cylinder head. Lift the manifold assemblies from the engine. Remove and discard the gaskets.

7. To separate the manifolds, remove the nuts joining the intake and exhaust manifolds.

8. Clean the mating surfaces of the cylinder head and the manifolds.

9. If the intake and exhaust manifolds have been separated, coat the mating surfaces lightly with graphite grease and place the exhaust manifold over the studs on the intake manifold. Install the lockwashers and nuts. Tighten them fingertight.

10. Install a new intake manifold gasket.

11. Coat the mating surfaces lightly with graphite grease. Place the manifold assemblies in position against the cylinder head. Make sure that the gaskets have not become dislodged. Install the attaching washers, bolts and nuts. Tighten the attaching nuts and bolts in the proper sequence to 26 ft lbs. If the intake and exhaust manifolds were separated, tighten the nuts joining them.

12. Position a new gasket on the muffler inlet pipe and connect the inlet pipe to the exhaust manifold.

13. Connect the crankcase vent hose to the intake manifold inlet tube and position the hose clamp.

14. Connect the fuel inlet line and the distributor vacuum line to the carburetor.

15. Connect the accelerator cable to the carburetor and install the retracting spring. Connect the choke cable to the carburetor.

16. On a vehicle with an automatic transmission, install the bellcrank assembly and the kick-down rod retracting spring. Adjust the transmission control linkage.

17. Install the air cleaner.

V8 except 400

1. Remove the air cleaner and intake duct assembly, including the crankcase ventilation hose.

2. Disconnect the exhaust manifold(s) from the inlet pipe(s).

3. Remove the attaching bolts and flat washers, then remove the exhaust manifold.

4. Clean the mating surfaces of the exhaust manifold(s) and cylinder head(s). Clean the mounting flange of the exhaust manifold and muffler inlet pipe.

5. Apply graphite grease to the mating surface of the exhaust manifold(s).

6. Position the exhaust manifold on the cylinder head and install the attaching bolts

and flat washers. Working from the center to the ends, tighten the bolts to the specified torque.

7. Position the air cleaner and intake duct assembly, including the crankcase ventilation hose.

400 V8

1. Remove the air cleaner if the manifold being removed has the carburetor heat stove attached to it. Remove the oil filter.

2. On vehicles with a column mounted automatic transmission lever, disconnect the selector lever cross-shaft for clearance.

3. Disconnect the exhaust pipe or catalytic converter from the exhaust manifold. Remove and discard the donut gasket.

4. Remove the exhaust manifold attaching screws and remove the manifold from the cylinder head.

5. Install the exhaust manifold in the reverse order of removal. Apply a light coat of graphite grease to the mating surface of the manifold. Install and tighten the attaching bolts, starting from the center and working to both ends alternately. Tighten to the proper specifications.

Timing Gear Cover
OIL SEAL REPLACEMENT
144, 170, 200 Six-Cylinder

1. Drain the cooling system and disconnect the radiator upper hose at the coolant outlet elbow and remove the two upper radiator retaining bolts.

2. Raise the vehicle and drain the crankcase.

3. Remove the splash shield and the automatic transmission oil cooling lines, if so equipped, then remove the radiator.

4. Loosen and remove the fan belt, fan and pulley.

5. Use a gear puller to remove the crankshaft pulley damper.

6. Remove the cylinder front cover retaining bolts and gently pry the cover away from the block. Remove the gasket.

7. Drive out the old seal with a pin punch from the rear of the cover. Clean out the recess in the cover.

8. Coat the new seal with grease and drive it into the cover until it is fully seated. Check the seal to make sure that the spring around the seal is in the proper position.

9. Clean the cylinder front cover and the gasket surface of the cylinder block. Apply an oil-resistant sealer to the new front cover gasket and install the gasket onto the cover.

10. Install the cylinder front cover onto the engine.

NOTE: *Trim away the exposed portion of the old oil pan gasket flush with the front of the engine block. Cut and position the required portion of a new gasket to the oil pan and apply sealer to both sides.*

11. Lubricate the hub of the crankshaft damper pulley with Lubriplate to prevent damage to the seal during installation or on initial starting of the engine.

12. Install and assemble the remaining components in the reverse order of removal, starting from Step 4. Start the engine and check for leaks.

240 and 300 Six-Cylinder

1. Drain the coolant and remove the radiator. Remove the fan, belts, and pulley.

2. Remove the bolt and washer and pull off the damper with a gear puller.

3. Remove the oil pan.

4. Remove the front cover and clean off the old gasket.

5. Drive out the crankshaft seal with a pin punch and clean out the cover recess. Coat the new seal with grease and drive it in until it is fully seated in the recess.

6. Use sealer on the gasket surfaces of the block and cover. Install the cover with a new gasket.

7. Lubricate the crankshaft and the damper seal rubbing surface. Align the damper keyway with the crankshaft key and install the damper.

8. Apply sealant to the cavities between the rear main bearing cap and cylinder block. Install a new oil pan rear seal in the rear main bearing cap and apply a bead of sealant to the tapered seal ends. Install new pan side gaskets with sealer. Place a new front cover seal on the pan.

9. Replace the oil pan and all the other parts removed.

V8

1. Drain the cooling system and the crankcase.

2. Disconnect the upper and lower radiator hoses from the water pump and remove the radiator.

3. Disconnect the heater hose from the water pump. Slide the water pump by-pass hose clamp toward the water pump.

4. Loosen the alternator pivot bolt and the bolt which secures the alternator adjusting arm to the water pump.

5. Remove the bolts holding the fan shroud to the radiator, if so equipped. Remove the fan, spacer, pulley and drive belts.

6. Remove the crankshaft pulley from the crankshaft damper. Remove the damper attaching bolt and washer and remove the damper with a puller.

7. Disconnect the fuel pump outlet line at the fuel pump. Disconnect the vacuum inlet and outlet lines from the fuel pump. Remove the fuel pump attaching bolts and lay the pump to one side with the fuel inlet line still attached.

8. Remove the oil level dipstick and the bolt holding the dipstick tube to the exhaust manifold.

9. Remove the oil pan-to-cylinder front cover attaching bolts. Use a sharp, thin cutting blade to cut the oil pan gasket flush with the cylinder block. Remove the front cover and water pump as an assembly.

10. Discard the front cover gasket.

11. See Steps 7 and 8 of the front cover oil seal replacement procedure for 170 6 cylinder engines.

12. Assemble the engine in the reverse order of disassembly, referring to Steps 9, 10 and 12 of the procedure for 170 6 cylinder engines. It may be necessary to force the cover downward slightly to compress the pan gasket and align the attaching bolt holes in the cover and the cylinder block. This operation can be accomplished by inserting a dowel or drift pin in the holes and aligning the cover with the block.

Timing Chain

REMOVAL AND INSTALLATION

All except 240, 300

1. Remove the front cover and the crankshaft front oil slinger.

2. With a socket wrench of the proper size on the crankshaft pulley bolt, gently rotate the crankshaft in a clockwise direction until all slack is removed from the left-side of the timing chain. Scribe a mark on the engine block parallel to the present position of the left-side of the chain. Next, turn the crankshaft in a counterclockwise direction to remove all slack from the right-side of the chain. Force the left-side of the chain outward with the fingers and measure the distance between the reference point and the

TIMING MARKS

Alignment of the timing marks on the crankshaft and camshaft timing chain sprockets of the 144, 170, 200 6-cylinder

present position of the chain. If the distance is more than ½ in., replace the chain and/or the sprockets.

3. Crank the engine until the timing marks are aligned.

4. Remove the camshaft sprocket capscrew, washers and fuel pump eccentric on the V8 engine. Slide both sprockets and the timing chain forward and remove them as an assembly.

5. Install the sprockets and chain in the reverse order of removal, making sure that when they are positioned onto the camshaft and crankshaft, the timing marks are aligned.

Timing Gears

REMOVAL AND INSTALLATION

240 and 300 Six-Cylinder Only

1. Drain the cooling system and remove the front cover.

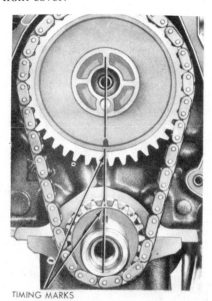

TIMING MARKS

Alignment of the timing marks on the crankshaft and camshaft timing chain sprockets on the V8

Alignment of the timing marks on the crankshaft and camshaft timing gears on the 240, 300 six-cylinder

2. Crank the engine until the timing marks on the camshaft and crankshaft gears are aligned.

3. Use a gear puller to remove both of the timing gears. Some 300 engines have a bolted-on camshaft gear.

4. Before installing the timing gears, be sure that the key and spacer are properly installed. Align the gear key way with the key and install the gear on the camshaft. Be sure that the timing marks line up on the camshaft and the crankshaft gears and install the crankshaft gear.

5. Install the front cover, and assemble the rest of the engine in the reverse order of disassembly. Fill the cooling system.

Camshaft

REMOVAL AND INSTALLATION

NOTE: *This procedure will probably require removal of the engine for 1961–67 models.*

144, 170, 200 Six-Cylinder

1. Remove the front cover, align the timing marks, and remove the timing chain and related parts as stated before.

2. Remove the cylinder head as previously outlined.

3. Disconnect the distributor primary wire at the ignition coil. Loosen the distributor lockbolt and remove the distributor.

4. Disconnect and plug the fuel inlet line at the fuel pump. Remove the fuel pump and gasket.

5. Remove the valve tappets with a magnet. Note that the tappets must be replaced in the same positions from which they are removed.

6. Remove the oil level dipstick.

7. Remove the headlight doors and disconnect the light ground wires and the screws. Disconnect the headlights and parking lights.

8. Remove the grille and hood lock as an assembly.

9. Remove the camshaft thrust plate.

10. Carefully withdraw the camshaft from the engine.

11. In preparation for installing the camshaft, clean the passage that feeds the rocker arm shaft by blowing compressed air into the opening in the block. Oil the camshaft journals and apply Lubriplate to all of the camshaft lobes. If a new camshaft is being installed, the spacer and dowel from the old camshaft must be used. Carefully slide the camshaft through the bearings.

12. Assemble the engine in the reverse order of disassembly.

240 and 300 Six-Cylinder

1. Remove the grille, radiator, and timing cover.

2. Remove the distributor, fuel pump, oil pan and oil pump.

3. Align the timing marks. Unbolt the camshaft thrust plate, working through the holes in the camshaft gear.

4. Loosen the rocker arms, remove the pushrods, take off the side cover and remove the valve lifters with a magnet.

5. Remove the camshaft very carefully to prevent nicking the bearings.

6. Oil the camshaft bearing journals and use Lubriplate® or something similar on the lobes. Install the camshaft, gear, and thrust plate, aligning the gear marks. Tighten down the thrust plate. Make sure that the camshaft end-play is not excessive.

7. The last item to be replaced is the distributor. The rotor should be at the firing position for no. 1 cylinder, with the timing gear marks aligned.

V8

1. Remove the grille, front cover, timing chain, and sprockets.

2. Disconnect the spark plug wires from the ignition harness bracket on the valve covers. Disconnect the ignition coil high-tension lead at the coil. Remove the distributor cap and the spark plug wire assembly.

3. Disconnect the wires from the ignition coil side terminals.

4. Disconnect the distributor vacuum

line from the carburetor. Remove the distributor lockbolt and clamp and remove the distributor from the engine.

5. Disconnect the heater hose from the intake manifold, the upper and lower radiator hoses at the engine and remove the radiator.

6. Disconnect the accelerator rod from the carburetor and the accelerator retracting spring.

7. Disconnect the water temperature sending unit wire from the sending unit and the engine ground strap at the engine.

8. Remove the PCV valve from the valve cover. Remove the valve covers. Loosen the rocker arm retaining nuts and rotate the rockers to the side, off the valve stems and pushrods.

9. Remove the intake manifold and carburetor as an assembly. Remove the intake manifold gaskets and seals.

10. Remove the valve pushrods in sequence so that they can be reinstalled in the same positions from which they were removed.

11. Remove the lifters and place them in order so that they too can be reinstalled in their original positions. Use either a magnet, or if the lifters are coated with varnish, a pair of pliers to remove them.

12. Remove the camshaft thrust plate and *carefully* remove the camshaft by sliding it out of the front of the engine.

13. In preparation for installation, oil the camshaft journals and apply Lubriplate to the lobes. Carefully slide the camshaft through the bearings and install the camshaft thrust plate.

NOTE: *Do not hammer the camshaft sprocket onto the camshaft because you might drive the plug out of the rear of the engine and cause an oil leak.*

14. Assemble the rest of the engine in the reverse order of disassembly.

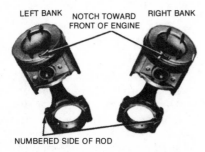

The proper positioning of the pistons and connecting rods in the V8

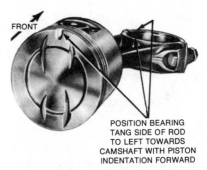

The proper positioning of the pistons and connecting rods in the 240 and 300 six-cylinder

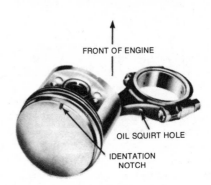

The proper positioning of the pistons and connecting rods in the 144, 170, and 200 six-cylinder

ENGINE LUBRICATION

Oil Pan

REMOVAL AND INSTALLATION

Six-Cylinder

1. Drain the crankcase and cooling system. Remove the oil level dipstick.

2. Remove the fan and water pump pulley.

3. Disconnect the radiator upper hose at the coolant outlet elbow.

4. Disconnect the flexible fuel line at the fuel pump.

5. Raise the vehicle and remove the air deflector shield (if so equipped) from below the radiator. Disconnect the radiator lower hose at the radiator.

6. Disconnect the starter cable at the starter. Remove the retaining bolts and remove the starter. Remove the air cleaner and carburetor on 1975 and later models.

7. Remove the attaching nuts and washers from the motor mounts, raise the front of the engine with a transmission jack and a block of wood. Place 2 in. thick wood

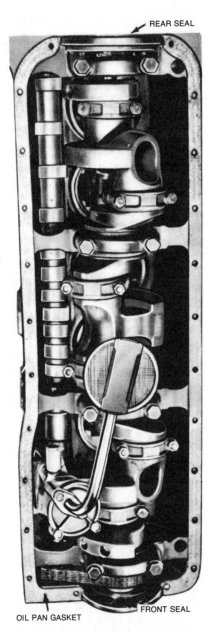

Positioning of the oil pan gaskets and seals on the 144, 170, and 200 six-cylinder

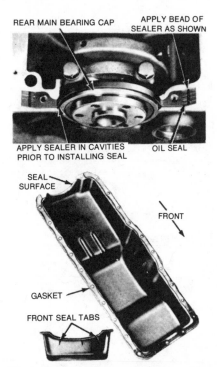

Positioning of the oil pan gaskets and seals on the 240 and 300 six-cylinder

blocks between the motor mounts on the engine and the mounting brackets. Lower the engine and remove the transmission jack.

8. Remove the oil pan retaining bolts. Remove the oil pump inlet tube retaining bolts, and remove the inlet tube and screen assembly from the oil pump. Leave it in the bottom of the oil pan. Remove the oil pan and gaskets. Remove the inlet tube and screen from the oil pan.

9. In preparation for installation, clean the gasket surfaces of the oil pump, oil pan and cylinder block. Remove the rear main bearing cap-to-oil pan seal and engine front cover-to-oil pan seal. Clean the seal grooves.

10. Position the oil pan front and rear seal on the engine front cover and the rear main bearing cap, respectively. Be sure that the tabs on the seals are over the oil pan gasket.

11. Clean the inlet tube and screen assembly and place it in the oil pan.

12. Position the oil pan under the engine and install the inlet tube and screen assembly on the oil pump with a new gasket. Position the oil pan against the cylinder block and install the retaining bolts.

13. Assemble the rest of the engine in the reverse order of disassembly, staring with Step 7.

302 V8

1. Raise the vehicle on a hoist.

2. Remove the bolts fastening the oil dipstick tube to the exhaust manifold and the oil pan. Position it to one side.

3. Drain the crankcase and remove the oil filter.

4. Disconnect the steering rod end at the idler arm.

5. Remove the nuts and washers attaching the engine front supports to the engine support crossmember.

REAR SEAL

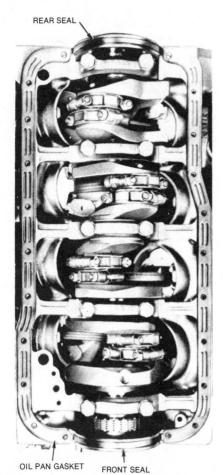

OIL PAN GASKET FRONT SEAL

Positioning of the oil pan gaskets and seals on the 302 V8

6. Position a support jack under the damper and raise the engine as required.

7. Remove the nuts attaching the engine support crossmember to the side rails and frame. Remove the engine support cross-member.

8. Lower the support jack and remove the oil pan attaching bolts and the oil pan with the inlet tube.

9. Clean the oil pan, inlet tube and gasket surfaces.

10. Position a new oil pan gasket and end seals to the cylinder block, then install the oil pump inlet tube.

11. Position the oil pan to the cylinder block and install the attaching bolts and tighten them.

12. Position a support jack under the damper and raise the engine as required.

13. Position the engine support cross-member of the side rails and frame. Install the attaching bolts and nuts and tighten them.

14. Lower the engine and remove the jack.

15. Install the washers and nuts attaching the engine supports and tighten.

16. Connect the steering rod end at the idler arm.

17. Connect the oil dipstick tube to the oil pan and exhaust manifold.

18. Install the oil filter.

19. Lower the vehicle and fill the crankcase. Start the engine and check for leaks.

351W, 400 and 460 V8

1. Remove the engine cover. Remove the air cleaner. Disconnect the battery. Remove or set aside the power steering pump, air conditioning compressor, fan shroud, dipstick tube, fuel line, fan and pulleys, transmission cooler lines, exhaust pipe, shift linkage, and driveshaft. The engine is going to be raised about 4 in. so virtually everything will have to be disconnected from the engine and transmission to prevent damage.

2. Unbolt the engine mounts and carefully raise the engine with a padded transmission jack about 4 in. off the mounts. Block it up for safety.

3. The oil pan may now be unbolted and removed.

Rear Main Oil Seal
REPLACEMENT

NOTE: *There are seal removal and installation tools available to make this job a lot easier.*

240 and 300 Six-Cylinder

1. Remove the starter.

2. Remove the transmission (see Transmission Removal and Installation). On standard transmission, remove pressure plate and cover assembly and the clutch disc.

3. Remove flywheel and engine rear cover plate.

4. Punch two holes with an awl on each side of the crankshaft just above the bearing cap to cylinder block split line.

5. Install two sheet metal screws, then pry on both at once to remove seal. Be careful not to damage or scratch oil seal surface. Clean out seal recess in cap and block.

6. Lightly oil crankshaft and seal, then carefully drive the seal straight in.

7. Install engine rear cover plate and flywheel. Coat the flywheel attaching bolt threads with oil-resistant sealer and tighten to the specified torque.

8. On standard transmission, install the clutch disc and pressure plate assembly (see Clutch Removal and Installation).

9. Install transmission.

All Except 240, 300 Six-Cylinder

1. Drain the crankcase and remove the oil pan, and as necessary, the oil pump.

2. Remove the lower half of the rear main bearing cap and, after removing the oil seal from the cap, drive out the pin in the bottom of the seal groove with a punch.

3. Loosen all the main bearing caps and allow the crankshaft to lower slightly.

NOTE: *Do not allow the crankshaft to drop more than* $1/32$ *in.*

4. With a 6 in. length of $3/16$ in. brazing rod, drive up on either exposed end of the top half of the oil seal. When the opposite end of the seal starts to protrude, grasp it with a pair of pliers and gently pull, while the driven end is being tapped.

5. After removing both halves of the old original rope seal and the retaining pin from the lower half of the bearing cap, carefully clean the seal grooves in the cap and block with solvent.

6. Soak the new rubber replacement seals in clean engine oil.

7. Install the upper half of the seal in the block with the undercut side of the seal toward the front of the engine. Slide the seal around the crankshaft journal until ⅜ in. protrudes beyond the base of the block.

8. Repeat the above procedure for the lower seal, allowing an equal amount of the seal to protrude beyond the opposite end of the bearing cap.

9. Install the rear bearing cap and torque all the main bearings to the proper specification. Apply sealer only to the rear of the seals.

10. Dip the bearing cap side seals in oil, then immediately install them. Do not use any sealer on the side seals. Tap the seals into place and do not clip the protruding ends.

11. Install the oil pump and oil pan. Fill the crankcase with oil, start the engine and check for leaks.

Oil Pump

REMOVAL AND INSTALLATION

1. Remove the oil pan.

2. Remove the oil pump inlet tube and screen assembly.

3. Remove the oil pump attaching bolts

and remove the oil pump gasket and intermediate driveshaft, if used.

4. Before installing the oil pump, prime it by filling the inlet and outlet port with engine oil and rotating the shaft of the pump to distribute it.

5. Position the intermediate driveshaft into the distributor socket.

6. Position the new gasket on the pump body and insert the intermediate driveshaft into the pump body.

7. Install the pump and intermediate driveshaft as an assembly. Do not force the pump if it does not seat readily. The driveshaft may be misaligned with the distributor shaft. To align it, rotate the intermediate driveshaft into a new position.

8. Install the oil pump attaching bolts and torque them to 12–15 ft lbs on the 6 cylinder engines and to 20–25 ft lbs on the V8 engines.

9. Install the oil pan.

ENGINE COOLING

The satisfactory performance of any engine is controlled to a great extent by the proper operation of the cooling system. The engine block is fully waterjacketed to prevent distortion of the cylinder walls. Directed cooling and water holes in the cylinder head causes water to flow past the valve seats, which are one of the hottest parts of any engine, to carry heat away from the valves and seats.

The minimum temperature of the coolant is controlled by the thermostat, mounted in the coolant outlet passage of the engine. When the coolant temperature is below the temperature rating of the thermostat, the thermostat remains closed and the coolant is directed through the radiator by-pass hose to the water pump and back into the engine. When the coolant temperature reaches the temperature rating of the thermostat, the thermostat opens and allows coolant to flow past it and into the top of the radiator. The radiator dissipates the excess engine heat before the coolant is recirculated through the engine.

The cooling system is pressurized and operating pressure is regulated by the rating of the radiator cap which contains a relief valve. The reason for a pressurized cooling system is to allow for higher engine operating temperatures with a higher coolant boiling point.

Radiator

REMOVAL AND INSTALLATION

1. Drain the cooling system.

2. Disconnect the transmission cooling lines from the bottom of the radiator, if so equipped.

3. Remove the retaining bolts at each of the 4 corners of the shroud, if so equipped, and position the shroud over the fan, clear of the radiator.

4. Disconnect the upper and lower hoses from the radiator.

5. Remove the radiator retaining bolts or the upper supports and lift the radiator from the vehicle. On some 240 sixes only, remove the right hood lock bracket and bolts from the radiator grille before removing the radiator.

6. Install the radiator in the reverse order of removal. Fill the cooling system and check for leaks.

Water Pump

REMOVAL AND INSTALLATION

Six-Cylinder

1. Drain the cooling system.

2. Disconnect the lower radiator hose from the water pump.

3. Remove the drive belt, fan and water pump pulley.

4. Disconnect the heater hose at the water pump.

5. Remove the water pump.

6. Before installing the old water pump, clean the gasket mounting surfaces on the pump and on the cylinder block. If a new water pump is being installed, remove the heater hose fitting from the old pump and install it on the new one. Coat the new gaskets with sealer on both sides and install the water pump in the reverse order of removal.

V8 Except 400

1. Remove the air cleaner and intake duct assembly, including the crankcase ventilation hose.

2. Drain the cooling system.

3. Disconnect the radiator upper hose at the engine and the lower hose at the radiator. Remove the radiator attaching bolts and nuts. Remove the radiator.

4. Loosen the alternator pivot bolt and the bolt attaching the alternator adjusting arm to the water pump.

5. Remove the drive belts, fan, spacer and the water pump pulley.

6. Disconnect the heater hose and the by-pass hose at the water pump.

7. Remove the bolts attaching the water pump to the cylinder front cover. Remove the water pump.

8. Remove all gasket material from the mounting surfaces of the cylinder front cover and the water pump.

9. Position a new gasket, coated on both sides with sealer, on the cylinder front cover; then install the water pump.

10. Connect the heater hose and the by-pass hose at the water pump.

11. Tighten the alternator pivot bolt and the bolt attaching the alternator adjusting arm to the water pump.

12. Install the water pump pulley, spacer and the fan drive belts.

13. Install the radiator, connecting the lower hose at the radiator and the upper hose at the engine.

14. Fill and bleed the cooling system. Operate the engine until normal operating temperatures have been reached and check for leaks.

15. Install the air cleaner and the intake duct assembly, including the crankcase ventilation hose.

400 V8

1. Drain the cooling system and remove the fan shroud attaching bolts.

2. Remove the fan assembly attaching screws and remove the shroud and fan.

3. Loosen the power steering pump attaching bolts.

4. If the truck is equipped with air conditioning, loosen the compressor attaching bolts, and remove the air conditioning compressor and power steering pump drive belts.

5. Loosen the alternator pivot bolt. Remove the two attaching bolts and spacer. Remove the drive belt, then rotate the bracket out of the way.

6. Remove the three air conditioning compressor attaching bolts and secure the compressor out of the way.

7. Remove the power steering pump attaching bolts and position the pump to one side.

8. Remove the air conditioner bracket attaching bolts and remove the bracket.

9. Disconnect the lower radiator hose and heater hose from the water pump.

10. Loosen the by-pass hose clamp at the water pump.

11. Remove the remaining water pump attaching bolts and remove the pump from the front cover. Remove the separator plate from the pump. Discard the gaskets.

12. Remove all gasket material from all of the mating surfaces.

13. Install the water pump, in the reverse order of removal, using a new gasket and waterproof sealer. When the water pump is first positioned to the front cover of the engine, install only those bolts not used to secure the air conditioner and alternator brackets.

Thermostat

REMOVAL AND INSTALLATION

1. Drain the cooling system to a level below the coolant outlet housing. Use the petcock valve at the bottom of the radiator to drain the system; it is not necessary to remove any of the hoses.

2. Remove the coolant outlet housing retaining bolts and slide the housing with the hose attached to one side.

3. Turn the thermostat counterclockwise to unlock it from the outlet.

4. Remove the gasket from the engine block and clean both mating surfaces.

5. To install the thermostat, coat a new gasket with water-resistant sealer and position it on the outlet of the engine. The gasket must be in place before the thermostat is installed.

6. Install the thermostat with the bridge (opposite end from the spring) inside the elbow connection and turn it clockwise to lock it in position with the bridge against the flat cast into the elbow connection.

7. Position the elbow connection onto the mounting surface of the outlet so that the thermostat flange is resting on the gasket and install the retaining bolts.

8. Fill the radiator and operate the engine until it reaches operating temperature. Check the coolant level and adjust as necessary.

NOTE: *It is a good practice to check the operation of a new thermostat before it is installed in an engine. Place the thermostat in a pan of boiling water. If it does not open more than ¼ in., do not install it in the engine.*

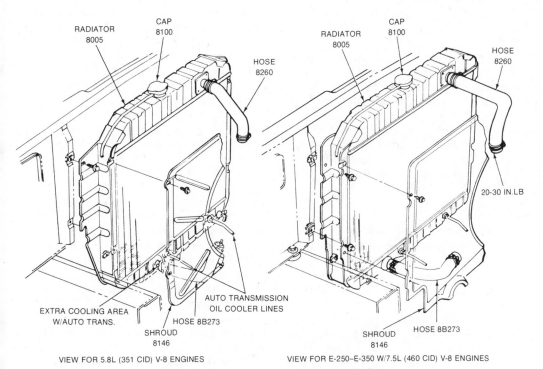

VIEW FOR 5.8L (351 CID) V-8 ENGINES

VIEW FOR E-250–E-350 W/7.5L (460 CID) V-8 ENGINES

Typical 8 cylinder engine radiator installation

ENGINE REBUILDING

Most procedures involved in rebuilding an engine are fairly standard, regardless of the type of engine involved. This section is a guide to accepted rebuilding procedures. Examples of standard rebuilding practices are illustrated and should be used along with specific details concerning your particular engine, found earlier in this chapter.

The procedures given here are those used by any competent rebuilder. Obviously some of the procedures cannot be performed by the do-it-yourself mechanic, but are provided so that you will be familiar with the services that should be offered by rebuilding or machine shops. As an example, in most instances, it is more profitable for the home mechanic to remove the cylinder heads, buy the necessary parts (new valves, seals, keepers, keys, etc.) and deliver these to a machine shop for the necessary work. In this way you will save the money to remove and install the cylinder head and the mark-up on parts.

On the other hand, most of the work involved in rebuilding the lower end is well within the scope of the do-it-yourself mechanic. Only work such as hot-tanking, actually boring the block or Magnafluxing (invisible crack detection) need be sent to a machine shop.

Tools

The tools required for basic engine rebuilding should, with a few exceptions, be those included in a mechanic's tool kit. An accurate torque wrench, and a dial indicator (reading in thousandths) mounted on a universal base should be available. Special tools, where required, are available from the major tool suppliers. The services of a competent automotive machine shop must also be readily available.

Precautions

Aluminum has become increasingly popular for use in engines, due to its low weight and excellent heat transfer characteristics. The following precautions must be observed when handling aluminum (or any other) engine parts:
—Never hot-tank aluminum parts.
—Remove all aluminum parts (identification tags, etc.) from engine parts before hot-tanking (otherwise they will be removed during the process).
—Always coat threads lightly with engine oil or anti-seize compounds before installation, to prevent seizure.
—Never over-torque bolts or spark plugs in aluminum threads. Should stripping occur, threads can be restored using any of a number of thread repair kits available (see next section).

Inspection Techniques

Magnaflux and Zyglo are inspection techniques used to locate material flaws, such as stress cracks. Magnaflux is a magnetic process, applicable only to ferrous materials. The Zyglo process coats the matrial with a fluorescent dye penetrant, and any material may be tested using Zyglo. Specific checks of suspected surface cracks may be made at lower cost and more readily using spot check dye. The dye is sprayed onto the suspected area, wiped off, and the area is then sprayed with a developer. Cracks then will show up brightly.

Overhaul

The section is divided into two parts. The first, Cylinder Head Reconditioning, assumes that the cylinder head is removed from the engine, all manifolds are removed, and the cylinder head is on a workbench. The camshaft should be removed from overhead cam cylinder heads. The second section, Cylinder Block Reconditioning, covers the block, pistons, connecting rods and crankshaft. It is assumed that the engine is mounted on a work stand, and the cylinder head and all accessories are removed.

Procedures are identified as follows:

Unmarked—Basic procedures that must be performed in order to successfully complete the rebuilding process.

Starred (*)—Procedures that should be performed to ensure maximum performance and engine life.

Double starred (**)—Procedures that may be performed to increase engine performance and reliability.

When assembling the engine, any parts that will be in frictional contact must be prelubricated, to provide protection on initial start-up. Any product specifically formulated for this purpose may be used. NOTE: *Do not use engine oil. Where semi-permanent* (locked but removable) installation of bolts or nuts is desired, threads should be cleaned and located with Loctite ® or a similar product (non-hardening).

Repairing Damaged Threads

Several methods of repairing damaged threads are available. Heli-Coil® (shown here), Keenserts® and Microdot® are among the most widely used. All involve basically the same principle—drilling out stripped threads, tapping the hole and installing a pre-wound insert—making welding, plugging and oversize fasteners unnecessary.

Two types of thread repair inserts are usually supplied—a standard type for most Inch Coarse, Inch Fine, Metric Coarse and Metric Fine thread sizes and a spark plug type to fit most spark plug port sizes. Consult the individual manufacturer's catalog to determine exact applications. Typical thread repair kits will contain a selection of pre-wound threaded inserts, a tap (corresponding to the outside diameter threads of the insert) and an installation tool. Spark plug inserts usually differ because they require a tap equipped with pilot threads and a combined reamer/tap section. Most manufacturers also supply blister-packed thread repair inserts separately in addition to a master kit containing a variety of taps and inserts plus installation tools.

Before effecting a repair to a threaded hole, remove any snapped, broken or damaged bolts or studs. Penetrating oil can be used to free frozen threads; the offending item can be removed with locking pliers or with a screw or stud extractor. After the hole is clear, the thread can be repaired, as follows:

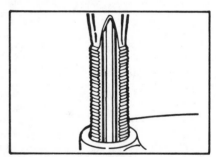
Drill out the damaged threads with specified drill. Drill completely through the hole or to the bottom of a blind hole

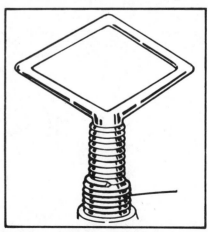
With the tap supplied, tap the hole to receive the thread insert. Keep the tap well oiled and back it out frequently to avoid clogging the threads

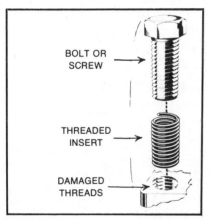
Damaged bolt holes can be repaired with thread repair inserts

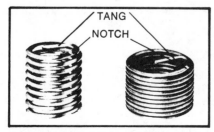
Standard thread repair insert (left) and spark plug thread insert (right)

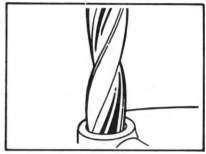
Screw the threaded insert onto the installation tool until the tang engages the slot. Screw the insert into the tapped hole until it is ¼–½ turn below the top surface. After installation break off the tang with a hammer and punch

Standard Torque Specifications and Fastener Markings

The Newton-metre has been designated the world standard for measuring torque and will gradually replace the foot-pound and kilogram-meter. In the absence of specific torques, the following chart can be used as a guide to the maximum safe torque of a particular size/grade of fastener.

- There is no torque difference for fine or coarse threads.
- Torque values are based on clean, dry threads. Reduce the value by 10% if threads are oiled prior to assembly.
- The torque required for aluminum components or fasteners is considerably less.

U. S. BOLTS

SAE Grade Number	1 or 2			5			6 or 7		

Bolt Markings

Manufacturer's marks may vary—number of lines always 2 less than the grade number.

Usage	Frequent			Frequent			Infrequent		
Bolt Size (inches)—(Thread)	Maximum Torque			Maximum Torque			Maximum Torque		
	Ft-Lb	kgm	Nm	Ft-Lb	kgm	Nm	Ft-Lb	kgm	Nm
¼—20	5	0.7	6.8	8	1.1	10.8	10	1.4	13.5
—28	6	0.8	8.1	10	1.4	13.6			
5⁄16—18	11	1.5	14.9	17	2.3	23.0	19	2.6	25.8
—24	13	1.8	17.6	19	2.6	25.7			
⅜—16	18	2.5	24.4	31	4.3	42.0	34	4.7	46.0
—24	20	2.75	27.1	35	4.8	47.5			
7⁄16—14	28	3.8	37.0	49	6.8	66.4	55	7.6	74.5
—20	30	4.2	40.7	55	7.6	74.5			
½—13	39	5.4	52.8	75	10.4	101.7	85	11.75	115.2
—20	41	5.7	55.6	85	11.7	115.2			
9⁄16—12	51	7.0	69.2	110	15.2	149.1	120	16.6	162.7
—18	55	7.6	74.5	120	16.6	162.7			
⅝—11	83	11.5	112.5	150	20.7	203.3	167	23.0	226.5
—18	95	13.1	128.8	170	23.5	230.5			
¾—10	105	14.5	142.3	270	37.3	366.0	280	38.7	379.6
—16	115	15.9	155.9	295	40.8	400.0			
⅞— 9	160	22.1	216.9	395	54.6	535.5	440	60.9	596.5
—14	175	24.2	237.2	435	60.1	589.7			
1— 8	236	32.5	318.6	590	81.6	799.9	660	91.3	894.8
—14	250	34.6	338.9	660	91.3	849.8			

METRIC BOLTS

NOTE: *Metric bolts are marked with a number indicating the relative strength of the bolt. These numbers have nothing to do with size.*

Description	Torque ft-lbs (Nm)			
Thread size x pitch (mm)	Head mark—4		Head mark—7	
6 x 1.0	2.2–2.9	(3.0–3.9)	3.6–5.8	(4.9–7.8)
8 x 1.25	5.8–8.7	(7.9–12)	9.4–14	(13–19)
10 x 1.25	12–17	(16–23)	20–29	(27–39)
12 x 1.25	21–32	(29–43)	35–53	(47–72)
14 x 1.5	35–52	(48–70)	57–85	(77–110)
16 x 1.5	51–77	(67–100)	90–120	(130–160)
18 x 1.5	74–110	(100–150)	130–170	(180–230)
20 x 1.5	110–140	(150–190)	190–240	(160–320)
22 x 1.5	150–190	(200–260)	250–320	(340–430)
24 x 1.5	190–240	(260–320)	310–410	(420–550)

NOTE: *This engine rebuilding section is a guide to accepted rebuilding procedures. Typical examples of standard rebuilding procedures are illustrated. Use these procedures along with the detailed instructions earlier in this chapter, concerning your particular engine.*

Cylinder Head Reconditioning

Procedure	Method
Remove the cylinder head:	See the engine service procedures earlier in this chapter for details concerning specific engines.
Identify the valves:	Invert the cylinder head, and number the valve faces front to rear, using a permanent felt-tip marker.
Remove the rocker arms (OHV engines only):	Remove the rocker arms with shaft(s) or balls and nuts. Wire the sets of rockers, balls and nuts together, and identify according to the corresponding valve.
Remove the camshaft (OHC engines only):	See the engine service procedures earlier in this chapter for details concerning specific engines.
Remove the valves and springs:	Using an appropriate valve spring compressor (depending on the configuration of the cylinder head), compress the valve springs. Lift out the keepers with needlenose pliers, release the compressor, and remove the valve, spring, and spring retainer. See the engine service procedures earlier in this chapter for details concerning specific engines.

Cylinder Head Reconditioning

Procedure	Method
Check the valve stem-to-guide clearance: 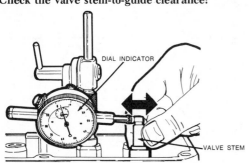 **Check the valve stem-to-guide clearance**	Clean the valve stem with lacquer thinner or a similar solvent to remove all gum and varnish. Clean the valve guides using solvent and an expanding wire-type valve guide cleaner. Mount a dial indicator so that the stem is at 90° to the valve stem, as close to the valve guide as possible. Move the valve off its seat, and measure the valve guide-to-stem clearance by rocking the stem back and forth to actuate the dial indicator. Measure the valve stems using a micrometer, and compare to specifications, to determine whether stem or guide wear is responsible for excessive clearance. *NOTE: Consult the Specifications tables earlier in this chapter.*
De-carbon the cylinder head and valves: 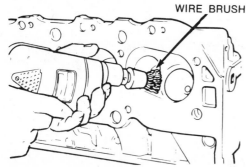 **Remove the carbon from the cylinder head with a wire brush and electric drill**	Chip carbon away from the valve heads, combustion chambers, and ports, using a chisel made of hardwood. Remove the remaining deposits with a stiff wire brush. *NOTE: Be sure that the deposits are actually removed, rather than burnished.*
Hot-tank the cylinder head (cast iron heads only): CAUTION: *Do not hot-tank aluminum parts.*	Have the cylinder head hot-tanked to remove grease, corrosion, and scale from the water passages. *NOTE: In the case of overhead cam cylinder heads, consult the operator to determine whether the camshaft bearings will be damaged by the caustic solution.*
Degrease the remaining cylinder head parts:	Clean the remaining cylinder head parts in an engine cleaning solvent. Do not remove the protective coating from the springs.
Check the cylinder head for warpage: 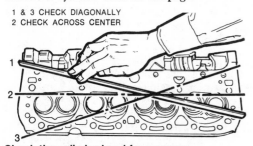 **Check the cylinder head for warpage**	Place a straight-edge across the gasket surface of the cylinder head. Using feeler gauges, determine the clearance at the center of the straight-edge. If warpage exceeds .003″ in a 6″ span, or .006″ over the total length, the cylinder head must be resurfaced. *NOTE: If warpage exceeds the manufacturer's maximum tolerance for material removal, the cylinder head must be replaced.* When milling the cylinder heads of V-type engines, the intake manifold mounting position is altered, and must be corrected by milling the manifold flange a proportionate amount.

Cylinder Head Reconditioning

Procedure	Method

*Knurl the valve guides:

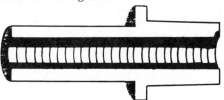

Cut-away view of a knurled valve guide

*Valve guides which are not excessively worn or distorted may, in some cases, be knurled rather than replaced. Knurling is a process in which metal is displaced and raised, thereby reducing clearance. Knurling also provides excellent oil control. The possibility of knurling rather than replacing valve guides should be discussed with a machinist.

Replace the valve guides:
NOTE: *Valve guides should only be replaced if damaged or if an oversize valve stem is not available.*

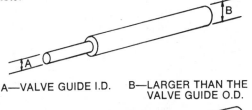

A—VALVE GUIDE I.D.   B—LARGER THAN THE VALVE GUIDE O.D.

WASHERS

A—VALVE GUIDE I.D.   B—LARGER THAN THE VALVE GUIDE O.D.

Valve guide installation tool using washers for installation

See the engine service procedures earlier in this chapter for details concerning specific engines. Depending on the type of cylinder head, valve guides may be pressed, hammered, or shrunk in. In cases where the guides are shrunk into the head, replacement should be left to an equipped machine shop. In other cases, the guides are replaced using a stepped drift (see illustration). Determine the height above the boss that the guide must extend, and obtain a stack of washers, their I.D. similar to the guide's O.D., of that height. Place the stack of washers on the guide, and insert the guide into the boss.
NOTE: *Valve guides are often tapered or beveled for installation.* Using the stepped installation tool (see illustration), press or tap the guides into position. Ream the guides according to the size of the valve stem.

Replace valve seat inserts:

Replacement of valve seat inserts which are worn beyond resurfacing or broken, if feasible, must be done by a machine shop.

Resurface (grind) the valve face:

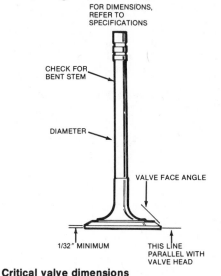

FOR DIMENSIONS, REFER TO SPECIFICATIONS

CHECK FOR BENT STEM

DIAMETER

VALVE FACE ANGLE

1/32" MINIMUM   THIS LINE PARALLEL WITH VALVE HEAD

Critical valve dimensions

Using a valve grinder, resurface the valves according to specifications given earlier in this chapter.
CAUTION: *Valve face angle is not always identical to valve seat angle.* A minimum margin of

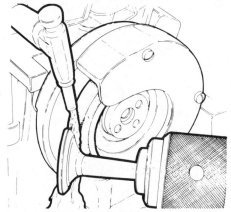

Valve grinding by machine

Cylinder Head Reconditioning

Procedure	Method
	$^1/_{32}''$ should remain after grinding the valve. The valve stem top should also be squared and resurfaced, by placing the stem in the V-block of the grinder, and turning it while pressing lightly against the grinding wheel. NOTE: *Do not grind sodium filled exhaust valves on a machine. These should be hand lapped.*
Resurface the valve seats using reamers or grinder: 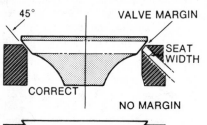  **Valve seat width and centering**  **Reaming the valve seat with a hand reamer**	Select a reamer of the correct seat angle, slightly larger than the diameter of the valve seat, and assemble it with a pilot of the correct size. Install the pilot into the valve guide, and using steady pressure, turn the reamer clockwise. CAUTION: *Do not turn the reamer counterclockwise.* Remove only as much material as necessary to clean the seat. Check the concentricity of the seat (following). If the dye method is not used, coat the valve face with Prussian blue dye, install and rotate it on the valve seat. Using the dye marked area as a centering guide, center and narrow the valve seat to specifications with correction cutters. NOTE: *When no specifications are available, minimum seat width for exhaust valves should be $^5/_{64}''$, intake valves $^1/_{16}''$.* After making correction cuts, check the position of the valve seat on the valve face using Prussian blue dye.
	To resurface the seat with a power grinder, select a pilot of the correct size and coarse stone of the proper angle. Lubricate the pilot and move the stone on and off the valve seat at 2 cycles per second, until all flaws are gone. Finish the seat with a fine stone. If necessary the seat can be corrected or narrowed using correction stones.
Check the valve seat concentricity:  **Check the valve seat concentricity with a dial gauge**	Coat the valve face with Prussian blue dye, install the valve, and rotate it on the valve seat. If the entire seat becomes coated, and the valve is known to be concentric, the seat is concentric.
	*Install the dial gauge pilot into the guide, and rest of the arm on the valve seat. Zero the gauge, and rotate the arm around the seat. Run-out should not exceed .002″.

Cylinder Head Reconditioning

Procedure	Method

*Lap the valves:
NOTE: *Valve lapping is done to ensure efficient sealing of resurfaced valves and seats.*

Lapping the valves by hand

Home-made valve lapping tool

HAND DRILL

ROD

SUCTION CUP

*Invert the cylinder head, lightly lubricate the valve stems, and install the valves in the head as numbered. Coat valve seats with fine grinding compound, and attach the lapping tool suction cup to a valve head.
NOTE: *Moisten the suction cup.* Rotate the tool between the palms, changing position and lifting the tool often to prevent grooving. Lap the valve until a smooth, polished seat is evident. Remove the valve and tool, and rinse away all traces of grinding compound.

**Fasten a suction cup to a piece of drill rod, and mount the rod in a hand drill. Proceed as above, using the hand drill as a lapping tool.
CAUTION: *Due to the higher speeds involved when using the hand drill, care must be exercised to avoid grooving the seat.* Lift the tool and change direction of rotation often.

Check the valve springs:

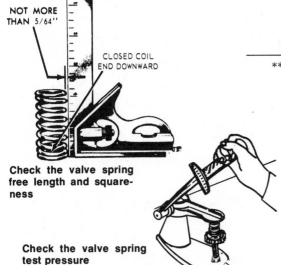

NOT MORE THAN 5/64"

CLOSED COIL END DOWNWARD

Check the valve spring free length and squareness

Check the valve spring test pressure

Place the spring on a flat surface next to a square. Measure the height of the spring, and rotate it against the edge of the square to measure distortion. If spring height varies (by comparison) by more than 1/16" or if distortion exceeds 1/16", replace the spring.

**In addition to evaluating the spring as above, test the spring pressure at the installed and compressed (installed height minus valve lift) height using a valve spring tester. Springs used on small displacement engines (up to 3 liters) should be ∓ 1 lb of all other springs in either position. A tolerance of ∓ 5 lbs is permissible on larger engines.

Cylinder Head Reconditioning

Procedure	Method
*Install valve stem seals: 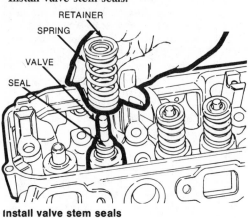 **Install valve stem seals**	* Due to the pressure differential that exists at the ends of the intake valve guides (atmospheric pressure above, manifold vacuum below), oil is drawn through the valve guides into the intake port. This has been alleviated somewhat since the addition of positive crankcase ventilation, which lowers the pressure above the guides. Several types of valve stem seals are available to rocker arms and balls, and install them on the the stem and guide boss, while others require that the boss be machined. Recently, Teflon guide seals have become popular. Consult a parts supplier or machinist concerning availability and suggested usages. **NOTE:** *When installing seals, ensure that a small amount of oil is able to pass the seal to lubricate the valve guides; otherwise, excessive wear may result.*
Install the valves:	See the engine service procedures earlier in this chapter for details concerning specific engines. Lubricate the valve stems, and install the valves in the cylinder head as numbered. Lubricate and position the seals (if used) and the valve springs. Install the spring retainers, compress the springs, and insert the keys using needle-nose pliers or a tool designed for this purpose. **NOTE:** *Retain the keys with wheel bearing grease during installation.*
Check valve spring installed height: 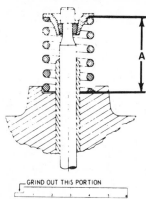 **Measure the valve spring installed height (A) with a modified steel rule** 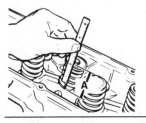 **Valve spring installed height (A)**	Measure the distance between the spring pad and the lower edge of the spring retainer, and compare to specifications. If the installed height is incorrect, add shim washers between the spring pad and the spring. **CAUTION:** *Use only washers designed for this purpose.*
Install the camshaft (OHC engines only) and check end-play:	See the engine service procedures earlier in this chapter for details concerning specific engines.

Cylinder Head Reconditioning

Procedure	Method
Inspect the rocker arms, balls, studs, and nuts (OHV engines only): 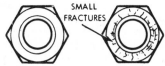 **Stress cracks in the rocker nuts**	Visually inspect the rocker arms, balls, studs, and nuts for cracks, galling, burning, scoring, or wear. If all parts are intact, liberally lubricate the rocker arms and balls, and install them on the cylinder head. If wear is noted on a rocker arm at the point of valve contact, grind it smooth and square, removing as little material as possible. Replace the rocker arm if excessively worn. If a rocker stud shows signs of wear, it must be replaced (see below). If a rocker nut shows stress cracks, replace it. If an exhaust ball is galled or burned, substitute the intake ball from the same cylinder (if it is intact), and install a new intake ball. NOTE: *Avoid using new rocker balls on exhaust valves.*
Replacing rocker studs (OHV engines only): 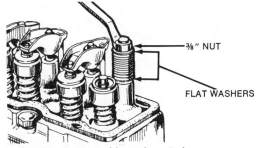 **Extracting a pressed-in rocker stud** 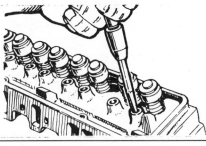 **Ream the stud bore for oversize rocker studs**	In order to remove a threaded stud, lock two nuts on the stud, and unscrew the stud using the lower nut. Coat the lower threads of the new stud with Loctite, and install. Two alternative methods are available for replacing pressed in studs. Remove the damaged stud using a stack of washers and a nut (see illustration). In the first, the boss is reamed .005–.006″ oversize, and an oversize stud pressed in. Control the stud extension over the boss using washers, in the same manner as valve guides. Before installing the stud, coat it with white lead and grease. To retain the stud more positively drill a hole through the stud and boss, and install a roll pin. In the second method, the boss is tapped, and a threaded stud installed.
Inspect the rocker shaft(s) and rocker arms (OHV engines only) 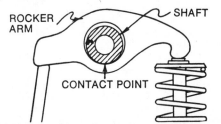 **Check the rocker arm-to-rocker shaft contact area**	Remove rocker arms, springs and washers from rocker shaft. NOTE: *Lay out parts in the order as they are removed.* Inspect rocker arms for pitting or wear on the valve contact point, or excessive bushing wear. Bushings need only be replaced if wear is excessive, because the rocker arm normally contacts the shaft at one point only. Grind the valve contact point of rocker arm smooth if necessary, removing as little material as possible. If excessive material must be removed to smooth and square the arm, it should be replaced. Clean out all oil holes and passages in rocker shaft. If shaft is grooved or worn, replace it. Lubricate and assemble the rocker shaft.

Cylinder Head Reconditioning

Procedure	Method
Inspect the pushrods (OHV engines only):	Remove the pushrods, and, if hollow, clean out the oil passages using fine wire. Roll each pushrod over a piece of clean glass. If a distinct clicking sound is heard as the pushrod rolls, the rod is bent, and must be replaced.
	*The length of all pushrods must be equal. Measure the length of the pushrods, compare to specifications, and replace as necessary.
Inspect the valve lifters (OHV engines only): 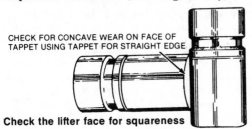 CHECK FOR CONCAVE WEAR ON FACE OF TAPPET USING TAPPET FOR STRAIGHT EDGE **Check the lifter face for squareness**	Remove lifters from their bores, and remove gum and varnish, using solvent. Clean walls of lifter bores. Check lifters for concave wear as illustrated. If face is worn concave, replace lifter, and carefully inspect the camshaft. Lightly lubricate lifter and insert it into its bore. If play is excessive, an oversize lifter must be installed (where possible). Consult a machinist concerning feasibility. If play is satisfactory, remove, lubricate, and reinstall the lifter.
*Testing hydraulic lifter leak down (OHV engines only):	Submerge lifter in a container of kerosene. Chuck a used pushrod or its equivalent into a drill press. Position container of kerosene so pushrod acts on the lifter plunger. Pump lifter with the drill press, until resistance increases. Pump several more times to bleed any air out of lifter. Apply very firm, constant pressure to the lifter, and observe rate at which fluid bleeds out of lifter. If the fluid bleeds very quickly (less than 15 seconds), lifter is defective. If the time exceeds 60 seconds, lifter is sticking. In either case, recondition or replace lifter. If lifter is operating properly (leak down time 15–60 seconds), lubricate and install it.

Cylinder Block Reconditioning

Procedure	Method
Checking the main bearing clearance: 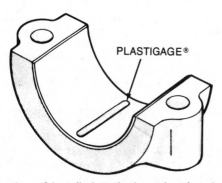 PLASTIGAGE® **Plastigage® installed on the lower bearing shell**	Invert engine, and remove cap from the bearing to be checked. Using a clean, dry rag, thoroughly clean all oil from crankshaft journal and bearing insert. NOTE: *Plastigage® is soluble in oil; therefore, oil on the journal or bearing could result in erroneous readings.* Place a piece of Plastigage along the full length of journal, reinstall cap, and torque to specifications. NOTE: *Specifications are given in the engine specifications earlier in this chapter.* Remove bearing cap, and determine bearing clearance by comparing width of Plastigage to the scale on Plastigage envelope. Journal taper is determined by comparing width of the Plastigage strip near its ends. Rotate crankshaft 90° and retest, to determine journal eccentricity. NOTE: *Do not rotate crankshaft with Plastigage*

Cylinder Block Reconditioning

Procedure	Method

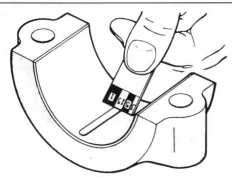

Measure Plastigage® to determine main bearing clearance

installed. If bearing insert and journal appear intact, and are within tolerances, no further main bearing service is required. If bearing or journal appear defective, cause of failure should be determined before replacement.

* Remove crankshaft from block (see below). Measure the main bearing journals at each end tiwce (90° apart) using a micrometer, to determine diameter, journal taper and eccentricity. If journals are within tolerances, reinstall bearing caps at their specified torque. Using a telescope gauge and micrometer, measure bearing I.D. parallel to piston axis and at 30° on each side of piston axis. Subtract journal O.D. from bearing I.D. to determine oil clearance. If crankshaft journals appear defective, or do not meet tolerances, there is no need to measure bearings; for the crankshaft will require grinding and/or undersize bearings will be required. If bearing appears defective, cause for failure should be determined prior to replacement.

Check the connecting rod bearing clearance:

Connecting rod bearing clearance is checked in the same manner as main bearing clearance, using Plastigage. Before removing the crankshaft, connecting rod side clearance also should be measured and recorded.

* Checking connecting rod bearing clearance, using a micrometer, is identical to checking main bearing clearance. If no other service is required, the piston and rod assemblies need not be removed.

Remove the crankshaft:

Using a punch, mark the corresponding main bearing caps and saddles according to position (i.e., one punch on the front main cap and saddle, two on the second, three on the third, etc.). Using number stamps, identify the corresponding connecting rods and caps, according to cylinder (if no numbers are present). Remove the main and connecting rod caps, and place sleeves of plastic tubing or vacuum hose over the connecting rod bolts, to protect the journals as the crankshaft is removed. Lift the crankshaft out of the block.

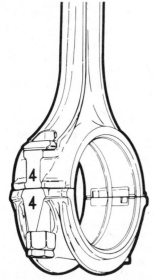

Match the connecting rod to the cylinder with a number stamp

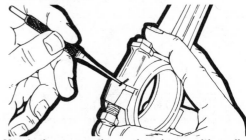

Match the connecting rod and cap with scribe marks

Cylinder Block Reconditioning

Procedure	Method
Remove the ridge from the top of the cylinder: 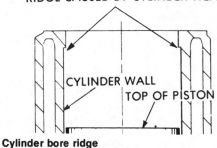 Cylinder bore ridge	In order to facilitate removal of the piston and connecting rod, the ridge at the top of the cylinder (unworn area; see illustration) must be removed. Place the piston at the bottom of the bore, and cover it with a rag. Cut the ridge away using a ridge reamer, exercising extreme care to avoid cutting too deeply. Remove the rag, and remove cuttings that remain on the piston. **CAUTION:** *If the ridge is not removed, and new rings are installed, damage to rings will result.*
Remove the piston and connecting rod: 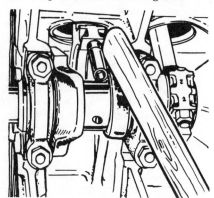 **Push the piston out with a hammer handle**	Invert the engine, and push the pistons and connecting rods out of the cylinders. If necessary, tap the connecting rod boss with a wooden hammer handle, to force the piston out. **CAUTION:** *Do not attempt to force the piston past the cylinder ridge* (see above).
Service the crankshaft:	Ensure that all oil holes and passages in the crankshaft are open and free of sludge. If necessary, have the crankshaft ground to the largest possible undersize.
	**Have the crankshaft Magnafluxed, to locate stress cracks. Consult a machinist concerning additional service procedures, such as surface hardening (e.g., nitriding, Tuftriding) to improve wear characteristics, cross drilling and chamfering the oil holes to improve lubrication, and balancing.
Removing freeze plugs:	Drill a small hole in the middle of the freeze plugs. Thread a large sheet metal screw into the hole and remove the plug with a slide hammer.
Remove the oil gallery plugs:	Threaded plugs should be removed using an appropriate (usually square) wrench. To remove soft, pressed in plugs, drill a hole in the plug, and thread in a sheet metal screw. Pull the plug out by the screw using pliers.
Hot-tank the block: NOTE: *Do not hot-tank aluminum parts.*	Have the block hot-tanked to remove grease, corrosion, and scale from the water jackets. **NOTE:** *Consult the operator to determine whether the camshaft bearings will be damaged during the hot-tank process.*

Illustration labels (top figure): RIDGE CAUSED BY CYLINDER WEAR / CYLINDER WALL / TOP OF PISTON

Cylinder Block Reconditioning

Procedure	Method
Check the block for cracks:	Visually inspect the block for cracks or chips. The most common locations are as follows: 　Adjacent to freeze plugs. 　Between the cylinders and water jackets. 　Adjacent to the main bearing saddles. 　At the extreme bottom of the cylinders. Check only suspected cracks using spot check dye (see introduction). If a crack is located, consult a machinist concerning possible repairs.
	** Magnaflux the block to locate hidden cracks. If cracks are located, consult a machinist about feasibility of repair. ﹒
Install the oil gallery plugs and freeze plugs:	Coat freeze plugs with sealer and tap into position using a piece of pipe, slightly smaller than the plug, as a driver. To ensure retention, stake the edges of the plugs. Coat threaded oil gallery plugs with sealer and install. Drive replacement soft plugs into block using a large drift as driver.
	* Rather than reinstalling lead plugs, drill and tap the holes, and install threaded plugs.
Check the bore diameter and surface: 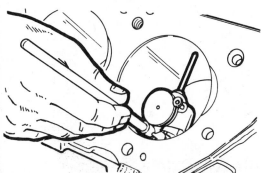 **Measure the cylinder bore with a dial gauge**	Visually inspect the cylinder bores for roughness, scoring, or scuffing. If evident, the cylinder bore must be bored or honed oversize to eliminate imperfections, and the smallest possible oversize piston used. The new pistons should be given to the machinist with the block, so that the cylinders can be bored or honed exactly to the piston size (plus clearance). If no flaws are evident, measure the bore diameter using a telescope gauge and micrometer, or dial gauge, parallel and perpendicular to the engine centerline, at the top (below the ridge) and bottom of the bore. Subtract the bottom measurements from the top to determine taper, and the parallel to the centerline measurements from the perpendicular measurements to determine eccentricity. If the measurements are not within specifications, the cylinder must be bored or honed, and an oversize piston installed. If the measurements are within specifications the cylinder may be used as is, with only finish honing (see below).

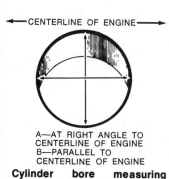

←—CENTERLINE OF ENGINE—→

A—AT RIGHT ANGLE TO CENTERLINE OF ENGINE
B—PARALLEL TO CENTERLINE OF ENGINE

Cylinder bore measuring points

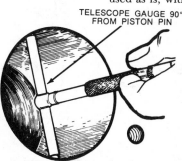

TELESCOPE GAUGE 90° FROM PISTON PIN

Measure the cylinder bore with a telescope gauge

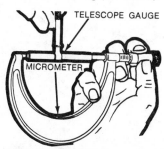

TELESCOPE GAUGE

MICROMETER

Measure the telescope gauge with a micrometer to determine the cylinder bore

Cylinder Block Reconditioning

Procedure	Method
	NOTE: *Prior to submitting the block for boring, perform the following operation(s).*
Check the cylinder block bearing alignment: 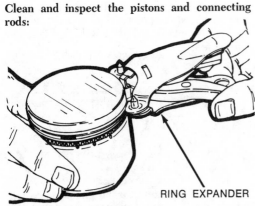 **Check the main bearing saddle alignment**	Remove the upper bearing inserts. Place a straightedge in the bearing saddles along the centerline of the crankshaft. If clearance exists between the straightedge and the center saddle, the block must be alignbored.
*Check the deck height:	The deck height is the distance from the crankshaft centerline to the block deck. To measure, invert the engine, and install the crankshaft, retaining it with the center main cap. Measure the distance from the crankshaft journal to the block deck, parallel to the cylinder centerline. Measure the diameter of the end (front and rear) main journals, parallel to the centerline of the cylinders, divide the diameter in half, and subtract it from the previous measurement. The results of the front and rear measurements should be identical. If the difference exceeds .005″, the deck height should be corrected. NOTE: *Block deck height and warpage should be corrected at the same time.*
Check the block deck for warpage:	Using a straightedge and feeler gauges, check the block deck for warpage in the same manner that the cylinder head is checked (see Cylinder Head Reconditioning). If warpage exceeds specifications, have the deck resurfaced. NOTE: *In certain cases a specification for total material removal (Cylinder head and block deck) is provided. This specification must not be exceeded.*
Clean and inspect the pistons and connecting rods: RING EXPANDER **Remove the piston rings**	Using a ring expander, remove the rings from the piston. Remove the retaining rings (if so equipped) and remove piston pin. NOTE: *If the piston pin must be pressed out, determine the proper method and use the proper tools; otherwise the piston will distort.* Clean the ring grooves using an appropriate tool, exercising care to avoid cutting too deeply. Thoroughly clean all carbon and varnish from the piston with solvent. CAUTION: *Do not use a wire brush or caustic solvent on pistons.* Inspect the pistons for scuffing, scoring, cracks, pitting, or excessive ring groove wear. If wear is evident, the piston must be replaced. Check the connecting rod length by measuring the rod from the inside of the large end to the

Cylinder Block Reconditioning

Procedure	Method

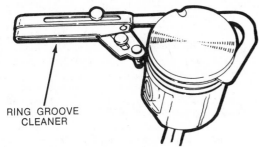

RING GROOVE
CLEANER

Clean the piston ring grooves

inside of the small end using calipers (see illustration). All connecting rods should be equal length. Replace any rod that differs from the others in the engine.

* Have the connecting rod alignment checked in an alignment fixture by a machinist. Replace any twisted or bent rods.

* Magnaflux the connecting rods to locate stress cracks. If cracks are found, replace the connecting rod.

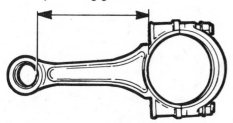

Check the connecting rod length (arrow)

Fit the pistons to the cylinders:

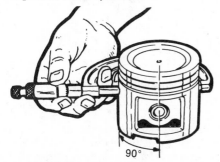

90°

Measure the piston prior to fitting

Using a telescope gauge and micrometer, or a dial gauge, measure the cylinder bore diameter perpendicular to the piston pin, 2½" below the deck. Measure the piston perpendicular to its pin on the skirt. The difference between the two measurements is the piston clearance. If the clearance is within specifications or slightly below (after boring or honing), finish honing is all that is required. If the clearance is excessive, try to obtain a slightly larger piston to bring clearance within specifications. Where this is not possible, obtain the first oversize piston, and hone (or if necessary, bore) the cylinder to size.

Assemble the pistons and connecting rods:

Install the piston pin lock-rings (if used)

Inspect piston pin, connecting rod small end bushing, and piston bore for galling, scoring, or excessive wear. If evident, replace defective part(s). Measure the I.D. of the piston boss and connecting rod small end, and the O.D. of the piston pin. If within specifications, assemble piston pin and rod.
CAUTION: *If piston pin must be pressed in, determine the proper method and use the proper tools; otherwise the piston will distort.*
Install the lock rings; ensure that they seat properly. If the parts are not within specifications, determine the service method for the type of engine. In some cases, piston and pin are serviced as an assembly when either is defective. Others specify reaming the piston and connecting rods for an oversize pin. If the connecting rod bushing is worn, it may in many cases be replaced. Reaming the piston and replacing the rod bushing are machine shop operations.

Cylinder Block Reconditioning

Procedure	Method
Clean and inspect the camshaft: 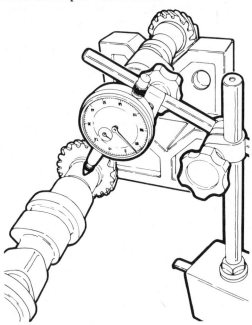 **Check the camshaft for straightness**	Degrease the camshaft, using solvent, and clean out all oil holes. Visually inspect cam lobes and bearing journals for excessive wear. If a lobe is questionable, check all lobes as indicated below. If a journal or lobe is worn, the camshaft must be reground or replaced. NOTE: *If a journal is worn, there is a good chance that the bushings are worn.* If lobes and journals appear intact, place the front and rear journals in V-blocks, and rest a dial indicator on the center journal. Rotate the camshaft to check straightness. If deviation exceeds .001″, replace the camshaft. *Check the camshaft lobes with a micrometer, by measuring the lobes from the nose to base and again at 90° (see illustration). The lift is determined by subtracting the second measurement from the first. If all exhaust lobes and all intake lobes are not identical, the camshaft must be reground or replaced. 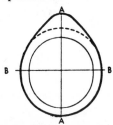 **Camshaft lobe measurement**
Replace the camshaft bearings (OHV engines only): 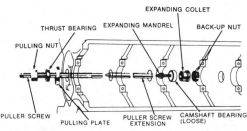 **Camshaft bearing removal and installation tool (OHV engines only)**	If excessive wear is indicated, or if the engine is being completely rebuilt, camshaft bearings should be replaced as follows: Drive the camshaft rear plug from the block. Assemble the removal puller with its shoulder on the bearing to be removed. Gradually tighten the puller nut until bearing is removed. Remove remaining bearings, leaving the front and rear for last. To remove front and rear bearings, reverse position of the tool, so as to pull the bearings in toward the center of the block. Leave the tool in this position, pilot the new front and rear bearings on the installer, and pull them into position: Return the tool to its original position and pull remaining bearings into position. NOTE: *Ensure that oil holes align when installing bearings.* Replace camshaft rear plug, and stake it into position to aid retention.
Finish hone the cylinders:	Chuck a flexible drive hone into a power drill, and insert it into the cylinder. Start the hone, and move it up and down in the cylinder at a rate which will produce approximately a 60° cross-hatch pattern. NOTE: *Do not extend the hone below the cylin-*

Cylinder Block Reconditioning

Procedure	Method

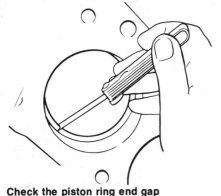

CROSS HATCH
PATTERN

50°-60°

Cylinder bore after honing

der bore. After developing the pattern, remove the hone and recheck piston fit. Wash the cylinders with a detergent and water solution to remove abrasive dust, dry, and wipe several times with a rag soaked in engine oil.

Check piston ring end-gap:

Check the piston ring end gap

Compress the piston rings to be used in a cylinder, one at a time, into that cylinder, and press them approximately 1″ below the deck with an inverted piston. Using feeler gauges, measure the ring end-gap, and compare to specifications. Pull the ring out of the cylinder and file the ends with a fine file to obtain proper clearance.
CAUTION: *If inadequate ring end-gap is utilized, ring breakage will result.*

Install the piston rings:

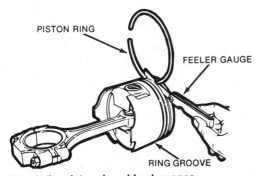

PISTON RING

FEELER GAUGE

RING GROOVE

Check the piston ring side clearance

Inspect the ring grooves in the piston for excessive wear or taper. If necessary, recut the grooves(s) for use with an overwidth ring or a standard ring and spacer. If the groove is worn uniformly, overwidth rings, or standard rings and spacers may be installed without recutting. Roll the outside of the ring around the groove to check for burrs or deposits. If any are found, remove with a fine file. Hold the ring in the groove, and measure side clearance. If necessary, correct as indicated above.
NOTE: *Always install any additional spacers above the piston ring.*
The ring groove must be deep enough to allow the ring to seat below the lands (see illustration). In many cases, a "go-no-go" depth gauge will be provided with the piston rings. Shallow grooves may be corrected by recutting, while deep grooves require some type of filler or expander behind the piston. Consult the piston ring sup-

Cylinder Block Reconditioning

Procedure	Method
	plier concerning the suggested method. Install the rings on the piston, lowest ring first, using a ring expander. NOTE: *Position the ring as specified by the manufacturer.* Consult the engine service procedures earlier in this chapter for details concerning specific engines.
Install the camshaft (OHV engines only):	Liberally lubricate the camshaft lobes and journals, and install the camshaft. CAUTION: *Exercise extreme care to avoid damaging the bearings when inserting the camshaft.* Install and tighten the camshaft thrust plate retaining bolts. See the engine service procedures earlier in this chapter for details concerning specific engines.
Check camshaft end-play (OHV engines only): Check the camshaft end-play with a feeler gauge	Using feeler gauges, determine whether the clearance between the camshaft boss (or gear) and backing plate is within specifications. Install shims behind the thrust plate, or reposition the camshaft gear and retest endplay. In some cases, adjustment is by replacing the thrust plate. See the engine service procedures earlier in this chapter for details concerning specific engines.
DIAL INDICATOR CAMSHAFT Check the camshaft end-play with a dial indicator	* Mount a dial indicator stand so that the stem of the dial indicator rests on the nose of the camshaft, parallel to the camshaft axis. Push the camshaft as far in as possible and zero the gauge. Move the camshaft outward to determine the amount of camshaft endplay. If the endplay is not within tolerance, install shims behind the thrust plate, or reposition the camshaft gear and retest. See the engine service procedures earlier in this chapter for details concerning specific engines.
Install the rear main seal:	See the engine service procedures earlier in this chapter for details concerning specific engines.
Install the crankshaft: 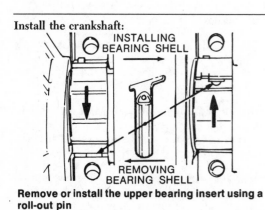INSTALLING BEARING SHELL REMOVING BEARING SHELL Remove or install the upper bearing insert using a roll-out pin	Thoroughly clean the main bearing saddles and caps. Place the upper halves of the bearing inserts on the saddles and press into position. NOTE: *Ensure that the oil holes align.* Press the corresponding bearing inserts into the main bearing caps. Lubricate the upper main bearings, and lay the crankshaft in position. Place a strip of Plastigage on each of the crankshaft journals, install the main caps, and torque to specifications. Remove the main caps, and compare the Plastigage to the scale on the Plastigage envelope. If clearances are within tolerances, remove the Plastigage, turn the crankshaft 90°, wipe off all oil and retest. If all clearances are correct, re-

Cylinder Block Reconditioning

Procedure	Method

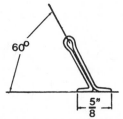

Home-made bearing roll-out pin

move all Plastigage, thoroughly lubricate the main caps and bearing journals, and install the main caps. If clearances are not within tolerance, the upper bearing inserts may be removed, without removing the crankshaft, using a bearing roll out pin (see illustration). Roll in a bearing that will provide proper clearance, and retest. Torque all main caps, excluding the thrust bearing cap, to specifications. Tighten the thrust bearing cap finger tight. To properly align the thrust bearing, pry the crankshaft the extent of its axial travel several times, the last movement held toward the front of the engine, and torque the thrust bearing cap to specifications. Determine the crankshaft end-play (see below), and bring within tolerance with thrust washers.

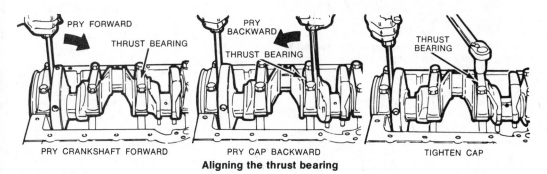

PRY CRANKSHAFT FORWARD   PRY CAP BACKWARD   TIGHTEN CAP

Aligning the thrust bearing

Measure crankshaft end-play:

Mount a dial indicator stand on the front of the block, with the dial indicator stem resting on the nose of the crankshaft, parallel to the crankshaft axis. Pry the crankshaft the extent of its travel rearward, and zero the indicator. Pry the crankshaft forward and record crankshaft end-play.

NOTE: *Crankshaft end-play also may be measured at the thrust bearing, using feeler gauges (see illustration).*

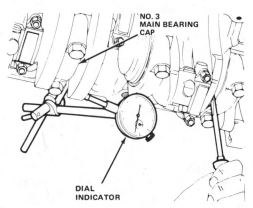

Check the crankshaft end-play with a dial indicator

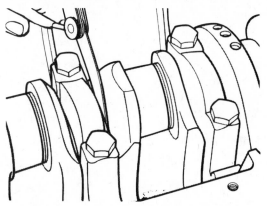

Check the crankshaft end-play with a feeler gauge

Cylinder Block Reconditioning

Procedure	Method

Install the pistons:

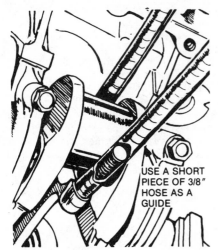

USE A SHORT PIECE OF 3/8" HOSE AS A GUIDE

Use lengths of vacuum hose or rubber tubing to protect the crankshaft journals and cylinder walls during piston installation

RING COMPRESSOR

Install the piston using a ring compressor

Press the upper connecting rod bearing halves into the connecting rods, and the lower halves into the connecting rod caps. Position the piston ring gaps according to specifications (see car section), and lubricate the pistons. Install a ring compresser on a piston, and press two long (8") pieces of plastic tubing over the rod bolts. Using the tubes as a guide, press the pistons into the bores and onto the crankshaft with a wooden hammer handle. After seating the rod on the crankshaft journal, remove the tubes and install the cap finger tight. Install the remaining pistons in the same manner. Invert the engine and check the bearing clearance at two points (90° apart) on each journal with Plastigage.
NOTE: *Do not turn the crankshaft with Plastigage installed.* If clearance is within tolerances, remove *all* Plastigage, thoroughly lubricate the journals, and torque the rod caps to specifications. If clearance is not within specifications, install different thickness bearing inserts and recheck.
CAUTION: *Never shim or file the connecting rods or caps.* Always install plastic tube sleeves over the rod bolts when the caps are not installed, to protect the crankshaft journals.

Check connecting rod side clearance:

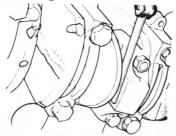

Check the connecting rod side clearance with a feeler gauge

Determine the clearance between the sides of the connecting rods and the crankshaft, using feeler gauges. If clearance is below the minimum tolerance, the rod may be machined to provide adequate clearance. If clearance is excessive, substitute an unworn rod, and recheck. If clearance is still outside specifications, the crankshaft must be welded and reground, or replaced.

Inspect the timing chain (or belt):

Visually inspect the timing chain for broken or loose links, and replace the chain if any are found. If the chain will flex sideways, it must be replaced. Install the timing chain as specified. Be sure the timing belt is not stretched, frayed or broken.
NOTE: *If the original timing chain is to be reused, install it in its original position.*

Cylinder Block Reconditioning

Procedure	Method
Check timing gear backlash and runout (OHV engines):	Mount a dial indicator with its stem resting on a tooth of the camshaft gear (as illustrated). Rotate the gear until all slack is removed, and zero the indicator. Rotate the gear in the opposite direction until slack is removed, and record gear backlash. Mount the indicator with its stem resting on the edge of the camshaft gear, parallel to the axis of the camshaft. Zero the indicator, and turn the camshaft gear one full turn, recording the runout. If either backlash or runout exceed specifications, replace the worn gear(s).

Check the camshaft gear backlash

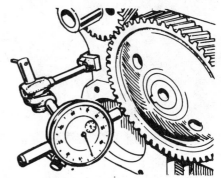

Check the camshaft gear run-out

Completing the Rebuilding Process

Following the above procedures, complete the rebuilding process as follows:

Fill the oil pump with oil, to prevent cavitating (sucking air) on initial engine start up. Install the oil pump and the pickup tube on the engine. Coat the oil pan gasket as necessary, and install the gasket and the oil pan. Mount the flywheel and the crankshaft vibration damper or pulley on the crankshaft. NOTE: *Always use new bolts when installing the flywheel.* Inspect the clutch shaft pilot bushing in the crankshaft. If the bushing is excessively worn, remove it with an expanding puller and a slide hammer, and tap a new bushing into place.

Position the engine, cylinder head side up. Lubricate the lifters, and install them into their bores. Install the cylinder head, and torque it as specified. Insert the pushrods (where applicable), and install the rocker shaft(s) (if so equipped) or position the rocker arms on the pushrods. Adjust the valves.

Install the intake and exhaust manifolds, the carburetor(s), the distributor and spark plugs. Adjust the point gap and the static ignition timing. Mount all accessories and install the engine in the car. Fill the radiator with coolant, and the crankcase with high quality engine oil.

Break-in Procedure

Start the engine, and allow it to run at low speed for a few minutes, while checking for leaks. Stop the engine, check the oil level, and fill as necessary. Restart the engine, and fill the cooling system to capacity. Check the point dwell angle and adjust the ignition timing and the valves. Run the engine at low to medium speed (800–2500 rpm) for approximately ½ hour, and retorque the cylinder head bolts. Road test the car, and check again for leaks.

Follow the manufacturer's recommended engine break-in procedure and maintenance schedule for new engines.

Emission Controls and Fuel System

EMISSION CONTROLS

There are three types of automobile pollutants that concern automotive engineers: crankcase fumes, exhaust gases and gasoline vapors from evaporation. The devices and systems used to limit these pollutants are commonly called emission control equipment.

Crankcase Emission Controls

The crankcase emission control equipment consists of a positive crankcase ventilation (PCV) valve, a closed or open oil filler cap and the hoses that connect this equipment.

When the engine is running, a small portion of the gases which are formed in the combustion chamber leak by the piston rings and enter the crankcase. Since these gases are under pressure they tend to escape from the crankcase and enter into the atmosphere. If these gases were allowed to remain in the crankcase for any length of time, they would contaminate the engine oil and cause sludge to build up. If the gases are allowed to escape into the atmosphere, they would pollute the air, as they contain unburned hydrocarbons. The crankcase emission control equipment recycles these gases back into the engine

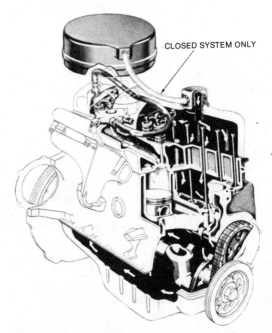

A cutaway view of the typical 6-cylinder positive crankcase ventilation system

combustion chamber, where they are burned.

Crankcase gases are recycled in the following manner. While the engine is running, clean filtered air is drawn into the crankcase either directly through the oil filler cap or through the carburetor air filter and then through a hose leading to the oil filler cap. As the air passes through the crankcase it picks up the combustion gases and carries them out of the crankcase, up through the PCV valve and into the intake manifold. After they enter the intake manifold they are drawn into the combustion chamber and are burned.

The most critical component of the system is the PCV valve. This vacuum-controlled valve regulates the amount of gases which are recycled into the combustion chamber. At low engine speeds the valve is partially closed, limiting the flow of gases into the intake manifold. As engine speed increases, the valve opens to admit greater quantities of the gases into the intake manifold. If the valve should become blocked or plugged, the gases will be prevented from escaping the crankcase by the normal route. Since these gases are under pressure, they will find their own way out of the crankcase. This alternate route is usually a weak oil seal or gasket in the engine. As the gas escapes by the gasket, it also creates an oil leak. Besides causing oil leaks, a clogged PCV valve also allows these gases to remain in the crankcase for an extended period of time, promoting the formation of sludge in the engine.

The above explanation and the troubleshooting procedure which follows applies to all of the engines installed in Ford vans, since all are equipped with PCV systems.

TROUBLESHOOTING

With the engine running, pull the PCV valve and hose from the valve rocker cover rubber grommet. Block off the end of the valve with your finger. A strong vacuum should be felt. Shake the valve; a clicking noise indicates it is free. Replace the valve if it is suspected of being blocked.

Removal

1. Pull the PCV valve and hose from the rubber grommet in the rocker cover.
2. Remove the PCV valve from the hose. Inspect the inside of the PCV valve. If it is dirty, disconnect it from the intake manifold and clean it in a suitable, safe solvent.

To install, proceed as follows:

1. If the PCV valve hose was removed, connect it to the intake manifold.
2. Connect the PCV valve to its hose.
3. Install the PCV valve into the rubber grommet in the valve rocker cover.

Exhaust Emission Controls
THERMACTOR SYSTEM

All 1968 models equipped with manual transmission, all 1974 models manufactured for sale in California, and all 1975–82 models are equipped with a Thermactor emission control system.

The Thermactor emission control system

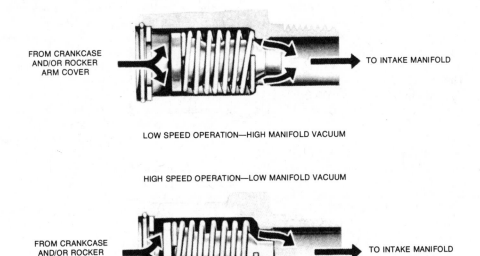

FROM CRANKCASE AND/OR ROCKER ARM COVER — TO INTAKE MANIFOLD

LOW SPEED OPERATION—HIGH MANIFOLD VACUUM

HIGH SPEED OPERATION—LOW MANIFOLD VACUUM

FROM CRANKCASE AND/OR ROCKER ARM COVER — TO INTAKE MANIFOLD

A cutaway view of a PCV valve showing its operation

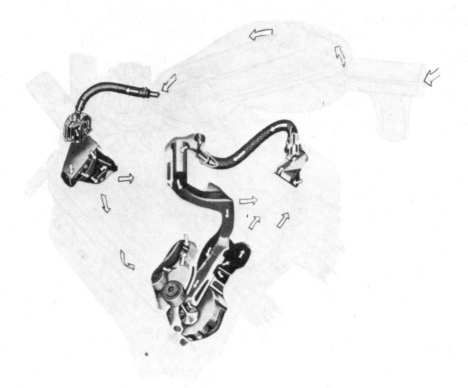

A cutaway view of the PCV system of the 302 V8

makes use of a belt-driven air pump to inject fresh air into the hot exhaust stream through the engine exhaust ports. The result is the extended burning of those fumes which were not completely ignited in the combustion chamber, and the subsequent reduction of some of the hydrocarbon and carbon monoxide content of the exhaust emissions into harmless carbon dioxide and water.

The Thermactor system is composed of the following components:

1. Air supply pump (belt-driven)
2. Air by-pass valve
3. Check valves
4. Air manifolds (internal or external)
5. Air supply tubes (on external manifolds only).

Air for the Thermactor system is cleaned by means of a centrifugal filter fan mounted on the air pump driveshaft. The air filter does not require a replaceable element.

To prevent excessive pressure, the air pump is equipped with a pressure relief valve which uses a replaceable plastic plug to control the pressure setting.

The Thermactor air pump has sealed bearings which are lubricated for the life of the unit, and pre-set rotor vane and bearing clearances, which do not require any periodic adjustments.

The air supply from the pump is controlled by the air by-pass valve, sometimes called a dump valve. During deceleration, the air by-pass valve opens, momentarily diverting the air supply through a silencer and into the atmosphere, thus preventing backfires within the exhaust system.

A check valve is incorporated in the air inlet side of the air manifolds. Its purpose is to prevent exhaust gases from backing up into the Thermactor system. This valve is especially important in the event of drive belt failure, and during deceleration, when the air by-pass valve is dumping the air supply.

The air manifolds and air supply tubes channel the air from the Thermactor air pump into the exhaust ports of each cylinder, thus completing the cycle of the Thermactor system.

IMPROVED COMBUSTION SYSTEM

All 1968 vans equipped with automatic transmission, all 1969 models and all 1970 and

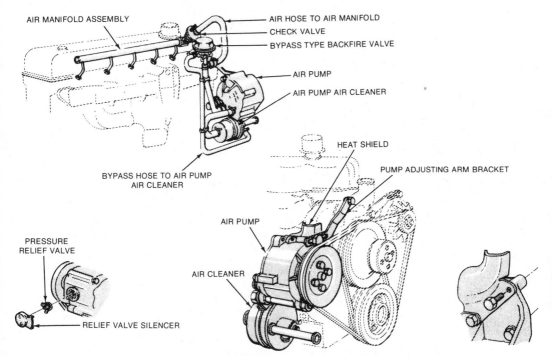

AIR MANIFOLD ASSEMBLY

AIR HOSE TO AIR MANIFOLD
CHECK VALVE
BYPASS TYPE BACKFIRE VALVE

AIR PUMP
AIR PUMP AIR CLEANER

HEAT SHIELD
PUMP ADJUSTING ARM BRACKET

BYPASS HOSE TO AIR PUMP
AIR CLEANER

AIR PUMP

PRESSURE
RELIEF VALVE

AIR CLEANER

RELIEF VALVE SILENCER

The Thermactor exhaust emission control system installed on a 240 six

later models (regardless of other exhaust emission control equipment) are equipped with the Improved Combustion (IMCO) System. The IMCO System controls emissions arising from the incomplete combustion of the air/fuel mixture in the cylinders. The IMCO system incorporates a number of modifications to the distributor spark control system, the fuel system, and the internal design of the engine.

Internal engine modifications include the following: elimination of surface irregularities and crevices as well as a low surface area-to-volume ratio in the combustion chambers, a high-velocity intake manifold combined with short exhaust ports, selective valve timing and a higher temperature and capacity cooling system.

Modifications to the fuel system include the following: recalibrated carburetors to achieve a leaner air/fuel mixture, more precise calibration of the choke mechanism, the installation of idle mixture limiter caps and a heated air intake system.

Modifications to the distributor spark control system include the following: a modified centrifugal advance curve, the use of dual diaphragm distributors in most applications, a ported vacuum switch, a deceleration valve and a spark delay valve.

CARBURETOR

The carburetors used on engines equipped with emission controls have specific flow characteristics that differ from the carburetors used on vehicles not equipped with emission control devices. Also, since 1968, all carburetors have limiter caps installed on the idle fuel mixture adjustment screws. These limiter caps prevent an overly rich mixture adjustment from being made. The correct adjustment can usually be reached within the range of the limiter caps. These carburetors are identified by number. The same type carburetor should be used when replacement is necessary.

THERMOSTATICALLY CONTROLLED AIR CLEANER SYSTEM (TAC)

This system consists of a heat shroud which is integral with the right-side exhaust manifold, a hot air hose and a special air cleaner assembly equipped with a thermal sensor and vacuum motor and air valve assembly.

The temperature of the carburetor intake air is thermostatically controlled by means of a valve plate and a vacuum override built into a duct assembly attached to the air cleaner. The exhaust manifold shroud tube is attached

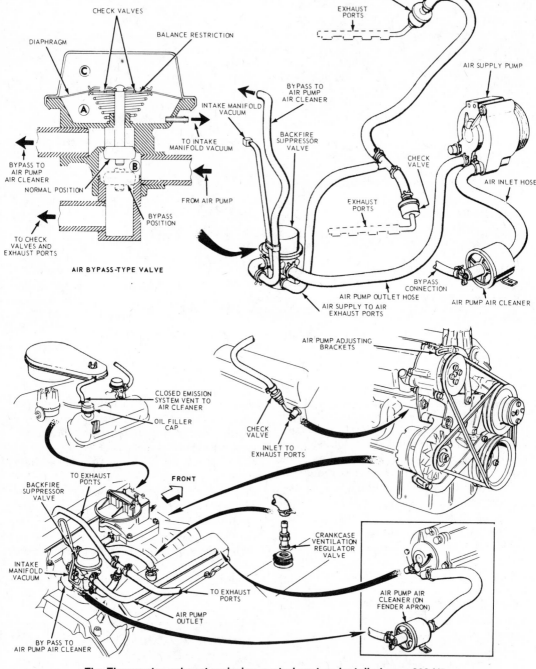

The Thermactor exhaust emission control system installed on a 302 V8

to the shroud over the exhaust manifold for the source of heated air.

The thermal sensor is attached to the air valve actuating lever, along with the vacuum motor lever, both of which control the position of the air valve to supply either heated air from the exhaust manifold or cooler air from the engine compartment.

During the warm-up period, when the under-the-hood temperatures are low, the thermal sensor doesn't exert enough tension on the air valve actuating lever to close (heat off) the air valve. Thus, the carburetor receives heated air from around the exhaust manifold.

As the temperature of the air entering the

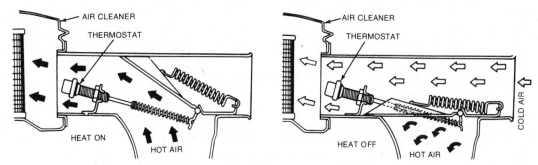

Operation of the thermostatically controlled air cleaner

air cleaner approaches approximately 110° F, the thermal sensor begins to push on the air valve actuating lever and overcome the spring tension which holds the air valve in the open (heat on) position. The air valve begins to move to the closed (heat off) position, allowing only under-the-hood air to enter the air cleaner.

The air valve in the air cleaner will also open, regardless of the air temperature, during heavy acceleration to obtain maximum airflow through the air cleaner. The extreme decrease in intake manifold vacuum during heavy acceleration permits the vacuum motor to override the thermostatic control. This opens the system to both heated air and air from the engine compartment.

DUAL DIAPHRAGM DISTRIBUTOR

The dual diaphragm distributor has two diaphragms which operate independently. The outer (primary) diaphragm makes use of carburetor vacuum to advance the ignition timing. The inner (secondary) diaphragm uses intake manifold vacuum to provide additional retardation of ignition timing during closed-throttle deceleration and idle, resulting in the reduction of hydrocarbon emissions.

DISTRIBUTOR MODULATOR (DIST-O-VAC) SYSTEM

1970 and 1971 models equipped with automatic transmission and the 240 engine are equipped with a Dist-O-Vac spark control system. This system is used in conjunction with all of the IMCO system equipment except the deceleration valve.

The three components of the Dist-O-Vac system are the speed sensor, the thermal switch, and the electronic control module. The electronic control module consists of two sub-assemblies: the electronic control amplifier and the three-way solenoid valve.

The speed sensor, a small unit mounted in

the speedometer cable, contains a rotating magnet and a stationary winding which is insulated from ground. The magnet, which rotates with the speedometer cable, generates a small voltage which increases directly with speed. This voltage is directed to the electronic control amplifier.

The thermal switch consists of a bimetallic-element switch which is mounted in the right door pillar and senses the temperature of the air. The switch is closed at 58° F or lower, and open at temperatures about 58° F. This switch is also connected to the electronic control amplifier.

Within the electronic control module case, there is a printed circuit board and an electronic amplifier. The speed sensor and thermal switch are connected to this assembly. The thermal switch is the dominant circuit. When the temperature of the outside air is 58° F or lower, the circuit is closed, so that regardless of speed, the electronic control amplifier will not trigger the three-way solenoid valve. At temperatures above 58° F, however, the thermal switch circuit is open, allowing the circuit from the speed sensor to take over and control the action of the solenoid valve.

The three-way solenoid valve is located within the electronic control module and below the printed circuit board of the amplifier. It is vented to the atmosphere at the top, and connected at the bottom of the carburetor spark port (small hose) and the primary (advance) side of the dual-diaphragm distributor (large hose). The large hose is also channeled through the temperature-sensing valve. The small hose is equipped with an air bleed to provide a positive airflow in the direction of the carburetor. The air bleed purges the hose of vacuum, thus assuring that raw gasoline will not be drawn through the hose and into the distributor diaphragm.

When the thermal switch is closed (air

temperature 58° F or lower), or when it is open and the speed sensor is not sending out a strong enough voltage signal (speeds below approximately 35 mph), the amplifier will not activate the solenoid valve and the valve is in the closed position, blocking the passage of air from the small tube through the large tube. With the valve in this position, the larger hose is vented to the atmosphere through the top opening in the three-way valve assembly. Consequently, no vacuum is being supplied to the primary diaphragm on the distributor, and, therefore, no vacuum advance.

When the air temperature is above 58° F and/or the speed of the car is sufficient to generate the required voltage (35 mph or faster), the valve opens, blocking the vent to the atmosphere while opening the vacuum line from the carburetor spark port to the primary diaphragm of the distributor.

TRANSMISSION REGULATED SPARK SYSTEM

1972 vans equipped with the 240 Six and automatic transmission use a transmission regulated spark control system.

The transmission regulated spark control system (TRS) differs from the Dist-O-Vac and ESC systems in that the speed sensor and amplifier are replaced by a switch on the transmission. The switch is activated by a mechanical linkage which opens the switch when the transmission is shifted into High gear. The switch, when opened, triggers the opening of the vacuum lines to the distributor, thus providing vacuum advance. So, in short, the TRS system blocks vacuum advance to the distributor only when the outside temperature is above 65° F and the transmission is in First or Second gear.

PORTED VACUUM SWITCH VALVE (PVS)

The PVS valve is a temperature sensing valve found on the distributor vacuum advance line, and is installed in the coolant outlet elbow. During prolonged periods of idle, or any other situation which causes engine operating temperatures to be higher than normal, the valve, which under normal conditions simply connects the vacuum advance diaphragm to its vacuum source within the carburetor, closes the normal source vacuum port and engages an alternate source vacuum port. This alternate source is from the intake manifold which, under idle conditions, main-

tains a high vacuum. This increase in vacuum supply to the distributor diaphragm advances the timing, increasing the idle speed. The increase in idle speed causes a directly proportional increase in the operation of the cooling system. When the engine has cooled sufficiently, the vacuum supply is returned to its normal source, the carburetor.

DECELERATION VALVE

Beginning in 1969, some engines were equipped with a distributor vacuum advance control valve (deceleration valve) which is used with dual diaphragm distributors to further aid in controlling ignition timing. The deceleration valve is in the vacuum line which runs from the outer (advance) diaphragm to the carburetor, the normal vacuum supply for the distributor. During deceleration, the intake manifold vacuum rises causing the deceleration valve to close off the carburetor vacuum source and connect the intake manifold vacuum source to the distributor advance diaphragm. The increase in vacuum provides maximum ignition timing advance, thus providing more complete fuel combustion and decreasing exhaust system backfiring.

EXHAUST GAS RECIRCULATION SYSTEM (EGR)

In this system, a vacuum-operated EGR flow valve is attached to the carburetor spacer. A passage in the carburetor spacer mates with a hole in the mounting face of the EGR valve or the intake manifold. The most common system allows exhaust gases to flow from the exhaust crossover, through the control valve and through the spacer into the intake manifold below the carburetor. For those engines where exhaust gases cannot be picked up from the exhaust crossover (6 cylinder) as described above, the gases are picked up from the choke stove located on the exhaust manifold or directly from the exhaust manifold. The exhaust gases are routed to the carburetor spacer through steel tubing.

The vacuum signal which operates the EGR valve originates at the EGR vacuum port in the carburetor. This signal is controlled by at least one, and sometimes two, series of valves.

A water temperature sensing valve (the EGR PVS) which is closed until the water temperature reaches either 60° F or 125° F, depending on application, is always used.

The position of the EGR vacuum port in

the carburetor and calibration of the EGR valve can be varied to give the required modulation of EGR during acceleration and low speed cruise conditions. However, a more complicated system using a second series valve is sometimes needed to provide control of EGR for engine operation at high speed cruise conditions. The second valve: the high speed modulator valve, is controlled as a function of vehicle speed.

The high speed EGR modulator subsystem consists of a speed sensor, an electronic module and a solenoid vacuum valve. The speed sensor, driven by the speedometer cable, provides an AC signal in relation to engine speed, to the electronic module. The elec-

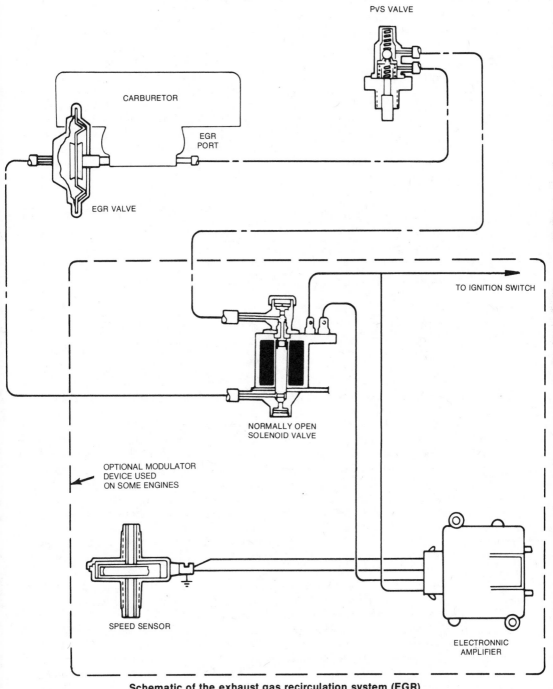

Schematic of the exhaust gas recirculation system (EGR)

tronic module processes the information from the speed sensor and sends a signal to the high speed modulator (vacuum solenoid) valve. When the vehicle speed exceeds the module trigger speed, the solenoid vacuum valve closes which, in turn, causes the EGR valve to close.

EGR/COOLANT SPARK CONTROL (CSC) SYSTEM

The EGR/CSC system is used on most 1974 and later models. It regulates both distributor spark advance and the EGR valve operation according to coolant temperature by sequentially switching vacuum signals.

The major EGR/CSC system components are:

1. 95° F EGR-PVS valve;
2. Spark Delay Valve (SDV);
3. Vacuum check valve.

When the engine coolant temperature is below 82° F, the EGR-PVS valve admits carburetor EGR port vacuum (occurring at about 2,500 rpm) directly to the distributor advance diaphragm, through the one-way check valve.

At the same time, the EGR-PVS valve shuts off carburetor EGR vacuum to the EGR valve and transmission diaphragm.

When engine coolant temperature is 95° F and above, the EGR-PVS valve is actuated and directs carburetor EGR vacuum to the EGR valve and transmission instead of the distributor. At temperatures between 82–95° F, the EGR-PVS valve may be open, closed, or in mid-position.

The SDV valve delays carburetor spark vacuum to the distributor advance diaphragm by restricting the vacuum signal through the SDV valve for a predetermined time. During normal acceleration, little or no vacuum is admitted to the distributor advance diaphragm until acceleration is completed, because of (1) the time delay of the SDV valve and (2) the re-routing of EGR port vacuum if the engine coolant temperature is 95° F or higher.

The check valve blocks off vacuum signal from the SDV to the EGR-PVS so that carburetor spark vacuum will not be dissipated when the EGR-PVS is actuated above 95° F.

The 235° F PVS is not part of the EGR/CSC system, but is connected to the distributor vacuum advance to prevent engine overheating while idling (as on previous models). At idle speed, no vacuum is generated at either the carburetor spark port or EGR port and engine timing is fully re-

tarded. When engine coolant temperature reaches 235° F, however, the valve is actuated to admit intake manifold vacuum to the distributor advance diaphragm. This advances the engine timing and speeds up the engine. The increase in coolant flow and fan speed lowers engine temperature.

COLD START SPARK ADVANCE (CSSA) SYSTEM

All 1975–78 Fords using the 460 V8 are equipped with the CSSA System. It is a modification of the existing spark control system to aid in cold start driveability. The system uses a coolant temperature sensing vacuum switch located on the thermostat housing. When the engine is cold (below 125° F), it permits full manifold vacuum to the distributor advance diaphragm. After the engine warms up, normal spark control (retard) resumes.

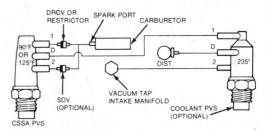

Typical CSSA system

VACUUM OPERATED HEAT CONTROL VALVE (VOHV)

To further aid cold start driveability during engine warmup, most 1975 and later engines use a VOHV located between the exhaust manifold and the exhaust inlet (header) pipe.

When the engine is first started, the valve is closed, blocking exhaust gases from exiting from one bank of cylinders. These gases are then diverted back through the intake manifold crossover passage under the carburetor. The result is quick heat to the carburetor and choke.

The VOHV is controlled by a ported vacuum switch which uses manifold vacuum to keep the vacuum motor on the valve closed until the coolant reaches a predetermined "warm-up" valve. When the engine is warmed-up, the PVS shuts off vacuum to the VOHV, and a strong return spring opens the VOHV butterfly.

SPARK DELAY VALVE

The spark delay valve is a plastic spring-loaded, color-coded valve in the vacuum line to the distributor vacuum advance chamber on some 1972 models. Under heavy throttle application, the valve will close, blocking carburetor vacuum to the distributor vacuum advance mechanism. After the designated period of time, the valve opens, restoring normal carburetor vacuum to the distributor.

CATALYTIC CONVERTER

Starting 1975, most models under 6000 lbs. GVW have an exhaust system catalytic converter. The converter is in the exhaust system ahead of the muffler. It contains a catalytic agent made of platinum and palladium, used to oxidize hydrocarbons (HC) and carbon monoxide (CO). The catalyst is expected to function without service of any kind for at least 50,000 miles. Use of leaded fuel would quickly cause catalyst failure; for this reason, a tank filler restriction prevents the entry of service station leaded fuel nozzles.

Evaporative Emission Controls

Beginning 1970, Ford vans produced for sale in California were equipped with evaporative emission controls on the fuel system. For 1971, the system was modified somewhat and used on all Ford vans as standard equipment.

Changes in atmospheric temperature cause fuel tanks to "breathe"; that is, the air within the tank expands and contracts with outside temperature changes. As the temperature rises, air escapes through the tank vent tube or the vent in the tank cap. The air which escapes contains gasoline vapors. In a similar manner, the gasoline which fills the carburetor float bowl expands when the engine is stopped. Engine heat causes this expansion. The vapors escape through the carburetor and air cleaner.

The Evaporative Emission Control System provides a sealed fuel system with the capability to store and condense fuel vapors. The system has three parts: a fill control vent system; a vapor vent and storage system; and a pressure and vacuum relief system (special fill cap).

The fill control vent system is a modification to the fuel tank. It uses an air space within the tank which is 10–12% of the tank's volume. The air space is sufficient to provide for the thermal expansion of the fuel. The space also serves as part of the in-tank vapor vent system.

The in-tank vent system consists of the air space previously described and a vapor separator assembly. The separator assembly is mounted to the top of the fuel tank and is secured by a cam-lockring, similar to the one which secures the fuel sending unit. Foam material fills the vapor separator assembly. The foam material separates raw fuel and vapors, thus retarding the entrance of fuel into the vapor line.

The sealed filler cap has a pressure vacuum relief valve. Under normal operating conditions, the filler cap operates as a check valve, allowing air to enter the tank to replace the fuel consumed. At the same time, it prevents vapors from escaping through the cap. In case of excessive pressure within the tank, the filler cap valve opens to relieve the pressure.

Because the filler cap is sealed, fuel vapors have but one place through which they may escape—the vapor separator assembly at the top of the fuel tank. The vapors pass through the foam material and continue through a single vapor line which leads to a canister in the engine compartment. The canister is filled with activated charcoal.

Another vapor line runs from the top of the carburetor float chamber to the charcoal canister.

As the fuel vapors (hydrocarbons), enter the charcoal canister, they are absorbed by the charcoal. The air is dispelled through the open bottom of the charcoal canister, leaving the hydrocarbons trapped within the charcoal. When the engine is started, vacuum causes fresh air to be drawn into the canister from its open bottom. The fresh air passes through the charcoal picking up the hydrocarbons which are trapped there and feeding them into the carburetor for burning with the fuel mixture.

Emission Control Service

Complete and detailed procedures for the servicing of the crankcase ventilation system are found in the "Maintenance" Section of Chapter 1.

THERMACTOR SYSTEM
Air By-Pass Valve Replacement

1. Disconnect the air and vacuum hoses at the air by-pass valve body.

2. Position the air by-pass valve and connect the respective hoses.

Check Valve Replacement

1. Disconnect the air supply hose at the valve. Use a 1¼ in. crowfoot wrench. The valve has a standard, right-hand pipe thread.

2. Clean the threads on the air manifold adapter (air supply tube on the V8 engines) with a wire brush. Do not blow compressed air through the check valve in either direction.

3. Install the check valve and tighten.

4. Connect the air supply hose.

Air Manifold Replacement
SIX-CYLINDER ENGINES

1. Disconnect the air supply hose at the check valve, position the hose out of the way and remove the valve.

2. Loosen all of the air manifold-to-cylinder head tube coupling nuts (compression fittings). Inspect the air manifold for damaged threads and fittings and for leaking connections. Repair or replace as required. Clean the manifold and associated parts with kerosene. Do not dry the parts with compressed air.

3. Position the air manifold on the cylinder head. Be sure that all of the tube coupling nuts are aligned with the cylinder head.

4. Screw each coupling nut into the cylinder head, one or two threads. Tighten the tube coupling nuts.

5. Install the check valve and tighten it.

6. Connect the air supply hose to the check valve.

Air Supply Tube Replacement
V8 ENGINE ONLY

1. Disconnect the air supply hose at the check valve and position the hose out of the way.

2. Remove the check valve.

3. Remove the air supply tube bolt and seal washer.

4. Carefully remove the air supply tube and seal washer from the cylinder head. Inspect the air supply tube for evidence of leaking threads or seal surfaces. Examine the attaching bolt head, seal washers, and supply tube surface for leaks. Inspect the attaching bolt and cylinder head threads for damage. Clean the air supply tube, seal washers, and bolt with kerosene. Do not dry the parts with compressed air.

5. Install the seal washer and air supply tube on the cylinder head. Be sure that it is positioned in the same manner as before removal.

6. Install the seal washer and mounting bolt. Tighten the bolt.

7. Install the check valve and tighten it.

8. Connect the air supply hose to the check valve.

Air Nozzle Replacement
SIX-CYLINDER ENGINES ONLY

Normally, air nozzles should be replaced during cylinder head reconditioning. A nozzle may be replaced, however, without removing the cylinder head, by removing the air manifold and using a hooked tool.

Clean the nozzle with kerosene and a stiff brush. Inspect the air nozzles for eroded tips.

Air Pump and Filter Fan Replacement

1. Loosen the air pump attaching bolts.

2. Remove the drive pulley attaching bolts and pull the pulley off the air pump shaft.

3. Pry the outer disc loose, then remove the centrifugal filter fan. Care must be used to prevent foreign matter from entering the air intake hole, especially if the fan breaks during removal. Do not attempt to remove the metal drive hub.

4. Install the new filter fan by drawing it into position with the pulley bolts.

NOTE: *Some 1966–67 air pumps have air filters with replaceable, noncleanable elements.*

Air Pump Replacement

1. Disconnect the air outlet hose at the air pump.

2. Loosen the pump belt tension adjuster.

3. Disengage the drive belt.

4. Remove the mounting bolt and air pump.

5. Position the air pump on the mounting bracket and install the mounting bolt.

6. Place the drive belt in the pulley and attach the adjusting arm to the air pump.

7. Adjust the drive belt tension and tighten the adjusting arm and mounting bolts.

8. Connect the air outlet hose to the air pump.

Relief Valve Replacement

Do not disassemble the air pump on the truck to replace the relief valve, but remove the pump from the engine.

1. Remove the relief valve on the pump housing and hold it in position with a block of wood.

3. Use a hammer to lightly tap the wood block until the relief valve is seated.

Relief Valve Pressure-Setting Plug Replacement

1. Compress the locking tabs inward (together) and remove the plastic pressure-setting plug.

2. Before installing the new plug, be sure that the plug is the correct one. The plugs are color-coded.

3. Insert the plug in the relief valve hole and push in until it snaps into place.

Distributor Temperature-Sensing Vacuum Control Valve Test

1. Check the routing and connection of all the vacuum hoses.

2. Attach a tachometer to the engine.

3. Bring the engine up to the normal operating temperature. The engine must not be overheated.

4. Note the engine rpm, with the transmission in Neutral, and the throttle at curb idle.

5. Disconnect the vacuum hose from the intake manifold at the temperature-sensing valve. Plug or clamp the hose.

6. Note the idle rpm with the hose disconnected. If there is no change in rpm, the valve is good. If there is a drop of 100 or more rpm, the valve should be replaced. Replace the vacuum line.

7. Check to make sure that the all-season coolant mixture meets specifications and that the correct radiator cap is in place and functioning.

8. Block the radiator airflow to induce a higher-than-normal temperature condition.

9. Continue to operate the engine until the temperature or heat indicator shows above normal.

If the engine speed, by this time, has increased 100 or more rpm, the temperature-sensing valve is satisfactory. If not, it should be replaced.

Distributor Deceleration Vacuum Control Valve Test

1. Connect a tachometer to the engine and bring the engine to the normal operating temperature.

2. Check the idle speed and set it to specifications with the headlights on high beam, as necessary.

3. Turn off the headlights and note the idle rpm.

4. Remove the plastic cover from the valve. Slowly turn the adjusting screw counterclockwise without pressing in. After 5, and no more than 6 turns, the idle speed should suddenly increase to about 1000 rpm. If the speed does not increase after six turns, push inward on the valve spring retainer and release. Speed should now increase.

5. Slowly turn the adjusting screw clockwise until the idle speed drops to the speed noted in Step 3. Make one more turn clockwise.

6. Increase the engine speed to 2000 rpm, hold for 5 seconds, and release the throttle. The engine speed should return to idle speed within 4 seconds. If idle is not resumed in 4 seconds, back off the dashpot adjustment and repeat the check. If the idle is not resumed in 3 seconds with the dashpot back off, turn the deceleration valve adjustment screw an additional quarter turn clockwise and repeat the check. Repeat the quarter turn adjustment and idle return checks until the engine returns to idle within the required time.

7. If it takes more than one complete turn from Step 5 to meet the idle return time specification, replace the valve.

Dual Diaphragm Vacuum Advance and Vacuum Retard Functional Check

1. To check vacuum advance, disconnect the vacuum lines from both the advance (outer) and retard (inner) diaphragms. Plug the line removed from the retard diaphragm.

Connect a tachometer and timing light to the engine. Increase the idle speed by setting the screw on the first step of the fast idle cam. Note the ignition timing setting, using a timing light.

Connect the carburetor vacuum line to the advance diaphragm. If the timing advances immediately, the advance unit is functioning properly. Adjust the idle speed to 550–600 rpm.

2. Check the vacuum retardation as follows: using a timing light, note the ignition timing. Remove the plug from the manifold vacuum line and connect the line to the inner diaphragm. Timing should retard immediately.

3. If vacuum retardation is not to specifications, replace the dual diaphragm advance unit. If the advance (vacuum) does not function properly, calibrate the unit on a distributor test stand. If the advance part of the unit cannot be calibrated, or if either diaphragm

is leaking, replace the dual diaphragm vacuum advance unit.

Evaporative Emission Control System Check

Other than a visual check to determine that none of the vapor lines are broken, there is no test for this equipment.

Electronic Spark Control System Operation Test

1. Raise the rear of the car until the rear wheels are clear of the ground by at least 4 in. Support the rear of the car with jackstands.

> CAUTION: *The rear of the van must be firmly supported during this test. If one of the rear wheels should come in contact with the ground while it is turning, the van will move forward very rapidly and unexpectedly. As an extra precaution, chock the front wheels and do not stand in front of the vehicle while the wheels are turning.*

2. Disconnect the vacuum hose from the distributor vacuum advance chamber. This is the outer hose on vans with dual diaphragm vacuum advance units.

3. Connect the hose to a vacuum gauge.

4. Pour hot water on the temperature sensing switch to make sure that it is above 65° F.

5. Start the engine and apply the foot brake. Depress the clutch and shift the transmission into High gear. Release the hand brake and slowly engage the clutch.

6. Have an assistant observe the vacuum gauge while you raise the speed of the engine until the speedometer reads 35 mph, at which time the vacuum gauge should show a reading.

7. If the vacuum gauge shows a reading below 35 mph, a component in the electronic spark control system is defective. If the vacuum gauge does not show a reading, even above 35 mph, there is either a defective component in the electronic spark control system, or there is a broken or clogged vacuum passage between the carburetor and the distributor.

Heated Air Intake Test

1. With the engine completely cold, look inside the cold air duct and make sure that the valve plate is fully in the up position (closing the cold air duct).

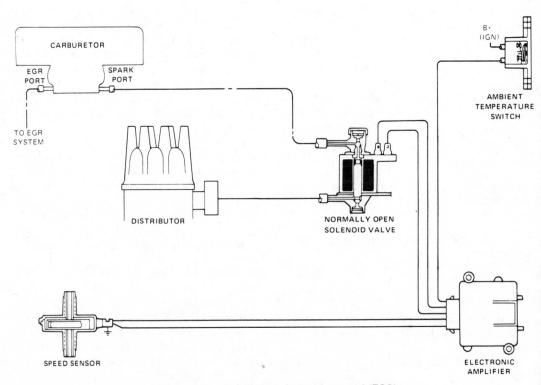

Schematic of the electronic spark control (ESC)

2. Start the engine and bring it to operating temperature.

3. Stop the engine and look inside the cold air duct again. The valve plate should be down. allowing an opening from the cold air duct into the air cleaner.

4. If the unit appears to be malfunctioning, remove it and examine it to make sure that the springs are not broken or disconnected, and replace the thermostat if all other parts appear intact and properly connected.

EXHAUST GAS RECIRCULATION SYSTEM

EGR Valve Cleaning

Remove the EGR valve for cleaning. Do not strike or pry on the valve diaphragm housing or supports, as this may damage the valve operating mechanism and/or change the valve calibration. Check orifice hole in the EGR valve body for deposits. A small hand drill of no more than 0.060 in. diameter may be used to clean the hole if plugged. Extreme care must be taken to avoid enlarging the hole or damaging the surface of the orifice plate.

VALVES WHICH CANNOT BE DISASSEMBLED

Valves which are riveted or otherwise permanently assembled should be replaced if highly contaminated; they cannot be cleaned.

VALVES WHICH CAN BE DISASSEMBLED

Separate the diaphragm section from the main mounting body. Clean the valve plates, stem, and the mounting plate, using a small power-driven rotary type wire brush. Take care not to damage the parts. Remove deposits between stem and valve disc by using a steel blade or shim approximately 0.028 in. thick in a sawing motion around the stem shoulder at both sides of the disc.

The poppet must wobble and move axially before reassembly.

Clean the cavity and passages in the main body of the valve with a power-driven rotary wire brush. If the orifice plate has a hole less than 0.450 in. it must be removed for cleaning. Remove all loosened debris using shop compressed air. Reassemble the diaphragm section on the main body using a new gasket between them. Torque the attaching screws to specification. Clean the orifice plate and the counterbore in the valve body. Reinstall the orifice plate using a small amount of contact cement to retain the plate in place during assembly of the valve to the carburetor spacer. Apply cement to only outer edges of the orifice plate to avoid restriction of the orifice.

EGR Supply Passages and Carburetor Space Cleaning

Remove the carburetor and carburetor spacer on engines so equipped. Clean the supply tube with a small power-driven rotary type wire brush or blast cleaning equipment. Clean the exhaust gas passages in the spacer using a suitable wire brush and/or scraper. The machined holes in the spacer can be cleaned by using a suitable round wire brush. Hard encrusted material should be probed loose first, then brushed out.

EGR Exhaust Gas Channel Cleaning

Clean the exhaust gas channel, where applicable, in the intake manifold, using a suitable carbon scraper. Clean the exhaust gas entry port in the intake manifold by hand passing a suitable drill bit thru the holes to auger out the deposits. Do not use a wire brush. The manifold riser bore(s) should be suitably plugged during the above action to prevent any of the residue from entering the induction system.

Transmission-Regulated Spark

TRANSMISSION VALVE TEST

1. Attach a test light to the wire which connects the transmission valve to the distributor modulator valve.

2. Jack up and support the vehicle, so that the rear wheels are free to turn.

3. Start the engine and engage the transmission in Low gear. Observe the test light, which should be lighted at this time.

4. On standard transmissions, engage High gear and check to see that the light goes out.

5. On automatic transmissions, place the vehicle in Drive and allow it to upshift. Upon the shift into High gear, the test light should go out.

6. If the test lamp fails to function properly, replace the transmission valve.

FUEL SYSTEM

Fuel Pump

Ford van engines use a camshaft eccentric-actuated combination fuel pump located on

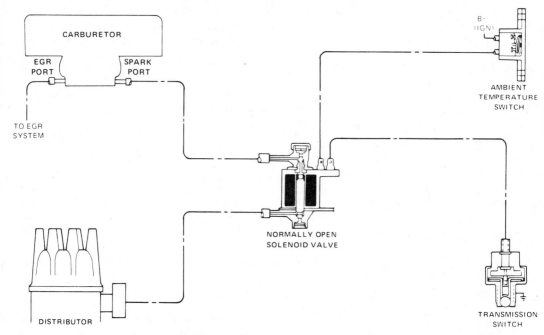

Schematic of the transmission regulated spark system

the lower left-side of the engine block on both 6 cylinder and V8 engines.

REMOVAL

1. Disconnect the fuel inlet and outlet lines at the fuel pump. Discard the fuel inlet retaining clamp.

2. Remove the pump retaining bolts then remove the pump assembly and gasket from the engine. Discard the gasket.

INSTALLATION

1. If a new pump is to be installed, remove the fuel line connector fitting from the old pump and install it in the new pump.

2. Remove all gasket material from the mounting pad and pump flange. Apply oil-resistant sealer to both sides of a new gasket.

3. Position the new gasket on the pump flange and hold the pump in position against the mounting pad. Make sure that the rocker arm is riding on the camshaft eccentric.

4. Press the pump tight against the pad, install the retaining bolts and alternately torque them to 12–15 ft lbs on 6 cylinder engines and 20–24 ft lbs on the V8. Connect the fuel lines. Use a new clamp on the fuel inlet line.

5. Operate the engine and check for leaks.

TESTING

Incorrect fuel pump pressure and low volume (flow rate) are the two most likely fuel

pump troubles that will affect engine performance. Low pressure will cause a lean mixture and fuel starvation at high speeds and excessive pressure will cause high fuel consumption and carburetor flooding.

To determine that the fuel pump is in satisfactory operating condition, tests for both fuel pump pressure and volume should be performed.

The tests are performed with the fuel pump installed on the engine and the engine at normal operating temperature and at idle speed.

Before the test, make sure that the replaceable fuel filter has been changed at the proper mileage interval. If in doubt, install a new filter.

Pressure Test

1. Remove the air cleaner assembly. Disconnect the fuel inlet line of the fuel filter at the carburetor. Use care to prevent fire, due to fuel spillage. Place an absorbent cloth under the connection before removing the line to catch any fuel that might flow out of the line.

2. Connect a pressure gauge, a restrictor and a flexible hose between the fuel filter and the carburetor.

3. Position the flexible hose and the restrictor so that the fuel can be discharged into a suitable, graduated container.

4. Before taking a pressure reading,

operate the engine at the specified idle rpm and vent the system into the container by opening the hose restrictor momentarily.

5. Close the hose restrictor, allow the pressure to stabilize and note the reading. The pressure should be as specified in the Tune Up Charts earlier in this book.

If the pump pressure is not within 4–6 psi and the fuel lines and filter are in satisfactory condition, the pump is defective and should be replaced.

If the pump pressure is within the proper range, perform the test for fuel volume.

Volume Test

1. Operate the engine at the specified idle rpm.

2. Open the hose restrictor and catch the fuel in the container while observing the time it takes to pump 1 pint. It should take 30 seconds for 1 pint to be expelled on all vehicles made prior to the 1974 model year. On 1974–82 vehicles, 1 pint should be expelled in 20 seconds. If the pump does not pump to specifications, check for proper fuel tank venting or a restriction in the fuel line leading from the fuel tank to the carburetor before replacing the fuel pump.

Carburetors

The carburetor identification tag is attached to the carburetor. The basic part number for all carburetors is 9510. To obtain replacement parts, it is necessary to know the part number prefix, suffix and, in some cases, the design change code. If the carburetor is ever replaced by a new unit, make sure that the identification tag stays with the new carburetor and the vehicle.

REMOVAL AND INSTALLATION

1. Remove the air cleaner.

2. Remove the throttle cable or rod from the throttle lever. Disconnect the distributor vacuum line, EGR vacuum line, if so equipped, the inline fuel filter and the choke heat tube at the carburetor.

3. Disconnect the choke clean air tube from the air horn. Disconnect the choke actuating cable, if so equipped.

4. Remove the carburetor retaining nuts then remove the carburetor. Remove the carburetor mounting gasket, spacer (if so equipped), and the lower gasket from the intake manifold.

5. Before installing the carburetor, clean the gasket mounting surfaces of the spacer and carburetor. Place the spacer between two new gaskets and position the spacer and gaskets on the intake manifold. Position the carburetor on the spacer and gasket and secure it with the retaining nuts. To prevent leakage, distortion or damage to the carburetor body flange, snug the nuts, then alternately tighten each nut in a criss-cross pattern.

6. Connect the inline fuel filter, throttle cable, choke heat tube, distributor vacuum line, EGR vacuum line, and choke cable.

7. Connect the choke clean air line to the air horn.

8. Adjust the engine idle speed, the idle fuel mixture and anti-stall dashpot (if so equipped). Install the air cleaner.

CARBURETOR TROUBLESHOOTING

The best way to diagnose a bad carburetor is to eliminate all other possible sources of the problem. If the carburetor is suspected to be the problem, first perform all of the adjustments given in this Section. If this doesn't correct the difficulty, then check the following. Check the ignition system to make sure that the spark plugs, breaker points, and condenser are in good condition and adjusted to the proper specifications. Examine the emission control equipment to make sure that all the vacuum lines are connected and none are blocked or clogged. See the first half of this Chapter. Check the ignition timing adjustment. Check all of the vacuum lines on the engine for loose connections, splits or breaks. Torque the carburetor and intake manifold attaching bolts to the proper specifications. If, after performing all of these checks and adjustments, the problem is still not solved, then you can safely assume that the carburetor is the source of the problem.

OVERHAUL

Efficient carburetion depends greatly on careful cleaning and inspection during overhaul since dirt, gum, water or varnish in or on the carburetor parts are often responsible for poor performance.

Overhaul the carburetor in a clean, dust-free area. Carefully disassemble the carburetor, referring often to the exploded views. Keep all similar and look-alike parts segregated during disassembly and cleaning to avoid accidental interchange during assembly. Make a note of all jet sizes.

When the carburetor is disassembled,

wash all parts (except diaphragms, electric choke units, pump plunger and any other plastic, leather, fiber, or rubber parts) in clean carburetor solvent. Do not leave the parts in the solvent any longer than is necessary to sufficiently loosen the dirt and deposits. Excessive cleaning may remove the special finish from the float bowl and choke valve bodies, leaving these parts unfit for service. Rinse all parts in clean solvent and blow them dry with compressed air or allow them to air dry, while resting on clean, lintless paper. Wipe clean all cork, plastic, leather and fiber parts with a clean, lint-free cloth.

Blow out all passages and jets with compressed air and be sure that there are no restrictions or blockages. Never use wire or similar tools to clean jets, fuel passages or air bleeds. Clean all jets and valves separately to avoid accidental interchange.

Examine all parts for wear or damage. If wear or damage is found, replace the defective parts. Especially, inspect the following:

1. Check the float needle and seat for wear. If wear is found, replace the complete assembly.

2. Check the float hinge pin for wear and the float(s) for dents or distortion. Replace the float if fuel has leaked into it.

3. Check the throttle and choke shaft bores for wear or an out-of-round condition. Damage or wear to the throttle arm, shaft or shaft bore will often require replacement of the throttle body. These parts require a close tolerance of fit; wear may allow air leakage, which could affect starting and idling.

NOTE: *Throttle shafts and bushings are not normally included in overhaul kits. They can be purchased separately.*

4. Inspect the idle mixture adjusting needles for burrs or grooves. Any such condition requires replacement of the needle, since you will not be able to obtain a satisfactory idle.

5. Test the accelerator pump check valves. They should pass air one way, but not the other. Test for proper seating by blowing and sucking on the valve. Replace the valve as necessary. If the valve is satisfactory, wash the valve again to remove moisture.

6. Check the bowl cover for warped surfaces with a straightedge.

7. Closely inspect the valves and seats for wear and damage, replacing as necessary.

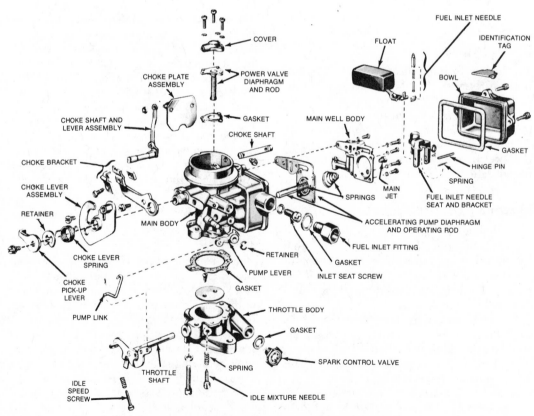

Holley 1904 carburetor assembly, exploded view

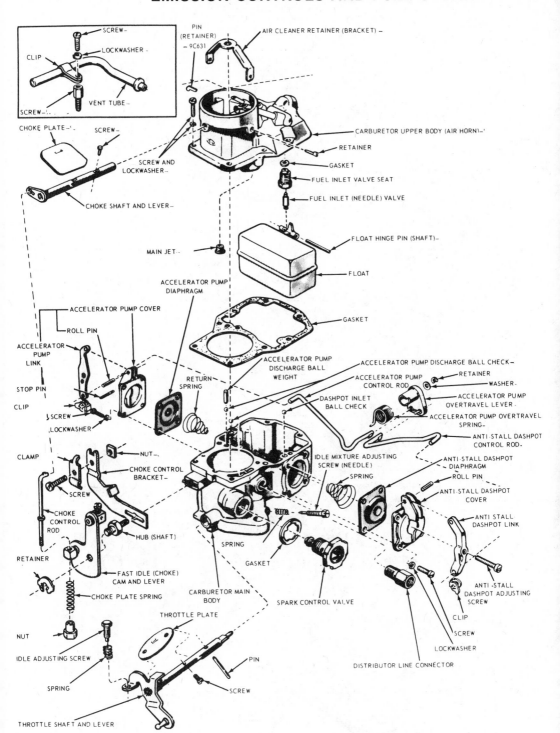

An exploded view of the Ford 1100 1-bb1 carburetor

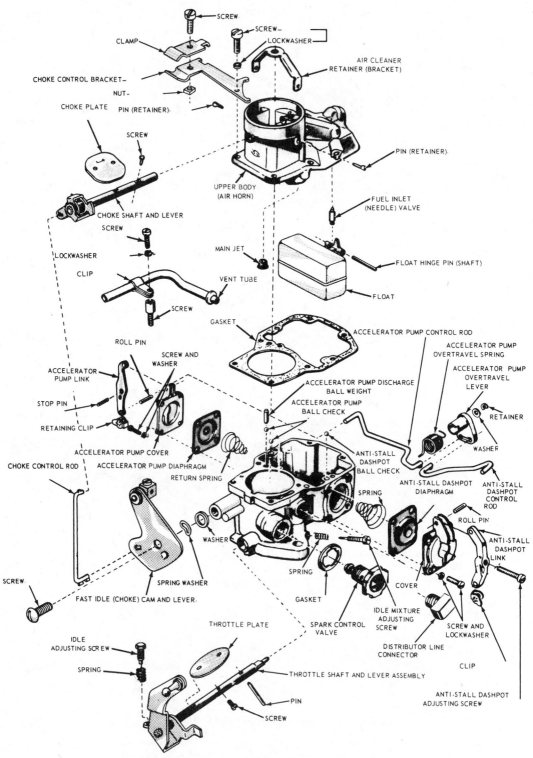

SCREW

SCREW—
LOCKWASHER

CLAMP

AIR CLEANER
RETAINER (BRACKET)

CHOKE CONTROL BRACKET—

NUT—

CHOKE PLATE   PIN (RETAINER)·

SCREW

PIN (RETAINER)·

UPPER BODY
(AIR HORN)

FUEL INLET
(NEEDLE) VALVE

CHOKE SHAFT AND LEVER

SCREW

LOCKWASHER

CLIP

MAIN JET

FLOAT HINGE PIN (SHAFT)

VENT TUBE

FLOAT

SCREW

ROLL PIN

GASKET

ACCELERATOR PUMP CONTROL ROD

ACCELERATOR PUMP
OVERTRAVEL SPRING

SCREW AND
WASHER

ACCELERATOR PUMP DISCHARGE
BALL WEIGHT

ACCELERATOR PUMP
OVERTRAVEL
LEVER

ACCELERATOR
PUMP LINK

ACCELERATOR PUMP
BALL CHECK

RETAINER

STOP PIN

RETAINING CLIP

WASHER

ACCELERATOR PUMP COVER

ANTI-STALL
DASHPOT
BALL CHECK

CHOKE CONTROL ROD

ACCELERATOR PUMP DIAPHRAGM

RETURN SPRING

ANTI-STALL DASHPOT
DIAPHRAGM

ANTI-STALL
DASHPOT
CONTROL
ROD

SPRING

ROLL PIN

ANTI-STALL
DASHPOT
LINK

SCREW·

WASHER

SPRING

SPRING WASHER

SPRING

FAST IDLE (CHOKE) CAM AND LEVER·

COVER

GASKET

IDLE MIXTURE
ADJUSTING
SCREW

SCREW AND
LOCKWASHER

IDLE
ADJUSTING SCREW

THROTTLE PLATE

SPARK CONTROL
VALVE

DISTRIBUTOR LINE
CONNECTOR

CLIP

SPRING

THROTTLE SHAFT AND LEVER ASSEMBLY

ANTI-STALL DASHPOT
ADJUSTING SCREW

PIN

SCREW

An exploded view of the Ford 1101 1-bbl carburetor

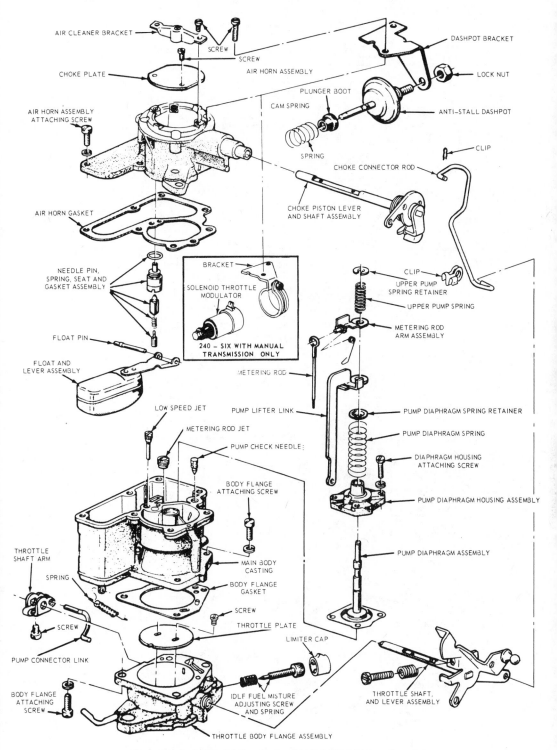

An exploded view of the Carter Model YF 1-bbl carburetor

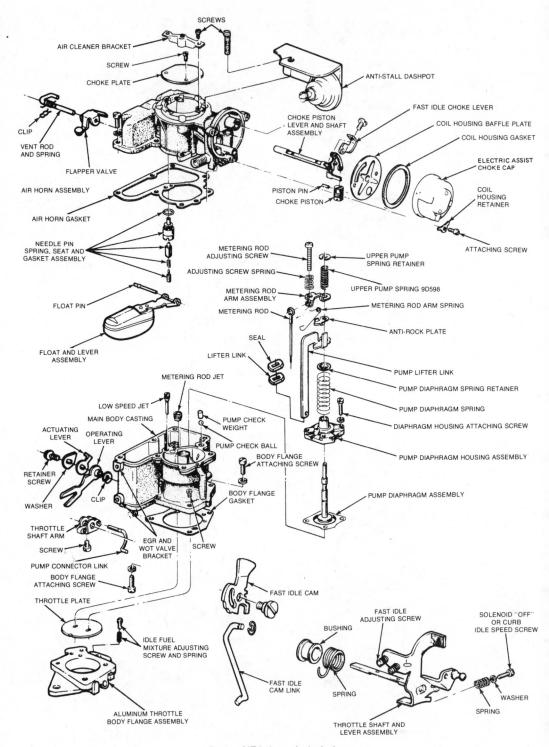

SCREWS

AIR CLEANER BRACKET

SCREW

CHOKE PLATE

ANTI-STALL DASHPOT

CLIP

VENT ROD AND SPRING

FLAPPER VALVE

AIR HORN ASSEMBLY

AIR HORN GASKET

CHOKE PISTON LEVER AND SHAFT ASSEMBLY

FAST IDLE CHOKE LEVER

COIL HOUSING BAFFLE PLATE

COIL HOUSING GASKET

ELECTRIC ASSIST CHOKE CAP

COIL HOUSING RETAINER

PISTON PIN

CHOKE PISTON

ATTACHING SCREW

NEEDLE PIN SPRING, SEAT AND GASKET ASSEMBLY

METERING ROD ADJUSTING SCREW

ADJUSTING SCREW SPRING

METERING ROD ARM ASSEMBLY

METERING ROD

FLOAT PIN

UPPER PUMP SPRING RETAINER

UPPER PUMP SPRING 9D598

METERING ROD ARM SPRING

ANTI-ROCK PLATE

SEAL

LIFTER LINK

FLOAT AND LEVER ASSEMBLY

METERING ROD JET

LOW SPEED JET

MAIN BODY CASTING

ACTUATING LEVER

OPERATING LEVER

PUMP CHECK WEIGHT

PUMP CHECK BALL

RETAINER SCREW

WASHER

CLIP

BODY FLANGE ATTACHING SCREW

BODY FLANGE GASKET

PUMP LIFTER LINK

PUMP DIAPHRAGM SPRING RETAINER

PUMP DIAPHRAGM SPRING

DIAPHRAGM HOUSING ATTACHING SCREW

PUMP DIAPHRAGM HOUSING ASSEMBLY

PUMP DIAPHRAGM ASSEMBLY

THROTTLE SHAFT ARM

SCREW

PUMP CONNECTOR LINK

BODY FLANGE ATTACHING SCREW

THROTTLE PLATE

EGR AND WOT VALVE BRACKET

SCREW

IDLE FUEL MIXTURE ADJUSTING SCREW AND SPRING

ALUMINUM THROTTLE BODY FLANGE ASSEMBLY

FAST IDLE CAM

FAST IDLE CAM LINK

BUSHING

SPRING

FAST IDLE ADJUSTING SCREW

THROTTLE SHAFT AND LEVER ASSEMBLY

SOLENOID "OFF" OR CURB IDLE SPEED SCREW

WASHER

SPRING

Carter YFA-1 exploded view

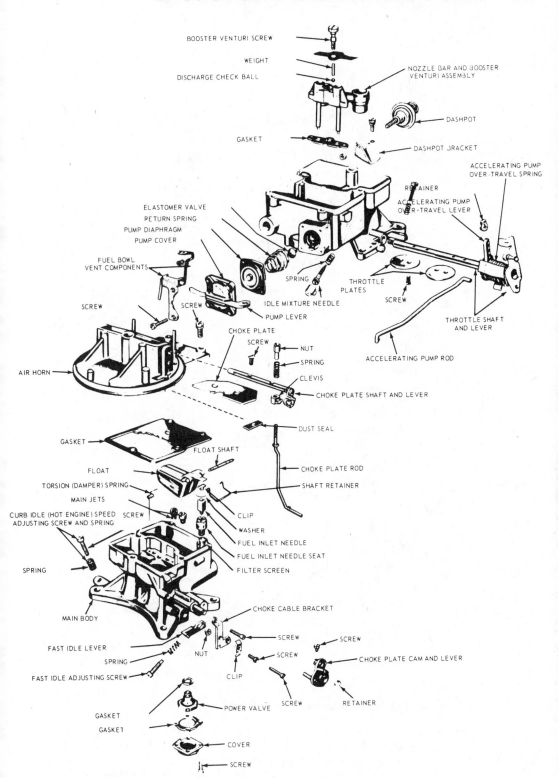

BOOSTER VENTURI SCREW

WEIGHT

DISCHARGE CHECK BALL

NOZZLE BAR AND BOOSTER VENTURI ASSEMBLY

DASHPOT

GASKET

DASHPOT BRACKET

ACCELERATING PUMP OVER-TRAVEL SPRING

RETAINER

ACCELERATING PUMP OVER-TRAVEL LEVER

ELASTOMER VALVE
RETURN SPRING
PUMP DIAPHRAGM
PUMP COVER

FUEL BOWL
VENT COMPONENTS

SPRING

THROTTLE PLATES

SCREW

THROTTLE SHAFT AND LEVER

SCREW

SCREW

IDLE MIXTURE NEEDLE

PUMP LEVER

ACCELERATING PUMP ROD

CHOKE PLATE

SCREW

NUT

SPRING

CLEVIS

CHOKE PLATE SHAFT AND LEVER

AIR HORN

DUST SEAL

GASKET

FLOAT SHAFT

CHOKE PLATE ROD

FLOAT

TORSION (DAMPER) SPRING

SHAFT RETAINER

MAIN JETS

CURB IDLE (HOT ENGINE) SPEED
ADJUSTING SCREW AND SPRING

SCREW

CLIP

WASHER

FUEL INLET NEEDLE

SPRING

FUEL INLET NEEDLE SEAT

FILTER SCREEN

MAIN BODY

CHOKE CABLE BRACKET

FAST IDLE LEVER

SCREW

SCREW

NUT

SPRING

SCREW

CHOKE PLATE CAM AND LEVER

FAST IDLE ADJUSTING SCREW

CLIP

GASKET

POWER VALVE

SCREW

RETAINER

GASKET

COVER

SCREW

An exploded view of the Autolite Model 2100 2-bbl carburetor

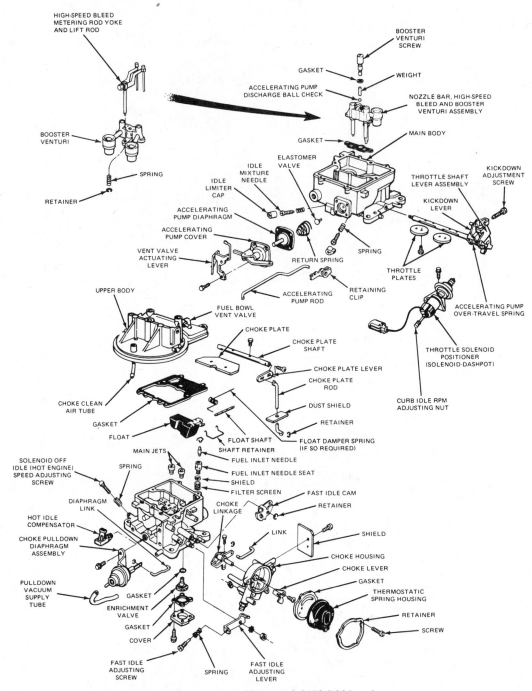

An exploded view of the Motorcraft 2150 2-bbl carburetor

8. After the carburetor is assembled, check the choke valve for freedom of operation.

Carburetor overhaul kits are recommended for each overhaul. These kits contain all gaskets and new parts to replace those which deteriorate most rapidly. Failure to replace all of the parts supplied with the kit (especially gaskets) can result in poor performance later.

Most carburetor manufacturers supply overhaul kits of three basic types: minor repair; major repair; and gasket kits. Basically, they contain the following:

Minor Repair Kits:
• All gaskets

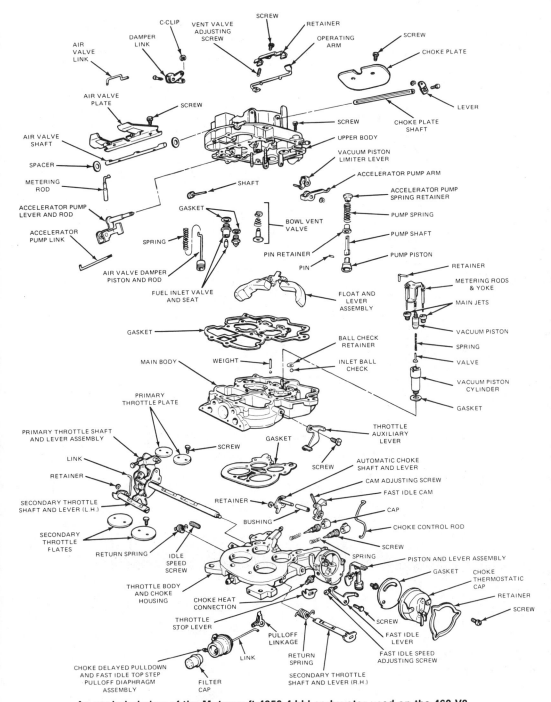

An exploded view of the Motorcraft 4350 4-bbl carburetor used on the 460 V8

- Float needle valve
- Mixture adjusting screws
- All diaphragms
- Spring for the pump diaphragm

Major Repair Kits:
- All jets and gaskets
- All diaphragms

- Float needle valve
- Mixture adjusting screws
- Pump ball valve
- Main jet carrier
- Float
- Some float bowl cover hold-down screws and washers

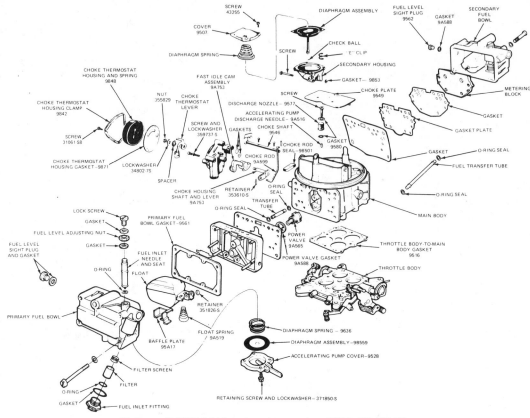

Motorcraft 4180 4-bbl carburetor used on 1981–82 460 V8

Gasket Kits:
• All gaskets

After cleaning and checking all components, reassemble the carburetor, using new parts and referring to the exploded view. When reassembling, make sure that all screws and jets are tight in their seats, but do not overtighten, as the tips will be distorted. Tighten all screws gradually, in rotation. Do not tighten needle valves into their seats; uneven jetting will result. Always use new gaskets. Be sure to adjust the float level.

FLOAT AND FUEL LEVEL ADJUSTMENTS

Holley 1904

1. Remove the carburetor from the engine.

2. Remove the float bowl cover.

3. Place a $^{23}/_{32}$ inch gauge under the float hinge bracket. Loosen the seat screw and allow the float to rest lightly on the gauge.

4. Tighten the seat screw. This sets the fuel level.

5. Remove the $^{23}/_{32}$ inch gauge and invert the carburetor.

6. Place an $^{11}/_{64}$ inch gauge between the top of the float and the top inside surface of the float bowl. To adjust the float level, bend the tab on the float arm. The gauge should pass lightly between float and bowl.

7. Turn the carburetor upright and slide a $^{3}/_{16}$ inch gauge between the bottom of the float and the bottom inside surface of the float bowl. Bend the upright tang on the float lever to adjust the float drop. The gauge should pass lightly between float and bowl.

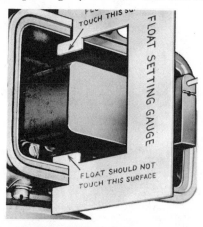

Holley 1904 bench float setting

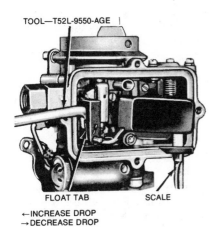

Holley 1904 float drop setting

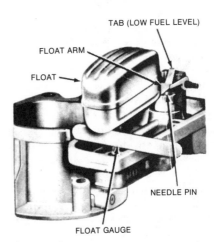

Float level adjustment for the Carter Model YF 1-bbl carburetor

8. Using a new bowl cover gasket and a new carburetor mounting gasket, install the cover on the bowl and the carburetor on the engine.

Ford Model 1100, 1101 1-bbl and Carter Model YF 1-bbl

1. Remove the carburetor air horn and gasket from the carburetor.

2. Invert the air horn assembly, and check the clearance from the top of the float to the bottom of the air horn. Hold the air horn at eye level when gauging the float level. The float arm (lever) should be resting on the needle pin. Do not load the needle when adjusting the float. Bend the float arm as necessary to adjust the float level (clearance). Do not bend the tab at the end of the float arm, because it prevents the float from striking the bottom of the fuel bowl when empty.

3. Turn the air horn over and hold it upright and let the float hang free. Measure the maximum clearance from the top of the

float to the bottom of the air horn with the float gauge. Hold the air horn at eye level when gauging the dimension. To adjust the float drop, bend the tab at the end of the float arm.

4. Install the carburetor air horn with a new gasket.

Autolite (Motorcraft) Model 2100, 2150 2-bbl (Wet Adjustment)

1. Operate the engine until it reaches normal operating temperature. Place the vehicle on a level surface and stop the engine.

2. Remove the carburetor air cleaner assembly.

3. Remove the air horn attaching screws and the carburetor identification tag. Temporarily, leave the air horn and gasket in position on the carburetor main body and start

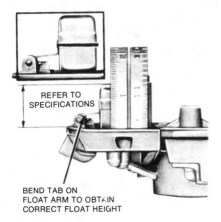

Float level adjustment for the Autolite (Ford) Model 1100 1-bbl carburetor

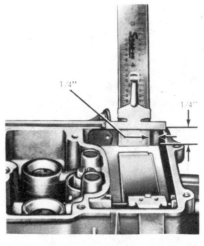

Float level adjustment for the Autolite Model 2100 and 2150 2-bbl carburetor

the engine. Let the engine idle for a few minutes, then rotate the air horn out of the way and remove the air horn gasket to provide access to the float assembly.

4. While the engine is idling, use a scale to measure the vertical distance from the top machined surface of the carburetor main body to the level of the fuel in the fuel bowl. The measurement must be made at least ¼ in. away from any vertical surface to assure an accurate reading, because the surface of the fuel is concave—being higher at the edges than in the center. Care must be exercised to measure the fuel level at the point of contact with the float.

5. If any adjustment is required, stop the engine to minimize the hazard of fire due to spilled gasoline. To adjust the fuel level, bend the float tab contacting the fuel inlet valve upward in relation to the original position to raise the fuel level, and downward to lower it. Each time the float is adjusted, the engine must be started and permitted to idle for a few minutes to stabilize the fuel level. Check the fuel level after each adjustment, until the specified level is obtained.

6. Assemble the carburetor in the reverse order of disassembly, using a new gasket between the air horn and the main carburetor body.

Motorcraft Model 4180

Dry Adjustment

NOTE: *The dry adjustment is a necessary preliminary to the wet adjustment, which is the real adjustment.*

1. With the carburetor installed, and the engine cold, remove the carburetor tops.

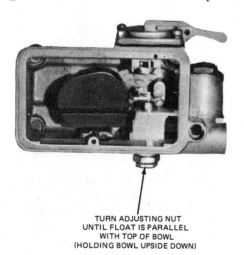

TURN ADJUSTING NUT
UNTIL FLOAT IS PARALLEL
WITH TOP OF BOWL
(HOLDING BOWL UPSIDE DOWN)

2. Invert the tops and adjust the floats so that they are parallel with the fuel bowls.

3. Install the carburetor top.

WET ADJUSTMENT

1. Run the engine to normal operating temperature and park the truck on level ground.

2. Remove the air cleaner.

3. Each bowl's level must be checked separately. Place a container under the fuel level sight plug. Remove the plug. The fuel should be at the bottom edge of the hole.

4. If the level is too high, loosen the level adjusting locknut. Turn the screw Clockwise until the level is BELOW the opening. The turn is counterclockwise until the level is just at the opening.

5. Tighten the locknut and install the plug. Wait until the level is stabilized and check again.

6. If the level is too low, Loosen the locknut and turn the screw counterclockwise until the level is just to the bottom edge of the hole.

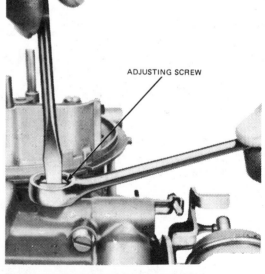

ADJUSTING SCREW

Wet float adjustment, Motorcraft 4180

Motorcraft Model 4350

1. Adjustments to the fuel level are best made with the carburetor removed from the engine.

2. Invert the air horn assembly and remove the gasket from the surface.

3. Use a T-scale to measure the distance from the floats to the air horn casting. Position the scale horizontally over the flat sur-

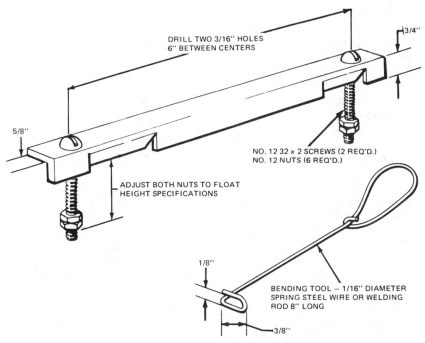

DRILL TWO 3/16" HOLES
6" BETWEEN CENTERS

3/4"

5/8"

NO. 12 32 x 2 SCREWS (2 REQ'D.)
NO. 12 NUTS (6 REQ'D.)

ADJUST BOTH NUTS TO FLOAT
HEIGHT SPECIFICATIONS

1/8"

BENDING TOOL – 1/16" DIAMETER
SPRING STEEL WIRE OR WELDING
ROD 8" LONG

3/8"

Motorcraft 4350 float gauge and bending tool fabrication details

face of both floats at the free ends and parallel to the air horn casting. Hold the lower end of the vertical scale in full contact with the smooth surface of the air horn.

CAUTION: *The end of the vertical scale must not come into contact with any gasket sealing ridges while measuring the float level.*

4. The free end of each float should just touch the horizontal scale. If one float is lower than the other, twist the float and lever assembly slightly to correct.

5. Adjust the float level by bending the tab which contacts the needle and seat assembly.

NOTE: *The illustrations show an alternate*

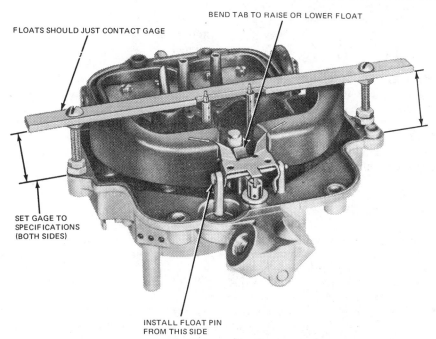

BEND TAB TO RAISE OR LOWER FLOAT

FLOATS SHOULD JUST CONTACT GAGE

SET GAGE TO
SPECIFICATIONS
(BOTH SIDES)

INSTALL FLOAT PIN
FROM THIS SIDE

Using the fabricated float level gauge on the Motorcraft 4350

method of adjusting the floats on the model 4300 carburetor.

The procedure includes the fabrication of a gauge and a bending device. After fabricating the gauge, it is possible to adjust it to the specified dimensions and insert it into the air horn outboard holes. Both pontoons should just touch the gauge.

A float tab bending tool is also shown and may be used in the following manner.

To raise the float: insert the open end of the bending tool to the RIGHT side of the float lever tab and between the needle and float hinge. Raise the float lever off of the needle and bend the tab downward.

To lower the float: insert the bending tool to the LEFT side of the float lever tab between the needle and float hinge, support the float lever, and bend the tab upward.

FAST IDLE SPEED ADJUSTMENT

Holley 1904, Ford Model 1100, 1101 1-bbl

The fast idle is controlled by the idle adjusting screw bearing against the bottom of the choke cam and lever during idle or closed-throttle conditions. The choke cam and lever opens the throttle slightly, through contact of the idle adjusting screw with the cam, as the manual choke position is selected. Higher engine idle speeds are automatically provided through contact of the idle adjusting screw with the cam. The curb idle must be adjusted correctly for the fast idle to be proper during application of the choke.

1963–74 Carter Model YF 1-bbl

1. Position the fast idle screw on the kickdown step of the fast idle cam against the shoulder of the high step.

2. Adjust by bending the choke plate connecting rod to obtain the specified clearance between the lower edge of the choke plate and the carburetor air horn. Use a drill bit inserted between the lower edge of the choke plate and the carburetor air horn.

3. With the engine at operating temperature, air cleaner removed and a tachometer attached according to the manufacturer's instructions, manually rotate the fast idle cam to the top or second step as specified while holding the choke plate fully open. Turn the fast idle adjustment screw inward or outward as required to obtain the specified speed.

4. When setting the fast idle speed, all distributor vacuum and EGR controls must

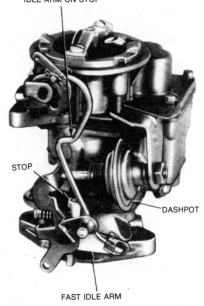

CHOKE WIDE OPEN—BEND FOR LIGHT CONTACT OF FAST IDLE ARM ON STOP

STOP

DASHPOT

FAST IDLE ARM

Fast idle speed adjustment on the Carter Model YF 1-bbl carburetor

be disconnected and plugged to insure proper speeds during cold operation.

1975–80 Carter YF, and YFA 1-bbl

1. Run the engine to normal operating temperature.

2. Remove the air cleaner and attach a tachometer to the engine according to the manufacturer's instructions.

3. Manually rotate the fast idle to the top step while holding the choke plate fully opened.

4. Rotate the cam until the fast idle adjusting screw rests on the cam step specified on the underhood emissions sticker.

5. Turn the fast idle speed adjusting screw to obtain the speed specified in the Tune-Up Charts.

NOTE: *When this operation is performed outdoors in cold weather, all vacuum controls to the distributor and EGR valve must be bypassed. This can be done by connecting a jumper hose from the DIST port on the carburetor to the vacuum advance port of the distributor and by disconnecting and plugging the EGR vacuum source hose.*

Autolite (Motorcraft) Model 2100, 2150 2-bbl

The fast idle speed adjustment is made in the same manner as for the Model YF carburetor, starting at Step 3.

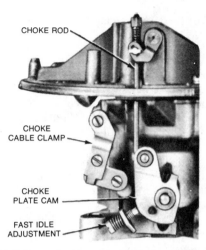

Fast idle speed adjustment on the Autolite Model 2100 2-bbl carburetor

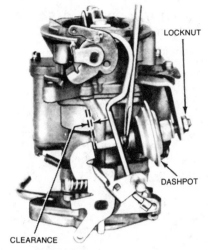

Anti-stall dashpot adjustment on the Carter Model YF 1-bbl carburetor

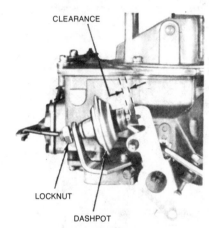

Anti-stall dashpot adjustment on the Autolite Model 2100 2-bbl carburetor

To adjust the model 2100 fast idle cam clearance, follow the procedure given below:

1. Rotate the choke thermostatic spring housing 90° in the rich direction.

2. Position the fast idle speed screw on the high step of the cam.

3. Depress the choke pulldown diaphragm against the diaphragm stop screw to place the choke in the pulldown position.

4. While holding the choke pulldown diaphragm depressed, open the throttle slightly and allow the fast idle cam to fall.

5. Close the throttle and check the position of the fast idle cam. The screw should contact the cam at the V mark on the cam.

6. Adjust the fast idle cam adjusting screw to obtain the proper setting.

Motorcraft 4180 and 4350 4-bbl

The fast idle speed adjustment is made in the same manner as for the Model YF carburetor, starting with Step 3.

DASHPOT ADJUSTMENT

1. Remove the air cleaner.

2. Loosen the anti-stall dashpot locknut.

3. With the choke plate open, hold the throttle plate closed (idle position), and check the clearance between the throttle lever and the dashpot plunger tip with a feeler gauge.

NOTE: *On the Ford Model 1100 1-bbl carburetor, turn the adjusting screw 3 turns in after the screw contacts the diaphragm assembly.*

Anti-stall dashpot adjustment on the Autolite (Ford) Model 1100 1-bbl carburetor

ACCELERATING PUMP CLEARANCE ADJUSTMENT

Ford 1100

1. Insert the roll pin in the lower hole (HI position in the lever stop hold).

2. Position the throttle and choke linkage so that the throttle plate will seat in the throttle bore. Hold the throttle plates in the closed position. Position a gauge or drill of the specified thickness between the roll pin and the cover surface. Bend the accelerating pump actuating rod to obtain the specified gauge or drill clearance between the pump cover and the roll pin in the pump lever.

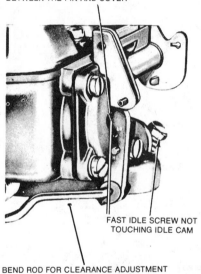

WITH THROTTLE PLATE CLOSED, INSERT A *GAUGE* THAT EQUALS THE SPECIFIED CLEARANCE BETWEEN THE PIN AND COVER

FAST IDLE SCREW NOT TOUCHING IDLE CAM

BEND ROD FOR CLEARANCE ADJUSTMENT

Accelerating pump clearance adjustment, Ford 1100

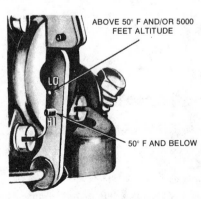

ABOVE 50° F AND/OR 5000 FEET ALTITUDE

LO

HI

50° F AND BELOW

Accelerating pump lever adjustment, Ford 1100

ACCELERATING PUMP STROKE ADJUSTMENTS

Ford 1100

Acceleration requirements in various climates are satisfied by controlling the amount of fuel discharged by the accelerating pump. The pump stroke is controlled by changing the location of the roll pin in the lever stop hole.

For operation in ambient temperatures 50° F and below, place the roll pin in the hole of the pump operating lever marked HI (lower hole). For best performance and economy at normal ambient temperatures and high altitude (above 50° F and/or above 5,000 feet altitude), place the roll pin in the LO (upper hole) of the lever.

Motorcraft 2150

The accelerating pump stroke has been factory set for a particular engine application and should not be readjusted. If the stroke has been changed from the specified hole reset to specifications by following these procedures.

1. To release the rod from the retaining clip, lift upward on the portion of the clip that snaps over the shaft and then disengage the rod.

2. Position the clip over the specified hole in the overtravel lever and insert the operating rod through the clip and the overtravel lever. Snap the end of the clip over the rod to secure.

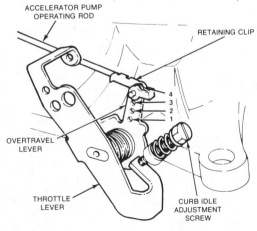

ACCELERATOR PUMP OPERATING ROD

RETAINING CLIP

4
3
2
1

OVERTRAVEL LEVER

THROTTLE LEVER

CURB IDLE ADJUSTMENT SCREW

Motorcraft 2150 accelerating pump stroke adjustment

CHILTON'S
FUEL ECONOMY
& TUNE-UP TIPS

Tune-up • Spark Plug Diagnosis • Emission Controls

Fuel System • Cooling System • Tires and Wheels

General Maintenance

CHILTON'S FUEL ECONOMY & TUNE-UP TIPS

Fuel economy is important to everyone, no matter what kind of vehicle you drive. The maintenance-minded motorist can save both money and fuel using these tips and the periodic maintenance and tune-up procedures in this Repair and Tune-Up Guide.

There are more than 130,000,000 cars and trucks registered for private use in the United States. Each travels an average of 10-12,000 miles per year, and, and in total they consume close to 70 billion gallons of fuel each year. This represents nearly ⅔ of the oil imported by the United States each year. The Federal government's goal is to reduce consumption 10% by 1985. A variety of methods are either already in use or under serious consideration, and they all affect you driving and the cars you will drive. In addition to "down-sizing", the auto industry is using or investigating the use of electronic fuel delivery, electronic engine controls and alternative engines for use in smaller and lighter vehicles, among other alternatives to meet the federally mandated Corporate Average Fuel Economy (CAFE) of 27.5 mpg by 1985. The government, for its part, is considering rationing, mandatory driving curtailments and tax increases on motor vehicle fuel in an effort to reduce consumption. The government's goal of a 10% reduction could be realized — and further government regulation avoided — if every private vehicle could use just 1 less gallon of fuel per week.

How Much Can You Save?

Tests have proven that almost anyone can make at least a 10% reduction in fuel consumption through regular maintenance and tune-ups. When a major manufacturer of spark plugs sur-

TUNE-UP

1. Check the cylinder compression to be sure the engine will really benefit from a tune-up and that it is capable of producing good fuel economy. A tune-up will be wasted on an engine in poor mechanical condition.

2. Replace spark plugs regularly. New spark plugs alone can increase fuel economy 3%.

3. Be sure the spark plugs are the correct type (heat range) for your vehicle. See the Tune-Up Specifications.

Heat range refers to the spark plug's ability to conduct heat away from the firing end. It must conduct the heat away in an even pattern to avoid becoming a source of pre-ignition, yet it must also operate hot enough to burn off conductive deposits that could cause misfiring.

The heat range is usually indicated by a number on the spark plug, part of the manufacturer's designation for each individual spark plug. The numbers in bold-face indicate the heat range in each manufacturer's identification system.

Periodically, check the spark plugs to be sure they are firing efficiently. They are excellent indicators of the internal condition of your engine.

Manufacturer	Typical Designation
AC	R **45** TS
Bosch (old)	WA **145** T30
Bosch (new)	HR **8** Y
Champion	RBL **15** Y
Fram/Autolite	4**15**
Mopar	P-**62** PR
Motorcraft	BRF-**42**
NGK	BP **5** ES-15
Nippondenso	W **16** EP
Prestolite	14GR **5** 2A

On AC, Bosch (new), Champion, Fram/Autolite, Mopar, Motorcraft and Prestolite, a higher number indicates a hotter plug. On Bosch (old), NGK and Nippondenso, a higher number indicates a colder plug.

4. Make sure the spark plugs are properly gapped. See the Tune-Up Specifications in this book.

5. Be sure the spark plugs are firing efficiently. The illustrations on the next 2 pages show you how to "read" the firing end of the spark plug.

6. Check the ignition timing and set it to specifications. Tests show that almost all cars have incorrect ignition timing by more than 2°.

veyed over 6,000 cars nationwide, they found that a tune-up, on cars that needed one, increased fuel economy over 11%. Replacing worn plugs alone, accounted for a 3% increase. The same test also revealed that 8 out of every 10 vehicles will have some maintenance deficiency that will directly affect fuel economy, emissions or performance. Most of this mileage-robbing neglect could be prevented with regular maintenance.

Modern engines require that all of the functioning systems operate properly for maximum efficiency. A malfunction anywhere wastes fuel. You can keep your vehicle running as efficiently and economically as possible, by being aware of your vehicle's operating and performance characteristics. If your vehicle suddenly develops performance or fuel economy problems it could be due to one or more of the following:

PROBLEM	POSSIBLE CAUSE
Engine Idles Rough	Ignition timing, idle mixture, vacuum leak or something amiss in the emission control system.
Hesitates on Acceleration	Dirty carburetor or fuel filter, improper accelerator pump setting, ignition timing or fouled spark plugs.
Starts Hard or Fails to Start	Worn spark plugs, improperly set automatic choke, ice (or water) in fuel system.
Stalls Frequently	Automatic choke improperly adjusted and possible dirty air filter or fuel filter.
Performs Sluggishly	Worn spark plugs, dirty fuel or air filter, ignition timing or automatic choke out of adjustment.

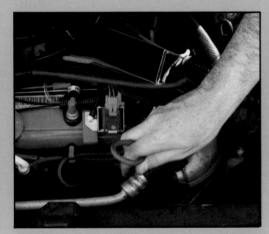

Check spark plug wires on conventional point type ignition for cracks by bending them in a loop around your finger.

Be sure that spark plug wires leading to adjacent cylinders do not run too close together. (Photo courtesy Champion Spark Plug Co.)

7. If your vehicle does not have electronic ignition, check the points, rotor and cap as specified.

8. Check the spark plug wires (used with conventional point-type ignitions) for cracks and burned or broken insulation by bending them in a loop around your finger. Cracked wires decrease fuel efficiency by failing to deliver full voltage to the spark plugs. One misfiring spark plug can cost you as much as 2 mpg.

9. Check the routing of the plug wires. Misfiring can be the result of spark plug leads to adjacent cylinders running parallel to each other and too close together. One wire tends to pick up voltage from the other causing it to fire "out of time".

10. Check all electrical and ignition circuits for voltage drop and resistance.

11. Check the distributor mechanical and/or vacuum advance mechanisms for proper functioning. The vacuum advance can be checked by twisting the distributor plate in the opposite direction of rotation. It should spring back when released.

12. Check and adjust the valve clearance on engines with mechanical lifters. The clearance should be slightly loose rather than too tight.

SPARK PLUG DIAGNOSIS

Normal

APPEARANCE: This plug is typical of one operating normally. The insulator nose varies from a light tan to grayish color with slight electrode wear. The presence of slight deposits is normal on used plugs and will have no adverse effect on engine performance. The spark plug heat range is correct for the engine and the engine is running normally.

CAUSE: Properly running engine.

RECOMMENDATION: Before reinstalling this plug, the electrodes should be cleaned and filed square. Set the gap to specifications. If the plug has been in service for more than 10-12,000 miles, the entire set should probably be replaced with a fresh set of the same heat range.

Oil Deposits

APPEARANCE: The firing end of the plug is covered with a wet, oily coating.

CAUSE: The problem is poor oil control. On high mileage engines, oil is leaking past the rings or valve guides into the combustion chamber. A common cause is also a plugged PCV valve, and a ruptured fuel pump diaphragm can also cause this condition. Oil fouled plugs such as these are often found in new or recently overhauled engines, before normal oil control is achieved, and can be cleaned and reinstalled.

RECOMMENDATION: A hotter spark plug may temporarily relieve the problem, but the engine is probably in need of work.

Incorrect Heat Range

APPEARANCE: The effects of high temperature on a spark plug are indicated by clean white, often blistered insulator. This can also be accompanied by excessive wear of the electrode, and the absence of deposits.

CAUSE: Check for the correct spark plug heat range. A plug which is too hot for the engine can result in overheating. A car operated mostly at high speeds can require a colder plug. Also check ignition timing, cooling system level, fuel mixture and leaking intake manifold.

RECOMMENDATION: If all ignition and engine adjustments are known to be correct, and no other malfunction exists, install spark plugs one heat range colder.

Photos Courtesy Fram Corporation

Carbon Deposits

APPEARANCE: Carbon fouling is easily identified by the presence of dry, soft, black, sooty deposits.

CAUSE: Changing the heat range can often lead to carbon fouling, as can prolonged slow, stop-and-start driving. If the heat range is correct, carbon fouling can be attributed to a rich fuel mixture, sticking choke, clogged air cleaner, worn breaker points, retarded timing or low compression. If only one or two plugs are carbon fouled, check for corroded or cracked wires on the affected plugs. Also look for cracks in the distributor cap between the towers of affected cylinders.

RECOMMENDATION: After the problem is corrected, these plugs can be cleaned and reinstalled if not worn severely.

MMT Fouled

APPEARANCE: Spark plugs fouled by MMT (Methycyclopentadienyl Maganese Tricarbonyl) have reddish, rusty appearance on the insulator and side electrode.

CAUSE: MMT is an anti-knock additive in gasoline used to replace lead. During the combustion process, the MMT leaves a reddish deposit on the insulator and side electrode.

RECOMMENDATION: No engine malfunction is indicated and the deposits will not affect plug performance any more than lead deposits (see Ash Deposits). MMT fouled plugs can be cleaned, regapped and reinstalled.

High Speed Glazing

APPEARANCE: Glazing appears as shiny coating on the plug, either yellow or tan in color.

CAUSE: During hard, fast acceleration, plug temperatures rise suddenly. Deposits from normal combustion have no chance to fluff-off; instead, they melt on the insulator forming an electrically conductive coating which causes misfiring.

RECOMMENDATION: Glazed plugs are not easily cleaned. They should be replaced with a fresh set of plugs of the correct heat range. If the condition recurs, using plugs with a heat range one step colder may cure the problem.

Ash (Lead) Deposits

APPEARANCE: Ash deposits are characterized by light brown or white colored deposits crusted on the side or center electrodes. In some cases it may give the plug a rusty appearance.

CAUSE: Ash deposits are normally derived from oil or fuel additives burned during normal combustion. Normally they are harmless, though excessive amounts can cause misfiring. If deposits are excessive in short mileage, the valve guides may be worn.

RECOMMENDATION: Ash-fouled plugs can be cleaned, gapped and reinstalled.

Detonation

APPEARANCE: Detonation is usually characterized by a broken plug insulator.

CAUSE: A portion of the fuel charge will begin to burn spontaneously, from the increased heat following ignition. The explosion that results applies extreme pressure to engine components, frequently damaging spark plugs and pistons.

Detonation can result by over-advanced ignition timing, inferior gasoline (low octane) lean air/fuel mixture, poor carburetion, engine lugging or an increase in compression ratio due to combustion chamber deposits or engine modification.

RECOMMENDATION: Replace the plugs after correcting the problem.

Photos Courtesy Champion Spark Plug Co.

EMISSION CONTROLS

13. Be aware of the general condition of the emission control system. It contributes to reduced pollution and should be serviced regularly to maintain efficient engine operation.

14. Check all vacuum lines for dried, cracked or brittle conditions. Something as simple as a leaking vacuum hose can cause poor performance and loss of economy.

15. Avoid tampering with the emission control system. Attempting to improve fuel econ-

FUEL SYSTEM

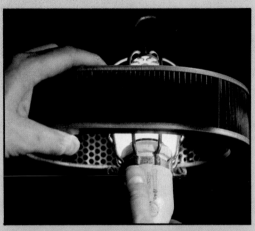

Check the air filter with a light behind it. If you can see light through the filter it can be reused.

Extremely clogged filters should be discarded and replaced with a new one.

18. Replace the air filter regularly. A dirty air filter richens the air/fuel mixture and can increase fuel consumption as much as 10%. Tests show that ⅓ of all vehicles have air filters in need of replacement.

19. Replace the fuel filter at least as often as recommended.

20. Set the idle speed and carburetor mixture to specifications.

21. Check the automatic choke. A sticking or malfunctioning choke wastes gas.

22. During the summer months, adjust the automatic choke for a leaner mixture which will produce faster engine warm-ups.

COOLING SYSTEM

29. Be sure all accessory drive belts are in good condition. Check for cracks or wear.

30. Adjust all accessory drive belts to proper tension.

31. Check all hoses for swollen areas, worn spots, or loose clamps.

32. Check coolant level in the radiator or expansion tank.

33. Be sure the thermostat is operating properly. A stuck thermostat delays engine warm-up and a cold engine uses nearly twice as much fuel as a warm engine.

34. Drain and replace the engine coolant at least as often as recommended. Rust and scale

TIRES & WHEELS

38. Check the tire pressure often with a pencil type gauge. Tests by a major tire manufacturer show that 90% of all vehicles have at least 1 tire improperly inflated. Better mileage can be achieved by over-inflating tires, but never exceed the maximum inflation pressure on the side of the tire.

39. If possible, install radial tires. Radial tires deliver as much as ½ mpg more than bias belted tires.

40. Avoid installing super-wide tires. They only create extra rolling resistance and decrease fuel mileage. Stick to the manufacturer's recommendations.

41. Have the wheels properly balanced.

omy by tampering with emission controls is more likely to worsen fuel economy than improve it. Emission control changes on modern engines are not readily reversible.

16. Clean (or replace) the EGR valve and lines as recommended.

17. Be sure that all vacuum lines and hoses are reconnected properly after working under the hood. An unconnected or misrouted vacuum line can wreak havoc with engine performance.

23. Check for fuel leaks at the carburetor, fuel pump, fuel lines and fuel tank. Be sure all lines and connections are tight.

24. Periodically check the tightness of the carburetor and intake manifold attaching nuts and bolts. These are a common place for vacuum leaks to occur.

25. Clean the carburetor periodically and lubricate the linkage.

26. The condition of the tailpipe can be an excellent indicator of proper engine combustion. After a long drive at highway speeds, the inside of the tailpipe should be a light grey in color. Black or soot on the insides indicates an overly rich mixture.

27. Check the fuel pump pressure. The fuel pump may be supplying more fuel than the engine needs.

28. Use the proper grade of gasoline for your engine. Don't try to compensate for knocking or "pinging" by advancing the ignition timing. This practice will only increase plug temperature and the chances of detonation or pre-ignition with relatively little performance gain.

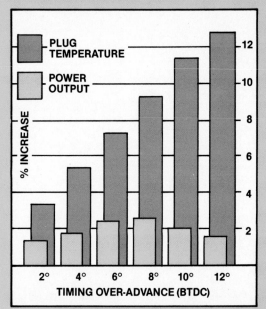

Increasing ignition timing past the specified setting results in a drastic increase in spark plug temperature with increased chance of detonation or preignition. Performance increase is considerably less. (Photo courtesy Champion Spark Plug Co.)

that form in the engine should be flushed out to allow the engine to operate at peak efficiency.

35. Clean the radiator of debris that can decrease cooling efficiency.

36. Install a flex-type or electric cooling fan, if you don't have a clutch type fan. Flex fans use curved plastic blades to push more air at low speeds when more cooling is needed; at high speeds the blades flatten out for less resistance. Electric fans only run when the engine temperature reaches a predetermined level.

37. Check the radiator cap for a worn or cracked gasket. If the cap does not seal properly, the cooling system will not function properly.

42. Be sure the front end is correctly aligned. A misaligned front end actually has wheels going in differed directions. The increased drag can reduce fuel economy by .3 mpg.

43. Correctly adjust the wheel bearings. Wheel bearings that are adjusted too tight increase rolling resistance.

Check tire pressures regularly with a reliable pocket type gauge. Be sure to check the pressure on a cold tire.

GENERAL MAINTENANCE

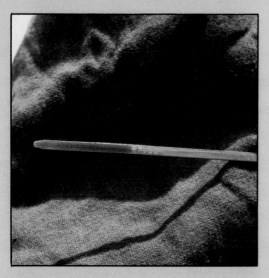

Check the fluid levels (particularly engine oil) on a regular basis. Be sure to check the oil for grit, water or other contamination.

A vacuum gauge is another excellent indicator of internal engine condition and can also be installed in the dash as a mileage indicator.

44. Periodically check the fluid levels in the engine, power steering pump, master cylinder, automatic transmission and drive axle.

45. Change the oil at the recommended interval and change the filter at every oil change. Dirty oil is thick and causes extra friction between moving parts, cutting efficiency and increasing wear. A worn engine requires more frequent tune-ups and gets progressively worse fuel economy. In general, use the lightest viscosity oil for the driving conditions you will encounter.

46. Use the recommended viscosity fluids in the transmission and axle.

47. Be sure the battery is fully charged for fast starts. A slow starting engine wastes fuel.

48. Be sure battery terminals are clean and tight.

49. Check the battery electrolyte level and add distilled water if necessary.

50. Check the exhaust system for crushed pipes, blockages and leaks.

51. Adjust the brakes. Dragging brakes or brakes that are not releasing create increased drag on the engine.

52. Install a vacuum gauge or miles-per-gallon gauge. These gauges visually indicate engine vacuum in the intake manifold. High vacuum = good mileage and low vacuum = poorer mileage. The gauge can also be an excellent indicator of internal engine conditions.

53. Be sure the clutch is properly adjusted. A slipping clutch wastes fuel.

54. Check and periodically lubricate the heat control valve in the exhaust manifold. A sticking or inoperative valve prevents engine warm-up and wastes gas.

55. Keep accurate records to check fuel economy over a period of time. A sudden drop in fuel economy may signal a need for tune-up or other maintenance.

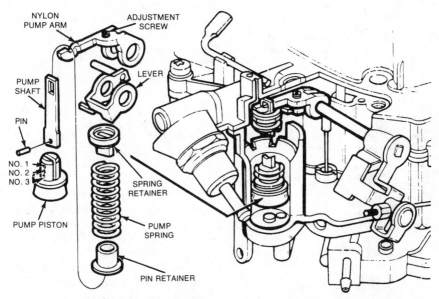

Motorcraft 4180, 4350 accelerating pump stroke adjustment

Motorcraft 4350

The accelerator pump has only one adjustment, a piston-to-shaft pin position which is set at the factory to deliver the proper amount of fuel for the engine on which it is installed. This setting should not be changed from the specified adjustment.

The control rod that operates the accelerator pump also operates the limiter that controls the height of the main metering rod piston.

Do not turn the vacuum limiter lever adjusting nut in order to adjust the stroke of the accelerator pump. This adjustment is set at the factory and changing it could affect drivability of the vehicle.

Remove the air horn assembly and invert it.

Disconnect the accelerator pump from the operating arm by holding downward on the spring and sliding the arm out of the pump shaft slot.

1. Disassemble the spring and nylon keeper that retains the adjustment pin. If the pin is not in the specified hole, remove it, reposition the shaft to the correct hole in the piston assembly and re-install the pin.

2. Slide the nylon retainer over the pin and position the spring on the shaft. Compress the spring on the shaft and install the pump on the pump arm.

ACCELERATING PUMP LEVER ADJUSTMENT
Motorcraft 4180

1. With the throttle plates wide open, insert a feeler gauge between the lever adjustment screw head and the pump arm when the arm is depressed manually.

2. If adjustment is required, loosen the adjusting screw locknut and turn the screw to obtain proper clearance.

CHOKE PULLDOWN ADJUSTMENT
Ford 1100

1. Insert a drill or gauge of the specified size between the choke plate and the inside of the air horn, and place the choke linkage in the full-choke position.

2. While maintaining the full-choke position, adjust the nut on the choke connector (pull-down) rod to just contact the swivel on the cam lever.

Carter YF, YFA

1. Remove the air cleaner. Remove the choke thermostatic spring housing from the carburetor.

2. Bend a 0.026 inch diameter wire gauge at a 90 degree angle approximately ⅛ inch from one end. Insert the bent end of the gauge between the choke piston slot and the

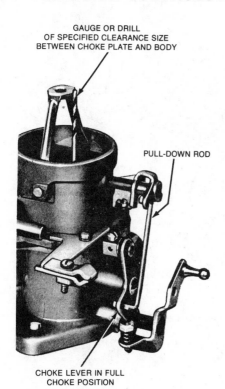

GAUGE OR DRILL
OF SPECIFIED CLEARANCE SIZE
BETWEEN CHOKE PLATE AND BODY

PULL-DOWN ROD

CHOKE LEVER IN FULL
CHOKE POSITION

Ford 1100 choke pull-down adjustment

right hand slot in the choke housing. Rotate the choke piston lever counterclockwise until the gauge is snug in the piston slot.

3. Exert a light pressure on the choke piston lever to hold the gauge in place, then use a drill gauge with a diameter equal to the specified clearance between the lower edge

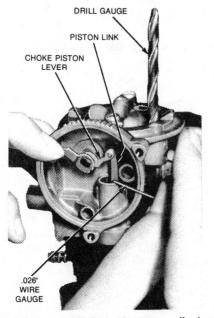

DRILL GAUGE

PISTON LINK

CHOKE PISTON
LEVER

.026"
WIRE
GAUGE

Carter YF choke pull-down clearance adjustment

of the choke plate and the carburetor bore to check clearance.

4. To adjust the choke plate pulldown clearance, bend the choke piston lever as required to obtain the specified setting. Remove the choke piston lever for bending to prevent distorting the piston link, causing erratic choke operation.

5. Install the choke thermostatic spring housing and gasket. Set the housing to specifications.

Autolite 2100

1. Remove the air cleaner.

2. With the engine at normal operating temperature, loosen the choke thermostatic spring housing retainer screws and set the housing 90 degrees in the rich direction.

3. Disconnect and remove the choke heat tube from the choke housing.

4. Turn the fast idle adjusting screw outward one full turn.

5. Start the engine, then check for the specified clearance between the lower edge of the choke plate and the air horn wall.

6. If the clearance is not within specifica- turn the diaphragm stop screw (located on the underside of the choke diaphragm housing) clockwise to decrease or counterclockwise to increase the clearance.

7. Connect the choke heat tube and set the choke thermostatic spring housing to specifications. Adjust the fast idle speed to specifications.

Motorcraft 2150

1. Set throttle on fast idle cam top step.

2. Note index position of choke bimetallic cap. Loosen retaining screws and rotate cap 90 degrees in the rich (closing) direction.

3. Activate pulldown motor by manually forcing pulldown control diaphragm link in the direction of applied vacuum or by applying vacuum to external vacuum tube.

4. Measure vertical hard gauge clearance between choke plate and center of carburetor air horn wall nearest fuel bowl.

Pulldown setting should be within specifications for minimum choke plate opening.

If choke plate pulldown is found to be out of specification, reset by adjusting diaphragm stop on end of choke pulldown diaphragm.

If pulldown is reset, cam clearance should be checked and reset if required.

After pulldown check is completed, reset choke bimetallic cap to recommended index position as specified in the Carburetor Speci-

Carburetor Specifications

HOLLEY 1904

Year	Engine	Float Setting (in.)	Fuel Level Setting (in.)	Float Drop (in.)	Idle Mixture Screw Adjustment	Power Valve Opens (in. Hg)	Spark Control Valve No.
1961–62	144	11/64	23/32	3/16	1–1½ turns out	4–7	728
	170	11/64	23/32	3/16	1–1½ turns out	7–10	35

MOTORCRAFT 4350

Year	Engine	Float Setting (in.)	Supplementary Valve Setting (in.)	Accelerator Pump Rod Location	Initial Choke Pulldown (in.)	Dechoke Minimum (in.)	Choke Cap Setting
1975	460 49s.	15/16	1/16	Inner #2	5/32	1/3	Index
	460 Cal.	31/32	1/16	Inner #2	5/32	1/3	Index
	460 H. Alt.	1	1/32	Inner #2	5/32	1/3	Index
1976	460	1	1/32	Inner #2	5/32	1/3	Index
1977	460	1	1/32	#3	5/32	1/3	Index
1978	460	1	1/32	#3	5/32	1/3	Index

FORD 1100

Year	Engine	Float Setting (in.)	Accelerator Pump Clearance (in.)	Choke Plate Pulldown Clearance (in.)	Dashpot Clearance (in.)	Idle Mixture Adjustment	Spark Control Valve Closes (in. Hg)
1963	144	1	$3/16$	$3/8$	—	$3/4$ turns out	6–8
	170	1	$3/16$	$3/8$	$3\frac{1}{2}$ turns in	$3/4$ turns out	6–8
1964	144	1	$3/16$	$3/8$	—	$1\frac{1}{2}$ turns out	9–10
	170 MT	1	$3/16$	$3/8$	—	$1\frac{1}{2}$ turns out	8–9
	170 AT	1	$3/16$	$3/8$	$3\frac{1}{2}$ turns in	$1\frac{1}{2}$ turns out	5.5–6.5
1965	170 MT	①	$3/16$	$3/8$	—	$1\frac{1}{2}$ turns out	8–9
	170 AT	①	$3/16$	$3/8$	$3\frac{1}{2}$ turns in	$1\frac{1}{2}$ turns out	8–9
	200	①	$3/16$	$3/8$	—	$1\frac{1}{2}$ turns out	8–9
	240	①	$7/32$	$3/8$	—	$1\frac{1}{2}$ turns out	6.0
1966	170 MT	$1\frac{1}{32}$	$3/16$	$3/8$	—	$1\frac{1}{2}$ turns out	8.5
	170 AT	$1\frac{1}{32}$	$3/16$	$3/8$	$3\frac{1}{2}$ turns in	$1\frac{1}{2}$ turns out	8.5
	240 MT	$1\frac{1}{32}$	$7/32$	—	—	$1\frac{1}{2}$ turns out	6.0
	240 AT	$1\frac{1}{32}$	$7/32$	—	$3\frac{1}{2}$ turns in	$1\frac{1}{2}$ turns out	6.0
	240②	$1\frac{1}{50}$	$7/32$	—	$3\frac{1}{2}$ turns in	$1\frac{1}{2}$ turns out	—

Year	Engine	Float Setting (in.)	Dechoke Minimum (in.)	Choke Pulldown (in.)	Dashpot Clearance (in.)	Throttle Plate Fast Idle Clearance (in.)	Fast Idle Speed (rpm)
1967–68	170 MT	$1\frac{3}{32}$	$\frac{3}{16}$	$\frac{3}{8}$	—	$1\frac{1}{2}$ turns out	—
	170 AT	$1\frac{3}{32}$	$\frac{3}{16}$	$\frac{3}{8}$	$3\frac{1}{2}$ turns in	$1\frac{1}{2}$ turns out	—
	170②	$1\frac{3}{32}$	$\frac{3}{16}$	$\frac{3}{8}$	2 turns in	$1\frac{1}{2}$ turns out	—
	240 MT	$1\frac{3}{32}$③	$\frac{7}{32}$	$\frac{3}{8}$	—	$1\frac{1}{2}$ turns out	—
1969	240 AT	$1\frac{3}{32}$	$\frac{7}{32}$	$1\frac{3}{32}$④	$3\frac{1}{2}$ turns in⑤	—	9.0

CARTER YF

Year	Engine	Float Setting (in.)	Dechoke Minimum (in.)	Choke Pulldown (in.)	Dashpot Clearance (in.)	Throttle Plate Fast Idle Clearance (in.)	Fast Idle Speed (rpm)
1969–70	170	$\frac{7}{32}$	$\frac{5}{64}$	$\frac{7}{32}$	$\frac{7}{64}$	$\frac{3}{64}$	—
	240 MT	$\frac{7}{32}$	$\frac{9}{32}$	$\frac{7}{32}$	$\frac{7}{64}$	$\frac{1}{32}$	—
	240 AT	$\frac{7}{32}$	$\frac{9}{32}$	$\frac{7}{32}$	—	—	850
1971	240 E-300	$\frac{3}{8}$	$\frac{9}{32}$	$\frac{8}{32}$	$\frac{7}{64}$	—	1750
	240	$\frac{3}{8}$	$\frac{9}{32}$	$\frac{8}{32}$	—	—	1750
1972–73	240	$\frac{3}{8}$	$\frac{9}{32}$	$\frac{8}{32}$	—	—	1750
	300	$\frac{3}{8}$	$\frac{9}{32}$	$\frac{8}{32}$	$\frac{3}{32}$	—	1750
1974	240	$\frac{3}{8}$	$\frac{9}{32}$	$\frac{8}{32}$	—	$\frac{6}{32}$	—

CARTER YF (cont.)

Year	Engine	Float Setting (in.)	Accelerator Pump Clearance (in.)	Choke Plate Pulldown Clearance (in.)	Dashpot Clearance (in.)	Idle Mixture Adjustment	Spark Control Valve Closes (in. Hg)
	300	3/8	9/32	10/32	3/32	4/32	—
1975	300	3/8	9/32	8/32	—	4/32	—
1976	300	3/8	9/32	10/32	—	4/32	—
	300 Canada	23/32	9/32	10/32	—	4/32	—
	300 Calif.	23/32	9/32	10/32	—	4/32	—
1977	300	25/32	9/32	10/32	—	4/32	—
1978	300	25/32	9/32	8/32	.070	.140	—
	300 E-350	23/32	9/32	8/32	—	4/32	—

For 1979–80 carburetor specifications, see the special section at the end of the carburetor charts.

AUTOLITE 2100

Year	Engine	Float Setting (in.)	Fuel Level (in.)	Fast Idle Cam Clearance (in.)	Choke Pulldown (in.)	Dechoke Minimum (in.)	Choke Cap Setting
1969	302	3/8	3/4	—	1/4	—	—
1970	302 AT	7/16	13/16	.140	3/16	1/16	Index
	302 MT	7/16	13/16	.150	3/16	1/16	2 Rich

Year	Engine	Float Setting (in.)	Fuel Level (in.)	Fast Idle Cam Clearance (in.)	Choke Pulldown (in.)	Accelerator Pump Rod Location	Choke Cap Setting
1971	302 Bus MT	7/16	13/16	.140	5/32	1/16	Index
	302 Bus AT	7/16	13/16	.140	5/32	1/16	Index
	302 Van⑥ MT	7/16	13/16	.140	5/32	1/16	Index
	302 Van⑥ AT	7/16	13/16	.140	5/32	1/16	1 Rich
1972–73	302	7/16	13/16	see text	see text	—	2 Rich
	302 E-300	7/16	13/16	.110	see text	—	2 Rich
1974	302	7/16	13/16	see text	see text	—	2 Rich

MOTORCRAFT 2150

Year	Engine	Float Setting (in.)	Fuel Level (in.)	Fast Idle Cam Clearance (in.)	Choke Pulldown (in.)	Accelerator Pump Rod Location	Choke Cap Setting
1975–76	351W MT	31/64	7/8	see text	5/32	#3	1 NR⑦
	351W AT	31/64	7/8	see text	5/32	#3	3 NR
	351W AT⑧	1/2	7/8	see text	5/32	#2	3 NR
1977	351W MT⑨	7/16	13/16	see text	3/16	#3	3 NR
	351W AT⑨	7/16	13/16	see text	3/16	#2	3 NR
	351W AT⑩	31/64	7/8	see text	3/16	#3	1 NR

MOTORCRAFT 2150 (cont.)

Year	Engine	Float Setting (in.)	Fuel Level (in.)	Fast Idle Cam Clearance (in.)	Choke Pulldown (in.)	Dechoke Minimum (in.)	Choke Cap Setting
	351W AT⑪	$31/64$	$7/8$	see text	$3/16$	#4	2 NR
	351W MT⑫	$31/64$	$7/8$	see text	$3/16$	#4	1 NR
	351W AT⑬	$31/64$	$7/8$	see text	$3/16$	#3	2 NR
1978	351W AT⑨	$31/64$	$7/8$	see text	$7/32$	#2	1 NR
	351W MT⑨	$31/64$	$7/8$	see text	$3/16$	#3	3 NR
	351W E-350	$31/64$	$7/8$	see text	$3/16$	#3	3 NR

For 1979–80 carburetor specifications, see the special section at the end of the carburetor charts.

① rubber float: 1 inch
   metal float: $1^{3}/_{32}$ inch
② with Thermactor
③ with Thermactor: $1^{1}/_{32}$ inch
④ with Imco: $9/32$ inch
⑤ with Thermactor or Imco: .10″ clearance between the plunger and lever
⑥ E-300 with GVW over 6,000 lb.
⑦ California: 3 NR
⑧ Canada
⑨ E-100 only
⑩ E-150, 250, 300 California
⑪ E-150, 250, 300 High Altitude
⑫ E-150, 250, 300 49 states
⑬ E-150, 250, 300 49 states before serial #Y0001
49s: 49 states (except California)
MT: Manual transmission
AT: Automatic transmission
NR: Notches rich

1979–80 Carburetor Specifications

Calibration Number ●	Choke Plate Pulldown Setting (inches)	Time for Choke Plate to Rotate (Come Off—Seconds—Maximum)	Air Flow (Pounds Per Minute)	Choke Setting	Fast Idle RPM		Curb Idle RPM		TSP Off RPM		Timing RPM
					High Cam	Kick Down	① A/C Off/On	Non-AC	AC	Non-AC	
9-51G-RO	.230	80	.06	Index		1600	700	700	500	500	500
9-51J-RO	.230	80	.06	Index		1600	700	700	500	500	500
9-51K-RO	.230	80	.06	Index		1600	700	700	500	500	500
9-51L-RO	.230	80	.06	Index		1600	700	700	500	500	500
9-51M-RO	.230	80	.06	Index		1600	700	700	500	500	500
9-51S-RO	.230	80	.06	Index		1600	700	700	500	500	500
9-51T-RO	.230	80	.06	Index		1600	700	700	500	500	500
9-52G-RO	.230	80	.06	Index		1600	550	550	500	500	500
9-52J-RO	.230	80	.06	Index		1600	550	550	500	500	500
9-52L-RO	.230	80	.06	Index		1600	550	550	500	500	500
9-52M-RO	.230	80	.06	Index		1600	550	550	500	500	500
9-53G-RO	.140	235	.085	3 Rich	2000		700	700			550
9-53H-RO	.140	125	.085	3 Rich	2000		700	700			550

1979–80 Carburetor Specifications (cont.)

Calibration Number ●	Choke Plate Pulldown Setting (inches)	Time for Choke Plate to Rotate (Come Off) (Seconds—Maximum)	Air Flow (Pounds Per Minute)	Choke Setting	Fast Idle RPM		Curb Idle RPM		TSP Off RPM		Timing RPM
					High Cam	Kick Down	①A/C Off/On	Non-AC	AC	Non-AC	
9-54G-RO	.145	150	.079	3 Rich	2000		600	600	550	550	550
9-54H-RO	.145	150	.079	3 Rich	2000		600	600	550	550	550
9-54J-RO	.145	135	.079	2 Rich	2000		600	600	550	550	550
9-54R-RO	.145	135	.079	3 Rich	2000		600	600	550	550	550
9-54S-RO	.136	75	.080	1 Rich	2400		650	650	550	550	550
9-54T-RO	.145	150	.079	3 Rich	2000		600	600	550	550	550
9-54U-RO	.136	75	.080	1 Rich	2400		650	650	550	550	550
9-59H-RO	.135	84	.074	Index	2000		650	650			650
9-59J-RO	.145	84	.074	Index	2000		650	650			650
9-59K-RO	.145	84	.074	Index	2000		650	650			650
9-59S-RO	.135	84	.07	Index	2000		650	650			650
9-59T-RO	.150	84	.07	Index	2000		650	650			650
9-60G-RO	.145	84	.079	Index	2000		550	550			500

Code									
9-60H-RO	.150	84	.08	Index	2000	550	550		500
9-60J-RO	.140	84	.079	Index	2000	550	550		500
9-60L-RO	.150	84	.08	Index	2000	550	550		500
9-60M-RO	.150	84	.08	Index	2000	550	550		500
9-60S-RO	.150	84	—	3 Rich	2100	550	550		500
9-61G-RO	.145	84	.074	Index	2000	650	650		650
9-61H-RO	.135	84	.076	Index	2000	650	650		650
9-62J-RO	.145	85	.079	Index	1900	550	550		550
9-62M-RO	.145	85	.079	Index	1900	550	550		500
9-63H-RO	.190	77	.06	Index	1500	800	800	500	500
9-64G-RO	.200	67	.06	Index	2200	600	600	500	500
9-64H-RO	.200	67	.06	Index	2200	600	600	500	500
9-64S-RO	.200	67	.06	Index	2200	600	600	500	500
9-66G-RO	.210	130	.09	5 Rich	1600	650②	650	800③	800 TSP Off

① Only for A/C-TSP equipped, A/C compressor electromagnetic clutch de-energized
② Energize A/C electromagnetic clutch
③ De-energize A/C electromagnetic clutch
• Refer to engine calibration code on underhood emissions sticker.

1981 Carburetor Specifications
Carter YFA

Check the carburetor part number tag to determine which specifications to use for your vehicle

Engine	Part Number	Choke Pulldown Setting	Fast Idle Cam Setting	Dechoke Setting	Choke Plate Come-Off Time	Float Setting (Dry)	Choke Cap Setting	Fast Idle
6-300	D9TE-9510-CA,VA E0TE-9510-AMA,FA	.290	.140	.280	—	.690	Index	1400
	E1TE-9510-UA,ARA, ARB	.230	.140	.280	110 sec.	.780	Index	1400
	E1TE-9510-EA,DA, ANA,TA,EB,ANB	.300	.140	.280	110 sec.	.780	Index	1400

Motorcraft 2150

Engine	Part Number	Choke Pulldown Setting	Fast Idle Cam Setting	Dechoke Setting	Float Level (Wet)	Float Level (Dry)	Accelerator Pump Lever Location	Choke Cap Setting	Fast Idle
8-302	E1TE-9510-CNA,CMA	.125	V-notch	.200	.810	7/16	#2	V-notch	1500
	E1TE-9510-CPA,CRA	.125	V-notch	.200	.810	7/16	#2	V-notch	1500
8-351	E1TE-9510-CCA	.155	V-notch	.250	.875	31/64	#4	V-notch	2000
	E1TE-9510-BHA	.140	V-notch	.200	.875	31/64	#2	3NR	2000
	E1TE-9510-BFA	.140	V-notch	.200	.875	31/64	#2	V-notch	2000
	E1UE-9510-FA	.120	V-notch	.200	.875	31/64	#3	Index	2000
	E1UE-9510-CA, JA	.120	V-notch	.200	.875	31/64	#3	V-notch	2000

Motorcraft 4180

Engine	Part Number	Choke Pulldown Setting	Dechoke Setting	Fuel Level	Choke Cap Setting	Pump Level Location
8-460	ALL	.195–.225	.295–.335	sight plug	5NR	#1

fications Chart. Check and reset fast idle speed to specifications if necessary.

Motorcraft 4180, 4350

1. Remove the choke thermostatic spring housing assembly.

2. Open throttle about half-throttle and position the fast idle adjusting screw on the high step of the fast idle cam.

3. Bend a 0.036 inch diameter wire gauge at a 90 degree angle approximately ⅛ inch from its end. Insert the bent end of the gauge between the choke piston slot and the upper edge of the right-hand slot in the choke housing.

4. Rotate the choke thermostat lever counterclockwise until the gauge is snug in the position slot. Hold the gauge in position with light force on the lever and move the top of the choke rod away from the carburetor while moving the bottom of the rod toward the carburetor to remove end play from linkage.

5. Using a drill gauge or equivalent, check initial choke pulldown clearance by placing the gauge against the inner wall of the choke air horn on the downstream side at approximately the longitudinal centerline of the carburetor and check clearance from wall to edge of choke plate.

6. If the measured clearance is not within specifications, adjust clearance by turning the hex head lock screw on the choke plate shaft in a clockwise direction three (3) full turns. (Note: Lock screw is left-hand threaded.) Pry choke lever from shaft to break taper lock. Choke lever should rotate freely on choke shaft.

7. Hold the drill gauge with diameter equal to specified pulldown clearance between the lower edge of the choke plate and air horn wall, maintaining light closing force on choke plate.

8. With choke piston snug against the 0.036 inch wire gauge, the top of the choke rod held away from the carburetor while moving the bottom of the rod toward the carburetor to remove end play from linkage, and the choke plate held against the drill gauge, tighten the hex head screw on the choke shaft.

9. Reinstall the choke thermostatic spring housing assembly.

DECHOKE ADJUSTMENT

All except 4350

1. Remove the air cleaner.

2. Hold the throttle plate fully open and close the choke plate as far as possible without forcing it. Use a drill of the proper diameter to check the clearance between the choke plate and air horn.

3. If the clearance is not within specification, adjust by bending the arm on the choke trip lever. Bending the arm downward will increase the clearance, and bending it upward will decrease the clearance. Always recheck the clearance after making any adjustment.

4. If the choke plate clearance and fast idle cam linkage adjustment was performed with the carburetor on the engine, adjust the engine idle speed and fuel mixture. Adjust the dashpot (if so equipped).

Motorcraft 4180, 4350

1. Open the throttle plate to the wide open position and hold.

2. Rotate the choke plate toward the closed position until the pawl on the fast idle speed lever contacts the fast idle cam.

3. Check the clearance between the lower edge of the choke plate and the air horn wall.

4. Adjust the clearance to specifications by bending the pawl on the fast idle speed lever forward to increase or backward to decrease the clearance

Chassis Electrical

HEATER

Blower Motor and/or Heater Core

REMOVAL AND INSTALLATION

1961–68

The heater blower motor may be removed without removing the heater case, by simply disconnecting the lead-in wires and removing the three attaching bolts.

1. Remove the right side grille-work from around the head light.
2. Working through the opening, remove the six heater case attaching screws.
3. Disconnect the water hoses from the bottom of the heater case.
4. Disconnect the defroster ducts from the case.
5. Remove the remaining attaching screws from inside the van.
6. Lower the heater case to the floor and disconnect the control cables and wiring.
7. Remove the case.
8. Installation is the reverse of removal. Replace any damaged sealer.

1969–74

1. Open the hood and remove the battery to gain access to the heater mounting bolts.

2. Drain the cooling system.
3. Disconnect the heater hoses at the heater.
4. Disconnect the heater resistor and motor leads.
5. From under the hood, remove the 3 heater-to-dash mounting bolts. Then, move the heater out of position to gain access to the control cable and disconnect the cable. Remove the heater assembly to a bench.
6. Separate the two halves of the heater case (16 screws and 1 clip).

For heater core replacement, use Steps 7, 8 and 14 through 18.

7. Remove the heater core.
8. Transfer the core pads to the new core, and position the core in the case.

For blower motor replacement, use Steps 9 through 18.

9. Remove the two screws and lift the motor and wheel from the front half of the heater housing.
10. Remove the blower wheel and motor mounting bracket.
11. Position the new motor in the mounting bracket and install the mounting bolts and nuts.
12. Install the blower wheel.
13. Position the motor assembly in the housing and install the mounting screws.

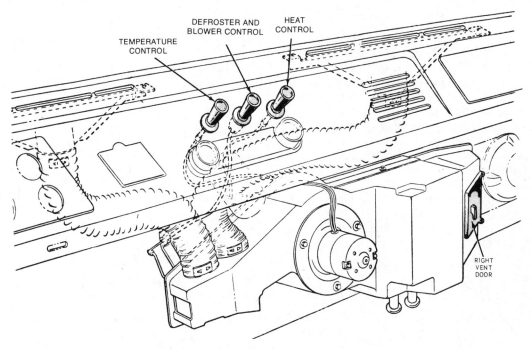

TEMPERATURE CONTROL

DEFROSTER AND BLOWER CONTROL

HEAT CONTROL

RIGHT VENT DOOR

Heater assembly used in the 1961–68 models

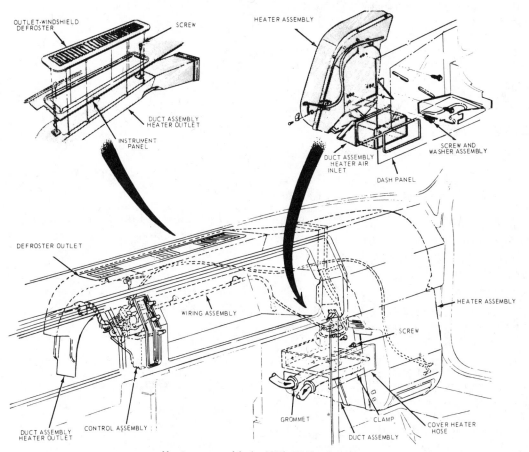

OUTLET-WINDSHIELD DEFROSTER

SCREW

DUCT ASSEMBLY HEATER OUTLET

INSTRUMENT PANEL

HEATER ASSEMBLY

DUCT ASSEMBLY HEATER AIR INLET

SCREW AND WASHER ASSEMBLY

DASH PANEL

DEFROSTER OUTLET

WIRING ASSEMBLY

HEATER ASSEMBLY

SCREW

DUCT ASSEMBLY HEATER OUTLET

CONTROL ASSEMBLY

GROMMET

CLAMP

DUCT ASSEMBLY

COVER HEATER HOSE

Heater assembly in 1970–74 Ford vans

14. Position both halves of the case together and install the screws and clip.

15. Place the heater controls in the Off position. Place the heater on the wheel housing as near the installed position as possible. Pull the air door closed (toward the rear of the vehicle) and connect the control cable.

16. Position the heater to the dash, and install the 3 mounting bolts. Use an assistant and make certain that the housing openings line up with the defroster and fresh air openings.

17. Connect the resistor and motor leads.

18. Connect the heater hoses.

19. Install the battery and fill the cooling system. Run the engine and check for leaks.

1975–82 Without Air Conditioning

HEATER CORE

1. Drain the coolant; remove the battery.

2. Disconnect the resistor wiring harness and the orange blower motor lead. Remove the ground wire screw from the firewall.

3. Detach the heater hoses and the plastic hose retaining strap.

4. Remove the five mounting screws inside the truck.

5. Remove the heater assembly.

6. Cut the seal at the top and bottom edge of the core retainer. Remove the two screws and the retainer. Slide the core and seal out of the case.

7. Reverse the procedure for installation.

BLOWER MOTOR

1. Disconnect the orange motor lead wire. Remove the ground wire screw from the firewall.

2. Disconnect the blower motor cooling tube.

3. Remove the four mounting plate screws and the motor assembly.

4. Reverse the procedure for installation.

1975–82 With Air Conditioning

HEATER CORE

1. Disconnect the resistor electrical leads on the front of the blower cover inside the truck. Detach the vacuum line from the vacuum motor. Remove the blower cover.

2. Remove the nut and push washer from the air door shaft. Remove the control cable from the bracket and the air door shaft.

3. Remove the blower motor housing and the air door housing.

4. Drain the coolant and detach the heater hoses.

5. Remove the heater core retaining brackets. Remove the core and seal assembly.

6. Reverse the procedure for installation.

BLOWER MOTOR

1. Disconnect the resistor electrical leads on the front of the blower cover inside the truck.

2. Remove the blower cover.

3. Push the wiring grommet forward out of the housing hole.

4. Remove the blower motor mounting plate. Remove the blower motor.

5. Reverse the procedure for installation.

Auxiliary Hot Water Heater

HEATER/BLOWER ASSEMBLY

1964–68

REMOVAL AND INSTALLATION

1. Disconnect the battery ground cable.

2. Raise the vehicle on hoist.

3. Remove the two hoses from the heater core and plug the hoses.

4. Remove the rubber insulators from the heater core tubes.

5. Remove the four nuts from the heater assembly retaining studs.

6. Lower the vehicle.

7. Disconnect the two electrical leads at the heater assembly.

8. Remove the heater from the vehicle.

9. Position the heater asembly in the vehicle, inserting the mounting studs through the floor pan.

10. Connect the two electrical leads at the heater assembly.

11. Raise the vehicle on hoist.

12. Install the four nuts on the heater assembly retaining studs.

13. Install the rubber insulators on the heater core tubes.

14. Remove the plugs from the heater hoses and install the hoses on the heater core tubes securing them with clamps.

15. Lower the vehicle.

16. Add required coolant to the cooling system.

17. Connect the battery ground cable.

AUXILIARY HEATER CORE

1964–68

REMOVAL AND INSTALLATION

1. Remove the heater assembly from the vehicle and place on work bench.

2. Remove the heater core from the heater case.

3. Remove the four rubber spacers from the core.

4. Using sealer, install the four rubber spacers to the heater core.

5. Install the core in the heater case and install the four mounting screws.

6. Install the heater assembly in the vehicle.

AUXILIARY HEATER BLOWER AND/OR CORE

1969–74

REMOVAL AND INSTALLATION

1. Disconnect the battery ground cable.

2. Raise the vehicle on a hoist.

3. Remove the two hoses from the heater core and plug the hoses.

4. Remove the rubber insulators from the heater core tubes.

5. Remove the four nuts from the heater assembly retaining studs.

6. Lower the vehicle.

7. Disconnect the two electrical leads at the heater assembly.

8. Remove the heater from the vehicle.

9. Position the heater assembly in the vehicle, inserting the mounting studs through the floor pan.

10. Connect the two electrical leads at the heater assembly.

11. Raise the vehicle on a hoist.

12. Install the four nuts on the heater assembly retaining studs.

13. Install the rubber insulators on the heater core tubes.

14. Remove the plugs from the heater hoses and install the hoses on the heater core tubes securing them with clamps.

15. Lower the vehicle.

16. Add required coolant to the cooling system.

17. Connect the battery ground cable.

AUXILIARY HEATER CASE (WITH OR WITHOUT A/C)

1975–82

REMOVAL AND INSTALLATION

1. Remove the first bench seat (if so equipped).

2. Remove the auxiliary heater and/or air conditioning cover assembly attaching screws and remove the cover.

3. Position the cover assembly to the body side panel and install the attaching screws.

4. Install the bench seat (if removed) and tighten the retaining bolts 25–45 ft lb.

AUXILIARY HEATER CORE AND SEAL ASSEMBLY

1975–82

REMOVAL AND INSTALLATION

1. Remove the first bench seat (if so equipped).

2. Remove auxiliary heater and/or air conditioning cover attaching screws (15) and remove the cover.

3. Partially drain the engine coolant from the cooling system.

4. Remove the heater hoses from the auxiliary heater core assembly (2 clamps).

5. Pull the wiring assembly away from the heater core seal.

6. Slide the heater core and seal assembly out of the housing slot.

7. Slide the heater core and seal assembly into the housing slot (position the wiring to one side).

8. Install the heater hoses to the heater core assembly (2 clamps).

9. Fill the cooling system to specification.

10. Position the cover assembly to the body side panel and install the attaching screws (15).

11. Install the bench seat (if removed) and tighten the retaining bolts 25–45 ft lb.

Auxiliary Gasoline Heater 1965–68

IGNITION BASE SERVICE

The breaker points, the breaker cam, and the condenser are referred to as the ignition base assembly. The assembly is mounted at one end of the hot air blower. The breaker points are protected from water and dirt by a metal snap-on cover.

To service the breaker points, remove the retaining screws, disconnect the Bowden cable from the thermostat and lift the cover from the blower assembly on the left side of the floor pan. Then, remove the breaker point snap-on cover and check as follows:

1. Clean and inspect the breaker points.

2. If the breaker points are in good condition, check the breaker points gap. If the gap on one lobe of the cam is .018 inch, a gap of .012 inch to .021 inch is permissible on the other lobe. Try to bring both gaps within the desired reading by loosening the two ignition

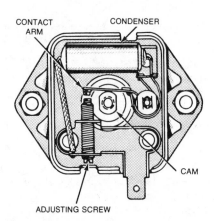

CONTACT ARM

CONDENSER

CAM

ADJUSTING SCREW

Ignition points adjustment

unit mounting nuts and shifting the assembly slightly as permitted by bolt hole clearance.

3. If the correct gap limits cannot be obtained by shifting the assembly, the complete ignition unit assembly should be replaced.

Do not attempt to change the gap on used points by turning the threaded stationary point. A cratering action occurs here normally in service.

4. Be sure that the condenser connections are tight. Connections that are loose can result in intermittent and weak sparks. A bright flash can be due to an open circuit at this point.

HEATER HOUSING ASSEMBLY REPAIR

Before performing any service operations, the housing lower cover has to be removed.

Raise the truck on a hoist, remove the retaining screws, then remove the lower cover from the housing. The components are now accessible.

HEAT EXCHANGER AND BURNER ASSEMBLY

Removal and Installation

1. Remove the four screws and nuts that join the outer and inner heater shields of the heat exchanger. Remove the overheat switch wire lead from the fuel solenoid, and disconnect the wire connector between the overheat switch and the terminal board. Lift the outer shield half off.

2. Remove the ignition coil high tension cable from the spark plug, and the combustion blower air duct at the burner unit. Also, remove the spark plug ground lead from the terminal board.

3. Disconnect the fuel line from the burner unit.

4. Remove the two screws and nuts that secure the heat exchanger exhaust outlet to the heat exchanger case side. Remove the holding plate, gasket and gasket retainer. Lift out the heat exchanger and burner assembly.

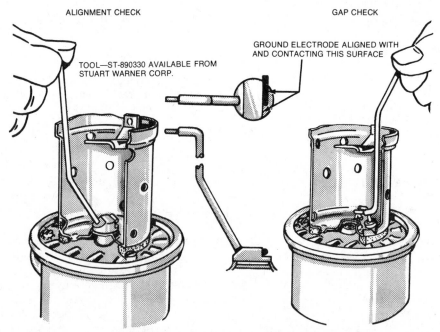

ALIGNMENT CHECK

GAP CHECK

TOOL—ST-890330 AVAILABLE FROM STUART WARNER CORP.

GROUND ELECTRODE ALIGNED WITH AND CONTACTING THIS SURFACE

Checking spark plug alignment and gap

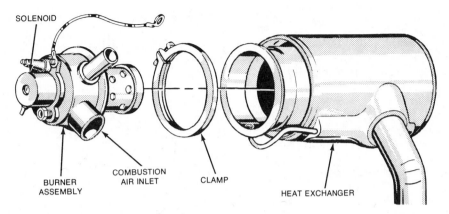

SOLENOID

BURNER
ASSEMBLY

COMBUSTION
AIR INLET

CLAMP

HEAT EXCHANGER

Heat exchanger and burner

5. Position the heat exchanger and burner assembly in the heater. Position the holding plate, gasket retainer, and gasket on the heat exchanger exhaust outlet and install the 2 attaching screws and nuts.

6. Connect the fuel line to the burner unit.

7. Connect the ignition coil high tension cable to the spark plug and the spark plug ground lead to the terminal board.

8. Install the combustion blower air duct to the burner.

9. Position the heat exchanger outer shield half and install the 4 retaining screws and nuts.

10. Connect the overheat switch wire to the fuel solenoid and connect the wire connector between the overheat switch and the terminal board.

IGNITION BASE ASSEMBLY

Removal and Installation

If the ignition base assembly has to be replaced, remove the retaining screws, disconnect the Bowden cable from the thermostat and lift the cover from the blower assembly on the left side of the floor pan.

Remove the two screws securing the assembly to the ventilator blower motor and pull off the unit. Unscrew the cam from the motor shaft.

After a new base has been installed, make adjustments of the breaker points by turning the threaded stationary point until the gap on each lobe of the cam conforms to the procedure outlined in Ignition Base Service, above. After readjustment is complete, lock the stationary point with rosin core solder.

THERMOSTAT AND CONTROL CABLE

Removal and Installation

Remove the heater cover retaining screws, disconnect the Bowden cable from the thermostat and lift the cover from the blower assembly on the left side of the floor pan. Then, separate the two wires from the connectors on the thermostat microswitch.

Disconnect the control cable and remove the thermostat retaining screws. When installing a new thermostat, adjust the control cable for satisfactory operation.

The thermostat is pre-set at the factory and is not adjustable in service. Any attempt to adjust the switch will almost certainly result in insufficient heater output, or in burned out heat exchanger.

IGNITION COIL

Removal and Installation

1. Disconnect the ignition coil cable from the spark plug at the burner unit.

2. Disconnect the ignition coil two wire leads from the terminal board.

3. Remove the coil mounting bracket two attaching nuts, together with washers and screws, and lift out the bracket and ignition coil and cable. To take the ignition coil from the bracket, remove or loosen the bracket screw.

4. Install the ignition coil in the bracket.

5. Position the coil and bracket in the heater case and install the 2 attaching nuts.

6. Connect the ignition coil terminal wires at the connectors. Connect the high tension lead to the spark plug and the ignition coil.

SPARK PLUG

Removal and Installation

To service a defective spark plug, the burner assembly should be removed from the heater housing. This can be done without removing the heat exchanger.

1. Disconnect the fuel line, then remove the ignition cable from the spark plug. Remove the spark plug ground wire from the terminal block.

2. Remove the wire terminal to the fuel solenoid.

3. Remove the clamp that secures the heat exchanger to the burner assembly.

4. Disconnect the combustion blower duct at the burner assembly and remove the burner from the housing.

5. After the burner assembly has been removed, take out the screws securing the spark plug retaining plate and remove the spark plug and its sealing copper washers from the burner unit. Give the spark plug a thorough check.

6. When installing the spark plug with the two washers into the burner housing, the spark plug electrode should point away from the large notch in the spark plug porcelain. The large notch indexes with a lug in the burner housing to provide correct electrode alignment. Before installing the spark plug, make certain that the spark plug electrode is in the center of the porcelain insulator.

7. The relationship of the ground electrode to the fuel nozzle is very important. This relationship can be checked by inserting gauge in the center hole of the mixer cup. The ground electrodes should lie flat against the flat surface of the gauge. If necessary, use long nose pliers to bend the ground electrode into proper position.

8. The other end of the tool gauge can be used to check the gap between the spark plug electrode and the ground electrode. This end is .085 inch thick. If necessary, bend the ground electrode to adjust the gap. But, after any bending, check once more the alignment of the ground electrode to the fuel nozzle.

9. Assemble the burner to the heat exchanger and connect the combustion blower direct.

10. Connect the wires and the fuel line.

COMBUSTION BLOWER AND FUEL PUMP

Removal and Installation

1. Remove the two clamps and disconnect the blower air hose at the burner and at the blower.

2. Remove the fuel lines from the burner unit inlet and from the fuel pump inlet.

3. Remove the blower motor ground lead from the terminal block and disconnect the wire connector between the terminal board and the blower motor.

4. Remove the large clamp that holds the blower assembly to the mounting bracket in the case. Lift out the blower assembly.

5. Position the blower to the mounting in the heater case and install the retaining clamp.

6. Connect the motor wire at the connector and the ground wire at the terminal block.

7. Connect the fuel lines to the burner inlet and the fuel pump inlet.

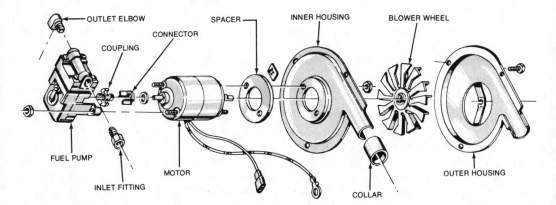

Exploded view of the combustion blower

8. Position the air hose to the blower and burner and install the 2 clamps.

BLOWER AND MOTOR

Removal and Installation

1. Remove the retaining screws, disconnect the Bowden cable from the thermostat and lift the cover from the blower assembly on the left side of the floor pan.

2. Loosen the clamp and disconnect the hot air duct from the blower housing.

3. Remove the three screws that secure the motor mounting plate to the blower housing.

4. Disconnect the motor ground wire at the passenger compartment deck panel. Also, disconnect the wire at the breaker points assembly and disconnect the wire connectors to the blower motor.

5. Lift the assembly from the blower housing.

6. Remove the set-screw that holds the blower wheel to the motor shaft and pull off the wheel.

7. Remove the screws that hold the mounting plate to the blower motor and remove the plate and the two spacers.

8. To remove the breaker points assembly, remove the two securing screws and lift off the assembly. Remove the breaker points cam from the motor shaft.

9. Install the breaker points cam on the motor shaft, then install the breaker points assembly. Check and adjust the points.

10. Place the two spacers on the motor mounting screws and install the mounting plate.

11. Install the blower wheel on the motor shaft.

12. Connect the blower motor and breaker assembly wires and connect the motor ground wire at the passenger compartment deck panel.

13. Mount the motor and blower assembly to the blower housing.

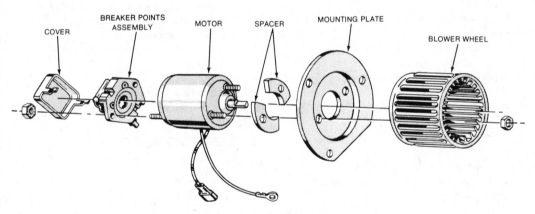

Exploded view of the hot air blower

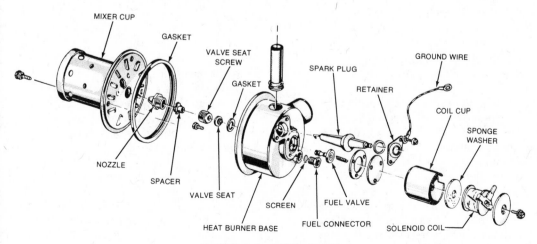

Exploded view of the burner

14. Connect the hot air duct to the blower housing.

15. Install the blower assembly cover and connect the thermostat Bowden cable.

RADIO

REMOVAL AND INSTALLATION

1961–68

1. Disconnect the lead wire at the fuse panel.

2. Detach the speaker leads at the radio.

3. Detach the antenna.

4. Pull off the control knobs. Remove the screws and take off the dial assembly.

5. Remove the shaft nuts and the retaining plate.

6. Remove the right and left support bracket nuts and remove the radio.

7. Reverse the procedure for installation.

1969–74

1. Disconnect the ground cable from the battery.

2. Remove the 8 screws attaching the instrument cluster to the instrument panel. Pull the cluster away from the instrument panel and disconnect the speedometer cable from the speedometer. Allow the instrument cluster to hang out of the opening.

3. Disconnect the radio power and light wires at the connectors.

4. From under the hood, remove the nut attaching the radio rear mounting bracket to the dash panel.

5. Remove the knobs from the radio control shafts.

6. Remove the 8 screws attaching the radio bezel to the instrument panel. Pull the bezel away from the radio and disconnect the speaker wires at the multiple connector.

7. Remove the radio power wire from the two clips over the instrument cluster opening.

8. Disconnect the antenna lead-in cable from the radio.

9. Remove the 3 screws attaching the radio and mounting bracket to the radio opening, and remove the radio and bracket from the vehicle.

To install the radio:

10. Position the radio and mounting bracket in the instrument panel opening. Route the power wire through the clips over the instrument cluster opening.

11. Install the 3 radio mounting bracket attaching screws.

12. Connect the antenna lead-in cable to the radio.

13. Connect the remaining components and install the instrument cluster in the reverse order of removal.

1975–82

1. Detach the battery ground cable.

2. Remove the heater and A/C control knobs. Remove the lighter.

3. Remove the radio knobs and discs.

4. If the truck has a lighter, snap out the name plate at the right side to remove the panel attaching screw.

5. Remove the five finish panel screws.

6. Very carefully pry out the cluster panel in two places.

7. Detach the antenna lead and speaker wires.

8. Remove the two nuts and washers and the mounting plate.

9. Remove the four front radio attaching screws. Remove the rear support nut and washer and remove the radio.

10. Reverse the procedure for installation.

WINDSHIELD WIPERS

Motor

REMOVAL AND INSTALLATION

1961–68

1. Disconnect the switch feed wire from the ignition switch, and the motor control wires at the terminals on the wiper control.

2. Remove the linkage arm retaining clip from the wiper arm lever, and remove the linkage arms.

3. Remove the wiper motor mounting bolts and remove the wiper motor and mounting bracket assembly from the instrument panel.

4. Transfer the mounting bracket from the old motor to the new motor.

5. Position the motor and bracket assembly to the retaining bracket under the instrument panel, and install the mounting bolts.

6. Place the linkage arms on the wiper arm lever and install the retaining clip.

7. Connect the motor control wires to the control assembly and the feed wire to the ignition switch. Check the operation of the wipers.

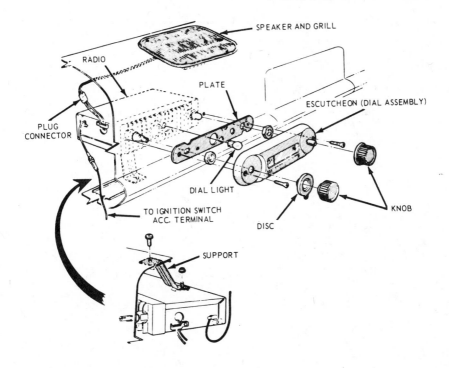

SPEAKER AND GRILL

RADIO

PLATE

ESCUTCHEON (DIAL ASSEMBLY)

PLUG CONNECTOR

DIAL LIGHT

KNOB

TO IGNITION SWITCH ACC. TERMINAL

DISC

KNOB

SUPPORT

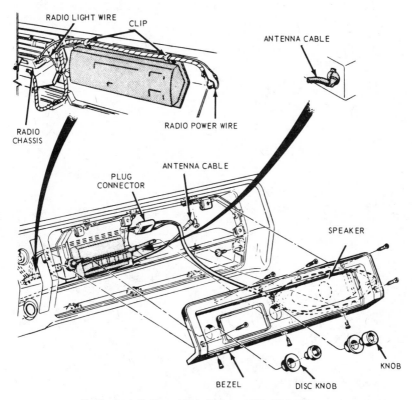

RADIO LIGHT WIRE   CLIP

ANTENNA CABLE

RADIO CHASSIS

RADIO POWER WIRE

ANTENNA CABLE

PLUG CONNECTOR

SPEAKER

KNOB

BEZEL   DISC KNOB

Radio installation, 1961–68 top; 1969–74 bottom

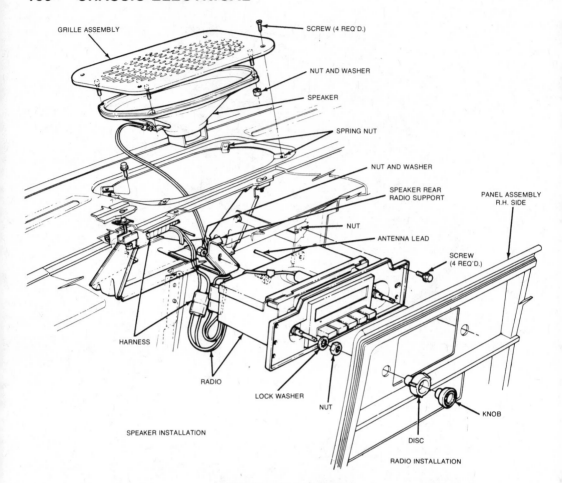

GRILLE ASSEMBLY

SCREW (4 REQ'D.)

NUT AND WASHER

SPEAKER

SPRING NUT

NUT AND WASHER

SPEAKER REAR
RADIO SUPPORT

PANEL ASSEMBLY
R.H. SIDE

NUT

ANTENNA LEAD

SCREW
(4 REQ'D.)

HARNESS

RADIO

LOCK WASHER

NUT

KNOB

DISC

SPEAKER INSTALLATION

RADIO INSTALLATION

1975–82 radio installation

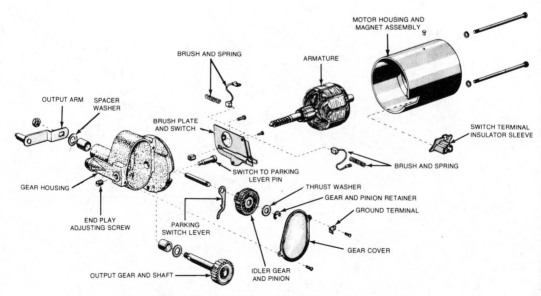

MOTOR HOUSING AND
MAGNET ASSEMBLY

BRUSH AND SPRING

ARMATURE

OUTPUT ARM   SPACER
WASHER

BRUSH PLATE
AND SWITCH

SWITCH TERMINAL
INSULATOR SLEEVE

BRUSH AND SPRING

GEAR HOUSING

SWITCH TO PARKING
LEVER PIN

THRUST WASHER

GEAR AND PINION RETAINER

GROUND TERMINAL

END PLAY
ADJUSTING SCREW

PARKING
SWITCH LEVER

GEAR COVER

OUTPUT GEAR AND SHAFT

IDLER GEAR
AND PINION

Exploded view of the 1961–64 single speed wiper motor

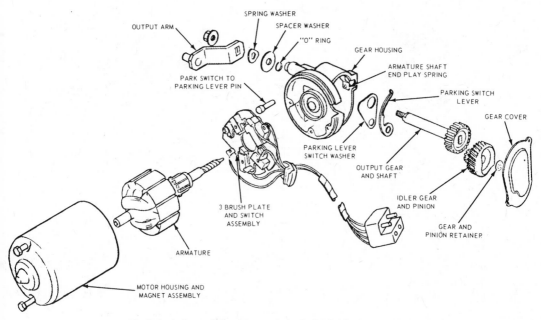

Exploded view of the two-speed windshield wiper motor

1969–74

1. Disconnect the battery ground cable.

2. Disconnect the wiper motor wires at the harness multiple connector or stud terminal.

3. Remove the clip which retains the motor drive arm to the linkage mounting arm and pivot shaft assembly.

4. Remove the wiper motor bracket attaching bolts and remove the motor and bracket from the vehicle. Then, remove the motor from the bracket.

5. Check the new motor to be sure that it is in the park position. Then, install the motor on the mounting bracket.

6. Remove the drive arm from the old motor and install it on the new motor in the park position (in the opposite direction from the ground strap).

7. Install the motor and bracket on the dash panel.

8. Connect the linkage mounting arm and pivot shaft assembly to the motor drive arm and install the retaining clip.

9. Connect the motor wires to the harness or stud terminal and the ground cable to the battery. Then check the operation of the wipers.

1975–82

1. Disconnect the battery ground cable. Remove the fuse panel and bracket.

2. Disconnect the motor wires.

3. Remove the arms and blades.

4. Remove the outer air inlet cowl. Take off the motor linkage clip.

5. Unbolt and remove the motor.

6. Reverse the procedure for installation.

Linkage

REMOVAL AND INSTALLATION

1961–68

1. Remove the wiper blade and arm assembly from the pivot shaft.

2. Remove the pivot shaft retaining nut and bezel.

3. Working under the instrument panel from inside the vehicle, remove the retaining clip and washer that secures the linkage to the wiper motor arm and remove the linkage and pivot shaft from the truck.

4. Position the pivot shaft and linkage in the mounting hole on the front panel. Secure the linkage to the motor arm with the washer and retaining clip.

5. Working from the outside of the vehicle, install the bezel and retaining nut to the pivot shaft.

6. Install the wiper arm and blade assembly to the pivot shaft and check the operation of the wipers.

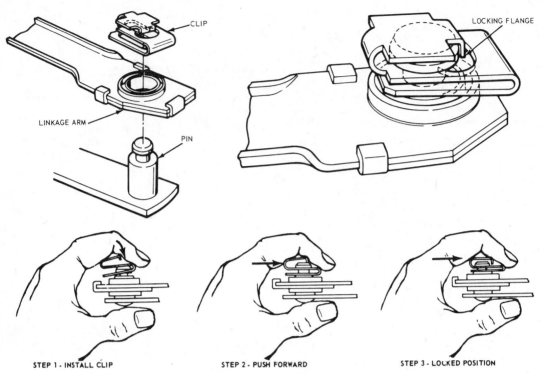

Installation of the wiper arm connecting clip

1969–74

1. Remove the wiper blade and arm assembly from the pivot shaft.

2. Working under the instrument panel from inside the vehicle, remove the six screws retaining the pivot shafts.

3. Remove the retaining clip that secures the linkage to the wiper motor arm and remove the linkage and pivot shafts from the vehicle.

4. Position the pivot shafts in the mounting holes on the front cowl panel. Secure the linkage to the motor arm with the retaining clip.

5. Install the six screws or two nuts retaining the pivot shafts to the cowl.

6. Install the wiper arm and blade assemblies to the pivot shafts and check the operation of the wipers.

1975–82

1. Disconnect the battery ground cable.

2. Remove the wiper blades and arms. Detach the washer hoses.

3. Remove the cowl grille.

4. Remove the linkage clips. Remove the pivot to cowl screws and remove the assembly.

INSTRUMENT CLUSTER

REMOVAL AND INSTALLATION

1961–68

1. Disconnect the battery ground cable.

2. Disconnect the speedometer cable at the speedometer head.

3. Remove the screws retaining the instrument cluster assembly to the instrument panel and lift the cluster out at the front of the panel.

4. Disconnect the instrument wires, remove the light sockets and remove the cluster assembly.

5. Position the cluster assembly, connect the instrument wires, and install the light sockets.

6. Install the cluster assembly to the instrument panel. When installing, make sure that all wiring and cables are moved away from the opening in the instrument panel.

7. Connect the speedometer cable and the battery ground cable. **Be careful not to kink the speedometer cable.**

8. Check the operation of all gauges, lights and signals.

1969–70

1. Disconnect the battery ground cable.

2. Remove the screws retaining the in-

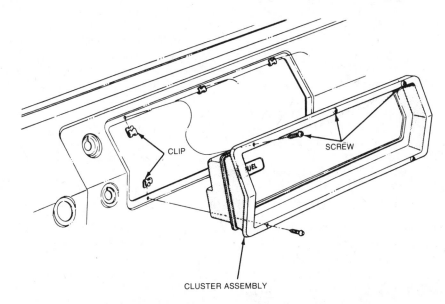

CLIP

SCREW

FUEL

CLUSTER ASSEMBLY

Removal and installation of the 1969–74 instrument cluster

strument cluster assembly to the instrument panel.

3. Carefully lift the cluster away from the instrument panel far enough to gain access to the speedometer cable at the head. The cluster is removed from the front of the panel. Disconnect the speedometer cable at the speedometer head.

4. Disconnect the multiple connector of the cluster wiring loom, and remove the cluster assembly. Individual cluster connections can be disconnected for service as necessary.

5. Connect the speedometer cable and tighten the nut to 18 to 24 in lbs. Connect the cluster wiring loom multiple connector.

6. Carefully move the instrument cluster into position at the instrument panel, guiding all wiring and cables into position to prevent damage. **Be careful not to kink the speedometer cable.**

7. Install the screws retaining the instrument cluster to the instrument panel.

8. Connect the battery ground cable and

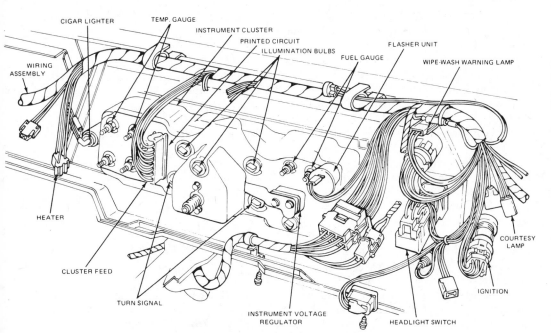

CIGAR LIGHTER   TEMP. GAUGE
INSTRUMENT CLUSTER
PRINTED CIRCUIT
ILLUMINATION BULBS
FUEL GAUGE
FLASHER UNIT
WIPE-WASH WARNING LAMP
WIRING ASSEMBLY
HEATER
COURTESY LAMP
CLUSTER FEED
IGNITION
TURN SIGNAL
INSTRUMENT VOLTAGE REGULATOR
HEADLIGHT SWITCH

Rear view of a 1974 instrument cluster

check the operation of all gauges, lights and signals.

1971–74

1. Disconnect the battery ground cable.
2. From the front of the cluster, remove the eight screws that retain the cluster to the instrument panel, and position the cluster part way out of the panel for access to the back of the cluster.
3. At the back of the cluster, disconnect the speedometer cable from the head and disconnect the multiple (feed) plug from the printed circuit.
4. Disconnect the wire from the flasher unit at the upper left hand corner of the cluster and remove the cluster assembly from the vehicle.
5. Hold the cluster near its opening in the instrument panel and connect: the wire to the flasher unit at the upper left hand corner of the cluster; the multiple feed plug to the printed circuit; and the speedometer cable to the head.
6. Position the cluster to the instrument panel and install the eight retaining screws.

1975–77

1. Disconnect the battery ground cable.
2. Remove seven instrument cluster-to-panel retaining screws.
3. Position cluster part away from the panel for access to the back of the cluster to disconnect the speedometer cable.

If there is not sufficient access to disengage the speedometer cable from the speedometer, it may be necessary to remove the speedometer cable at the transmission and pull cable through cowl, to allow room to reach the speedometer quick disconnect.

4. Disconnect the harness connector plug from the printed circuit board and remove the cluster assembly from the instrument panel.
5. Remove the cluster.
6. Apply approximately $3/16$ inch diameter ball of silicone lubricant or equivalent in the drive hole of the speedometer head.
7. Position the cluster near its opening in the instrument panel.
8. Connect the harness connector plug to the printed circuit board.
9. Connect the speedometer cable (quick disconnect) to the speedometer head.

Connect the speedometer cable and housing assembly to the transmission (if removed).

10. Install the seven instrument cluster-to-panel retaining screws and connect the battery ground cable.
11. Check operation of all gauges, lights, and signals.

1978–82

1. Disconnect the battery ground cable.
2. Remove two steering column shroud to panel retaining screws and remove shroud.
3. Loosen bolts which attach the column to the Band C Support to provide sufficient clearance for cluster removal. (Required for tilt steering column vehicles only).
4. Remove seven instrument cluster to panel retaining screws.
5. Position cluster part away from the panel for access to the back of the cluster to disconnect the speedometer.

If there is not sufficient access to disengage the speedometer cable from the speedometer, it may be necessary to remove the speedometer cable at the transmission and pull cable through cowl, to allow room to reach the speedometer quick disconnect.

6. Disconnect the harness connector plug from the printed circuit board and remove the cluster assembly from the instrument panel.
7. Apply approximately $3/16$ inch diameter ball of silicone lubricant or equivalent in the drive hole of the speedometer head.
8. Position the cluster near its opening in the instrument panel.
9. Connect the harness connector plug to the printed circuit board.
10. Connect the speedometer cable (quick disconnect) to the speedometer head.

Connect the speedometer cable and housing assembly to the transmission (if removed).

11. Install the seven instrument cluster-to-panel retaining screws and connect the battery ground cable.
12. Check operation of all gauges, lights, and signals.
13. Reinstall the steering column.
14. Position steering column shroud to instrument panel and install two screws.

HEADLIGHTS

Removal and Installation

1. Remove the attaching screws and remove the trim ring, or door. This isn't necessary on 1975–82 models.

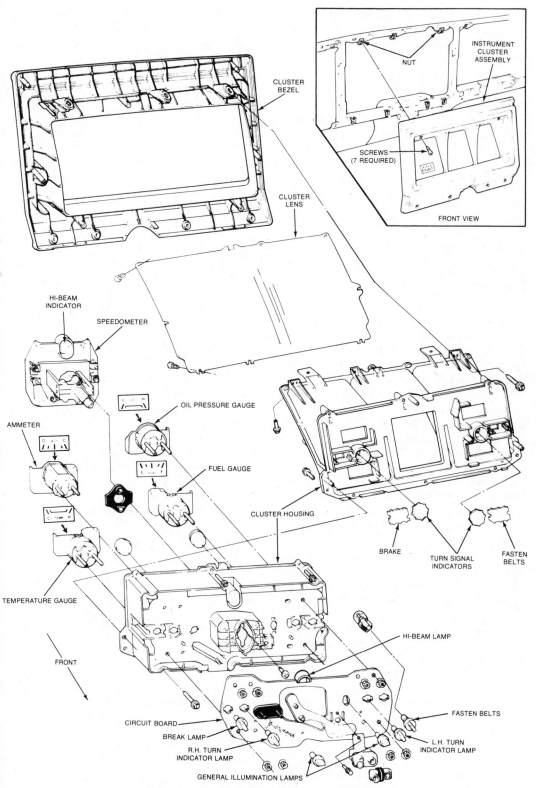

CLUSTER BEZEL

NUT

INSTRUMENT CLUSTER ASSEMBLY

SCREWS (7 REQUIRED)

FRONT VIEW

CLUSTER LENS

HI-BEAM INDICATOR

SPEEDOMETER

AMMETER

OIL PRESSURE GAUGE

FUEL GAUGE

CLUSTER HOUSING

BRAKE

TURN SIGNAL INDICATORS

FASTEN BELTS

TEMPERATURE GAUGE

FRONT

HI-BEAM LAMP

CIRCUIT BOARD

BREAK LAMP

R.H. TURN INDICATOR LAMP

GENERAL ILLUMINATION LAMPS

FASTEN BELTS

L.H. TURN INDICATOR LAMP

Rear view of the 1975–82 instrument cluster

2. Loosen or remove the headlight retaining ring screws and remove the retaining ring by rotating it counterclockwise. Do not disturb the adjusting screw settings.

3. Pull the headlight bulb forward and disconnect the wiring assembly plug from the bulb.

4. Connect the wiring assembly plug to the new bulb. Place the bulb in position, making sure that the locating tabs of the bulb are fitted in the positioning slots.

5. Install the headlight retaining ring.

6. Place the headlight trim ring or door into position, and install the retaining screws.

Ignition Switch and Lock Cylinder

1961–68

1. Disconnect the negative cable from the battery.

2. Turn the ignition key to the accessory position. Slightly depress the pin in the lockface, turn the key counterclockwise, and pull the key and lock cylinder out of the switch assembly. If only the lock cylinder is to be replaced, proceed to Step 9.

3. Press in on the rear of the switch and rotate the switch ⅛ turn counterclockwise (as viewed from the terminal end). Remove the bezel, switch and spacer.

4. Remove the nut from the back of the ignition switch. Remove the accessory and gauge feed wires from the accessory terminal of the switch. Pull off the insulated plug from the rear of the switch.

5. If a new ignition switch is to be installed, insert a screwdriver into the lock opening of the ignition switch and turn the slot in the switch to a full counterclockwise position.

6. Connect the insulated plug with wires to the back of the ignition switch. Position the accessory and gauge wires onto the ignition switch stud and install the retaining nut.

7. Position the retainer on the switch with the open face away from the switch.

8. Place the switch and spacer to the switch opening and press the switch toward the instrument panel and install the bezel.

9. If a new lock cylinder is to be installed, insert the key in the cylinder and turn the key to the accessory position. Place the lock and key in the ignition switch, depress the pin slightly, and turn the key counterclockwise. Push the new lock cylinder into the switch. Turn the key to check the lock cylinder operation.

10. Connect the battery cable and check the ignition switch operation.

1969–82

1. Disconnect the battery ground cable.

2. Insert the ignition key in the switch. Turn the key to the accessory position and insert a wire pin in the hole on the ignition switch. Slightly depress the pin while turning the key counterclockwise past the accessory position; this will release the lock cylinder from the switch assembly. Pull the lock cylinder from the switch with the key. If only the lock cylinder is to be replaced proceed to Step 7.

3. Remove the bezel nut retaining the switch to the instrument panel and lower the switch.

4. Depress the tabs securing the multiple connector to the rear of the ignition switch with a small screwdriver. Pull the multiple connector from the switch and remove the switch.

5. Depress the tabs on the multiple connector and plug the connector into the switch assembly, being sure that the tabs lock in place.

6. Position the switch to the instrument panel and install the bezel nut.

7. Insert the key in the lock cylinder and turn the key to the accessory position. Place the cylinder and key in the switch. Push the cylinder into the switch until it is fully seated, then turn the key to the lock position. Turn the key to check the operation of the lock cylinder.

8. Connect the battery ground cable to the battery and check the operation of the switch assembly.

CIRCUIT PROTECTION

Fuses

1961–68

The fuses are mounted in the fuse panel which is attached to the headlight switch. To replace the fuses it may be necessary to remove the battery ground cable and remove the headlight switch and fuse panel to a position below the lower edge of the instrument panel.

1969–82

The fuse panel is part of the instrument panel wiring assembly. It is mounted on the left side of the engine housing, above and to the right of the accelerator pedal.

In-line Fuses

Some circuits are protected by in-line cartridge fuses. These are replaced by squeezing together, twisting, and pulling the cartridge apart.

Circuit Breakers

Increasing numbers of circuits are protected by automatically resetting circuit breakers. These circuits include:
—Cigar lighter
—1962 and later wiper motor
—1974 and later tail, license, marker lights and horn.

Fuse Link

The fuse link is a short length of special, Hypalon (high temperature) insulated wire, integral with the engine compartment wiring harness and should not be confused with standard wire. It is several wire gauges smaller than the circuit which it protects. Under no circumstances should a fuse link replacement repair be made using a length of standard wire cut from bulk stock or from another wiring harness.

To repair any blown fuse link use the following procedure:

1. Determine which circuit is damaged, its location and the cause of the open fuse link. If the damaged fuse link is one of three fed by a common No. 10 or 12 gauge feed wire, determine the specific affected circuit.

2. Disconnect the negative battery cable.

3. Cut the damaged fuse link from the wiring harness and discard it. If the fuse link is one of three circuits fed by a single feed wire, cut it out of the harness at each splice end and discard it.

4. Identify and procure the proper fuse link and butt connectors for attaching the fuse link to the harness.

5. To repair any fuse link in a 3-link group with one feed:

a. After cutting the open link out of the harness, cut each of the remaining undamaged fuse links close to the feed wire weld.

b. Strip approximately ½ inch of insulation from the detached ends of the two good fuse links. Then insert two wire ends into one end of a butt connector and care-

fully push one stripped end of the replacement fuse link into the same end of the butt connector and crimp all three firmly together.

NOTE: *Care must be taken when fitting the three fuse links into the butt connector as the internal diameter is a snug fit for three wires. Make sure to use a proper crimping tool. Pliers, side cutters, etc. will not apply the proper crimp to retain the wires and withstand a pull test.*

c. After crimping the butt connector to the three fuse links, cut the weld portion from the feed wire and strip approximately ½ inch of insulation from the cut end. Insert the stripped end into the open end of the butt connector and crimp very firmly.

d. To attach the remaining end of the replacement fuse link, strip approximately ½ inch of insulation from the wire end of the circuit from which the blown fuse link was removed, and firmly crimp a butt connector or equivalent to the stripped wire. Then, insert the end of the replacement link into the other end of the butt connector and crimp firmly.

e. Using rosin core solder with a consistency of 60 percent tin and 40 percent lead, solder the connectors and the wires at the repairs and insulate with electrical tape.

Fuse Link Location Chart All Models

Circuit	Location	Protective Device
Air Conditioner, Clutch, Blower Relay	Fuse Panel	30 Amp
Air Conditioner	Starter Motor Relay	16 Gauge Fuse Link
Alternator	Starter Motor Relay	16 Gauge * Fuse Link
Alternator	Electric Choke	20 Gauge Fuse Link
Dual Batteries	Starter Motor Relay	14 Gauge Fuse Link

* 14 gauge for 70 and 100 amp alternators

REMOVE EXISTING VINYL TUBE SHIELDING
REINSTALL OVER FUSE LINK BEFORE CRIMPING
FUSE LINK TO WIRE ENDS

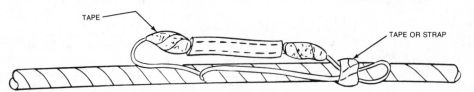

TAPE

TAPE OR STRAP

TYPICAL REPAIR USING THE SPECIAL #17 GA. (9.00′ LONG-YELLOW) FUSE LINK REQUIRED FOR THE AIR/COND.
CIRCUITS (2) #687E and #261A LOCATED IN THE ENGINE COMPARTMENT

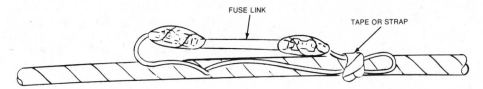

FUSE LINK

TAPE OR STRAP

TYPICAL REPAIR FOR ANY IN-LINE FUSE LINK USING THE SPECIFIED GAUGE FUSE LINK FOR THE SPECIFIC CIRCUIT

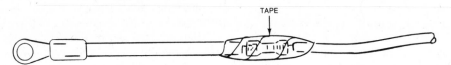

TAPE

TYPICAL REPAIR USING THE EYELET TERMINAL FUSE LINK OF THE SPECIFIED GAUGE FOR ATTACHMENT TO A CIRCUIT WIRE END

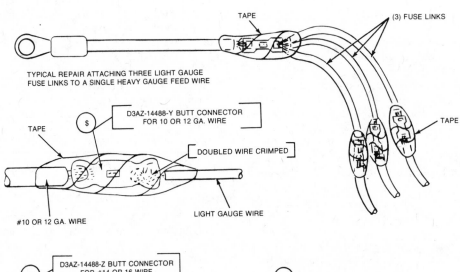

TAPE

(3) FUSE LINKS

TYPICAL REPAIR ATTACHING THREE LIGHT GAUGE
FUSE LINKS TO A SINGLE HEAVY GAUGE FEED WIRE

D3AZ-14488-Y BUTT CONNECTOR
FOR 10 OR 12 GA. WIRE

$

TAPE

DOUBLED WIRE CRIMPED

TAPE

LIGHT GAUGE WIRE

#10 OR 12 GA. WIRE

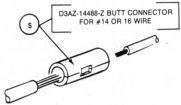

D3AZ-14488-Z BUTT CONNECTOR
FOR #14 OR 16 WIRE

$

$

FUSIBLE LINK REPAIR PROCEDURE

General fuse link repair procedure

6. To replace any fuse link on a single circuit in a harness, cut out the damaged portion, strip approximately ½ inch of insulation from the two wire ends and attach the appropriate replacement fuse link to the stripped wire ends with two proper size butt connectors. Solder the connectors and wires and insulate with tape.

7. To repair any fuse link which has an eyelet terminal on one end such as the charging circuit, cut off the open fuse link behind the weld, strip approximately ½ inch of insulation from the cut end and attach the appropriate new eyelet fuse link to the cut stripped wire with an appropriate size butt connector. Solder the connectors and wires at the repair and insulate with tape.

8. Connect the negative battery cable to the battery and test the system for proper operation.

NOTE: *Do not mistake a resistor wire for a fuse link. The resistor wire is generally longer and has print stating, "Resistor-don't cut or splice."*

NOTE: *When attaching a single No. 16, 17, 18 or 20 gauge fuse link to a heavy gauge wire, always double the stripped wire end of the fuse link before inserting and crimping it into the butt connector for positive wire retention.*

WIRING DIAGRAMS

Wiring diagrams have been left out of this book. As vans have become more complex, and available with longer and longer option lists, wiring diagrams have grown in size and complexity also. It has become virtually impossible to provide a readable reproduction in a reasonable number of pages. Information on ordering wiring diagrams from the vehicle manufacturer can be obtained from your dealer.

Clutch and Transmission

MANUAL TRANSMISSION

The 3-speed used in all Ford vans is a Ford Model 3.03 three-speed manual transmission; the shifter is mounted on the steering column. The number 3.03 is the distance in inches between the centerlines of the countershaft and the input shaft.

In 1964 only, Ford offered a 4-speed option on E-100 models. This unit was the British built Dagenham unit, identical to the unit used in the early Falcon passenger cars. The unit is fully synchronized in all forward gears; reverse is in constant mesh.

Beginning in 1978 Ford offered an optional 4-speed overdrive transmission. The 4-speed overdrive transmission is of the fully synchronized type with all gears except the reverse sliding gear being in constant mesh. All forward-speed changes are accomplished with synchronizer sleeves.

All forward-speed gears in the transmission are helical-type. However, the reverse sliding gear and the external teeth of the first- and second-speed synchronizer sleeve are spur-type.

A transmission service identification tag is located on the right side of the case at the front. The first line on the tag will show the transmission model and service identification code when required. The second line will show the transmission serial number. Additionally, a serial number is stamped on the top side of the flange on the case for further identification.

The 4-speed shift control unit is serviced as a unit only. It is not to be disassembled. The only parts to be removed from the shifter assembly are the 3 shift rods, the in-cab shift lever, back-up switch bracket, and the back-up light switch. The shift pattern for the control unit is imprinted on the shift knob. The automatically adjusted back-up light switch is assembled to the backside of the shift control unit.

REMOVAL AND INSTALLATION—3 SPEED

1. Raise the vehicle on a hoist and drain the lubricant from the transmission by removing the lower extension housing-to-transmission bolt.

2. Disconnect the driveshaft from the flange at the transmission. Secure the front end of the driveshaft out of the way by tying it up with a length of wire.

3. Disconnect the speedometer cable from the extension housing and disconnect the gearshift rods from the transmission. Disconnect the transmission regulated spark switch, if so equipped.

4. Position a transmission jack under the

transmission. Chain the transmission to the jack.

5. On 1961–68 vehicles, remove the transmission rear support bolts. Lower the engine enough to drop the transmission extension housing from the rear support.

On 1969 and later vehicles, raise the transmission slightly and remove the 4 bolts which retain the transmission support crossmember to the frame side rails. Remove the bolt which retains the transmission extension housing to the crossmember.

6. Remove the 4 transmission-to-flywheel housing bolts.

7. On the 1969 and later vehicles, position a bar under the rear of the engine to support it.

8. Remove the transmission from the vehicle by lowering the jack.

To install the transmission:

9. Make sure that the machined surfaces of the transmission case and the flywheel housing are free of dirt, paint, and burrs.

10. Install a guide pin in each lower mounting bolt hole.

11. Start the input shaft through the release bearing. Align the splines on the input shaft with the splines in the clutch disc. Move the transmission forward on the guide pins until the input shaft pilot enters the bearing or bushing in the crankshaft. If the transmission front bearing retainer binds up on the clutch release bearing hub, work the release bearing lever until the hub slides onto the transmission front bearing retainer. Install the two upper mounting bolts and lockwashers which attach the flywheel housing to the transmission. Remove the two guide pins and install the lower mounting bolts and lockwashers.

12. On 1961–68 vehicles, raise the jack enough to align the extension housing with the mounting holes in the hanger bracket. Install the attaching bolts. Remove the jack.

13. On 1969 and later vehicles, raise the jack slightly and remove the engine support bar. Position the support crossmember on the frame side rails and install the retaining bolts. Install the extension housing-to-crossmember retaining bolt.

14. Connect the gearshift rods and the speedometer cable. Connect the transmission regulated spark switch lead, if so equipped.

15. Install the driveshaft.

16. Fill the transmission to the bottom of the filler hole with the proper lubricant.

17. Adjust the clutch pedal free-play and the shift linkage as required.

REMOVAL AND INSTALLATION—4 SPEED

1. Disconnect the drive shaft from the U-joint flange on the transmission and tie the shaft up and out of the way.

2. Disconnect the shift rods from the shift levers on the transmission.

3. Remove the dust cover attaching bolts from the flywheel housing and remove the cover.

4. Remove the nut and lock washer that secures the starter cable to the starter. Lift the cable off the stud.

5. Remove the starter motor attaching bolts and lock washers and remove the starter.

6. Disconnect and remove the clutch release lever retracting spring.

7. Secure the transmission to a transmission jack.

8. Remove the speedometer cable clamp attaching bolt. Disconnect the cable from the extension housing.

9. Remove the four flywheel housing-to-engine attaching bolts and lock washers.

10. Remove the extension housing-to-engine rear support attaching bolt and lock washer.

11. Lower the transmission and at the same time, move it away from the flywheel housing being careful not to drop the spacer plate from between the transmission and housing.

12. Move the transmission from under the vehicle and remove it from the jack.

13. Secure the transmission to the jack.

14. Install two threaded guide pins in the flywheel housing lower mounting holes. Position the spacer plate on the guide pins.

15. Raise the transmission into place and align the input shaft with the clutch hub.

16. Move the transmission into place onto the two guide pins and against the flywheel housing. If necessary to align the input shaft splines with those in the clutch hub, place the transmission into reverse and rotate the output shaft slowly.

17. Install the two transmission-to-flywheel housing upper attaching bolts and lock washers. Remove the two guide pins and install the two lower attaching bolts and lock washers. Tighten the attaching bolts to the 32–36 ft lb.

18. Raise or lower the transmission as

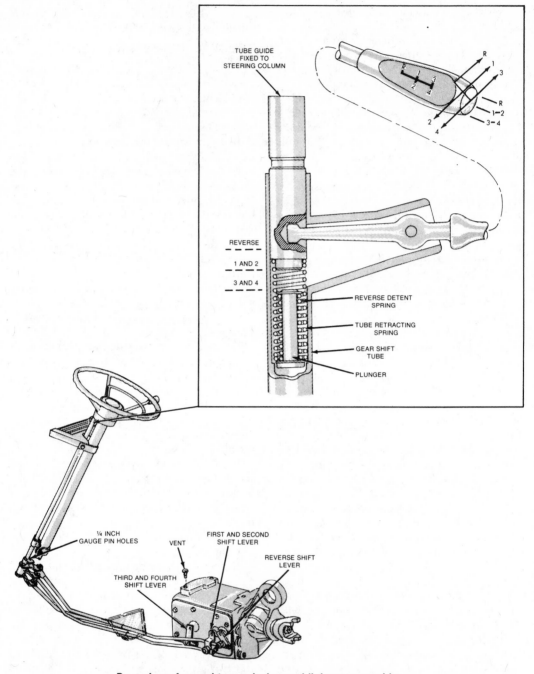

TUBE GUIDE FIXED TO STEERING COLUMN

REVERSE

1 AND 2

3 AND 4

REVERSE DETENT SPRING

TUBE RETRACTING SPRING

GEAR SHIFT TUBE

PLUNGER

¼ INCH GAUGE PIN HOLES

VENT

FIRST AND SECOND SHIFT LEVER

REVERSE SHIFT LEVER

THIRD AND FOURTH SHIFT LEVER

Dagenham 4-speed transmission and linkage assembly

required and install the extension housing-to-support attaching bolt, lock washer, and nut.

19. Remove the transmission jack.

20. Connect the drive shaft to the U-joint flange on the output shaft. Torque the retaining nuts to 60–80 ft lb.

21. Connect the speedometer cable to the extension housing and secure it with a bolt and lock washer.

22. Position the starter against the flywheel housing and secure it with the three attaching bolts and lock washers. Torque the bolts to 25–30 ft lb.

23. Connect the cable to the terminal on the starter.

24. Secure the dust cover to the flywheel housing with the attaching bolts and lock washers.

25. Install the clutch release lever retracting spring.

26. Connect the shift rods to the shift levers on the transmission.

27. Adjust the shift linkage, if required.

28. Fill the transmission to the correct level with the approved lubricant.

REMOVAL AND INSTALLATION—4 SPEED OVERDRIVE

1. Raise the vehicle on a hoist.

2. Mark the driveshaft so that it may be installed in the same relative position. Disconnect the drive shaft from the rear U-joint flange. Slide the driveshaft off the transmission output shaft and install the extension housing seal installation tool into the extension housing to prevent lubricant leakage.

3. Disconnect the speedometer cable from the extension housing.

4. Remove the retaining clips, flat washers, and spring washers that secure the shift rods to the shift levers. Remove the bolts connecting the shift control to the transmission extension housing. Remove the nut connecting the shift control to the transmission case.

NOTE: *A '6' and '8' is stamped on transmission extension housing by the shift control plate bolt holes. The '6' and '8' refer to either a 6 or 8 cylinder engine application. The shift control plate bolts must be placed in the right holes for proper plate positioning dependent upon engine application.*

5. Remove the rear transmission support connecting bolts attaching the support on the crossmember to the transmission extension housing.

6. Support the engine with a transmission jack and remove the extension housing-to-engine rear support attaching bolts.

7. Raise the rear of the engine high enough to remove the weight from the crossmember. Remove the bolts retaining the crossmember to the frame side supports and remove the crossmember.

8. Support the transmission on a jack and remove the bolts that attach the transmission to the flywheel housing.

9. Move the transmission and jack rearward until the transmission input shaft clears the flywheel housing. If necessary, lower the engine enough to obtain clearance for transmission removal. **Do not depress the clutch pedal while the transmission is removed.**

10. Make sure that the mounting surfaces of the transmission and the flywheel housing are free of dirt, paint, and burrs. Install two guide pins in the flywheel housing lower mounting bolt holes. Move the transmission forward on the guide pins until the input shaft splines enter the clutch hub splines and the case is positioned against the flywheel housing.

11. Install the two upper transmission to flywheel housing mounting bolts snug, and then remove the two guide pins. Install the two lower mounting bolts. Tighten all mounting bolts to 40–45 ft lb.

12. Raise the rear of the engine and install the crossmember. Install and torque the crossmember attaching bolts to 20–30 ft lb, then lower the engine.

13. With the transmission extension housing resting on the engine rear support, install the transmission extension housing attaching bolts. Tighten the bolts to 42–50 ft lb.

14. Install the transmission support bolts and tighten to 40–50 ft lb.

15. Position the shift control bracket on the stud on the transmission case and on the bolt attaching holes (holes marked either '6' or '8' dependent upon 6 or 8 cylinder engine application) on the transmission extension housing. Install and hand tighten connecting bolts.

NOTE: *The bracket must be placed in the proper position for correct shift control operation.*

Tighten the nut connecting the bracket to the transmission case to 22–30 ft lbs. Tighten the bolts to 22–30 ft lbs.

16. Secure each shift rod to its respective lever with the spring washer, flat washer, and retaining pin.

17. Connect the speedometer cable to the extension housing.

18. Remove the extension housing installation tool and slide the forward end of the drive shaft over the transmission output shaft. Connect the driveshaft to the rear U-joint flange. Adjust the linkage.

19. Fill the transmission to the proper level with the specified lubricant.

20. Lower the vehicle. Check the shift and crossover motion for full shift engagement and smooth crossover operation.

SHIFT LINKAGE ADJUSTMENT—3 SPEED

1. Place the gearshift lever in the Neutral position.

2. Loosen the adjustment nuts on the

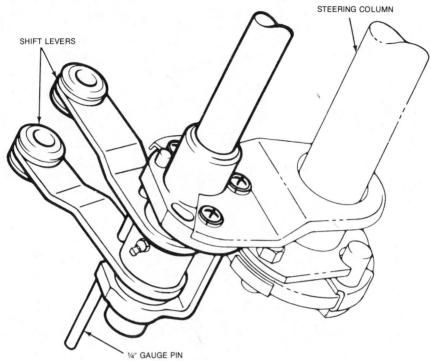

1961–75 shift linkage adjustment—3-speed

transmission shift levers sufficiently to allow the shift rods to slide freely on the transmission shift levers.

3. Insert a ¼ in. rod (³/₁₆ in. for 1976–80) through the pilot hole in the shift tube mounting bracket (1961–75 only) until it enters the adjustment hole of both the upper and lower shift lever.

4. Place the transmission shift levers in the Neutral position and tighten the adjustment nuts on the transmission shift levers.

5. Remove the ¼ in. rod from the pilot hole, and check the operation of the gearshift lever in all gear positions.

SHIFT LINKAGE ADJUSTMENT—4 SPEED

1. Place the gear shift lever in the neutral position.

2. Loosen the trunnion nuts at the transmission shift levers until the shift rods can slide freely in their trunnions.

3. Insert a ¼-inch rod through the hole in the lever locating bracket and the three shift levers.

4. Tighten the transmission lever trunnion nuts.

5. Remove the ¼-inch rod from the levers and locating bracket.

6. Check the operation of the shift lever in all range positions.

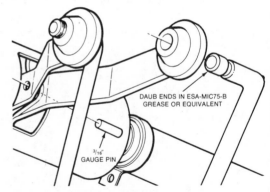

1976–82 shift linkage adjustment

SHIFT LINKAGE ADJUSTMENT—4 SPEED OVERDRIVE

1. Disconnect the 3 shift rods from the shifter assembly.

2. Insert a .25″ diameter pin through the alignment hole in the shifter assembly. Make sure the levers are in the neutral position.

3. Align the 3 transmission levers as follows: forward lever (3rd-4th lever) in the mid-position (neutral), rearward lever (1st-2nd lever) in the mid-position (neutral), and middle lever (reverse lever) rotate counterclockwise to the neutral position.

4. Rotate the output shaft to assure that the transmission is in neutral.

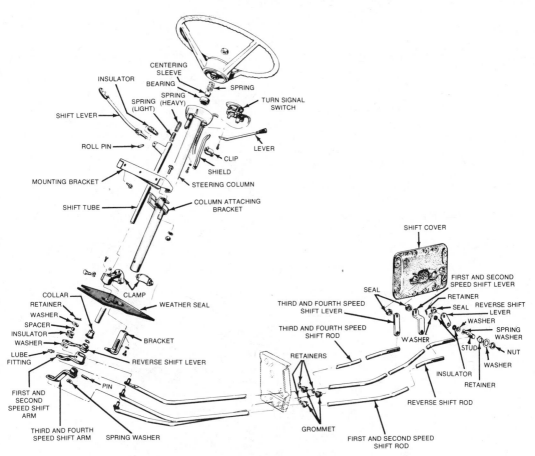

Dagenham 4-speed linkage, exploded view

5. Attach the slotted end of the shift rods over the slots of the studs in the shifter assembly. Install and tighten the locknuts to 15–20 ft-lbs.

6. Remove the alignment pin. Check for proper operation.

CLUTCH

REMOVAL AND INSTALLATION

1. Disconnect the cable from the starter and remove the starter.

2. Remove the transmission.

3. Disconnect the release lever retracting spring and release the rod.

4. Remove the hub and release bearing assembly.

5. Remove the flywheel housing-to-engine bolts, and lower the flywheel housing.

6. Remove the pressure plate and the disc from the flywheel. Unscrew the attaching bolts a few turns at a time, in a staggered sequence to prevent distortion of the pressure plate.

7. Wash the flywheel surface with alcohol. Do not use an oil-base cleaner, carbon tetrachloride or gasoline.

To install the clutch:

8. Place the clutch disc and the pressure plate and cover assembly in position on the flywheel. Start the retaining bolts until finger-tight.

9. Align the clutch disc with a clutch arbor (an old mainshaft works well) and then evenly torque the bolts to 23–28 ft lbs.

10. Lightly lubricate the release lever fulcrum and ends with lithium-base grease and position the release lever in the flywheel housing. Do not grease the release lever pivot assembly on 1975–80 models. Crimp the dust seal tabs flush against the flywheel housing. Attach the springs of the release bearing hub to the ends of the release fork. Be careful not to distort the springs.

11. Fill the groove in the clutch release bearing hub with lithium-base grease. Wipe the excess grease from the hub.

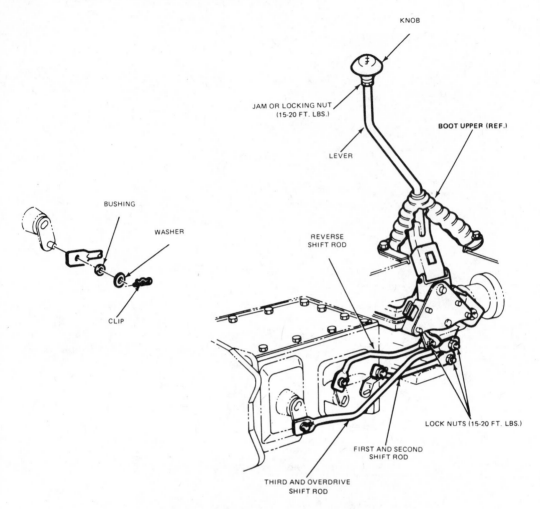

KNOB

JAM OR LOCKING NUT
(15-20 FT. LBS.)

BOOT UPPER (REF.)

LEVER

BUSHING

WASHER

REVERSE
SHIFT ROD

CLIP

LOCK NUTS (15-20 FT. LBS.)

FIRST AND SECOND
SHIFT ROD

THIRD AND OVERDRIVE
SHIFT ROD

4-speed Overdrive shift linkage adjustment

12. Position the flywheel housing and release lever assembly, and install the mounting bolts. Make sure that the muffler front hanger is in place on the flywheel housing.

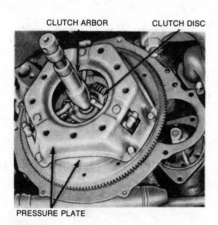

CLUTCH ARBOR   CLUTCH DISC

PRESSURE PLATE

Installing the clutch, using an alignment arbor to align the clutch disc spline

Install the dust cover, and tighten the attaching bolts.

13. Remove any dirt, paint, or burrs from the mounting surfaces of the flywheel housing and the transmission.

14. Install the transmission.

15. Install the starter and connect the starter cable.

16. Adjust the clutch pedal free-play and check the operation of the clutch.

CLUTCH PEDAL ADJUSTMENT

To check and adjust the pedal free travel, measure and note the distance from the floor pan to the top of the pedal; then depress the pedal slowly until the clutch release fingers contact the clutch release bearing. Measure and record the distance. The difference between the reading with the pedal in the depressed position and the reading with the pedal in the fully released position is the

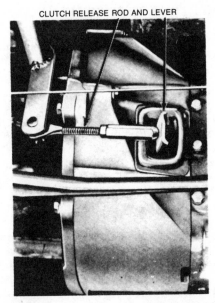

Clutch linkage (pedal travel) adjustment point at the bellhousing

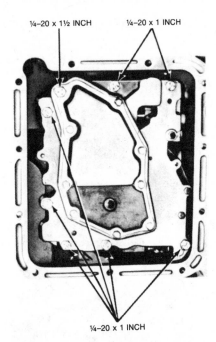

¼–20 x 1½ INCH   ¼–20 x 1 INCH

¼–20 x 1 INCH

View of the underside of the C4 transmission with the pan removed showing the location of the transmission filter screen

pedal free travel. The free travel should be as specified. If the free travel is not within specifications, loosen the jam nut on the clutch release rod. Adjust the rod length until the free travel is correct, then tighten the nut.

The clutch pedal height should be within 7½–7¾ in. from the floor pan to the center of the clutch pedal on 1969–74 models. On other models, the pedal height is not adjustable. Pedal height is adjusted by loosening the nut securing the clutch pedal eccentric bumper and rotating the bumper until the proper clutch pedal height is within the proper range.

Clutch Pedal Free Travel (in.)

Year	Free Travel
1961–67	⅞–1⅛
1968–69	1⅛–1⅜
1970–72	1⅛–1½
1973–74	¾–1½
1975–82	¾–1½, 1¼–1½ preferred

AUTOMATIC TRANSMISSION

The C4 automatic transmission is used on all models through 1974 and the 1975–77 E-100 and 150 sixes; the heavier-duty C6 is used on all other 1975–77 models. The C6 is used on all 1978–82 models except 1982 E-100 and

150 models. These models use the new C5. The C4 is identified by the letter G in the TRANS space on the Vehicle Certification Label; W indicates the C5; Z indicates the C6. Fluid changing and pan removal is covered in Chapter 1.

FRONT BAND (INTERMEDIATE) ADJUSTMENT

All

1. Clean all dirt from the adjusting screw and remove and discard the locknut.

2. Install a new locknut on the adjusting screw. Using a torque wrench, tighten the adjusting screw to 10 ft lbs.

3. Back off the adjusting screw EXACTLY 1¾ TURNS FOR THE C4, 4¼ TURNS FOR THE C5, 1½ TURNS FOR THE C6.

Adjusting the front (Intermediate) band

4. Hold the adjusting screw steady and tighten the locknut to 35–45 ft lbs.

REAR BAND (LOW-REVERSE) ADJUSTMENT

C4, C5

1. Clean all dirt from around the band adjusting screw and remove and discard the locknut.

2. Install a new locknut on the adjusting screw. Using a torque wrench, tighten the adjusting screw to 10 ft lbs.

3. Back off the adjusting screw EXACTLY 3 FULL TURNS.

4. Hold the adjusting screw steady and tighten the locknut to 35–45 ft lbs.

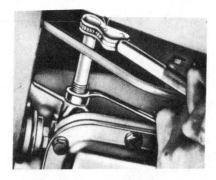

Adjusting the Low-Reverse band

GAUGE PIN HOLES   LOWER END OF STEERING COLUMN

FRONT GRILLE   ¼ INCH GAUGE PIN

Installation of the gauge pin through 1968

SHIFT LINKAGE ADJUSTMENT

1. On models through 1968, place the shift lever in the Neutral position. On all other model years, place the shift lever in the Drive position (parking brake applied, engine off).

NOTE: *On 1978–82 models, it will be necessary to hold the lever against the "D" stop with an eight pound weight attached to the end of the lever.*

2. Disconnect the manual shift rod from the shift lever on the transmission.

3. On models through 1968 shift the transmission shift lever at the transmission into the Neutral position (fourth detent from the rear). On all other models, move the transmission shift lever at the transmission to the Drive position (second detent from the rear).

4. On models through 1968 insert a ¼ in. gauge pin through the steering column shift rod actuating lever and the steering column shift tube bracket to hold the shift rod linkage in the Neutral position.

On all other models, just make sure that the steering column shift lever remains in the Drive position.

5. With the linkage in the position mentioned above (Drive or Neutral) at the steering column shift lever and the shift lever on the transmission, adjust the trunnion on the transmission end of the shift rod so that it slips into the manual lever on the transmission easily.

NOTE: *On 1974–82 models, the end of the shift rod is slotted and can be connected to the transmission at this point in the procedure. Tighten the attaching nut. This ends the linkage adjustment procedure for all 1974–82 models.*

6. On models through 1968 turn the trunnion 1 complete turn counterclockwise to lengthen the rod. On 1969–71 models, turn the trunnion 4 complete turns counterclockwise to lengthen the rod. On 1972 and 1973 models, lock the trunnion in the original position described in Step 5.

7. Connect the trunnion to the shift lever at the transmission. Remove the gauge pin on models through 1968.

8. Check the operation of the linkage and the transmission.

NEUTRAL START SWITCH ADJUSTMENT

1. With the manual shift linkage adjusted properly, loosen the two switch attaching bolts.

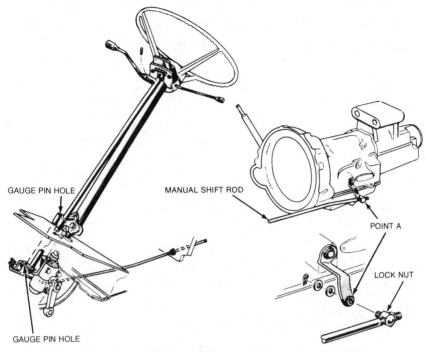

GAUGE PIN HOLE

MANUAL SHIFT ROD

POINT A

LOCK NUT

GAUGE PIN HOLE

Automatic transmission shift control linkage through 1968

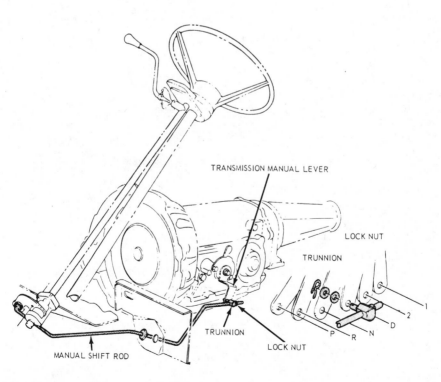

TRANSMISSION MANUAL LEVER

LOCK NUT

TRUNNION

TRUNNION

LOCK NUT

MANUAL SHIFT ROD

P   R   N   D

1   2

Automatic transmission shift control linkage for 1969–73. On the 1972–73 models there are two locknuts on either side of the trunnion

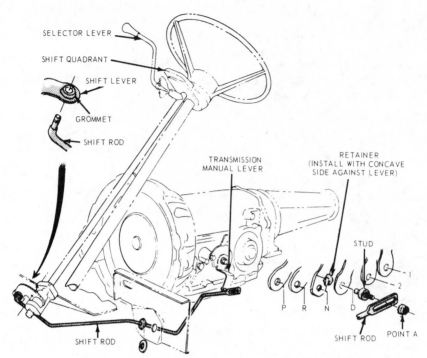

1974–82 automatic transmission shift control linkage

2. Place the transmission manual lever in Neutral. Rotate the switch and insert a No. 43 drill shank end into the gauge pin holes of the switch. The gauge pin (No. 43 drill) has to be inserted a full $^{31}/_{64}$ in. into the 3 holes of the switch.

3. Tighten the two neutral start switch attaching bolts 15 in. lbs. Remove the gauge pin from the switch.

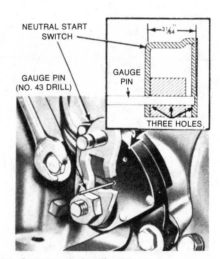

Neutral start switch adjustment

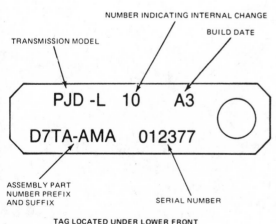

Typical automatic transmission identification tag

REMOVAL AND INSTALLATION
Through 1968
REMOVAL

1. Raise the engine compartment door and remove the throttle linkage bracket to top of converter housing attaching bolts.

2. Disconnect the neutral start switch wires at the starter relay, and the back-up light wires at the connector.

3. Raise the vehicle and loosen the transmission oil pan attaching bolts. On vehicles equipped with a 170 engine, lower one edge of the oil pan to drain the fluid.

4. At the front lower edge of the converter housing, remove the dust cover attaching bolts and cover.

5. Remove the converter to flywheel attaching nuts. As the flywheel is being rotated, remove the converter drain plugs and drain the fluid from the converter.

6. Disconnect the drive shaft from the transmission companion flange. Position the end of the drive shaft on top of the muffler to keep it out of the way. Remove the speedometer driven gear from the extension housing.

7. Disconnect the oil cooler lines from the transmission. Disconnect the vacuum line from the vacuum unit and retaining clips.

8. Disconnect the starter cable. Remove the starter to converter housing attaching bolts. Remove the starter.

9. Remove the downshift lever return spring from the retaining clip on the low-reverse servo cover.

10. Disconnect the manual and downshift linkage rods from the transmission control levers.

11. Install the converter drain plugs. If the converter is not going to be cleaned, torque the drain plugs to specifications.

12. Disconnect the neutral start switch wires from their retaining clips.

13. Position the transmission jack to support the transmission. Install the safety chain to hold the transmission on the jack.

14. Remove the converter housing to engine attaching bolts. Remove the extension housing to crossmember mounting bolts.

15. Lower the back of the transmission to clear the crossmember. Move the transmission and converter back from the engine. Lower the transmission and remove it from under the vehicle.

INSTALLATION

1. Position the transmission on the jack and secure the transmission and converter to the jack with the safety chain.

2. Raise the transmission and guide the transmission and converter into vehicle position. The converter to flywheel retaining studs must line up with the holes in the flywheel. The converter hub must enter the end of the crankshaft.

3. Install the converter housing to engine attaching bolts. Torque the bolts to specification. Install the converter to flywheel attaching nuts.

4. Install the extension housing to crossmember mounting bolts and retaining nuts, torque the bolts.

5. Remove the transmission jack and safety chain. Make sure the transmission fluid filler tube is properly installed in the transmission with the retaining bracket in alignment with the hole in the starter pocket of the housing.

6. Install the starter, starter cable retaining clip, oil filler tube, and attaching bolts. Torque the bolts.

7. Install the converter dust shield and torque the bolts to specification.

8. Install the vacuum line in the retaining clips and on the vacuum unit at the rear of the transmission.

9. Secure the oil cooler lines in the clips and connect them to the transmission.

10. Connect the transmission linkage rods to the control levers. Install the downshift lever return spring at the lever and clip on the low-reverse servo cover.

11. Secure the neutral start switch wires in the retaining clips.

12. Install the speedometer driven gear into the extension housing. Torque the attaching bolt.

13. Connect the drive shaft to the transmission. Torque the attaching nuts.

14. From underneath the vehicle, install the downshift linkage bracket onto the top of the converter housing. Install the attaching bolts finger tight.

15. Lower the vehicle and torque the linkage bracket attaching bolts.

16. Connect the neutral start wires at the starter relay, and the back-up light wires to the connector.

17. Add five quarts of transmission fluid. Run the engine at idle speed for about one minute. Re-check the transmission fluid level, add fluid if necessary.

18. Adjust the throttle and manual linkage. Check transmission for fluid leakage.

1969 and Later
REMOVAL

1. Working from inside the vehicle, remove the engine compartment cover.

2. Disconnect the neutral start switch wires at the plug connector.

3. If the vehicle is equipped with a V-8

engine, remove the flexhose from the air cleaner heat tube.

4. Remove the upper converter housing-to-engine attaching bolts (three bolts on 6-cylinder engine; four bolts on 8-cylinder engines).

5. Raise the vehicle on a hoist.

6. Place the drain pan under the transmission fluid pan. Starting at the rear of the pan and working toward the front, loosen the attaching bolts and allow the fluid to drain. Finally remove all of the pan attaching bolts except two at the front, to allow the fluid to further drain. With fluid drained, install two bolts on the rear side of the pan to temporarily hold it in place.

7. Remove the converter drain plug access cover from the lower end of the converter housing.

8. Remove the converter-to-flywheel attaching nuts. Place a wrench on the crankshaft pulley attaching bolt to turn the converter to gain access to the nuts.

9. With the wrench on the crankshaft pulley attaching bolt, turn the converter to gain access to the converter drain plug. Place a drain pan under the converter to catch the fluid. Then, remove the plug. With fluid drained, re-install the plug.

10. Disconnect the drive shaft.

11. Remove fluid filler tube.

12. Disconnect the starter cable at the starter. Remove the starter-to-converter housing attaching bolts and remove the starter.

13. Position the engine support bar (Tool T65E-6000-JO) to the frame and engine oil pan flanges.

14. Disconnect the cooler lines from the transmission. Disconnect the vacuum line from the vacuum diaphragm unit. Remove the vacuum line from the retaining clip at the transmission.

15. Remove the speedometer driven gear from the extension housing.

16. Disconnect the manual and downshift linkage rods from the transmission control levers.

17. Position a transmission jack to support the transmission. Install the safety chain to hold the transmission.

18. Remove the bolts and nuts securing the rear support and insulator assembly to the crossmember. Remove the six bolts retaining the crossmember to the side rails and remove the two support gussets. Raise the transmis-

sion with the jack and remove the crossmember.

19. Remove the bolt that retains the transmission filler tube to the cylinder block. Lift the filler tube and dipstick from the transmission.

20. Remove the remaining converter housing-to-engine attaching bolts. Lower the jack and remove the converter and transmission assembly from under the vehicle.

21. Remove the converter and mount the transmission in a holding fixture.

INSTALLATION

1. Tighten the converter drain plug to specification as listed at the end of this Part.

2. Position the converter on the transmission making sure the converter drive flats are fully engaged in the pump gear.

3. With the converter properly installed, place the transmission on the jack. Secure the transmission to the jack with the safety chain.

4. Rotate the converter until the studs and drain plug are in alignment with their holes in the flywheel.

5. Move the converter and transmission assembly forward into position, using care not to damage the flywheel and the converter pilot.

The converter must rest squarely against the flywheel. This indicates that the converter pilot is not binding in the engine crankshaft.

6. Install the lower converter housing-to-engine attaching bolts. Tighten the bolts. Install the converter-to-flywheel attaching nuts. Tighten the nuts.

7. Install the crossmember. Install the rear support and insulator assembly-to-crossmember attaching bolts and nuts. Tighten the bolts.

8. Remove the safety chain and remove the jack from under the vehicle. Remove the engine support bar.

9. Install a new O-ring on the lower end of the transmission filler tube and insert the tube and dipstick in the case.

10. Connect the vacuum line to the vacuum diaphragm making sure the line is secured in the retaining clip.

11. Connect the cooler lines to the transmission.

12. Install the speedometer driven gear into the extension housing. Tighten the attaching bolt.

13. Connect the transmission linkage rods

to the transmission control levers. When making transmission control attachments new retaining ring and grommet should always be used. Attach the shift rod to the steering column shift lever. Align the flats of the adjusting stud with the flats of the rod slot and insert the stud through the rod. Assemble the adjusting stud nut and washer to a loose fit. Perform a linkage adjustment.

14. Install the converter housing access cover and tighten the attaching bolts.

15. Position the starter into the converter housing and install the attaching bolts. Tighten the bolts. Install the starter cable.

16. Install the driveshaft.

17. Lower the vehicle.

18. Install the upper converter housing-to-engine attaching bolts. Tighten the bolts.

19. On V-8 engines, install the flex hose to the air cleaner heat tube. Install the bolt that retains the filler tube to the cylinder block.

20. Connect the neutral start switch wires at the plug connector.

21. Make sure the transmission fluid pan is securely attached, and fill the transmission to the proper level.

22. Raise the vehicle and check for transmission fluid leakage. Lower the vehicle and adjust the downshift and manual linkage.

23. Install the engine compartment cover.

Drive Train

DRIVELINE

Driveshaft

Short wheelbase vans use a single-piece driveshaft; long wheelbase models use a two-piece driveshaft with a support bearing and a sliding spline yoke at the center.

The driveshaft is joined to the transmission output shaft with sliding splines on all manual transmission short wheelbase models and some 1973–82 automatic transmission mod-

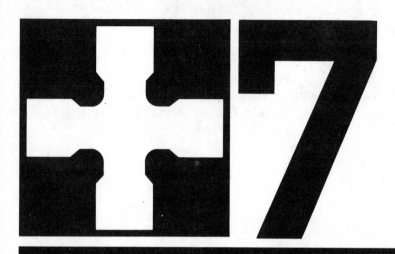

An exploded view of the driveshaft used on 1961–72 short wheelbase and automatic transmission models

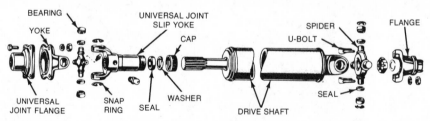
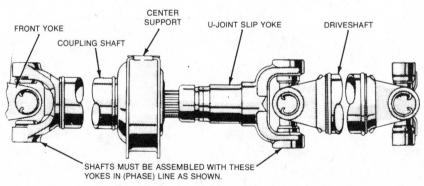

The driveshaft used on all long wheelbase manual transmission and 1961–72 long wheelbase automatic transmission models

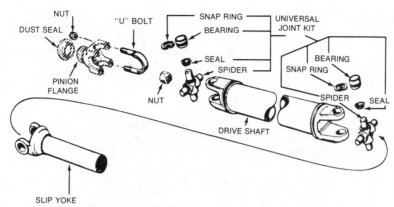

The driveshaft assembly used on all short wheelbase models with manual transmission and 1973–77 short wheelbase automatic transmission models

els; it connects to a fixed yoke on the output shaft on all long wheelbase manual transmission models and 1964–72 automatic transmission models.

REMOVAL AND INSTALLATION

One-Piece Driveshaft

1. If there are no alignment marks, match-mark the rear driveshaft yoke and the rear axle flange.

2. Unbolt the rear U-joint from the rear axle flange. Tape the bearing caps in place.

3. Unbolt the front U-joint from the transmission output shaft yoke on 1964–72 automatic transmission.

4. Pull the driveshaft back and remove it. You may have to plug the transmission extension housing to prevent leakage.

5. Reverse the procedure for installation. Grease the sliding splines used on all models except 1964–72 automatic transmission. Align the matchmarks.

NOTE: *If there is vibration in the drive-line, try unbolting the driveshaft from the rear axle flange and turning it 180°.*

Two-Piece Driveshaft

THROUGH 1977

1. If there are no alignment marks, match-mark the rear driveshaft yoke and the rear axle flange. Also matchmark the two drive-shaft halves.

2. Unbolt the rear U-joint from the rear axle flange. Tape the bearing caps in place.

3. Slide the rear half of the driveshaft off the coupling shaft splines.

4. Unbolt and support the center bearing.

5. Unbolt the front U-joint from the transmission output shaft yoke except on automatic transmission.

6. Pull the front half of the driveshaft back and remove it. You may have to plug the transmission extension housing to prevent leakage.

7. Reverse the procedure for installation. Grease the sliding splines used on automatic transmission. Align all matchmarks, making sure that all U-joints are in the same horizontal plane.

1978–82

NOTE: *To maintain driveline balance, mark the relationship of the rear driveshaft yoke and the rear axle pinion flange before disassembly.*

1. Disconnect the driveshaft from the rear axle flange and disconnect the driveshaft slip yoke from the coupling shaft yoke. Wrap tape around the loose bearing caps to prevent the bearings from falling off the universal joint spiders.

2. Remove the two center bearing support brackets (coupling shaft) to the frame crossmember attaching bolts. Remove the coupling shaft assembly from the transmission extension. Install a clean rag in the transmission housing to prevent leakage.

3. Slide the slip yoke off of the driveshaft. Remove the dust cap, cork seal and spacers from the slip yoke.

4. Clean the male splines of the drive-shaft with a wire brush and a suitable solvent. Remove all hardened grease deposits, dirt or rust. Inspect for worn or galled splines. Remove any nicks, gouges or burrs using a file or emery cloth. If the driveshaft is worn, warped, or cracked, replace the driveshaft and slip yoke assembly.

5. Using a suitable cleaning fluid, clean all dirt from the slip yoke internal splines and the slip yoke assembly. Carefully inspect the

slip yoke splines for wear or evidence of twisting. Check the clearance between the slip yoke splines and the driveshaft splines.

6. Wash all parts except the sealed center bearing and rubber insulator in suitable cleaning fluid. Do not immerse the sealed bearing in the cleaning fluid. Wipe the bearing and rubber insulator clean with a cloth dampened with cleaning fluid.

NOTE: *Inspect the slip yoke cork seal, replace if necessary.*

7. Check the center support bearing for wear or rough action by rotating the inner race while holding the outer race. If any wear or roughness is evident, replace the bearing.

8. Examine the rubber insulator for evidence of hardening, cracking, or deterioration. Replace if damaged in any way.

9. Lubricate the coupling shaft front slip yoke splines with chassis lube. The splines are sealed so that the transmission fluid does not wash away the spline lubricant. Remove the rag from the transmission housing. Install the front yoke of the coupling shaft assembly on the transmission output shaft. Do not allow the slip yoke assembly to bottom on the output shaft with excessive force.

10. Secure the center bearing support bracket to the frame crossmember with the center supporting attaching bolts. Tighten the bolts to 40–50 ft lb.

11. Slide the dust cap, cork seal, and spacers onto the splined shaft of the driveshaft. Apply a coating of chassis lube to the entire splined stub shaft end of the driveshaft assembly prior to the assembling of the driveshaft and the slip yoke.

12. Using a clean long handle (stencil type) brush apply chassis lube spread evenly on all the female splines of the slip yoke.

13. Assemble the driveshaft slip yoke to the coupling shaft. Tighten the U-bolt nuts to 60–70 ft lb.

14. Slide the splined end (front) of the driveshaft into the slip yoke (rear) on the coupling shaft, being certain that the splines are in "phase"; the arrow stamped on the slip yoke must be aligned with the arrow stamped on the stub shaft (splined) end of the driveshaft.

15. Connect the rear U-joint of the driveshaft to the rear axle pinion flange and tighten the U-bolt nuts to 60–70 ft lb.

16. Using a hand type grease gun, lubricate the driveshaft slip yoke through the zerk fitting with chassis lube.

NOTE: *To assure complete lubrication of the slip yoke splines, temporarily plug the vent hole in the "welch" type plug located at the yoke-end of the slip yoke while applying grease through the zerk fitting.*

U-Joints

OVERHAUL

1. Remove the driveshaft from the vehicle and place it in a vise, being careful not to damage it.

2. Remove the snap-rings which retain the bearings in the flange and in the driveshaft.

3. Remove the driveshaft tube from the vise and position the U-joint in the vise with a socket smaller than the bearing cap on one side and a socket larger than the bearing cap on the other side.

4. Slowly tighten the jaws of the vise so that the smaller socket forces the U-joint spider and the opposite bearing into the larger socket.

5. Remove the other side of the spider in the same manner (if applicable) and remove the spider assembly from the driveshaft. Discard the spider assemblies.

6. Clean all foreign matter from the yoke areas at the end of the driveshaft(s). Grease the new bearings.

7. Start the new spider and one of the bearing cap assemblies into a yoke by positioning the yoke in a vise with the spider positioned in place with one of the bearing cap assemblies positioned over one of the holes in the yoke. Slowly close the vise, pressing the bearing cap assembly in the yoke. Press the cap in far enough so that the retaining snap-ring can be installed. Use the smaller socket to recess the bearing cap.

8. Open the vise and position the opposite bearing cap assembly over the proper hole in the yoke with the socket that is smaller than the diameter of the bearing cap located on the cap. Slowly close the vise, pressing the bearing cap into the hole in the yoke with the socket. Make sure that the spider assembly is in line with the bearing cap as it is pressed in. Press the bearing cap in far enough so that the retaining snap-ring can be installed.

9. Install all remaining U-joints in the same manner.

10. Install the driveshaft.

Center Bearing

REMOVAL AND INSTALLATION

1. Remove the driveshafts.

2. Remove the two center support bearing attaching bolts and remove the assembly from the vehicle.

3. Do not immerse the sealed bearing in any type of cleaning fluid. Wipe the bearing and cushion clean with a cloth dampened with cleaning fluid.

4. Check the bearing for wear or rough action by rotating the inner race while holding the outer race. If wear or roughness is evident, replace the bearing.

Examine the rubber cushion for evidence of hardening, cracking, or deterioration. Replace it if it is damaged in any way.

5. Place the bearing in the rubber support and the rubber support in the U-shaped support and install the bearing in the reverse order of removal. Torque the support nuts to 40–50 ft lb.

REAR AXLE

The axle ratio is on a tag attached by one of the differential carrier or rear cover bolts. Ford axles with limited slip are indicated by an L replacing the axle ratio decimal point; Dana axles are marked L-S.

Introduction

The rear axle must transmit power through 90°. To accomplish this, straight cut bevel gears or spiral bevel gears were used. This type of gear is satisfactory for differential side gears, but since the centerline of the gears must intersect, they rapidly become unsuited for ring and pinion gears. The lowering of the driveshaft brought about a variation of the bevel gear, which is called the hypoid gear. This type of gear does not require a meeting of the gear centerlines and can therefore be underslung, relative to the centerline of the ring gear.

GEAR RATIOS

The drive axle of a vehicle is said to have a certain axle ratio. This number (usually a whole number and a decimal fraction) is actually a comparison of the number of gear teeth on the ring gear and the pinion gear. For example, a 4.11 rear means that theoretically, there are 4.11 teeth on the ring gear and one tooth on the pinion. Actually on a 4.11 rear, there are 37 teeth on the ring gear and nine teeth on the pinion gear. By dividing the number of teeth on the pinion gear into the number of teeth on the ring gear, the numerical axle ratio (4.11) is obtained. This also provides a good method of ascertaining exactly which axle ratio one is dealing with.

DIFFERENTIAL OPERATION

The differential is an arrangement of gears which permits the rear wheels to turn at different speeds when cornering and divides the torque between the axle shafts. The differential gears are mounted on a pinion shaft and the gears are free to rotate on this shaft. The pinion shaft is fitted in a bore in the differential case and is at right angles to the axle shafts.

Power flow through the differential is as follows. The drive pinion, which is turned by

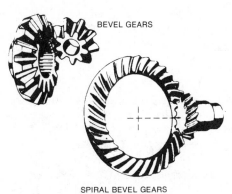

BEVEL GEARS

SPIRAL BEVEL GEARS

BEVEL GEAR APPLICATION
(© CHEVROLET DIV., G.M. CORP)

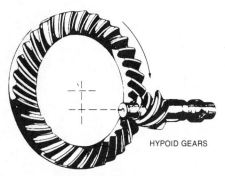

HYPOID GEARS

HYPOID GEAR APPLICATION
(© CHEVROLET DIV., G.M. CORP)

The three different designs of ring and pinion gears

the driveshaft, turns the ring gear. The ring gear, which is bolted to the differential case, rotates the case. The differential pinion forces the pinion gears against the side gears. In cases where both wheels have equal traction, the pinion gears do not rotate on the pinion shaft, because the input force of the pinion gear is divided equally between the two side gears. Consequently the pinion gears revolve with the pinion shaft, although they do not revolve on the pinion shaft itself. The side gears, which are splined to the axle shafts, and meshed with the pinion gears, rotate the axle shafts.

When it becomes necessary to turn a corner, the differential becomes effective and allows the axle shafts to rotate at different speeds. As the inner wheel slows down, the side gear splined to the inner wheel axle shaft also slows down. The pinion gears act as balancing levers by maintaining equal tooth loads to both gears while allowing unequal speeds of rotation at the axle shafts. If the vehicle speed remains constant, and the inner wheel slows down to 90 percent of vehicle speed, the outer wheel will speed up to 110 percent.

LIMITED-SLIP DIFFERENTIAL OPERATION

Limited-slip differentials provide driving force to the wheel with the best traction

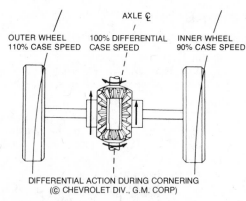

AXLE ℄

| OUTER WHEEL | 100% DIFFERENTIAL | INNER WHEEL |
| 110% CASE SPEED | CASE SPEED | 90% CASE SPEED |

DIFFERENTIAL ACTION DURING CORNERING
(© CHEVROLET DIV., G.M. CORP)

Differential action during turning

before the other wheel begins to spin. This is accomplished through clutch plates or cones. The clutch plates or cones are located between the side gears and inner wall of the differential case. When they are squeezed together through spring tension and outward force from the side gears, three reactions occur. Resistance on the side gears causes more torque to be exerted on the clutch packs or clutch cones. Rapid one-wheel spin cannot occur, because the side gear is forced to turn at the same speed as the case. Most important, with the side gear and the differential case turning at the same speed, the other wheel is forced to rotate in the same direction and at the same speed as the differen-

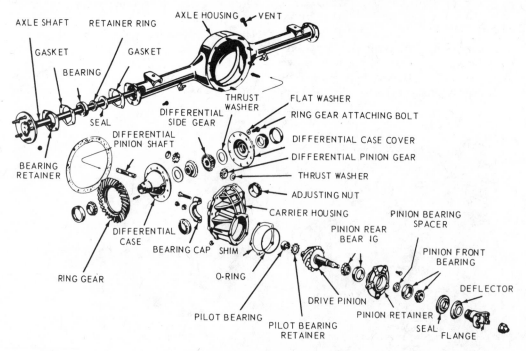

An exploded view of the Ford removable carrier rear axle with semi-floating axle shafts

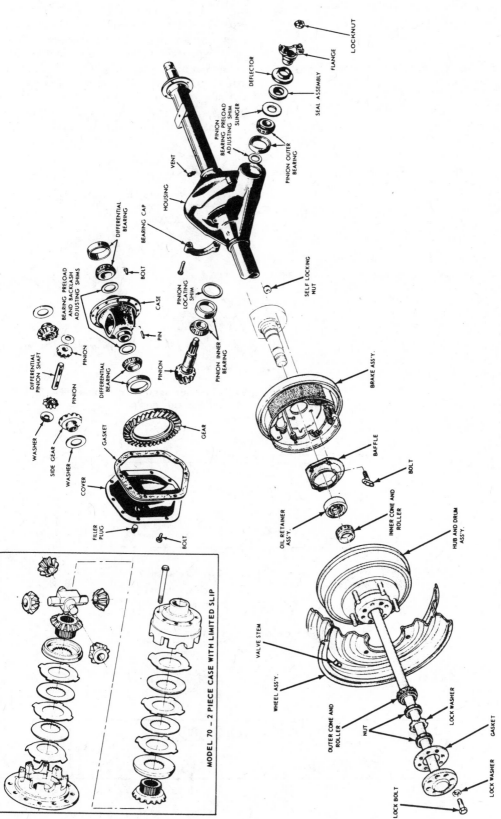

LOCKNUT

FLANGE

DEFLECTOR

SLINGER

SEAL ASSEMBLY

PINION
BEARING PRELOAD
ADJUSTING SHIM

PINION OUTER
BEARING

VENT

HOUSING

BEARING CAP

DIFFERENTIAL
BEARING

BOLT

SELF LOCKING
NUT

BEARING PRELOAD
AND BACKLASH
ADJUSTING SHIMS

CASE

PINION
LOCATING
SHIM

PIN

DIFFERENTIAL
PINION SHAFT

PINION

DIFFERENTIAL
BEARING

PINION

PINION INNER
BEARING

BRAKE ASS'Y.

WASHER

PINION

SIDE GEAR

WASHER

GASKET

GEAR

BAFFLE

BOLT

COVER

INNER CONE AND
ROLLER

OIL RETAINER
ASS'Y.

HUB AND DRUM
ASS'Y.

FILLER
PLUG

BOLT

VALVE STEM

WHEEL ASS'Y.

LOCK WASHER

OUTER CONE AND
ROLLER

NUT

GASKET

LOCK WASHER

LOCK BOLT

MODEL 70 – 2 PIECE CASE WITH LIMITED SLIP

An exploded view of the Dana integral carrier axle with full-floating axle shafts

tial case. Thus driving force is applied to the wheel with the better traction.

Axle Shaft, Bearing, and Seal
REMOVAL AND INSTALLATION
E-100, E-150, and E-200

1. Raise and support the vehicle and remove the wheel/tire assembly from the brake drum.

2. Remove the clips which secure the brake drum to the axle flange, then remove the drum from the flange.

3. Working through the hole provided in each axle shaft flange, remove the nuts which secure the wheel bearing retainer plate.

4. Pull the axle shaft assembly out of the axle housing. You may need a slide hammer.

NOTE: *The brake backing plate must not be dislodged. Install one nut to hold the plate in place after the axle shaft is removed.*

5. If the axle has ball bearings:
Loosen the bearing retainer ring by nicking it in several places with a cold chisel, then slide it off the axle shaft. On 1977–82 models, drill a ¼ to ½ in. hole part way through the ring,

then break it with a cold chisel. A hydraulic press is needed to press the bearing off and to press the new one on. Press the new bearing and the new retainer ring on separately. Use a slide hammer to pull the old seal out of the axle housing. Use sealer on the outer edge of the new seal through 1975. Carefully drive the new seal evenly into the axle housing, preferably with a seal driver tool.

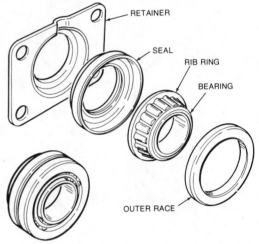

Tapered roller bearings on some 1974–82 E-100, 150, and 200 axle shafts

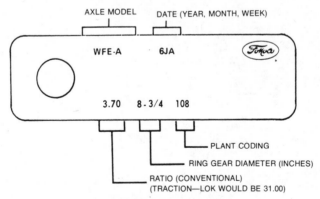

Ford axle identification tag

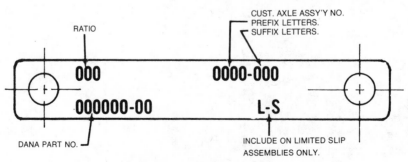

Dana axle identification tag

6. If the axle has tapered roller bearings (1974–82 only):
Use a slide hammer to remove the bearing cup from the axle housing. Drill a ¼ to ½ in. hole part way through the bearing retainer ring, then break it with a cold chisel. A hydraulic press is needed to press the bearing off and remove the seal. Press on the new seal and bearing, then the new retainer ring. Do not press the bearing and ring on together. Put the cup on the bearing, not in the housing, and lubricate the outer diameter of the cup and seal.

7. With ball bearings:
Place a new gasket between the housing flange and backing plate. Carefully slide the axle shaft into place. Turn the shaft to start the splines into the side gear and push it in.

8. With tapered roller bearings:
Move the seal out toward the axle shaft flange so there is at least $3/32$ between the edge of the outer seal and the bearing cup, to prevent snagging on installation. Carefully slide the axle shaft into place. Turn the shaft to start the splines into the side gear and push it in.

9. Install the bearing retainer plate.

10. Replace the brake drum and the wheel and tire.

E-250, E-300, and E-350

These procedures are thoroughly covered in Chapter 1 under Rear Wheel Bearing Packing and Adjustment.

Suspension and Steering

FRONT AND REAR SUSPENSION

The front axle in all 1961 to 1968 model Ford vans consists of a solid "I"-beam axle with the front wheel spindles attached to the ends of the axle spindle bolt (kingpin). Beginning with the 1969 models, all Ford vans have used two "I"-beam type front axles; one for each wheel. One end of each axle is attached to the spindle and a radius arm and the other end is attached to a frame pivot bracket on the opposite side of the vehicle. The spindles are held onto the axles by pivot bolts (kingpins).

Semi-elliptical leaf springs are used on the rear axles of all Ford vans. The front springs of 1961–68 models are also semi-elliptical leaf springs. The front springs on 1969 and later models are coil type springs.

Front Springs

REMOVAL AND INSTALLATION
Coil Springs
1969–74

1. Remove the floor mat (if so equipped) retainer from the lower end of the door opening. Fold the mat to one side to gain access to the shock absorber cover plate.

2. Remove the two cover plate attaching screws and remove the plate.

3. Remove the two spring upper retainer attaching screws and remove the retainer insulator and clamp.

4. Support the frame side rails with jackstands.

5. Place a jack under the axle, then remove the spring lower retainer attaching bolt. Remove the spring support and lower retainer.

6. Lower the jack slowly to relieve the spring tension, then remove the spring.

To install the front coil spring:

7. Position the spring on the axle with the pigtails toward the rear.

8. Position the spring lower support and retainer, and install the attaching bolt loosely.

9. Position the upper insulator on the spring.

10. Raise the jack high enough to apply light tension on the spring.

11. Install the spring upper retainer and the clamp in the following manner:

    a. Check the retainer assembly to ensure that the bolts are approximately flush with the bottom of the clamp bar.

    b. Insert the retainer assembly into the hole in the floor with the clamp bar pointing toward the right-side of the vehicle.

    c. Rotate the retainer assembly about

that the clamp bar has trapped the tang on the upper end of the spring.

12. Tighten the upper and lower attaching bolts. Remove the jackstands.

13. Install the shock absorber cover plate and floor mat, if so equipped.

1975–82

1. Raise the van with jack stands under the frame and a jack under the axle.

2. Disconnect the lower end of the shock absorber.

3. Remove the two spring upper retainer bolts from the top of the upper spring seat. Take off the retainer strap.

4. Remove the nut holding the lower spring retainer disc to the seat and axle. Remove the retainer.

5. Carefully lower the axle and remove the extended spring.

6. On installation, put the spring in place and raise the axle. Install the lower retainer and nut. Install the lower retainer and nut. Install the upper retainer strap. Connect the shock absorber.

Leaf Springs

1. Raise the front of the vehicle and support the chassis with jackstands. Support the front axle with a floor jack or hoist.

2. Remove the front splash shield.

3. Disconnect the lower end of the shock

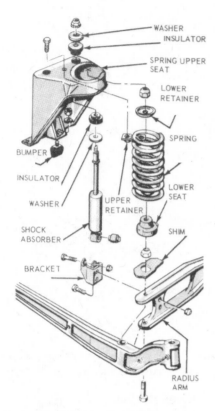

Typical 1969–80 front suspension

90° clockwise until the oval retainer seats properly to the oval hole and secure the two bolts.

d. Visually inspect the spring to ensure

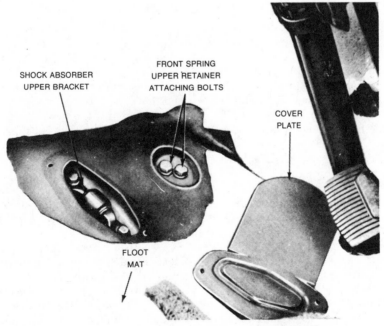

The 1969–74 upper shock absorber and spring mounting cover plate

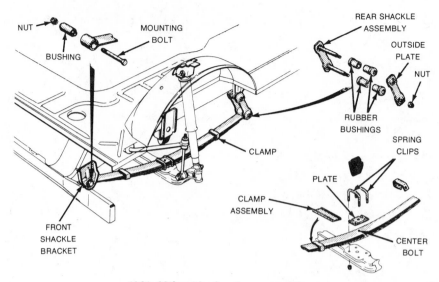

1961–68 front leaf spring assembly

absorber from the anchor bolt in the front axle.

4. Remove the two spring clips (U-bolts) and the spring clip plate.

5. Lower the spring, and remove the rear shackle nuts and outside plate.

6. Pull the rear shackle assembly and rubber bushings from the bracket and spring.

7. Remove the nut and mounting bolt which secure the front end of the spring, and remove the spring from the front shackle bracket.

To install the front leaf spring:

8. Install new rubber bushings in the rear shackle bracket and in the rear eye of the replacement spring.

9. Position the spring assembly and connect the front eye of the spring to the front shackle bracket by installing the front mounting bolt and nut. Do not tighten the nut.

10. Mount the rear end of the spring by inserting the upper stud of the rear shackle assembly through the rear shackle bracket, and the lower stud through the rear eye of the spring.

11. Install the outside plate to the rear shackle studs, and install the shackle nuts. Do not tighten the nuts at this time.

12. Position the spring center bolt to the pilot hole in the axle, and install the spring clips and plate. Do not tighten the attaching nuts at this time.

13. Raise the axle with the floor jack until the vehicle is free of the jackstands, and connect the lower end of the shock absorber to the anchor bolt in the front axle. Install the washer and nut.

14. Tighten the spring front mounting bolt and nut, the rear shackle nuts, and the spring clip nuts.

15. Install the front splash shield.

16. Remove the jackstands and lower the vehicle.

Rear Springs

REMOVAL AND INSTALLATION

E-100, E-150, and E-200

1. Raise the rear of the vehicle and support the chassis with jackstands. Support the rear axle with a floor jack or hoist.

2. Disconnect the lower end of the shock absorber from the bracket on the axle housing.

3. Remove the two U-bolts and plate.

4. Lower the axle and remove the upper and lower rear shackle bolts.

5. Pull the rear shackle assembly and rubber bushings from the bracket and spring.

6. Remove the nut and mounting bolt which secure the front end of the spring. Remove the spring assembly from the front shackle bracket.

7. Install new rubber bushings in the rear shackle bracket and in the rear eye of the replacement spring.

8. Assemble the front eye of the spring to the front shackle bracket with the front mounting bolt and nut. Do not tighten the nut.

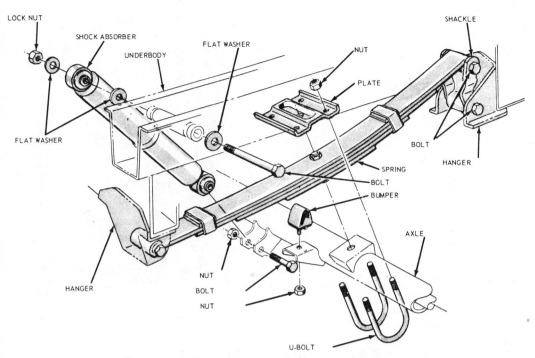

The rear spring assembly of E-100, E-150, and E-200 vans

9. Mount the rear end of the spring with the upper bolt of the rear shackle assembly passing through the eye of the spring. Insert the lower bolt through the rear spring hanger.

10. Assemble the spring center bolt in the pilot hole in the axle and install the plate. In-

stall the U-bolts through the plate. Do not tighten the attaching nuts at this time.

11. Raise the axle with a floor jack or hoist until the vehicle is free of the jackstands. Connect the lower end of the shock absorber to the bracket on the axle housing.

12. Tighten the spring front mounting bolt

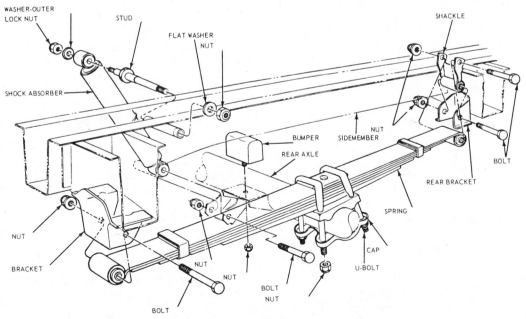

The rear spring assembly of E-250, E-300 and E-350 vans

and nut, the rear shackle nuts and the U-bolt nuts.

13. Remove the jackstands and lower the vehicle.

E-250, E-300, and E-350

1. Raise the rear of the vehicle and support the chassis with jackstands. Support the rear axle with a floor jack or hoist.

2. Disconnect the lower end of the shock absorber from the bracket on the axle housing.

3. Remove the two spring U-bolts and the spring cap.

4. Lower the axle and remove the spring front bolt from the hanger.

5. Remove the two attaching bolts from the rear of the spring. Remove the spring and shackle.

6. Assemble the upper end of the shackle to the spring with the attaching bolt.

7. Connect the front of the spring to the front bracket with the attaching bolt.

8. Assemble the spring and shackle to the rear bracket with the attaching bolt.

9. Place the spring plate over the head of the center bolt.

10. Raise the axle with a jack. Install the center bolt through the pilot hole in the pad on the axle housing.

11. Install the spring U-bolts, cap and attaching nuts. Tighten the nuts snugly.

12. Connect the lower end of the shock absorber to the lower bracket.

13. Tighten the spring front mounting bolt and nut, the rear shackle nuts and the spring U-bolt nuts.

14. Remove the jackstands and lower the vehicle.

Shock Absorbers

REMOVAL AND INSTALLATION

1961–68

1. Raise the vehicle on a hoist.

2. Remove the shock absorber lower attaching nut and washer.

3. On the rear shock absorbers, swing the lower end free of the mounting bracket on the axle housing.

4. Remove the upper attaching nut or bolt and remove the shock absorber from the vehicle.

5. Transfer the sleeves from the upper and lower bushings of the rear shocks and only the lower bushing of the front shock absorber

STABILIZER BAR   LINK

ANCHOR   AXLE   SHOCK LOWER MOUNT
BOLT

1961–68 front shock absorber and stabilizer link lower connections

to the new shocks. If the sleeves are worn or damaged, replace them with new ones.

6. Install the shock absorbers in the reverse order of removal.

1969–74

NOTE: *Replace the rear shock absorbers in the same manner as outlined for 1961–68 vehicles.*

1. Remove the bolt which attaches the lower end of the shock absorber to the radius arm bracket.

2. Remove the floor mat retainer from the lower end of the door opening. Fold the mat to one side to gain access to the shock absorber cover plate.

3. Remove the two cover plate attaching screws and remove the plate.

4. Remove the two shock absorber bracket attaching bolts and lift the shock absorber and bracket up through the floor pan.

5. Position the shock absorber and install and tighten the two attaching bolts.

6. Install the shock absorber cover plate.

7. Position the floor mat and install the retainer.

8. Connect the lower end of the shock absorber to the bracket.

1975–82

NOTE: *Replace the rear shock absorbers in the same way as outlined previously for 1961–68 models.*

To replace front shocks:

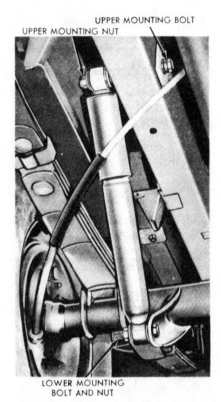

The rear shock absorber mounting for all models

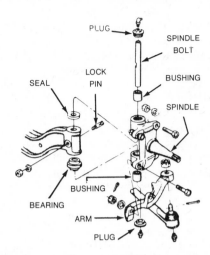

1969–74 E-100, 200 front spindle assembly

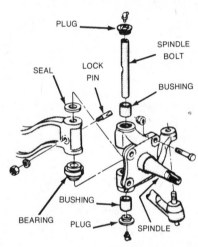

1969–74 E-300 and all 1975–82 front spindle assembly

1. Insert a wrench from the rear side of the upper spring seat to hold the upper shock retaining nut. Loosen the stud by using another wrench on the hex on the shaft.

2. Remove the bolt and nut at the lower end.

3. On installation, make sure to get the washers and insulators in the right place. Tighten the upper nut by turning the hex on the shaft. Replace the lower bolt. It is recommended that new rubber insulators be used.

Front Wheel Spindles and King Pins

REMOVAL AND INSTALLATION

1. Raise the vehicle until the front wheel clears the floor and place a support under the axle.

2. Back off the brake adjustment as necessary, and remove the wheel, wheel bearing, hub and drum as an assembly.

3. On 1969–74 E-100 and E-200 models, remove the brake backing plate and spindle-to-spindle arm attaching bolt. Remove the spindle arm and the brake backing plate from the spindle. Support the brake backing plate hose. On disc brake models, remove the cali-

per assembly and wire it up. Remove the dust cap, cotter pin, nut, washer, outer bearing, and rotor (disc). Take off the inner bearing cone and seal. Remove the brake dust shield.

4. On 1969–74 E-300 and all 1975–82 models, disconnect the steering linkage from the integral spindle and the spindle arm.

5. Remove the nut and lockwasher from the locking pin, and remove the locking pin.

6. Remove the upper and lower spindle bolt plugs; then, drive the spindle bolt out from the top of the axle and remove the spindle and bearing. Knock out the seal.

7. Make sure that the spindle bolt hole in the axle is free of nicks, burrs or foreign material. Install a new seal and coat the spindle bolt bushings and the spindle bolt hole in the axle with oil; then place the spindle in position on the axle.

8. Pack the spindle thrust bearing with chassis lubricant and insert the bearing into the spindle with the open end (lip side) of the bearing seal facing downward into the spindle.

9. Install the spindle pin in the spindle with the locking pin notch in the spindle bolt lined up with the locking pin hole in the axle. Drive the spindle bolt through the axle from the top side until the spindle bolt locking pin notch is lined up with the locking pin hole.

10. Make sure that the notch in the spindle pin is lined up with the locking pin hole in the axle and install a new locking pin. Install the locking pin lockwasher and nut. Tighten the nut and install the spindle bolt plugs at the top and bottom of the spindle.

11. On 1969–74 E-100 and E-200, install the brake backing plate and spindle arm. Torque the brake backing plate and spindle-to-spindle arm bolt and nut to 30–50 ft lbs. Advance the castellated nut as required to install the cotter pin.

12. Connect the steering linkage to the spindle on 1969–74 E-300 and all 1975–82 models. Tighten the nut to 50–75 ft lbs and advance the nut as required to install the cotter pin.

13. Install the wheel, hub and drum or disc brake assembly, and adjust the wheel bearing.

14. Lubricate the spindle assembly.

15. Check and adjust the toe-in setting.

Drag Link Replacement
1961–68

1. Raise the front of the vehicle and install safety stands under the axle.

2. Remove the cotter pin and nut, and disconnect the rear end of the drag link from the spindle arm with a ball joint puller.

3. Remove the cotter pin and nut, and disconnect the front end of the drag link from the Pitman arm with a ball joint puller.

4. Connect the front end of the new drag link to the sector shaft arm, and install the retaining nut and cotter pin.

5. Connect the rear end of the drag link to the spindle arm and install the retaining nut and cotter pin.

6. Transfer the two lubrication fittings to the new drag link, and lubricate after installation.

7. Remove the safety stands, and lower the vehicle.

Spindle Arm Connecting Rod End Replacement
1961–68

The spindle arm connecting rod ends have non-adjustable ball studs. A rod end should be replaced when excessive looseness at the ball is noticed.

1. Remove the cotter pin and the retain-

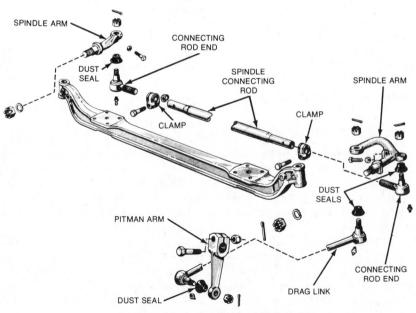

SPINDLE ARM — CONNECTING ROD END — DUST SEAL — SPINDLE CONNECTING ROD — CLAMP — SPINDLE ARM — CLAMP — DUST SEALS — PITMAN ARM — DUST SEAL — DRAG LINK — CONNECTING ROD END

1961–68 steering linkage, exploded view

ing nut, and disconnect the spindle arm from the connecting rod with a ball joint puller.

2. Loosen the clamp bolt, and turn the rod end out of the rod.

3. After lubricating the threads of the new rod end, turn it into the rod about the same distance as the old rod end was installed. This will provide an approximate toe-in setting.

4. Install the ball stud in the spindle arm, tighten the nut to 45–55 ft lb and install the cotter pin.

5. Check the toe-in. If necessary loosen the other connecting rod end clamp, and adjust the toe-in. Be sure to tighten the rod end clamps after adjusting the toe-in. The clamps should be positioned $3/16$ inch from the end of the rod, and with the clamp bolt horizontally located below the rod.

Tie Rod and Link Assembly

1969–82

Replace the drag link if a ball stud is excessively loose or if the drag link is bent. **Do not attempt to straighten a drag link.**

Replace the connecting rod if the ball stud is excessively loose, if the connecting rod is bent or if the threads are stripped. Do not attempt to straighten connecting rod.

After installing a connecting rod or adjusting toe-in check to insure that the adjustment sleeve clamps are correctly positioned on the E-100 and E-150 and to insure that the clamp stop is correctly installed on the E-250 and E-350.

1. Remove the cotter pins and nuts from the drag link, ball studs and from the right connecting rod ball stud.

2. Remove the right connecting rod ball stud from the drag link.

3. Remove the drag link ball studs from the spindle and the pitman arm.

4. Position the new drag link, ball studs in the spindle, and pitman arm and install nuts.

5. Position the right connecting rod ball stud in the drag link and install nut.

6. Tighten the nuts to 50–75 ft lbs and install the cotter pins.

7. Remove the cotter pin and nut from the connecting rod.

8. Remove the ball stud from the mating part.

9. Loosen the clamp bolt and turn the rod out of the adjustment sleeve.

10. Lubricate the threads of the new connecting rod, and turn it into the adjustment sleeve to about the same distance the old rods were installed. This will provide an approximate toe-in setting. Position the connecting rod ball studs in the spindle arms.

11. Install the nuts on to the connecting rod ball studs, tighten the nut to 50–75 ft lbs and install the cotter pin.

12. Check the toe-in and adjust, if necessary. After checking or adjusting toe-in, center the adjustment sleeve clamps between the locating nibs, position the clamps and tighten the nuts to 29–41 ft lbs.

Radius Arm (1969–82)

REMOVAL AND INSTALLATION

1. Raise the front of the vehicle and place safety stands under the frame and a jack under the wheel or axle.

2. Disconnect the shock absorber from the radius arm bracket.

3. Remove the two spring upper retainer attaching bolts from the top of the spring upper seat and remove the retainer.

4. Remove the nut which attaches the spring lower retainer to the lower seat and axle and remove the retainer.

5. Lower the axle and remove the spring.

6. Disconnect the steering rod from the spindle arm.

7. Remove the spring lower seat and shim from the radius arm. Then, remove the bolt and nut which attach the radius arm to the axle.

8. Remove the cotter pin, nut and washer from the radius arm rear attachment.

9. Remove the bushing from the radius arm and remove the radius arm from the vehicle.

10. Remove the inner bushing from the radius arm.

11. Position the radius arm to the axle and install the bolt and nut finger-tight.

12. Install the inner bushing on the radius arm and position the arm to the frame bracket.

13. Install the bushing, washer, and attaching nut. Tighten the nut and install the cotter pin.

14. Connect the steering rod to the spindle arm and install the attaching nut. Tighten the nut and install the cotter pin.

15. Tighten the radius arm-to-axle attaching bolt and nut.

16. Position the shim over the radius arm-

to-axle attaching nut and install the spring lower seat.

17. Place the spring in position and raise the front axle.

18. Position the spring lower retainer over the stud and lower the seat, and install the attaching nut.

19. Position the upper retainer over the spring coil and against the spring upper seat, and install the two attaching bolts.

20. Tighten the upper retainer attaching bolts and lower retainer attaching nut.

21. Connect the shock absorber to the lower bracket. Remove the jack and safety stands and lower the vehicle.

22. Check and adjust the toe-in setting.

Front End Alignment
CASTER AND CAMBER

The caster and camber angles of the front axle(s) of Ford vans are designed into the front axle(s) at the factory. Excessive negative camber on twin I-beams, causing wear on the inside edges of the tires, can be corrected by installation of front spring shims, available as Ford parts. Suspension misalignment caused by bent axles can be corrected by cold-bending in a shop with the suitable heavy equipment, probably a truck frame and alignment specialist. The caster angle of vehicles with solid front axles is adjusted by inserting tapered metal wedges between the springs and the spring pads on the axle. Toe-in is adjustable in the normal manner (by adjusting the tie-rods) and the procedure is given later on in this Section.

If you start to notice abnormal tire wear patterns and handling characteristics (steering wheel is hard to return to the straight-ahead position after negotiating a turn), then front end misalignment can be suspected.

NOTE: *It is very important that the tires be rotated at least at the intervals shown in the Maintenance Intervals Chart in Chapter 1 in order to get even tread wear on trucks with twin I-beam front suspension.*

However, toe-in alignment maladjustment, rather than caster or camber, is more likely to be the cause of excessive or uneven tire wear. Seldom is it necessary to correct caster or camber. The toe-in alignment should be checked before the caster and camber angles after making the following checks:

1. Check the air pressure in all the tires.

Make sure that the pressures agree with those specified for the tires and vehicle model being checked.

2. Raise the front of the vehicle off the ground. Grasp each front tire at the top and bottom, and push the wheel inward and outward. If any free-play is noticed between the brake drum and the brake backing plate, adjust the wheel bearings.

NOTE: *There is supposed to be a very, very small amount of free-play present. A common cause of excessive wear on the inside edge of the front tires is worn king-pins.*

3. Check all steering linkage for wear or maladjustment. Adjust and/or replace all worn parts.

4. Check the torque on the steering gear mounting bolts and tighten as necessary.

5. Rotate each front wheel slowly, and observe the amount of lateral or side run-out. If the wheel run-out exceeds ⅛ in., replace the wheel or install the wheel on the rear.

6. Inspect the twin I-beam radius arms to be sure that they are not bent or damaged. Inspect the bushings at the radius arm-to-axle attachment and radius arm-to-frame attachment points for wear or looseness. Repair or replace parts as required.

7. Raising the rear of the van, whether by suspension modifications or by using tall rear tires, will reduce the caster angle.

TOE-IN ADJUSTMENT

Toe-in can be measured by either a front end alignment machine or by the following method:

With the front wheels in the straight-ahead position, measure the distance between the extreme front and the extreme rear of the front wheels. In other words, measure the distance across the under-carriage of the vehicle between the two front edges and the two rear edges of the two front wheels. Both of these measurements (front and rear of the two wheels) must be taken at an equal distance from the floor and at the approximate centerline of the spindle. The difference between these two distances is the amount that the wheels toe-in or toe-out. The wheels should always be adjusted to toe-in according to specifications.

1. Loosen the clamp bolts at each end of the tie-rod sleeve. Rotate the connecting rod tube until the correct toe-in is obtained, then tighten the clamp bolts.

2. Recheck the toe-in to make sure that no

Wheel Alignment Specifications

Year	Model	CASTER Range (deg.)	CASTER Preferred Setting (deg)	CAMBER Range (deg)	CAMBER Preferred Setting (deg)	Toe-in (in.)	Steering Axis Inclination (deg)
1961–65	All	$4\frac{1}{4}$P to $5\frac{3}{4}$P	5P	$\frac{1}{8}$P to $\frac{5}{8}$P	$\frac{3}{8}$P	$\frac{1}{16}$ to $\frac{1}{8}$	$7\frac{1}{2}$
1966	All	$4\frac{1}{2}$P to 6P	$5\frac{1}{4}$P	$\frac{1}{8}$P to $\frac{5}{8}$P	$\frac{3}{8}$P	$\frac{1}{16}$ to $\frac{1}{8}$	$7\frac{1}{2}$
1967–68	All	$4\frac{1}{4}$P to $5\frac{3}{4}$P	5P	$\frac{1}{8}$P to $\frac{5}{8}$P	$\frac{3}{8}$P	$\frac{1}{16}$ to $\frac{1}{8}$	$7\frac{1}{2}$
1969	All	$4\frac{1}{4}$P to $5\frac{3}{4}$P	5P	0 to 1P	$\frac{1}{2}$P	$\frac{1}{16}$ to $\frac{3}{16}$	4
1970	All	$\frac{1}{2}$P to $5\frac{1}{2}$P	3P	$\frac{1}{2}$P to $3\frac{1}{2}$P	2P	$\frac{1}{16}$ to $\frac{3}{16}$	4
1971	E-100, 200	$\frac{1}{2}$P to $5\frac{1}{2}$P	3P	$\frac{1}{2}$P to $3\frac{1}{2}$P	2P	$\frac{1}{32}$ to $\frac{7}{32}$	4
	E-300	$2\frac{1}{2}$P to $7\frac{1}{2}$P	5P	$\frac{1}{2}$P to $3\frac{1}{2}$P	2P	$\frac{1}{32}$ to $\frac{7}{32}$	4
1972–73	E-100, 200	$3\frac{1}{2}$P to $8\frac{1}{2}$P	6P	$\frac{1}{2}$P to $3\frac{1}{2}$P	2P	$\frac{1}{32}$ to $\frac{7}{32}$	4
	E-300	$2\frac{1}{2}$P to $7\frac{1}{2}$P	5P	$\frac{1}{2}$P to $3\frac{1}{2}$P	2P	$\frac{1}{32}$ to $\frac{7}{32}$	4
1974–76	E-100, 200	$\frac{1}{2}$P to $8\frac{1}{2}$P	$4\frac{1}{2}$P	$\frac{1}{2}$P to $3\frac{1}{2}$P	2P	$\frac{3}{32}$ out to $\frac{5}{32}$ in	4
	E-300	$2\frac{1}{2}$P to $7\frac{1}{2}$P	5P	$\frac{1}{2}$P to $3\frac{1}{2}$P	2P	$\frac{3}{32}$ out to $\frac{5}{32}$ in	4
1977	E-100, 150	2P to $5\frac{3}{4}$P	$3\frac{7}{8}$P	$\frac{3}{4}$N to $1\frac{3}{4}$P	$\frac{1}{2}$P	$\frac{3}{32}$ out to $\frac{5}{32}$ in	4
	E-250, 350	4P to $8\frac{1}{4}$P	$6\frac{1}{8}$P	$\frac{1}{2}$N to $2\frac{1}{4}$P	$\frac{7}{8}$P	$\frac{3}{32}$ out to $\frac{5}{32}$ in	4

Beginning in 1973, Ford has stated that no adjustments by bending or any other means may be made to effect changes in the caster or camber of its twin I-beam front axles. Adjustment is by replacement of parts, only. 1977 was the last year Ford furnished general specifications for checking caster and camber on these vehicles. Use the following charts to determine the proper caster and camber for a specific vehicle, beginning with the 1978 model year.

Year	Ride Height (inches)	E-100, 150 Caster (deg)	E-100, 150 Camber (deg)	E-250, 350 Caster (deg)	E-250, 350 Camber (deg)
1978①	4.00 to 4.25	$3\frac{3}{4}$P to $6\frac{1}{2}$P	$\frac{3}{4}$N to $\frac{1}{2}$P	$6\frac{1}{4}$P to 9P	1N to $\frac{3}{4}$P
	4.25 to 4.50	$3\frac{1}{4}$P to $5\frac{3}{4}$P	$\frac{1}{2}$N to $\frac{3}{4}$P	$5\frac{3}{4}$P to $8\frac{1}{4}$P	$\frac{1}{2}$N to $1\frac{1}{4}$P
	4.50 to 4.75	$2\frac{1}{2}$P to $5\frac{1}{4}$P	0 to $1\frac{1}{4}$P	$5\frac{1}{4}$P to $7\frac{3}{4}$P	0 to $1\frac{3}{4}$P

Wheel Alignment Specifications (cont.)

Year	Ride Height (inches)	E-100, 150 Caster (deg)	E-100, 150 Camber (deg)	E-250, 350 Caster (deg)	E-250, 350 Camber (deg)
1978① (cont.)	4.75 to 5.00	2P to 4½P	½P to 1¾P	4½P to 7¼P	½P to 2¼P
	5.00 to 5.25	1¼P to 4P	1¼P to 2½P	4P to 6½P	1P to 2¾P
	5.25 to 5.50	¾P to 3¼P	1¾P to 3¼P	3¼P to 6P	1½P to 3¼P
	5.50 to 5.75	0 to 2¾P	1½P to 3¾P	—	—
1979–82 ②	3.25 to 3.50	6¼P to 8P	1¾N to ¼N	9P to 10½P	1¾N to ¼N
	3.50 to 3.75	5¾P to 7¼P	1½N to ¼P	8½P to 9¾P	1½N to ¼P
	3.75 to 4.00	5P to 6¾P	1N to ¾P	7⅞P to 9P	1N to ¾P
	4.00 to 4.25	4½P to 5¾P	½N to 1¼P	7⅛P to 8½P	½N to 1¼P
	4.25 to 4.50	4P to 5¼P	0 to 1¾P	6½P to 7¾P	0 to 1¾P
	4.50 to 4.75	3¼P to 4½P	½P to 2¼P	5¾P to 7P	½P to 2¼P
	4.75 to 5.00	2½P to 4P	1P to 2¾P	5¼P to 6½P	1P to 2¾P
	5.00 to 5.25	2P to 3¼P	1½P to 3¼P	4⅝P to 6P	1½P to 3¼P
	5.25 to 5.50	1½P to 2¾P	2P to 3¾P	4P to 5½P	2P to 3¾P

① toe-in: E-100, 150—0 to ¼ inch
E-250, 350—³⁄₃₂ inch out to ⁵⁄₃₂ inch in

② toe-in: all models—¹⁄₃₂ inch
P: Positive   N: Negative

changes occurred when the bolts were tightened.

NOTE: *The clamps should be positioned with the clamp bolts in a vertical position in front of the tube, with the nut down.*

STEERING

Steering Wheel

REMOVAL AND INSTALLATION

1. Disconnect the battery ground cable or the horn wire connector. Remove the horn button or ring by pressing down and turning counterclockwise. Remove the horn pad on later models by removing the screws on the back of the wheel spokes, unclip the wires, and remove the horn switch. On vehicles with speed control, squeeze or pinch the "J" clip ground terminal firmly and pull it out of the hole in the steering wheel.

2. Remove the steering wheel nut.

3. Make sure that the wheels are in the straight-ahead position and mark the steering wheel and steering column so that the steering wheel can be reassembled in the same position from which it is removed.

4. Remove the steering wheel with a puller.

5. Install the steering wheel in the reverse order of removal. Tighten the nut to 35 ft lbs.

Turn Signal/Hazard Warning Switch

REMOVAL AND INSTALLATION

1961–74

1. Disconnect the turn signal wires under the instrument panel.

2. Turn the turn signal lever counterclockwise to remove it. Remove the cover which retains the turn indicator wires to the steering column.

3. Remove the two retaining screws under the steering column cup, and lift the horn contact plate and turn the indicator assembly from the steering column cup.

4. Install the turn signal switch in the reverse order of removal.

1975–82

1. Disconnect the battery ground cable. Remove the steering wheel and horn switch.

2. Unscrew the turn signal switch lever.

3. Disconnect the switch wiring plug by lifting up on the tabs and separating. Remove the screws holding the switch to the column.

4. Remove the wires and terminals from the steering column connector plug, after noting the location and color of each.

5. Remove the protective wire cover from the harness and remove the switch and wires through the top of the column.

6. Tape the loose ends of the new switch wires to a wire and pull them through the steering column.

7. Install the switch retaining screws.

8. Install the wires into the column wire connector and connect the terminals.

9. Replace the turn signal lever, the steering wheel, and the horn switch.

Steering Column
REMOVAL AND INSTALLATION
1961–68

1. Disconnect the horn and turn signal wires under the instrument panel.

2. Move the floormat, pull up the rubber seal, and remove the column floor pan cover.

3. Loosen the three column support attaching bolts. Remove the clamp bolts holding the support to the column.

4. Disconnect the shift rods at the lower end of the column.

5. Remove the three steering gear mounting bolts and the pitman arm clamp bolt. Spread the pitman arm with a chisel. Separate the pitman arm and the steering gear.

6. Lift the column and steering gear assembly out through the inside of the van.

7. Reverse the procedure for installation.

1969–74

1. Disconnect the horn, turn signal and back-up lamp wires.

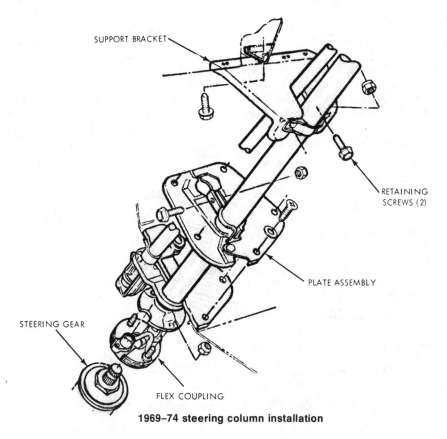

1969–74 steering column installation

2. Remove the steering wheel.

3. Disconnect the shift rods at the column shift levers.

4. Disconnect the flex coupling from the steering gear.

5. Remove the clamp holding the column to the support bracket on the instrument panel.

6. Remove the screws holding the plate assembly to the floor pan.

7. Remove the bolt and nut from the plate assembly clamp.

8. Lift the column from the vehicle. To install the steering column:

9. Position the column in the vehicle.

10. Install the screws which hold the column bracket to the support bracket on the instrument panel.

11. Align the flex coupling on the steering gear and install the retaining nuts.

12. Install the screws which hold the plate assembly to the floor pan.

13. Install the bolt and nut into the plate assembly clamp.

14. Connect the shift rods to the column shift levers.

15. Install the steering wheel.

16. Connect the back-up light, turn signal and horn wires.

1975–82

1. Remove the steering wheel as explained earlier.

2. Remove the two screws and the modesty cover from the instrument panel.

3. Disconnect the ignition switch wire connector and the backup and neutral start switch wires.

4. Disconnect the shift rods at the bottom of the column.

5. Remove the two nuts holding the steering shaft flange to the flexible coupling, after matchmarking it. Remove the three bolts holding the firewall opening cover plate.

6. Remove the column upper bracket to brake support bracket bolts.

7. Remove the column assembly through the inside of the truck.

8. Install the column, attach the flexible coupling, pull the column up slightly so that the coupling is either flat or curved up less than $3/32$ in., then tighten the column support brackets. Make sure that the flexible coupling pins are not binding. You can do this by putting a .010 in. shim around the right pin and turning the wheel. If it can be pulled out after turning the wheel, alignment is good.

Manual and Power Assisted Steering Gear (Recirculating Ball Type)

ADJUSTMENTS

These adjustments apply to the manual steering gear for all years and to the linkage-assisted power steering used through 1974. They do not apply to 1975–82 integral power steering.

Steering gear adjustments are normally required only after extensive mileage.

1. Be sure that the steering column is properly aligned and is not causing excessive turning effort.

2. On 1961–68 models, disconnect the steering linkage and remove the column floor pan cover for access. On 1969–82 models, the steering gear must be removed from the truck.

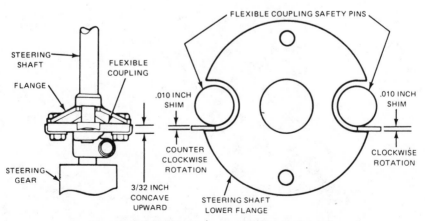

Checking the 1975–82 steering column alignment

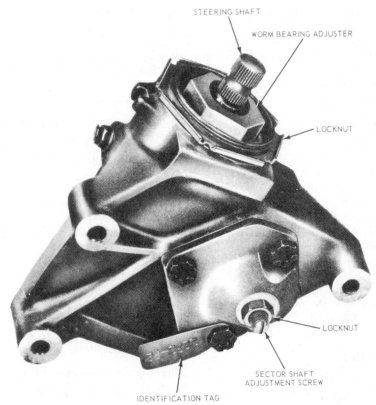

STEERING SHAFT

WORM BEARING ADJUSTER

LOCKNUT

LOCKNUT

SECTOR SHAFT
ADJUSTMENT SCREW

IDENTIFICATION TAG

The recirculating ball type steering gear used in all Ford vans

3. Be sure that the ball nut assembly and the sector gear are properly adjusted as follows to maintain minimum steering shaft endplay and backlash between the sector gear and ball nut (preload adjustment).

4. Loosen the sector shaft adjusting screw locknut and turn the adjusting screw counterclockwise approximately 3 times.

5. Measure the worm bearing preload by attaching an in. lbs torque wrench to the input shaft. Measure the torque required to rotate the input shaft about 1½ turns 2½ for 1975–82 in either direction. The worm bearing preload should be as specified.

6. To adjust the worm bearing preload, loosen the input shaft bearing adjuster locknut, and tighten or loosen the bearing adjuster to bring the preload within the speci-

Worm Bearing Preload

Model	Worm Bearing Preload (in. lbs)
1961–73 manual	4–5
1971–73 power	3–4
1974 manual	3–8
1974 power	2–6
1975–76 manual	5–8
1977–82 manual	3–8

Total Center Meshload

Model	Total Center Meshload (in. lbs)
1961–73 manual	9–10
1971–73 power	8–9
1974 manual	10–16
1974 power	7–12
1975–76 manual	4–10
1977–82 manual	10–16

fied limits. Tighten the locknut and recheck the preload.

7. Turn the input shaft slowly to either stop. Turn gently against the stop to avoid possible damage to the ball return guides. Then rotate the shaft approximately 3 turns to center the ball nut.

8. Turn the sector shaft adjusting screw clockwise until the specified pull is obtained to rotate the worm past its center.

With the steering gear in the center position, hold the sector shaft to prevent rotation and check the lash between the ball nuts, balls and worm shaft by applying a 15 in. lb torque on the steering gear input shaft, in both right and left turn directions. Total travel of the wrench should not exceed 1¼ in. when applying a 15 in. lbs torque on the steering shaft.

9. Tighten the sector shaft adjusting screw locknut, and recheck the backlash adjustment.

Power Steering

Ford vans were first equipped with power steering in 1971. This is a hydraulically-controlled linkage assist type system which includes a power steering pump, a control valve, a power cylinder, 4 fluid lines, and the steering linkage. The only adjustments that can be made in addition to the steering gear

(same as for manual steering) are the pitman arm stops.

1975–80 models have an integral power steering system in which the power assist is combined with the steering gear assembly.

ADJUSTMENTS

Pitman Arm Stops—1971–74

1. Loosen the locknut on both pitman arm stops and turn the adjusting screws inward several turns.

2. Turn the steering wheel to the right, until the right spindle steering arm contacts the stop.

3. Adjust the forward pitman arm stop outward until it contacts the pitman arm. Tighten the locknut.

4. Turn the steering wheel to the left until the left spindle steering arm contacts the stop.

5. Adjust the rearward pitman arm stop outward until it contacts the pitman arm. Tighten the locknut.

Steering Gear Meshload—1975–82

This adjustment is only for the 1975–82 integral power steering. It is normally required only after extensive mileage.

1. Make sure that the steering column is correctly aligned as explained in Step 8 of Steering Column Removal and Installation.

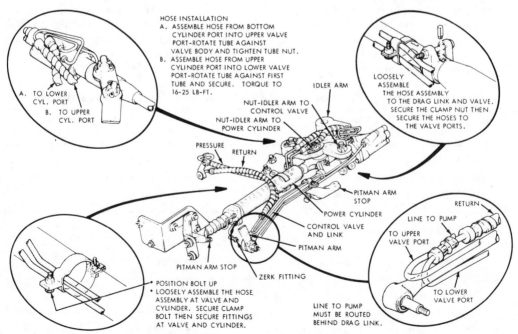

The 1971–74 linkage assist power steering mechanism

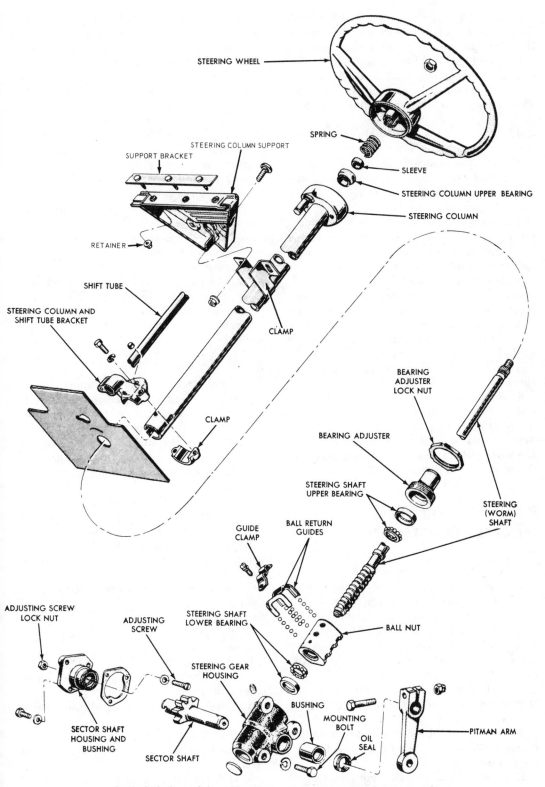

STEERING WHEEL

SPRING

SLEEVE

STEERING COLUMN UPPER BEARING

STEERING COLUMN

STEERING COLUMN SUPPORT

SUPPORT BRACKET

RETAINER

SHIFT TUBE

STEERING COLUMN AND
SHIFT TUBE BRACKET

CLAMP

CLAMP

BEARING
ADJUSTER
LOCK NUT

BEARING ADJUSTER

STEERING SHAFT
UPPER BEARING

STEERING
(WORM)
SHAFT

GUIDE
CLAMP

BALL RETURN
GUIDES

ADJUSTING SCREW
LOCK NUT

ADJUSTING
SCREW

STEERING SHAFT
LOWER BEARING

BALL NUT

STEERING GEAR
HOUSING

BUSHING

MOUNTING
BOLT

PITMAN ARM

OIL
SEAL

SECTOR SHAFT
HOUSING AND
BUSHING

SECTOR SHAFT

Exploded view of the 1961–68 steering gear and column assembly

2. Disconnect the steering linkage from the pitman arm on the steering gear. Remove the horn pad as explained under Steering Wheel Removal and Installation.

3. Disconnect the fluid reservoir return line and cap the reservoir return line tube. Place the end of the return line in a clean container and turn the steering wheel back and forth several times to empty the steering gear.

4. Turn the steering wheel nut with an inch pound torque wrench slowly. Find the torque required at: ½ turn off right and left stops, ½ turn off center both right and left, and over-center (full turn). The over-center torque should be 4–6 in. lb more than the end readings, but the total over-center torque must not exceed 14 in. lb.

5. To correct, back off the pitman shaft adjuster all the way, then back in ½ turn. Recheck the over-center torque. Loosen the locknut and tighten the sector shaft adjusting screw until the over-center torque reads 4–6 in. lb higher, but doesn't exceed 14 in. lb. Tighten the adjusting screw locknut and recheck.

6. Refill the system with the fluid specified in Chapter 1. Bleed the system of air by turning the steering wheel all the way to the right and left several times with the engine warmed up. Do not hold the steering against the stops or pump damage will result.

Power Steering Pump
REMOVAL AND INSTALLATION
1971–74

1. Raise the vehicle on a hoist.

2. Place a drain pan beneath the power steering pump and disconnect the pressure and return lines at the pump and drain the pump. If a suction gun is available, use it to remove the fluid from the pump reservoir. Lower six-cylinder engine equipped vehicles.

3. Loosen the power steering pump retaining bolts and move the drive belt out of the way.

4. Disconnect the reservoir hose from the pump on those models equipped with a remote reservoir.

5. On six-cylinder engine equipped vehicles, remove the nuts which hold the pump bracket to the cylinder block. Remove the pump and bracket from under the vehicle.

6. On V8 engine equipped vehicles, re-

move the bolts which hold the pump to the mounting bracket and lay the pump on the crossmember. Loosen the bolts and nuts which hold the mounting bracket to the cylinder block, allowing the bracket to move forward, and remove the pump from the vehicle.

NOTE: *If the power steering pump is being removed from the engine in order to facilitate the removal of some other component, and it is not necessary to completely remove the pump from the vehicle, it is not necessary and is not recommended that the pressure and return hoses be disconnected from the pump.*

7. Install the power steering pump in the reverse order of removal. Follow the procedure given below for initial start-up after the power steering pump or power cylinder have been disconnected from the system. This procedure is necessary to remove any air that might be trapped in the system.

INITIAL START-UP PROCEDURE

Upon initial engine start-up after a power cylinder or pump replacement, there is, more often than not, much noise and aeration. This is due to air trapped in the replaced unit which mixes with the surging fluid and causes aeration. The problem can be minimized, if the following procedure is employed:

1. Disconnect the coil wire.

2. Fill the power steering reservoir with the proper power steering fluid.

3. Crank the engine with the starter and continue adding fluid until the level stabilizes.

4. Rotate the steering wheel about 30° to each side of center, while continuing to crank the engine.

5. Recheck the fluid level and fill as required.

6. Reconnect the coil wire.

7. Start the engine and allow it to run for several minutes.

8. Rotate the steering wheel from stop to stop.

9. Shut off the engine and recheck the fluid level in the reservoir. Add fluid as necessary.

NOTE: *Check for fluid leaks before starting the engine and during the time the engine is running. If a leak is noticed, depending on its severity, shut the engine off and make the necessary adjustments to stop the leak. The pump could be damaged by being operated in the absence of fluid, since the fluid lubricates the pump.*

1975–82

1. Disconnect and plug the fluid lines.
2. Loosen the drive belt.
3. Unbolt the pump bracket from the air conditioning bracket, if any.

4. Remove the pump, mounting bracket, and pulley as an assembly.
5. Reverse the procedure for installation. Refill the system with the fluid specified in Chapter 1. Bleed the system of air by turning the steering wheel all the way to the right and left several times with the engine warmed up. Do not hold the steering against the stops or pump damage will result.

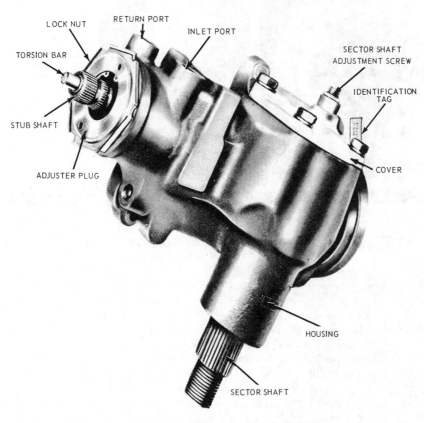

1975–80 Integral power steering gear

Brakes

BRAKE SYSTEM

Single-anchor, internal-expanding, duo-servo, self-adjusting, hydraulic drum brakes with a safety, dual master cylinder are used on Ford vans. Disc front brakes are used on 1975 and later models; dual piston on E-250 and 350, single piston on E-100 and 150.

The dual, safety-type master cylinder contains a double hydraulic cylinder with two fluid reservoirs, two hydraulic pistons (a primary and a secondary), and two residual check valves on all-drum systems, located in the outlet ports. The master cylinder's primary and secondary pistons function simultaneously when both the primary and secondary systems are fully operative.

Failure in either the front or rear brake system does not result in failure of the entire hydraulic brake system. Should hydraulic failure occur in the rear system, the hydraulic pressure from the primary piston (which actuates the front brakes) causes the secondary piston to bottom out in its bore, due to the lack of hydraulic pressure. The primary piston then actuates the front brakes with the continued stroke of the brake pedal.

Clean, high-quality brake fluid is essential to the safe and proper operation of the brake system. You should always buy the highest quality brake fluid that is available. If the brake fluid becomes contaminated, drain and flush the system and fill the master cylinder with new fluid.

NOTE: *Never reuse any brake fluid. Any brake fluid that is removed from the system should be discarded.*

The system has a pressure differential valve that activates a warning light if either hydraulic circuit is losing pressure. On 1975 and later models, the pressure differential valve is combined with a metering valve that restricts flow to the front brakes until the rear brakes overcome their retracting spring to prevent front brake lockup, and a proportioning valve that limits rear brake hydraulic pressure to prevent rear brake lockup.

Adjustment

The drum brakes on 1961–63 models require periodic adjustment. On 1964 and later they are self-adjusting; they require manual adjustment only after brake shoe replacement. The disc brakes are inherently self-adjusting and have no provision for manual adjustment.

To adjust the brakes, follow the procedure given below:

1. Raise the vehicle and support it with safety stands.

2. Remove the rubber plug from the adjusting slot on the backing plate.

3. Insert a brake adjusting spoon into the

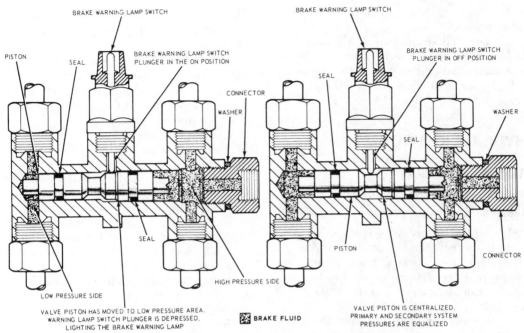

A cutaway view of the 1965–74 pressure differential valve system

slot and engage the lowest possible tooth on the starwheel. Move the end of the brake spoon downward to expand the adjusting screw. Repeat this operation until the brakes lock the wheel.

4. Insert a small screwdriver or piece of firm wire (coathanger wire) into the adjusting slot and push the automatic adjusting lever out and free of the starwheel on the adjusting screw and hold it there.

5. Engage the topmost tooth possible on the starwheel with the brake adjusting spoon. Move the end of the adjusting spoon upward to contract the adjusting screw. Back off the adjusting screw starwheel until the wheel spins freely without any drag. Keep track of the number of turns that the starwheel is backed off, or the number of strokes taken with the brake adjusting spoon.

6. Repeat this operation for the other side. When backing off the brakes on the other side, the starwheel adjuster must be backed off the same number of turns to prevent side-to-side brake pull.

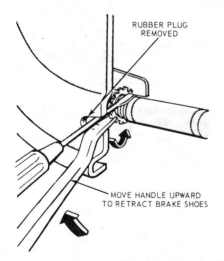

Positioning and operation of the brake adjusting tools during the adjustment procedure on E-100, E-150, and E-200 models—backing off the brakes

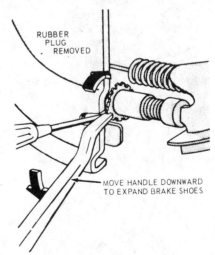

Positioning and operation of the brake adjusting tools during the adjustment procedure on E-250, E-300, and E-350 models—expanding the brakes

7. Repeat this operation on the other drum brakes.

8. When all drum brakes are adjusted, make several stops while backing the vehicle, to equalize the brakes at all of the wheels.

9. Remove the safety stands and lower the vehicle. Road test the vehicle.

HYDRAULIC SYSTEM

Master Cylinder
REMOVAL AND INSTALLATION
1961–68

1. Unbolt the forward splash shield.

2. Disconnect the pedal return spring.

3. Remove the locknut and eccentric bolt connecting the return spring bracket and master cylinder pushrod to the brake panel bracket.

4. Remove the snap ring from the pedal pivot pin.

5. Disconnect the brake lines and the stoplight switch.

6. Remove the mounting bolts and swing the cylinder down. Remove it from the pedal pivot pin and remove the pivot pin bushings.

7. On installation, adjust the eccentric bolt so that there is ¼–⁷/₁₆ in. pedal free-travel.

8. Bleed the system of air.

1969–74

1. Disconnect the wires from the stop-light switch.

2. Disconnect the hydraulic system brake lines at the master cylinder.

3. Remove the shoulder bolt and nut retaining the pushrod to the brake pedal. Remove the pushrod bushing.

4. Slide the master cylinder pushrod off the brake pedal pin. Remove the bushings and washers.

5. Remove the master cylinder retaining bolts and remove the master cylinder.

To install the master cylinder:

6. Position the master cylinder assembly on the firewall and install the retaining bolts.

7. Connect the hydraulic brake system lines to the master cylinder.

8. Lubricate the pushrod bushing. Insert the bushing in the pushrod and install the shoulder bolt which secures the pushrod to the brake pedal.

9. Connect the stoplight switch wires to the switch.

10. Bleed the hydraulic brake system.

1975 and Later
POWER BRAKES

1. Push the pedal down to release the vacuum from the booster. Release the pedal.

2. Disconnect the hydraulic lines.

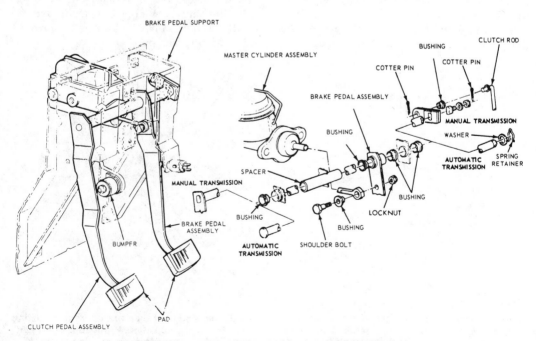

The 1969–74 master cylinder and brake pedal installation

3. Unbolt the master cylinder from the booster.

4. Before installation, check that the booster pushrod protrudes .980–.995 in. for 1970–82 E-350, .931–.946 for 1977–82 E100–250 and .880–.895 in. for 1975–76 beyond the base of the master cylinder mounting studs. Adjust as necessary.

5. Bleed the system of air after installation.

NON-POWER BRAKES

1. Disconnect the stoplight switch. Disconnect the dust boot from the rear of the master cylinder at the firewall.

2. Remove the shoulder bolt holding the cylinder pushrod to the brake pedal. Remove the stoplight switch from the pedal.

3. Remove the boot from the pushrod.

4. Disconnect the hydraulic lines.

5. Unbolt the master cylinder from the firewall.

6. Reverse the procedure for installation. Grease the pushrod bushing. Bleed the system of air after installation.

OVERHAUL

The most most thing to remember when rebuilding the master cylinder is cleanliness. Work in clean surroundings with clean tools and clean cloths or paper for drying purposes. Have plenty of clean alcohol and brake fluid on hand to clean and lubricate the internal components. There are service repair kits available for overhauling the master cylinder. Rebuilt master cylinders are also available.

1. Clean the outside of the master cylinder and remove the filler cap and gasket (diaphragm). Pour out any fluid that remains in the cylinder reservoir. Do not use any fluids other than brake fluid or alcohol to clean the master cylinder.

2. Unscrew the piston stop from the bottom of the cylinder body. Remove the O-ring seal from the piston stop. Discard the seal.

3. Remove the pushrod boot, if so equipped, from the groove at the rear of the master cylinder and slide the boot away from the rear of the master cylinder.

4. Remove the snap-ring which retains the primary and secondary piston assemblies within the cylinder body.

5. Remove the pushrod (if so equipped) and primary piston assembly from the master cylinder. Discard the piston assembly, including the boot (if so equipped).

6. Apply an air hose to the rear brake outlet port of the cylinder body and carefully blow the secondary piston out of the cylinder body.

7. Remove the return spring, spring retainer, cup protector, and cups from the secondary piston. Discard the cup protector and cups.

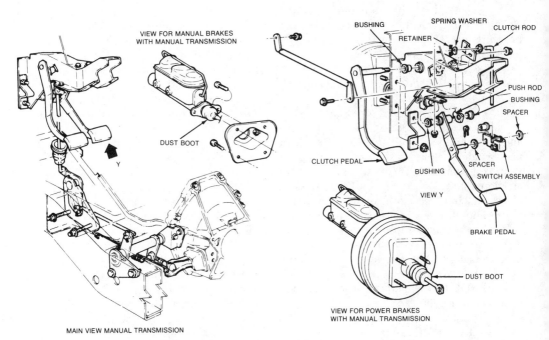

MAIN VIEW MANUAL TRANSMISSION

1975–82 brake pedal installation

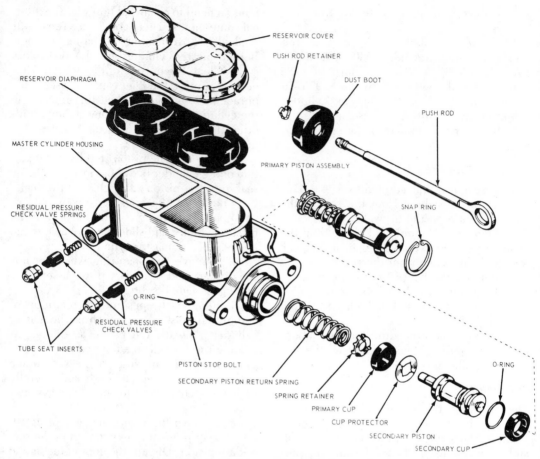

RESERVOIR COVER

PUSH ROD RETAINER

DUST BOOT

RESERVOIR DIAPHRAGM

PUSH ROD

MASTER CYLINDER HOUSING

PRIMARY PISTON ASSEMBLY

SNAP RING

RESIDUAL PRESSURE
CHECK VALVE SPRINGS

O-RING

RESIDUAL PRESSURE
CHECK VALVES

TUBE SEAT INSERTS

PISTON STOP BOLT

SECONDARY PISTON RETURN SPRING

SPRING RETAINER

PRIMARY CUP

CUP PROTECTOR

O-RING

SECONDARY PISTON

SECONDARY CUP

An exploded view of the 1969–82 master cylinder

8. Clean all of the remaining parts in clean isoprophyl alcohol and inspect the parts for chipping, excessive war or damage. Replace them as required.

NOTE: *When using a master cylinder repair kit, install all the parts supplied in the kit.*

9. Check all recesses, openings and internal passages to be sure that they are open and free from foreign matter. Use compressed air to blow out dirt and cleaning solvent remaining after the parts have been cleaned in the alcohol. Place all the parts on a clean pan, lint-free cloth, or paper to dry.

10. Dip all the parts, except the cylinder body, in clean brake fluid.

11. Assemble the two secondary cups, back-to-back, in the grooves near the end of the secondary piston.

12. Install the secondary piston assembly in the master cylinder.

13. Install a new O-ring on the piston stop, and start the stop into the cylinder body.

14. Position the boot, snap-ring and pushrod retainer on the pushrod. Make sure that the pushrod retainer is seated securely on the ball end of the rod. Seat the pushrod in the primary piston assembly.

15. Install the primary piston assembly in the master cylinder. Push the primary piston inward and tighten the secondary piston stop to retain the secondary piston in the bore.

16. Press the pushrod and pistons inward and install the snap-ring in the cylinder body.

17. Before the master cylinder is installed on the vehicle, the unit must be bled: support the master cylinder body in a vise, and fill both fluid reservoirs with brake fluid.

18. Loosely install plugs in the front and rear brake outlet bores. Depress the primary piston several times until air bubbles cease to appear in the brake fluid.

19. Tighten the plugs and attempt to depress the piston. The piston travel should be restricted after all air is expelled.

20. Remove the plugs. Install the cover

and gasket (diaphragm) assembly, and make sure that the cover retainer is tightened securely.

21. Install the master cylinder in the vehicle and bleed the hydraulic system.

Bleeding the Brakes

When any part of the hydraulic system has been disconnected for repair or replacement, air may get into the lines and cause spongy pedal action (because air can be compressed and brake fluid cannot). To correct this condition, it is necessary to bleed the hydraulic system after it has been properly connected to be sure that all air is expelled from the brake cylinders and lines.

When bleeding the brake system, bleed one brake cylinder at a time, beginning at the cylinder with the longest hydraulic line (farthest from the master cylinder) first. Keep the master cylinder reservoir filled with brake fluid during the bleeding operation. Never use brake fluid that has been drained from the hydraulic system, no matter how clean it is.

It will be necessary to centralize the pressure differential valve after a brake system failure has been corrected and the hydraulic system has been bled.

During the entire bleeding operation, do not allow the reservoir to run dry. Keep the master cylinder reservoirs filled with brake fluid.

NOTE: *When bleeding disc brake systems, the bleeder rod of the metering valve on the end of the pressure differential/metering/proportioning valve must be held out on the E-100 and 150, and in on the E-250 and 350. This is done to allow fluid flow to the front brakes.*

1. Clean all dirt from around the master cylinder fill cap, remove the cap and fill the master cylinder with brake fluid until the level is within ¼ in. of the top edge of the reservoir.

2. Clean off the bleeder screws at all 4 wheel cylinders. The bleeder screws are located on the inside of the brake backing plate or splash shield.

3. Attach a length of rubber hose over the nozzle of the bleeder screw at the wheel to be done first. Place the other end of the hose in a clean jar, submerged in brake fluid.

4. Open the bleeder screw valve ½–¾ turn.

5. Have an assistant slowly depress the

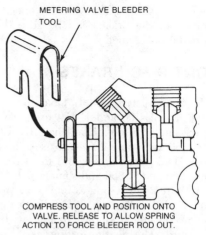

METERING VALVE BLEEDER TOOL

COMPRESS TOOL AND POSITION ONTO VALVE. RELEASE TO ALLOW SPRING ACTION TO FORCE BLEEDER ROD OUT.

A spring clip can be used to hold the pressure differential/metering/proportioning valve's bleeder valve out on E-100 and 150 disc brake systems

brake pedal. Close the bleeder screw valve and tell your assistant to allow the brake pedal to return slowly. Continue this pumping action to force any air out of the system. When bubbles cease to appear at the end of the bleeder hose, close the bleeder valve and remove the hose.

6. Check the master cylinder fluid level and add fluid accordingly. Do this after bleeding each wheel.

7. Repeat the bleeding operation at the remaining 3 wheels, ending with the one closest to the master cylinder. Fill the master cylinder reservoir.

CENTRALIZING THE PRESSURE DIFFERENTIAL VALVE

After any repair or bleeding of the primary (front brake) or secondary (rear brake) system, the dual-brake system warning light will usually remain illuminated due to the pressure differential valve remaining in the off-center position.

To centralize the pressure differential valve and turn off the warning light after the systems have been bled, follow the procedure below.

1. Turn the ignition switch to the ACC or ON position.

2. Check the fluid level in the master cylinder reservoirs and fill them to within ¼ in. of the top with brake fluid, as necessary.

3. Depress the brake pedal and the piston should center itself causing the brake warning light to go out.

4. Turn the ignition switch to the OFF position.

5. Before driving the vehicle, check the operation of the brakes and be sure that a firm pedal is obtained.

FRONT DISC BRAKES

All 1975 and later models have front disc brakes. The E-100 and E-150 use a sliding caliper, single piston brake; the 1975 E-250 and E-350 and some 1979–82 use a floating caliper, dual piston brake; and the 1976 and later E-250 and E-350 and some 1979–82 E-100, 150 use a rail sliding caliper, dual piston brake. Both the floating and sliding calipers are allowed to move slightly to align with the disc (rotor). The floating caliper is retained by through-bolts, and the sliding caliper by a key.

Pads

INSPECTION

1. Support the front end on jackstands.
2. Remove the wheel and tire.
3. Visually inspect the thickness of the pad linings through the ends and top of the caliper. Minimum acceptable pad thickness is $1/32$ in. lining thickness on bonded linings. Unless you want to remove the pads to measure the actual thickness from the rivet heads, you will have to make the limit for riveted lining visual inspection $1/16$ in. or more. The same applies if you don't know what kind of lining you have.

NOTE: *These manufacturer's specifications may not agree with your state inspection law.*

REMOVAL AND INSTALLATION

E-100 and E-150
EXCEPT 1979–82 SLIDING CALIPER

1. Remove and discard some of the fluid from the master cylinder without contaminating the contents to avoid overflow later on.
2. Support the front suspension on jackstands. Remove the wheel and tire.
3. Put an 8 in. C-clamp over the caliper and use it to push the outer pad in and pull the caliper out. This bottoms the caliper piston in its bore.
4. Remove the key retaining screw. Drive the caliper support key and spring out toward the outside, using a brass drift.
5. Push the caliper down and rotate the upper end up and out. Support the caliper, so as not to damage the brake hose.
6. Remove the outer pad from the caliper. You may have to tap it to loosen it. Remove the inner pad, removing the anti-rattle clip from the lower end of the shoe.
7. Thoroughly clean the sliding contact areas on the caliper and spindle assembly.
8. Put the new anti-rattle clip on the lower end of the new inner pad. Put the pad and clip in the pad abutment with the clip tab against the abutment and the loop-type spring away from the disc. Compress the clip and slide the upper end of the pad into place.
9. If the caliper piston isn't bottomed, bottom it with a C-clamp.
10. The replacement outer pad may differ slightly from the original equipment. Put the outer pad in place and press the tabs into place with your fingers. You can press the

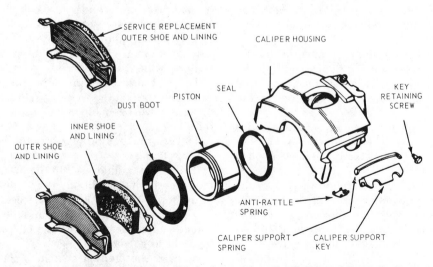

The sliding caliper, single piston, disc brake used on the E-100 and E-150 through 1978

pad in with a C-clamp, but be careful of the lining.

11. Position the caliper on the spindle assembly by pivoting it around the upper mounting surface. Be careful of the boot.

12. Use a screwdriver to hold the upper machined surface of the caliper against the support assembly. Drive a new key and spring assembly into place with a plastic mallet. Install the retaining screw and tighten to 12–20 ft lbs.

13. Replace the wheels and tires and lower the truck to the floor. Fill the master cylinder as specified in Chapter 1. Depress the brake pedal firmly several times to seat the pads on the disc. Don't drive until you get a firm pedal.

1975 E-250 and E-350 and 1979–82 with Floating Caliper

1. Remove with discard some of the fluid from the master cylinder without contaminating the contents to avoid overflow later on.

2. Support the front suspension on jackstands. Remove the wheel and tire.

3. Remove the pad mounting pins, anti-rattle springs, and the pads.

4. Loosen the piston housing to caliper mounting bolts enough to put in the new pads. Do not move the pistons.

5. Install the new pads, mounting pins, and anti-rattle springs. Be sure the spring tangs engage the pad holes. Tighten the pad mounting pins to 17–23 ft lbs.

6. Tighten the piston housing bolts evenly and squarely to reset the pistons in the cylinders. Torque them to 155–185 ft lbs.

7. Replace the wheels and tires and lower the truck to the floor. Fill the master cylinder as specified in Chapter 1. Depress the brake pedal firmly several times to seat the pads on the disc. Don't drive till you get a firm pedal.

1976–82 E-250 and E-350, 1979–82 E-100 and E-150 Sliding Caliper

1. Remove and discard some of the fluid from the master cylinder without contaminating the contents to avoid overflow later on.

2. Support the front suspension on jackstands. Remove the wheel and tire.

3. Remove the key retaining screw. Drive the key and spring out toward the inside, using a bass drift.

4. Rotate the key end of the caliper out

and away from the disc. Slide the opposite end clear and support the caliper, to prevent brake hose damage.

5. Remove the pad anti-rattle spring and both pads.

6. Thoroughly clean the sliding contact areas on the caliper and support.

7. Put the old inner pad back in place and use a C-clamp to force the pad and pistons back, until the pistons bottom. Make sure the pistons are bottomed.

8. Install the new pads and anti-rattle spring.

9. Put the caliper rail into the support slide and rotate the caliper onto the disc.

10. Put the key and spring in place and start them by hand. The spring should be between the key and caliper and the spring ends should overlap the key. If necessary, use a screwdriver to hold the caliper against the support assembly. Drive the key and spring into position, aligning the correct notch with the hole in the support. Install the key retaining screw and tighten to 12–20 ft lbs.

11. Replace the wheels and tires and lower the truck to the floor. Fill the master cylinder as specified in Chapter 1. Depress the brake pedal firmly several times to seat the pads on the disc. Don't drive till you get a firm pedal.

Caliper
REMOVAL AND INSTALLATION
E-100 and E-150 Floating Caliper

1. Support the front end on jackstands. Remove the wheel and tire.

2. Disconnect the brake hose. Cap the hose and plug the caliper.

3. Remove the caliper and pads as described under Pad Removal and Installation.

4. Check for leakage. A small amount of wetness inside the boot is normal. Clean the sliding contact areas on the support and caliper.

5. Replace the pads and caliper, connect the hose with a new washer, and bleed the system of air.

6. Replace the wheel and tire.

E-250, 350 1975–82 Floating Caliper

1. Support the front end on jackstands. Remove the wheel and tire.

2. Disconnect the brake hose. Cap the hose and plug the caliper.

3. Remove the pins and nuts holding the

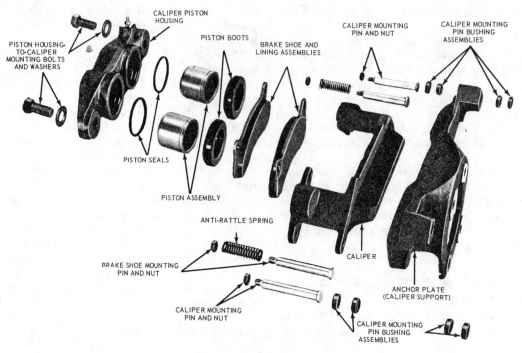

CALIPER PISTON
HOUSING

PISTON HOUSING-
TO-CALIPER
MOUNTING BOLTS
AND WASHERS

PISTON BOOTS

BRAKE SHOE AND
LINING ASSEMBLIES

CALIPER MOUNTING
PIN AND NUT

CALIPER MOUNTING
PIN BUSHING
ASSEMBLIES

PISTON SEALS

PISTON ASSEMBLY

ANTI-RATTLE SPRING

BRAKE SHOE MOUNTING
PIN AND NUT

CALIPER

CALIPER MOUNTING
PIN AND NUT

ANCHOR PLATE
(CALIPER SUPPORT)

CALIPER MOUNTING
PIN BUSHING
ASSEMBLIES

E-250, 350 floating caliper dual piston disc brake

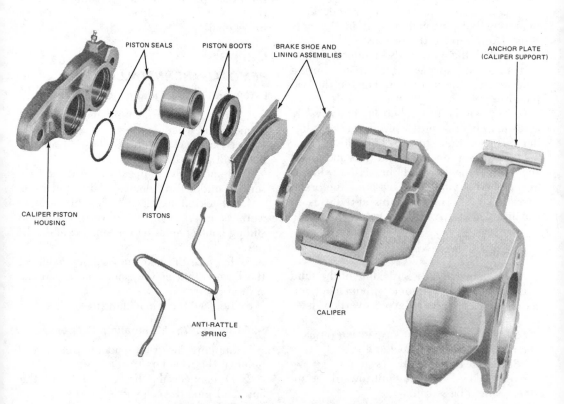

PISTON SEALS

PISTON BOOTS

BRAKE SHOE AND
LINING ASSEMBLIES

ANCHOR PLATE
(CALIPER SUPPORT)

CALIPER PISTON
HOUSING

PISTONS

ANTI-RATTLE
SPRING

CALIPER

E-250, 350 rail sliding caliper dual piston disc brake

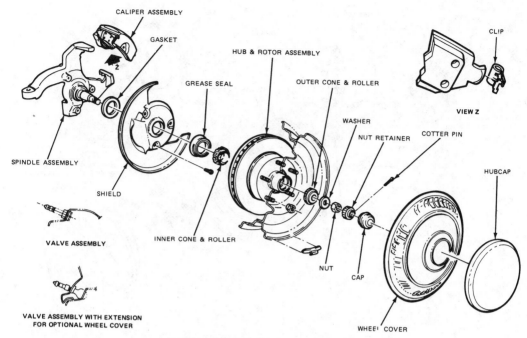

CALIPER ASSEMBLY

GASKET

HUB & ROTOR ASSEMBLY

GREASE SEAL

OUTER CONE & ROLLER

CLIP

VIEW Z

WASHER

NUT RETAINER

COTTER PIN

HUBCAP

SPINDLE ASSEMBLY

SHIELD

VALVE ASSEMBLY

INNER CONE & ROLLER

NUT

CAP

WHEEL COVER

VALVE ASSEMBLY WITH EXTENSION
FOR OPTIONAL WHEEL COVER

E-100 and E-150 disc brake installation

caliper to the anchor plate and remove the caliper.

4. Grease the pins lightly before installation. Tighten the nuts to 17–23 ft lbs. Use a new brake hose washer.

5. Bleed the system of air.

6. Replace the wheel and tire.

All Sliding Caliper

1. Support the front end on jackstands. Remove the wheel and tire.

2. Disconnect the brake hose. Cap the hose and plug the caliper.

3. Remove the key retaining screw and drive the key out with a brass drift.

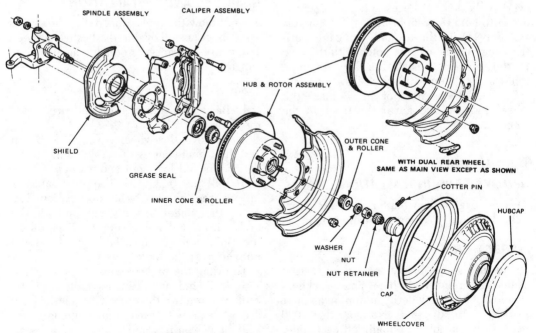

SPINDLE ASSEMBLY

CALIPER ASSEMBLY

HUB & ROTOR ASSEMBLY

SHIELD

GREASE SEAL

INNER CONE & ROLLER

OUTER CONE
& ROLLER

WITH DUAL REAR WHEEL
SAME AS MAIN VIEW EXCEPT AS SHOWN

COTTER PIN

HUBCAP

WASHER

NUT

NUT RETAINER

CAP

WHEELCOVER

1975 E-250 and E-350 disc brake installation

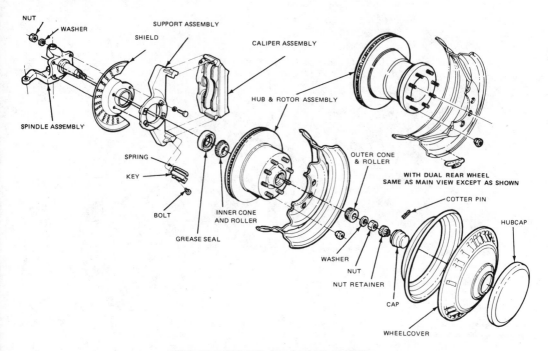

1976–82 E-250, 350 disc brake installation

4. Rotate the key end of the caliper out and slide the other end out.

5. Thoroughly clean the sliding areas.

6. To install, position the caliper rail into the slide on the support and rotate the caliper onto the rotor. Start the key and spring by hand. The spring should be between the key and caliper and the spring ends should overlap the key. If necessary, use a screwdriver to hold the caliper against the support assembly. Drive the key and spring into position, aligning the correct notch with the hole in the support. Install the key retaining screw and tighten to 12–20 ft lbs.

7. Bleed the system of air. Replace the wheel and tire and lower the truck to the floor.

Disc (Rotor)

REMOVAL AND INSTALLATION

This is covered in Chapter 1 under Front Wheel Bearing Packing and Adjustment.

INSPECTION

If the disc shows heavy scoring or rust, it should be refinished. The final thickness should not be less than the minimum amount marked on the disc hub. No more than .020 in. may be machined equally off each side. Runout, measured at a point 1 in. from the edge with a dial indicator, must not exceed .010 in. total within a 6 in. span.

DRUM BRAKES

Brake Drums

REMOVAL AND INSTALLATION

Do not blow the brake dust out of the drums with an air hose. Powdered asbestos has been found to be a cancer producing agent, when inhaled.

Front

1. Raise the vehicle until the tire clears the floor.

2. Remove the wheel cover or hub cap and the wheel bearing dust cap. Remove the cotter pin, nut lock, nut and washer.

3. Pull the brake drum approximately 2 in. out, then push it back into position. Remove the wheel bearing and pull off the brake drum and hub assembly. Back off on the brake adjustment if the brake drum will not slip over the brake shoes.

To install the brake drums:

4. If the hub and drum assembly are to be replaced, remove the protective coating from a new drum with carburetor degreaser. Install new bearings and a new grease seal. Pack the wheel bearings. If the original drum

is being used, be sure that the hub is clean and lubricated adequately.

5. Install the drum assembly, outer wheel bearing, washer, and adjusting nut.

6. Adjust the wheel bearing, install the nut lock and cotter pin, and the grease cap.

7. Install the wheel and hub cap. Adjust the brake shoes if they were backed off to remove the drum.

Rear

E-100, E-150, AND E-200

1. Raise the vehicle so that the wheel to be worked on is clear of the floor and install jackstands under the vehicle.

2. Remove the hub cap and the wheel/tire assembly. Remove the 3 retaining nuts and remove the brake drum. It may be necessary to back off the brake shoe adjustment in order to remove the brake drum. This is because the drum might be grooved or worn from being in service for an extended period of time.

3. Before installing a new brake drum, be sure to remove any protective coating with carburetor degreaser.

4. Install the brake drum in the reverse order of removal and adjust the brakes.

E-250, E-300, AND E-350

This procedure is covered thoroughly in Chapter 1 under Rear Wheel Bearing Packing and Adjustment. It requires removing the axle shaft.

INSPECTION

After the brake drum has been removed from the vehicle, it should be inspected for run-out, severe scoring, cracks, and the proper inside diameter.

Minor scores on a brake drum can be removed with fine emery cloth, provided that all grit is removed from the drum before it is installed on the vehicle.

A badly scored, rough, or out-of-round (run-out) drums can be ground or turned on a brake drum lathe. Do not remove any more material from the drum than is necessary to provide a smooth surface for the brake shoe to contact. The maximum diameter of the braking surface is shown on the inside of each brake drum. Brake drums that exceed the maximum braking surface diameter shown on the brake drum, either through wear or refinishing, must be replaced. This is because after the outside wall of the brake drum reaches a certain thickness (thinner than the

original thickness) the drum loses its ability to dissipate the heat created by the friction between the brake drum and the brake shoes, when the brakes are applied. Also, the brake drum will have more tendency to warp and/or crack.

The maximum braking surface diameter specification, which is shown on each drum, allows for a 0.060 in. machning cut over the original nominal drum diameter plus 0.030 in. additional wear before reaching the diameter where the drum must be discarded. Use a brake drum micrometer to measure the inside diameter of the brake drums.

Brake Shoes
REMOVAL AND INSTALLATION
E-100, E-150, and E-200

1. Raise and support the vehicle and remove the wheel and brake drum from the wheel to be worked on.

NOTE: *If you have never replaced brakes before and are not too familiar with the procedures involved, only disassemble and assemble one side at a time, leaving the other side intact as a reference during reassembly.*

2. Install a clamp over the ends of the wheel cylinder to prevent the pistons of the wheel cylinder from coming out, causing loss of fluid and much grief.

3. Contract the brake shoes by pulling the self-adjusting lever away from the star-wheel adjustment screw and turn the star-wheel up and back until the pivot nut is drawn onto the starwheel as far as it will come.

4. Pull the adjusting lever, cable and automatic adjuster spring down and toward the rear to unhook the pivot hook from the large hole in the secondary shoe web. Do not attempt to pry the pivot hook from the hole.

5. Remove the automatic adjuster spring and the adjusting lever.

6. Remove the secondary shoe-to-anchor spring with a brake tool. (Brake tools are very common implements and are available at auto parts stores). Remove the primary shoe-to-anchor spring and unhook the cable anchor. Remove the anchor pin plate.

7. Remove the cable guide from the secondary shoe.

8. Remove the shoe hold-down springs, shoes, adjusting screw, pivot nut, and socket. Note the color of each hold-down spring for assembly. To remove the hold-down springs,

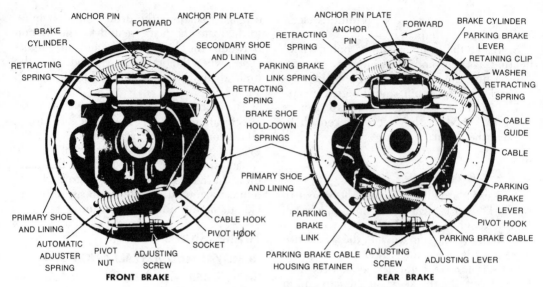

The front and rear brake assemblies for E-100, E-150, and E-200 vehicles

reach behind the brake backing plate and place one finger on the end of one of the brake hold-down spring mounting pins. Using a pair of pliers, grasp the washer-type retainer on top of the hold-down spring that corresponds to the pin which you are holding. Push down on the pliers and turn them 90° to align the slot in the washer with the head on the spring mounting pin. Remove the spring and washer retainer and repeat this operation on the hold-down spring on the other shoe.

9. On rear brakes, remove the parking brake link and spring. Disconnect the parking brake cable from the parking brake lever.

10. After removing the rear brake secondary shoe, disassemble the parking brake lever from the shoe by removing the retaining clip and spring washer.

To assemble and install the brake shoes:

11. On rear brakes, assemble the parking brake lever to the secondary shoe and secure it with the spring washer and retaining clip.

12. Apply a *light* coating of Lubriplate® at the points where the brake shoes contact the backing plate.

13. Position the brake shoes on the backing plate, and install the hold-down spring pins, springs, and spring washer-type retainers. On the rear brake, install the parking brake link, spring and washer. Connect the parking brake cable to the parking brake lever.

14. Install the anchor pin plate, and place the cable anchor over the anchor pin with the crimped side toward the backing plate.

15. Install the primary shoe-to-anchor spring with the brake tool.

16. Install the cable guide on the secondary shoe web with the flanged holes fitted into the hole in the secondary shoe web. Thread the cable around the cable guide groove.

17. Install the secondary shoe-to-anchor (long) spring. Be sure that the cable end is not cocked or binding on the anchor pin when installed. All of the parts should be flat on the anchor pin. Remove the wheel cylinder piston clamp.

18. Apply Lubriplate® to the threads and the socket end of the adjusting starwheel

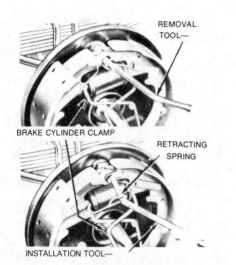

Removing and installing the brake shoe retracting springs with a brake spring tool

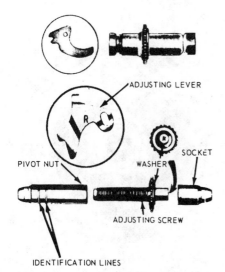

Identification of the rear brake adjusting screws and self-adjusting lever components, the one at the top is for the E-250, E-300, and E-350

screw. Turn the adjusting screw into the adjusting pivot nut to the limit of the threads and then back off ½ turn.

NOTE: *Interchanging the brake shoe adjusting screw assemblies from one side of the vehicle to the other would cause the brake shoes to retract rather than expand each time the automatic adjusting mechanism operated. To prevent this, the socket end of the adjusting screw is stamped with an "R" or an "L" for RIGHT or LEFT. The adjusting pivot nuts can be distinguished by the number of lines machined around the body of the nut; one line indicates left-hand nut and two lines indicates a right-hand nut.*

19. Place the adjusting socket on the screw and install this assembly between the shoe ends with the adjusting screw nearest to the secondary shoe.

20. Place the cable hook into the hole in the adjusting lever from the backing plate side. The adjusting levers are stamped with an "R" (right) or an "L" (left) to indicate their installation on the right or left-hand brake assembly.

21. Position the hooked end of the adjuster spring in the primary shoe web and connect the loop end of the spring to the adjuster lever hole.

22. Pull the adjuster lever, cable and automatic adjuster spring down toward the rear to engage the pivot hook in the large hole in the secondary shoe web.

23. After installation, check the action of the adjuster by pulling the section of the cable between the cable guide and the adjusting lever toward the secondary shoe web far enough to lift the lever past a tooth on the adjusting screw starwheel. The lever should snap into position behind the next tooth, and release of the cable should cause the adjuster spring to return the lever to its original position. This return action of the lever will turn the adjusting screw starwheel one tooth. The lever should contact the adjusting screw starwheel one tooth above the centerline of the adjusting screw.

If the automatic adjusting mechanism does not perform properly, check the following:

1. Check the cable and fittings. The cable ends should fill or extend slightly beyond the crimped section of the fittings. If this is not the case, replace the cable.

2. Check the cable guide for damage. The cable groove should be parallel to the shoe web, and the body of the guide should lie flat against the web. Replace the cable guide if this is not so.

3. Check the pivot hook on the lever. The hook surfaces should be square with the body on the lever for proper pivoting. Repair or replace the hook as necessary.

4. Make sure that the adjusting screw starwheel is properly seated in the notch in the shoe web.

E-250, E-300, and E-350

1. Raise and support the vehicle.

2. Remove the wheel and drum.

3. On a front wheel, remove the spring clip retainer fastening the adjustment cable anchor fitting to the brake anchor pin. On a rear wheel, remove the parking brake lever assembly retaining nut from behind the backing plate and remove the parking brake lever assembly.

NOTE: *From this point on, the removal of the front and rear brakes is the same.*

4. Remove the adjusting cable assembly from the anchor pin, cable guide, and adjusting lever.

5. Remove the brake shoe retracting springs.

6. Remove the brake shoe hold-down spring from each shoe.

7. Remove the brake shoes and adjusting screw assembly.

8. Disassemble the adjusting screw assembly.

To install the brake shoes:

9. Clean the ledge pads on the backing

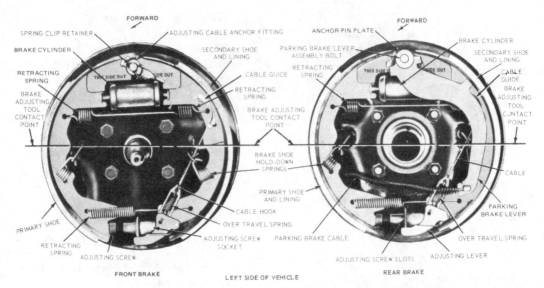

The front and rear brake assemblies for E-250, E-300 and E-350 vehicles

plate. Apply a light coat of Lubriplate to the ledge pads (where the brake shoes rub the backing plate).

10. Apply Lubriplate to the adjusting screw assembly and the hold-down and retracting spring contacts on the brake shoes.

11. Install the upper retracting spring on the primary and secondary shoes and position the shoe assembly on the backing plate with the wheel cylinder pushrods in the shoe slots.

12. Install the brake shoe hold-down springs.

13. Install the brake shoe adjustment screw assembly with the slot in the head of the adjusting screw toward the primary shoe, lower retracting spring, adjusting lever spring, adjusting lever assembly, and connect the adjusting cable to the adjusting lever. Position the cable in the cable guide and install the cable anchor fitting on the anchor pin.

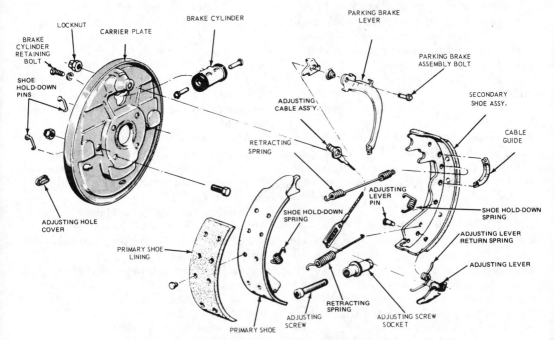

E-250, E-300, and E-350 rear brake details

14. Install the adjusting screw assemblies in the same locations from which they were removed. Interchanging the brake shoe adjusting screws from one side of the vehicle to the other will cause the brake shoes to retract rather than expand each time the automatic adjusting mechanism is operated. To prevent incorrect installation, the socket end of each adjusting screw is stamped with an R or an L to indicate their installation on the right or left-side of the vehicle. The adjusting pivot nuts can be distinguished by the number of lines machined around the body of the nut. Two lines indicate a right-hand nut; one line indicates a left-hand nut.

15. On a rear wheel, install the parking brake assembly in the anchor pin and secure with the retaining nut behind the backing plate.

16. Adjust the brakes before installing the brake drums and wheels. Install the brake drums and wheels.

17. Lower the vehicle and road test the brakes. New brakes may pull to one side or the other before they are seated. Continued pulling or erratic braking should not occur.

Wheel Cylinders

Front brake lining life can be increased on 1969–74 E-200 and E-300 models by decreasing the size of the front wheel cylinders and increasing the size of the rear. Front cylinders are decreased from $1\frac{1}{8}$ in. to $1\frac{1}{16}$ in., E-200 rear cylinders are increased from $\frac{13}{16}$ in. to $\frac{7}{8}$ in., E-300 rear cylinders are increased from $\frac{7}{8}$ in. to $\frac{15}{16}$ in. The necessary part numbers are given in Ford Technical Service Bulletin No. 86 of March 21, 1975.

OVERHAUL

Wheel cylinder rebuilding kits are available for reconditioning the wheel cylinders. The kits usually contain new cup springs, cylinder cups, and in some cases, new boots. The most important factor to keep in mind when rebuilding wheel cylinders is cleanliness. Keep all dirt away from the wheel cylinders when you are reassembling them.

1. To remove the wheel cylinder, jack up the vehicle and remove the wheel, hub, and drum.

2. Disconnect the brake line at the fitting on the brake backing plate.

3. Remove the brake assemblies.

4. Remove the screws which hold the

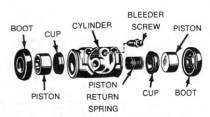

An exploded view of a wheel cylinder

wheel cylinder to the backing plate and remove the wheel cylinder from the vehicle.

5. Remove the rubber dust covers on the ends of the cylinder. Remove the pistons and piston cups and the spring. Remove the bleeder screw and make sure that it is not plugged.

6. Discard all of the parts which the rebuilding kit will replace.

7. Examine the inside of the cylinder. If it is severely rusted, pitted or scratched, then the cylinder must be replaced as the piston cups won't be able to seal against the walls of the cylinder.

8. Using a wheel cylinder hone or emery cloth and crocus cloth, polish the inside of the cylinder. The purpose of this is to put a new surface on the inside of the cylinder. Keep the inside of the cylinder coated with brake fluid while honing.

9. Wash out the cylinder with clean brake fluid after honing.

10. When reassembling the cylinder, dip all of the parts in clean brake fluid. Assemble the wheel cylinder in the reverse order of removal and disassembly.

Brake Backing Plate

REMOVAL AND INSTALLATION

1. In order to remove the brake backing plate, the brake assemblies must be removed.

2. Disconnect the hydraulic line from the wheel cylinder and submerge the end of the line in a container of brake fluid to minimize brake fluid loss and bleeding.

3. Remove the wheel cylinder.

4. On rear brakes, remove the parking brake lever from the cable. Rotate the flanged axle shaft so that the hole in the axle shaft flange aligns with the backing plate retaining nuts, then remove the nuts. Remove the axle shaft. Lift off the backing plate.

5. On the front brake assemblies, remove the capscrews which retain the backing plate to the spindle and remove the backing plate.

Brake Specifications

Year	Model	Master Cylinder Bore	Caliper Bore	Wheel Cylinder Bore Front	Wheel Cylinder Bore Rear	Rotor Diameter	Rotor Minimum Thickness	Rotor Maximum Run-out	Brake Drum Diameter Front	Brake Drum Diameter Rear	Machined Oversize Front	Machined Oversize Rear
1961–69	All	1.00	—	1.125	.8125	—	—	—	10.0	10.0	10.06	10.06
1970	E-100	1.00	—	1.125	.8125	—	—	—	10.0	10.0	10.06	10.06
	E-200	1.00	—	1.125	.8125	—	—	—	10.0	10.0	10.06	10.06
	E-300	1.00	—	1.125	.8750	—	—	—	12.0	12.0	12.06	12.06
1971–74	E-100	1.00	—	1.125	.8125	—	—	—	10.0	10.0	10.06	10.06
	E-200	1.00	—	1.125	.8125	—	—	—	11.03	11.03	11.09	11.09
	E-300	1.00	—	1.125	.8750	—	—	—	12.0	12.0	12.06	12.06
1975	E-100, 150	1.00	2.875	—	.8125	11.72	.940	.003	—	10.0	—	10.06
	E-250	1.062	2.180	—	.8125	12.55	1.120	.003	—	11.03	—	11.09
	E-350	1.062	2.180	—	.8750	12.55	1.120	.003	—	12.0	—	12.06
1976	E-100, 150	1.00	2.875	—	.9375	11.54	1.180	.003	—	11.03	—	11.09
	E-250	1.062	2.180	—	1.000	12.50	1.120	.003	—	12.0	—	12.06
	E-350	1.062	2.180	—	1.060	12.50	1.120	.003	—	12.0	—	12.06

Year	Model										
1977	E-100, 150	1.00	2.875	—	.9375	11.54	1.180	.003	11.03	—	11.09
	E-250	1.062	2.180	—	1.000	12.50	1.120	.003	12.0	—	12.06
	E-350	1.062	2.180	—	1.062	12.50	1.120	.003	12.0	—	12.06
1978	E-100, 150	1.00	2.875	—	.9375	11.54	1.180	.003	11.03	—	11.09
	E-250	1.062	2.180	—	1.000	12.50	1.120	.003	12.0	—	12.06
	E-350	1.062	2.180	—	1.062	12.50	1.120	.003	12.0	—	12.06
1979–82	E-100, 150	1.00	2.875	—	.9375	11.54	1.180	.003	11.03	—	11.09
	E-250	1.062	2.180	—	1.000	12.50	1.120	.003	12.0	—	12.06
	E-350	1.062	2.180	—	1.062	12.50	1.120	.003	12.0	—	12.06

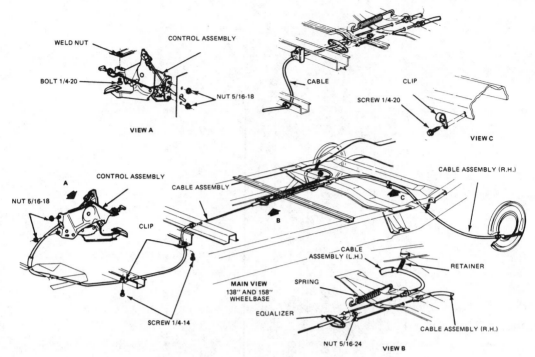

WELD NUT
CONTROL ASSEMBLY
BOLT 1/4-20
NUT 5/16-18
VIEW A

CABLE
CLIP
SCREW 1/4-20
VIEW C

CONTROL ASSEMBLY
CABLE ASSEMBLY
CABLE ASSEMBLY (R.H.)
NUT 5/16-18
A
CLIP
B
C
CABLE ASSEMBLY (L.H.)
RETAINER
MAIN VIEW
138" AND 158"
WHEELBASE
SPRING
EQUALIZER
CABLE ASSEMBLY (R.H.)
SCREW 1/4-14
NUT 5/16-24   VIEW B

1975–82 pedal operated parking brake linkage

6. Install the backing plate in the reverse order of removal.

PARKING BRAKE

Adjustment

1961–68

1. Make a few stops in reverse to make sure the rear drum brakes are fully adjusted.
2. Raise and support the rear axle.
3. Pull the parking brake handle up one notch from the release position.
4. Loosen the locknut on the cable equalizer (under the truck).
5. Tighten the adjusting nut until a slight drag is felt when turning the rear wheels forward.
6. Tighten the locknut to hold the adjustment.

7. Release the parking brake handle. There should be no drag at the rear wheels.

1969–82

The factory-recommended procedure is to use a tension gauge on the cables with the handle fully applied (1969–74) or with the pedal pushed down two clicks (1975–82). Tension should be 300 lbs for 1969–74 E-100 and 200, 225 lbs for 1969–74 E-300, and 70 lbs for 1975–82. If the tension gauge is not available, a method similar to that explained for 1961–68 models can be used. The most important point is to make sure that there is no drag when the brake is released and that the brake locks the wheel when fully applied. If there is brake shoe drag after adjustment on E-250, 300, and 350 models, remove the drums and check the clearance between the parking brake operating lever and the cam plate. It should be .015 in. with the parking brake released.

Body

10

DOORS

REMOVAL AND INSTALLATION

Front Doors

1. Remove the screws which hold the door to the hinge (1969–82 models) or the hinge to the door post (1961–68 models). Remove any access panels to gain access to the retaining bolts.

2. Slide the door off the hinges (1969–82 models) or lift the door from the vehicle with the hinges attached (1961–68 models).

NOTE: *The 1961–68 models have rivets which retain the door to the hinges. In order to remove the hinges from the door,*

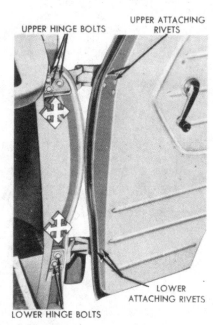

UPPER HINGE BOLTS   UPPER ATTACHING RIVETS

LOWER HINGE BOLTS   PLUG BUTTONS   LOWER ATTACHING RIVETS

1961–68 rear cargo door hinge adjustment

UPPER HINGE BOLTS   UPPER ATTACHING RIVETS

LOWER ATTACHING RIVETS

LOWER HINGE BOLTS

1961–68 front door hinge adjustment

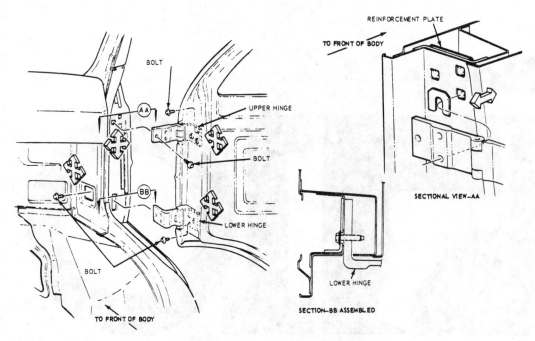

1969–74 front door hinge adjustment

the rivets must be drilled out with a 1 in. drill and replaced with nuts, bolts, and lockwashers.

3. Install the doors in the reverse order of removal. Do not tighten any of the attaching bolts until the door and door latch are aligned with the latch striker and the surrounding body panels. On the 1969–82 models, all of the attaching bolt holes are elongated to be adjustable in all directions. On the 1961–68 models, only the hinge-to-body attaching bolts are adjustable.

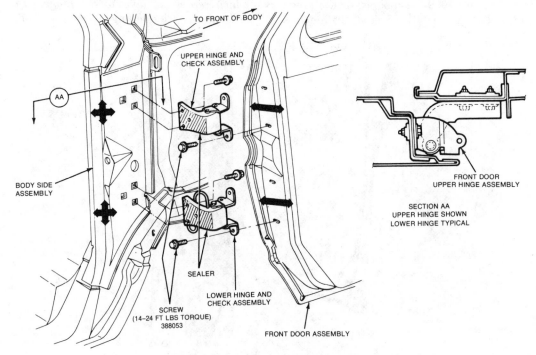

1975–82 front door hinge adjustment

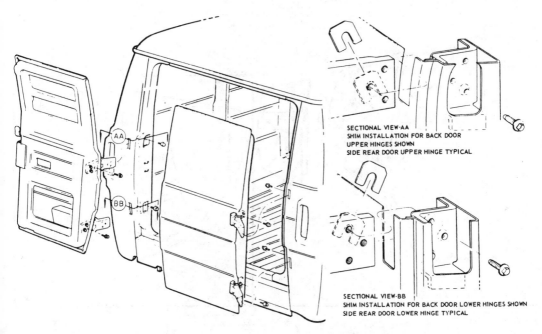

SECTIONAL VIEW-AA
SHIM INSTALLATION FOR BACK DOOR
UPPER HINGES SHOWN
SIDE REAR DOOR UPPER HINGE TYPICAL

SECTIONAL VIEW-BB
SHIM INSTALLATION FOR BACK DOOR LOWER HINGES SHOWN
SIDE REAR DOOR LOWER HINGE TYPICAL

1969–80 rear cargo door hinge adjustment

Side and Rear Hinged Cargo Doors

The rear and side cargo doors are removed, installed and adjusted in the same manner as described above for the front doors.

SLIDING DOOR ADJUSTMENT

1. To adjust the upper edge of the door in or out, loosen the upper roller retaining nut and move the roller in or out.

2. To adjust the lower front door edge in or out, support the door so it won't move up or down and loosen the guide assembly retaining screws. Move it forward to bring the door in and back to move it out.

3. To move the front of the door up or down, loosen the three lower guide attaching screws and rotate the guide around the lower screw. Loosen the upper roller bracket assembly screws and adjust so that the bottom edge of the roller assembly is about $1/16$ in. from the bottom flange of the upper track.

4. To move the rear edge of the door up or down, remove the trim panel or plug buttons. With the door open, loosen the hinge assembly screws and move the hinge assembly up or down.

5. The rear latch striker assembly can be adjusted up or down and in or out.

6. To adjust the door fore and aft, remove the nuts holding the center track shield. Re-

move the nuts and screws from outside the truck. Remove the shield. Loosen the three hinge check bolts. Remove the B pillar post trim panel. Loosen the two striker bolts and remove the striker. Fit the door and adjust the door check so that it is fully engaged with the upper hinge lever and the check bumper is fully depressed with the hinge casting. Install the front striker and add or remove shims to obtain proper front latch operations.

HOOD

ALIGNMENT

On those vehicles equipped with a hood, the hood can be adjusted fore and aft and up and down to obtain the proper clearance. To adjust the hood, loosen the hood-to-hinge attaching screws until they are just snug. Then, reposition the hood as required, and tighten the attaching screws. On 1969–74 models, the hood is adjusted up and down by placing shims between the hinge and the body. On 1975–82 models, loosen the hinge to cowl attaching screws for up and down adjustment. After the hood has been adjusted, check the hood latch and striker adjustment. Adjust the hood latch and striker as required.

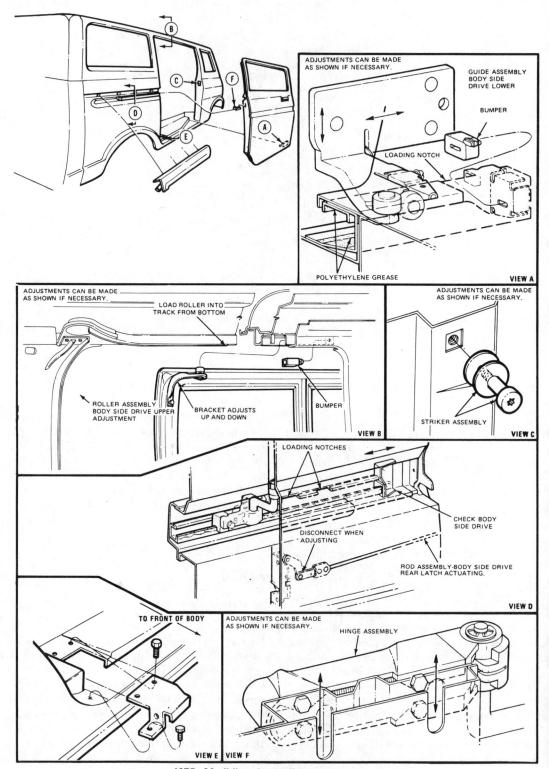

ADJUSTMENTS CAN BE MADE
AS SHOWN IF NECESSARY.

GUIDE ASSEMBLY
BODY SIDE
DRIVE LOWER

BUMPER

LOADING NOTCH

POLYETHYLENE GREASE

VIEW A

ADJUSTMENTS CAN BE MADE
AS SHOWN IF NECESSARY.

LOAD ROLLER INTO
TRACK FROM BOTTOM

ROLLER ASSEMBLY
BODY SIDE DRIVE UPPER
ADJUSTMENT

BRACKET ADJUSTS
UP AND DOWN

BUMPER

VIEW B

ADJUSTMENTS CAN BE MADE
AS SHOWN IF NECESSARY.

STRIKER ASSEMBLY

VIEW C

LOADING NOTCHES

CHECK BODY
SIDE DRIVE

DISCONNECT WHEN
ADJUSTING

ROD ASSEMBLY-BODY SIDE DRIVE
REAR LATCH ACTUATING.

VIEW D

TO FRONT OF BODY

VIEW E

ADJUSTMENTS CAN BE MADE
AS SHOWN IF NECESSARY.

HINGE ASSEMBLY

VIEW F

1975–82 sliding door adjustments, part one

PICKUP TAILGATE

REMOVAL AND INSTALLATION

1. Remove the 2 bolts which retain the hinges to the rear lower body panel, discon-nect the support arms, and remove the tailgate and hinges from the truck.

2. Position the tailgate and hinges to the rear lower body panel and install the hinge retaining bolts.

3. Connect the support arms.

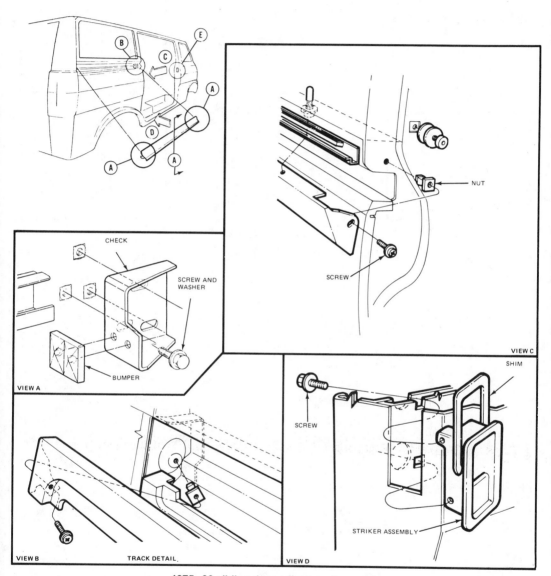

1975–82 sliding door adjustments, part two

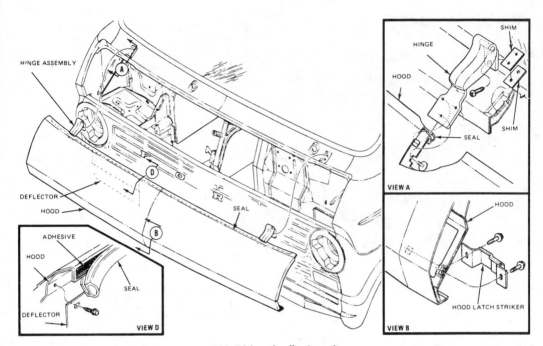

HINGE ASSEMBLY

DEFLECTOR

HOOD

ADHESIVE

HOOD

SEAL

DEFLECTOR

VIEW D

SEAL

A

D

B

SHIM

HINGE

HOOD

SEAL

SHIM

VIEW A

HOOD

HOOD LATCH STRIKER

VIEW B

1969–74 hood adjustments

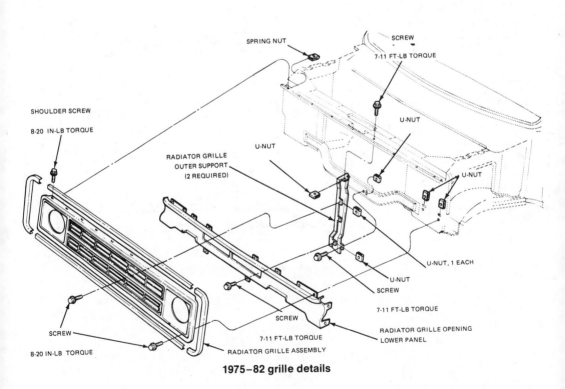

SPRING NUT

SCREW

7-11 FT-LB TORQUE

SHOULDER SCREW

8-20 IN-LB TORQUE

U-NUT

RADIATOR GRILLE
OUTER SUPPORT
(2 REQUIRED)

U-NUT

U-NUT

U-NUT

U-NUT, 1 EACH

U-NUT

SCREW

7-11 FT-LB TORQUE

RADIATOR GRILLE OPENING
LOWER PANEL

SCREW

SCREW

8-20 IN-LB TORQUE

7-11 FT-LB TORQUE

RADIATOR GRILLE ASSEMBLY

1975–82 grille details

BODY REPAIR

You can repair most minor auto body damage yourself. Minor damage usually falls into one of several categories: (1) small scratches and dings in the paint that can be repaired without the use of body filler, (2) deep scratches and dents that require body filler, but do not require pulling, or hammering metal back into shape and (3) rust-out repairs. The repair sequences illustrated in this chapter are typical of these types of repairs. If you want to get involved in more complicated repairs including pulling or hammering sheet metal back into shape, you will probably need more detailed instructions. Chilton's *Minor Auto Body Repair, 2nd Edition* is a comprehensive guide to repairing auto body damage yourself.

TOOLS AND SUPPLIES

The list of tools and equipment you may need to fix minor body damage ranges from very basic hand tools to a wide assortment of specialized body tools. Most minor scratches, dings and rust holes can be fixed using an electric drill, wire wheel or grinder attachment, half-round plastic file, sanding block, various grades of sandpaper (#36, which is coarse through #600, which is fine) in both wet and dry types, auto body plastic, primer, touch-up paint, spreaders, newspaper and masking tape.

Most manufacturers of auto body repair products began supplying materials to professionals. Their knowledge of the best, most-used products has been translated into body repair kits for the do-it-yourselfer. Kits are available from a number of manufacturers and contain the necessary materials in the required amounts for the repair identified on the package.

Kits are available for a wide variety of uses, including:

• Rusted out metal
• All purpose kit for dents and holes
• Dents and deep scratches
• Fiberglass repair kit
• Epoxy kit for restyling.

Kits offer the advantage of buying what you need for the job. There is little waste and little chance of materials going bad from not being used. The same manufacturers also merchandise all of the individual products used—spreaders, dent pullers, fiberglass cloth, polyester resin, cream hardener, body filler, body files, sandpaper, sanding discs and holders, primer, spray paint, etc.

CAUTION: *Most of the products you will be using contain harmful chemicals, so be extremely careful. Always read the complete label before opening the containers. When you put them away for future use, be sure they are out of children's reach!*

Most auto body repair kits contain all the materials you need to do the job right in the kit. So, if you have a small rust spot or dent you want to fix, check the contents of the kit before you run out and buy any additional tools.

ALIGNING BODY PANELS

Doors

There are several methods of adjusting doors. Your vehicle will probably use one of those illustrated.

Whenever a door is removed and is to be reinstalled, you should matchmark the position of the hinges on the door pillars. The holes of the hinges and/or the hinge attaching points are usually oversize to permit alignment of doors. The striker plate is also moveable, through oversize holes, permitting up-and-down, in-and-out and fore-and-aft movement. Fore-and-aft movement is made by adding or subtracting shims from behind the striker and pillar post. The striker should be adjusted so that the door closes fully and remains closed, yet enters the lock freely.

DOOR HINGES

Don't try to cover up poor door adjustment with a striker plate adjustment. The gap on each side of the door should be equal and uniform and there should be no metal-to-metal contact as the door is opened or closed.

1. Determine which hinge bolts must be loosened to move the door in the desired direction.

2. Loosen the hinge bolt(s) just enough to allow the door to be moved with a padded pry bar.

3. Move the door a small amount and check the fit, after tightening the bolts. Be sure that there is no bind or interference with adjacent panels.

4. Repeat this until the door is properly positioned, and tighten all the bolts securely.

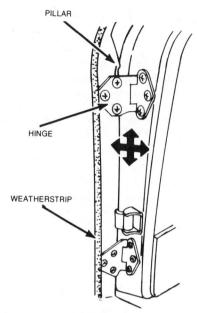

Door hinge adjustment

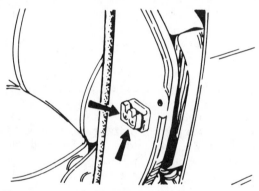

Move the door striker as indicated by arrows

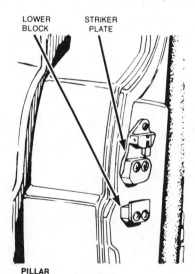

PILLAR

Striker plate and lower block

Hood, Trunk or Tailgate

As with doors, the outline of hinges should be scribed before removal. The hood and trunk can be aligned by loosening the hinge bolts in their slotted mounting holes and moving the hood or trunk lid as necessary. The hood and trunk have adjustable catch locations to regulate lock engagement. Bumpers at the front and/or rear of the hood provide a vertical adjustment and the hood lockpin can be adjusted for proper engagement.

The tailgate on the station wagon can be

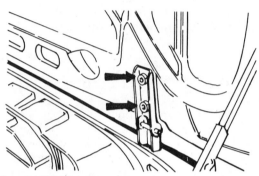

Loosen the hinge boots to permit fore-and-aft and horizontal adjustment

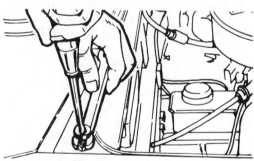

The hood is adjusted vertically by stop-screws at the front and/or rear

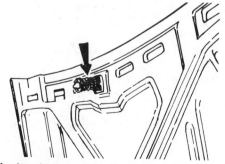

The hood pin can be adjusted for proper lock engagement

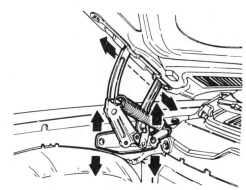

The height of the hood at the rear is adjusted by loosening the bolts that attach the hinge to the body and moving the hood up or down

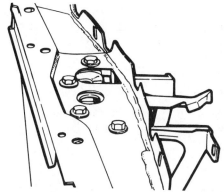

The base of the hood lock can also be repositioned slightly to give more positive lock engagement

adjusted by loosening the hinge bolts in their slotted mounting holes and moving the tailgate on its hinges. The latchplate and latch striker at the bottom of the tailgate opening can be adjusted to stop rattle. An adjustable bumper is located on each side.

RUST, UNDERCOATING, AND RUSTPROOFING

Rust

Rust is an electrochemical process. It works on ferrous metals (iron and steel) from the inside out due to exposure of unprotected surfaces to air and moisture. The possibility of rust exists practically nationwide—anywhere humidity, industrial pollution or chemical salts are present, rust can form. In coastal areas, the problem is high humidity and salt air; in snowy areas, the problem is chemical

salt (de-icer) used to keep the roads clear, and in industrial areas, sulphur dioxide is present in the air from industrial pollution and is changed to sulphuric acid when it rains. The rusting process is accelerated by high temperatures, especially in snowy areas, when vehicles are driven over slushy roads and then left overnight in a heated garage.

Automotive styling also can be a contributor to rust formation. Spot welding of panels creates small pockets that trap moisture and form an environment for rust formation. Fortunately, auto manufacturers have been working hard to increase the corrosion protection of their products. Galvanized sheet metal enjoys much wider use, along with the increased use of plastic and various rust retardant coatings. Manufacturers are also designing out areas in the body where rust-forming moisture can collect.

To prevent rust, you must stop it before it gets started. On new vehicles, there are two ways to accomplish this.

First, the car or truck should be treated with a commercial rustproofing compound. There are many different brands of franchised rustproofers, but most processes involve spraying a waxy "self-healing" compound under the chassis, inside rocker panels, inside doors and fender liners and similar places where rust is likely to form. Prices for a quality rustproofing job range from $100–$250, depending on the area, the brand name and the size of the vehicle.

Ideally, the vehicle should be rustproofed as soon as possible following the purchase. The surfaces of the car or truck have begun to oxidize and deteriorate during shipping. In addition, the car may have sat on a dealer's lot or on a lot at the factory, and once the rust has progressed past the stage of light, powdery surface oxidation rustproofing is not likely to be worthwhile. Professional rustproofers feel that once rust has formed, rustproofing will simply seal in moisture already present. Most franchised rustproofing operations offer a 3–5 year warranty against rust-through, but will not support that warranty if the rustproofing is not applied within three months of the date of manufacture.

Undercoating should not be mistaken for rustproofing. Undercoating is a black, tar-like substance that is applied to the underside of a vehicle. Its basic function is to deaden noises that are transmitted from under the car. It simply cannot get into the crevices and seams where moisture tends to collect. In fact, it may clog up drainage holes and ventilation passages. Some undercoatings also tend to crack or peel with age and only create more moisture and corrosion attracting pockets.

The second thing you should do immediately after purchasing the car is apply a paint sealant. A sealant is a petroleum based product marketed under a wide variety of brand names. It has the same protective properties as a good wax, but bonds to the paint with a chemically inert layer that seals it from the air. If air can't get at the surface, oxidation cannot start.

The paint sealant kit consists of a base coat and a conditioning coat that should be applied every 6–8 months, depending on the manufacturer. The base coat must be applied before waxing, or the wax must first be removed.

Third, keep a garden hose handy for your car in winter. Use it a few times on nice days during the winter for underneath areas, and it will pay big dividends when spring arrives. Spraying under the fenders and other areas which even car washes don't reach will help remove road salt, dirt and other build-ups which help breed rust. Adjust the nozzle to a high-force spray. An old brush will help break up residue, permitting it to be washed away more easily.

It's a somewhat messy job, but worth it in the long run because rust often starts in those hidden areas.

At the same time, wash grime off the door sills and, more importantly, the under portions of the doors, plus the tailgate if you have a station wagon or truck. Applying a coat of wax to those areas at least once before and once during winter will help fend off rust.

When applying the wax to the under parts of the doors, you will note small drain holes. These holes often are plugged with undercoating or dirt. Make sure they are cleaned out to prevent water build-up inside the doors. A small punch or penknife will do the job.

Water from the high-pressure sprays in car washes sometimes can get into the housings for parking and taillights, so take a close look. If they contain water merely loosen the retaining screws and the water should run out.

Repairing Scratches and Small Dents

Step 1. This dent (arrow) is typical of a deep scratch or minor dent. If deep enough, the dent or scratch can be pulled out or hammered out from behind. In this case no straightening is necessary

Step 2. Using an 80-grit grinding disc on an electric drill grind the paint from the surrounding area down to bare metal. This will provide a rough surface for the body filler to grab

Step 3. The area should look like this when you're finished grinding

Step 4. Mix the body filler and cream hardener according to the directions

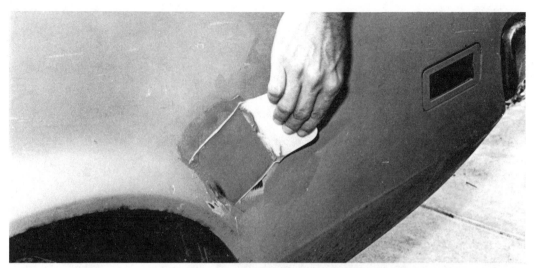

Step 5. Spread the body filler evenly over the entire area. Be sure to cover the area completely

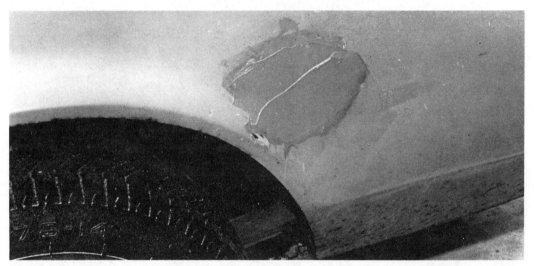

Step 6. Let the body filler dry until the surface can just be scratched with your fingernail

Step 7. Knock the high spots from the body filler with a body file

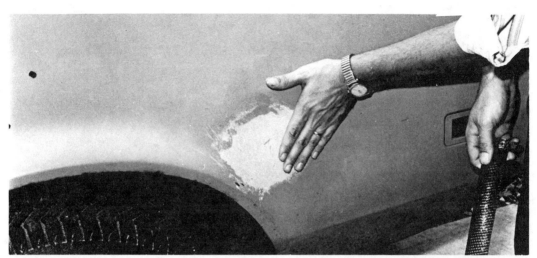

Step 8. Check frequently with the palm of your hand for high and low spots. If you wind up with low spots, you may have to apply another layer of filler

Step 9. Block sand the entire area with 320 grit paper

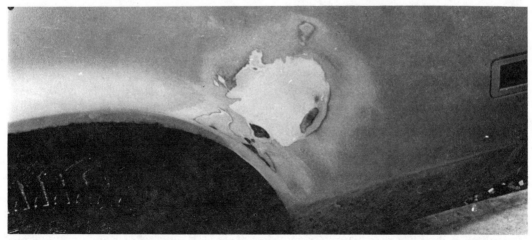

Step 10. When you're finished, the repair should look like this. Note the sand marks extending 2—3 inches out from the repaired area

Step 11. Prime the entire area with automotive primer

Step 12. The finished repair ready for the final paint coat. Note that the primer has covered the sanding marks (see Step 10). A repair of this size should be able to be spotpainted with good results

REPAIRING RUST HOLES

One thing you have to remember about rust: even if you grind away all the rusted metal in a panel, and repair the area with any of the kits available, *eventually* the rust will return. There are two reasons for this. One, rust is a chemical reaction that causes pressure under the repair from the inside out. That's how the blisters form. Two, the back side of the panel (and the repair) is wide open to moisture, and unpainted body filler acts like a sponge. That's why the best solution to rust problems

is to remove the rusted panel and install a new one or have the rusted area cut out and a new piece of sheet metal welded in its place. The trouble with welding is the expense; sometimes it will cost more than the car or truck is worth.

One of the better solutions to do-it-your-self rust repair is the process using a fiberglass cloth repair kit (shown here). This will give a strong repair that resists cracking and moisture and is relatively easy to use. It can be used on large or small holes and also can be applied over contoured surfaces.

Step 1. Rust areas such as this are common and are easily fixed

Step 2. Grind away all traces of rust with a 24-grit grinding disc. Be sure to grind back 3—4 inches from the edge of the hole down to bare metal and be sure all traces of rust are removed

AUTO BODY CARE

There are hundreds—maybe thousands—of products on the market, all designed to protect or aid your car's finish in some manner. There are as many different products as there are ways to use them, but they all have one thing in common—the surface must be clean.

Washing

The primary ingredient for washing your car is water, preferably "soft" water. In many areas of the country, the local water supply is "hard" containing many minerals. The little rings or film that is left on your car's surface after it has dried is the result of "hard" water.

Since you usually can't change the local water supply, the next best thing is to dry the surface before it has a chance to dry itself.

Into the water you usually add soap. Don't use detergents or common, coarse soaps. Your car's paint never truly dries out, but is always evaporating residual oils into the air. Harsh detergents will remove these oils, causing the paint to dry faster than normal.

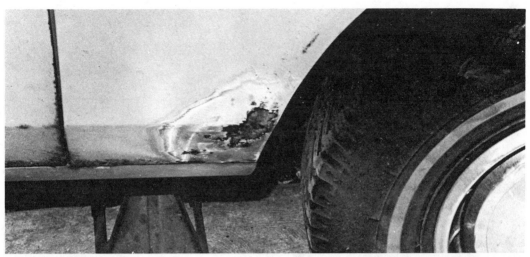

Step 3. Be sure all rust is removed from the edges of the metal. The edges must be ground back to un-rusted metal

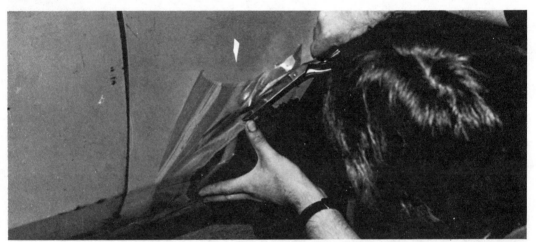

Step 4. If you are going to use release film, cut a piece about 2″ larger than the area you have sanded. Place the film over the repair and mark the sanded area on the film. Avoid any unnecessary wrinkling of the film

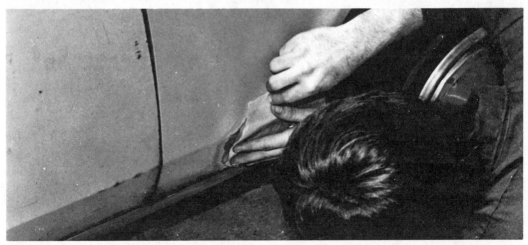

Step 5. Cut 2 pieces of fiberglass matte. One piece should be about 1″ smaller than the sanded area and the second piece should be 1″ smaller than the first. Use sharp scissors to avoid loose ends

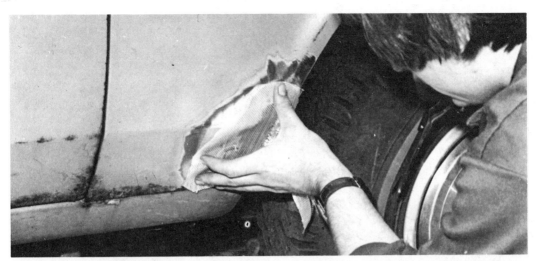

Step 6. Check the dimensions of the release film and cloth by holding them up to the repair area

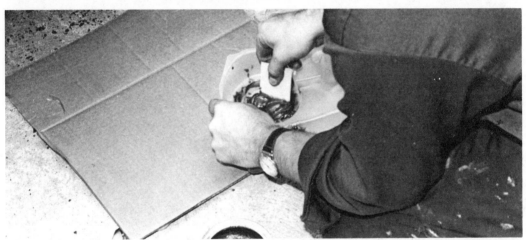

Step 7. Mix enough repair jelly and cream hardener in the mixing tray to saturate the fiberglass material or fill the repair area. Follow the directions on the container

Step 8. Lay the release sheet on a flat surface and spread an even layer of filler, large enough to cover the repair. Lay the smaller piece of fiberglass cloth in the center of the sheet and spread another layer of repair jelly over the fiberglass cloth. Repeat the operation for the larger piece of cloth. If the fiberglass cloth is not used, spread the repair jelly on the release film, concentrated in the middle of the repair

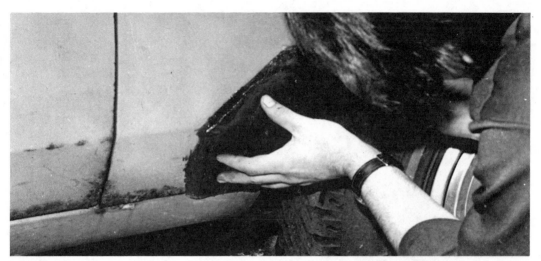

Step 9. Place the repair material over the repair area, with the release film facing outward

Step 10. Use a spreader and work from the center outward to smooth the material, following the body contours. Be sure to remove all air bubbles

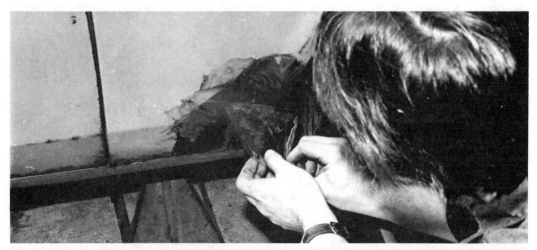

Step 11. Wait until the repair has dried tack-free and peel off the release sheet. The ideal working temperature is 65—90° F. Cooler or warmer temperatures or high humidity may require additional curing time

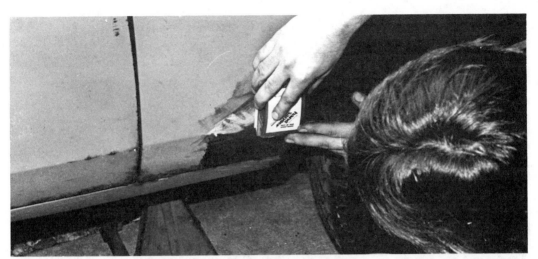

Step 12. Sand and feather-edge the entire area. The initial sanding can be done with a sanding disc on an electric drill if care is used. Finish the sanding with a block sander

Step 13. When the area is sanded smooth, mix some topcoat and hardener and apply it directly with a spreader. This will give a smooth finish and prevent the glass matte from showing through the paint

Step 14. Block sand the topcoat with finishing sandpaper

Step 15. To finish this repair, grind out the surface rust along the top edge of the rocker panel

Step 16. Mix some more repair jelly and cream hardener and apply it directly over the surface

Step 17. When it dries tack-free, block sand the surface smooth

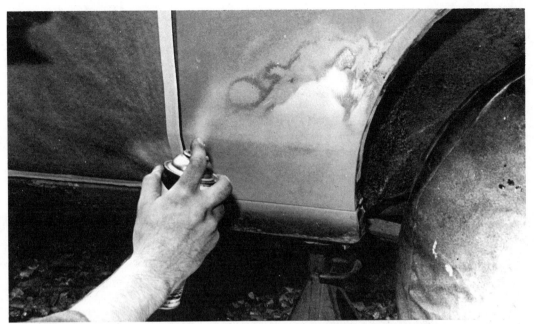

Step 18. If necessary, mask off adjacent panels and spray the entire repair with primer. You are now ready for a color coat

Instead use warm water and a non-detergent soap made especially for waxed surfaces or a liquid soap made for waxed surfaces or a liquid soap made for washing dishes by hand. Other products that can be used on painted surfaces include baking soda or plain soda water for stubborn dirt.

Wash the car completely, starting at the top, and rinse it completely clean. Abrasive grit should be loaded off under water pressure; scrubbing grit off will scratch the finish. The best washing tool is a sponge, cleaning mitt or soft towel. Whichever you choose, replace it often as each tends to absorb grease and dirt.

Other ways to get a better wash include:

• Don't wash your car in the sun or when the finish is hot.

• Use water pressure to remove caked-on dirt.

• Remove tree-sap and bird effluence immediately. Such substances will eat through wax, polish and paint.

One of the best implements to dry your car is a turkish towel or an old, soft bath towel. Anything with a deep nap will hold any dirt in suspension and not grind it into the paint.

Harder cloths will only grind the grit into the paint making more scratches. Always start drying at the top, followed by the hood and trunk and sides. You'll find there's always more dirt near the rocker panels and wheelwells which will wind up on the rest of the car if you dry these areas first.

Cleaners, Waxes and Polishes

Before going any farther you should know the function of various products.

Cleaners—remove the top layer of dead pigment or paint.

Rubbing or polishing compounds—used to remove stubborn dirt, get rid of minor scratches, smooth away imperfections and partially restore badly weathered paint.

Polishes—contain no abrasives or waxes; they shine the paint by adding oils to the paint.

Waxes—are a protective coating for the polish.

CLEANERS AND COMPOUNDS

Before you apply any wax, you'll have to remove oxidation, road film and other types of pollutants that washing alone will not remove.

The paint on your car never dries completely. There are always residual oils evaporating from the paint into the air. When enough oils are present in the paint, it has a healthy shine (gloss). When too many oils evaporate the paint takes on a whitish cast known as oxidation. The idea of polishing and waxing is to keep enough oil present in the painted surface to prevent oxidation; but when it occurs, the only recourse is to remove the top layer of "dead" paint, exposing the healthy paint underneath.

Products to remove oxidation and road film are sold under a variety of generic names—polishes, cleaner, rubbing compound, cleaner/polish, polish/cleaner, self-polishing wax, pre-wax cleaner, finish restorer and many more. Regardless of name there are two types of cleaners—abrasive cleaners (sometimes called polishing or rubbing compounds) that remove oxidation by grinding away the top layer of "dead" paint, or chemical cleaners that dissolve the "dead" pigment, allowing it to be wiped away.

Abrasive cleaners, by their nature, leave thousands of minute scratches in the finish, which must be polished out later. These should only be used in extreme cases, but are usually the only thing to use on badly oxidized paint finishes. Chemical cleaners are much milder but are not strong enough for severe cases of oxidation or weathered paint.

The most popular cleaners are liquid or paste abrasive polishing and rubbing compounds. Polishing compounds have a finer abrasive grit for medium duty work. Rubbing compounds are a coarser abrasive and for heavy duty work. Unless you are familiar with how to use compounds, be very careful. Excessive rubbing with any type of compound or cleaner can grind right through the paint to primer or bare metal. Follow the directions on the container—depending on type, the cleaner may or may not be OK for your paint. For example, some cleaners are not formulated for acrylic lacquer finishes.

When a small area needs compounding or heavy polishing, it's best to do the job by hand. Some people prefer a powered buffer for large areas. Avoid cutting through the paint along styling edges on the body. Small, hand operations where the compound is applied and rubbed using cloth folded into a thick ball allow you to work in straight lines along such edges.

To avoid cutting through on the edges when using a power buffer, try masking tape. Just cover the edge with tape while using power. Then finish the job by hand with the tape removed. Even then work carefully. The paint tends to be a lot thinner along the sharp ridges stamped into the panels.

Whether compounding by machine or by hand, only work on a small area and apply the compound sparingly. If the materials are spread too thin, or allowed to sit too long, they dry out. Once dry they lose the ability to deliver a smooth, clean finish. Also, dried out polish tends to cause the buffer to stick in one spot. This in turn can burn or cut through the finish.

WAXES AND POLISHES

Your car's finish can be protected in a number of ways. A cleaner/wax or polish/cleaner followed by wax or variations of each all provide good results. The two-step approach (polish followed by wax) is probably slightly better but consumes more time and effort. Properly fed with oils, your paint should never need cleaning, but despite the best polishing job, it won't last unless it's protected with wax. Without wax, polish must be renewed at least once a month to prevent oxidation. Years ago (some still swear by it today), the best wax was made from the Brazilian palm, the Carnuba, favored for its vegetable base and high melting point. However, modern synthetic waxes are harder, which means they protect against moisture better, and chemically inert silicone is used for a long lasting protection. The only problem with silicone wax is that it penetrates all layers of paint. To repaint or touch up a panel or car protected by silicone wax, you have to completely strip the finish to avoid "fisheyes."

Under normal conditions, silicone waxes will last 4–6 months, but you have to be careful of wax build-up from too much waxing. Too thick a coat of wax is just as bad as no wax at all; it stops the paint from breathing.

Combination cleaners/waxes have become popular lately because they remove the old layer of wax plus light oxidation, while putting on a fresh coat of wax at the same time. Some cleaners/waxes contain abrasive cleaners which require caution, although many cleaner/waxes use a chemical cleaner.

Applying Wax or Polish

You may view polishing and waxing your car as a pleasant way to spend an afternoon, or as a boring chore, but it has to be done to keep the paint on your car. Caring for the paint doesn't require special tools, but you should follow a few rules.

1. Use a good quality wax.
2. Before applying any wax or polish, be

sure the surface is completely clean. Just because the car looks clean, doesn't mean it's ready for polish or wax.

3. If the finish on your car is weathered, dull, or oxidized, it will probably have to be compounded to remove the old or oxidized paint. If the paint is simply dulled from lack of care, one of the non-abrasive cleaners known as polishing compounds will do the trick. If the paint is severely scratched or really dull, you'll probably have to use a rubbing compound to prepare the finish for waxing. If you're not sure which one to use, use the polishing compound, since you can easily ruin the finish by using too strong a compound.

4. Don't apply wax, polish or compound in direct sunlight, even if the directions on the can say you can. Most waxes will not cure properly in bright sunlight and you'll probably end up with a blotchy looking finish.

5. Don't rub the wax off too soon. The result will be a wet, dull looking finish. Let the wax dry thoroughly before buffing it off.

6. A constant debate among car enthusiasts is how wax should be applied. Some maintain pastes or liquids should be applied in a circular motion, but body shop experts have long thought that this approach results in barely detectable circular abrasions, especially on cars that are waxed frequently. They advise rubbing in straight lines, especially if any kind of cleaner is involved.

7. If an applicator is not supplied with the wax, use a piece of soft cheesecloth or very soft lint-free material. The same applies to buffing the surface.

SPECIAL SURFACES

One-step combination cleaner and wax formulas shouldn't be used on many of the special surfaces which abound on cars. The one-step materials contain abrasives to achieve a clean surface under the wax top coat. The abrasives are so mild that you could clean a car every week for a couple of years without fear of rubbing through the paint. But this same level of abrasiveness might, through repeated use, damage decals used for special trim effects. This includes wide stripes, wood-grain trim and other appliques.

Painted plastics must be cleaned with care. If a cleaner is too aggressive it will cut through the paint and expose the primer. If bright trim such as polished aluminum or chrome is painted, cleaning must be performed with even greater care. If rubbing compound is being used, it will cut faster than polish.

Abrasive cleaners will dull an acrylic finish. The best way to clean these newer finishes is with a non-abrasive liquid polish. Only dirt and oxidation, not paint, will be removed.

Taking a few minutes to read the instructions on the can of polish or wax will help prevent making serious mistakes. Not all preparations will work on all surfaces. And some are intended for power application while others will only work when applied by hand.

Don't get the idea that just pouring on some polish and then hitting it with a buffer will suffice. Power equipment speeds the operation. But it also adds a measure of risk. It's very easy to damage the finish if you use the wrong methods or materials.

Caring for Chrome

Read the label on the container. Many products are formulated specifically for chrome, but others contain abrasives that will scratch the chrome finish. If it isn't recommended for chrome, don't use it.

Never use steel wool or kitchen soap pads to clean chrome. Be careful not to get chrome cleaner on paint or interior vinyl surfaces. If you do, get it off immediately.

Troubleshooting

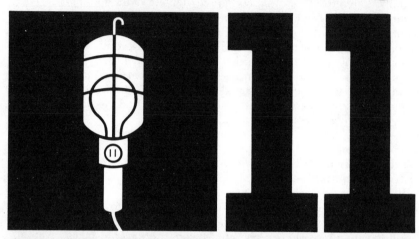

This section is designed to aid in the quick, accurate diagnosis of automotive problems. While automotive repairs can be made by many people, accurate troubleshooting is a rare skill for the amateur and professional alike.

In its simplest state, troubleshooting is an exercise in logic. It is essential to realize that an automobile is really composed of a series of systems. Some of these systems are interrelated; others are not. Automobiles operate within a framework of logical rules and physical laws, and the key to troubleshooting is a good understanding of all the automotive systems.

This section breaks the car or truck down into its component systems, allowing the problem to be isolated. The charts and diagnostic road maps list the most common problems and the most probable causes of trouble. Obviously it would be impossible to list every possible problem that could happen along with every possible cause, but it will locate MOST problems and eliminate a lot of unnecessary guesswork. The systematic format will locate problems within a given system, but, because many automotive systems are interrelated, the solution to your particular problem may be found in a number of systems on the car or truck.

USING THE TROUBLESHOOTING CHARTS

This book contains all of the specific information that the average do-it-yourself mechanic needs to repair and maintain his or her car or truck. The troubleshooting charts are designed to be used in conjunction with the specific procedures and information in the text. For instance, troubleshooting a point-type ignition system is fairly standard for all models, but you may be directed to the text to find procedures for troubleshooting an individual type of electronic ignition. You will also have to refer to the specification charts throughout the book for specifications applicable to your car or truck.

TOOLS AND EQUIPMENT

The tools illustrated in Chapter 1 (plus two more diagnostic pieces) will be adequate to troubleshoot most problems. The two other tools needed are a voltmeter and an ohmmeter. These can be purchased separately or in combination, known as a VOM meter.

In the event that other tools are required, they will be noted in the procedures.

Troubleshooting Engine Problems

See Chapters 2, 3, 4 for more information and service procedures.

Index to Systems

System	To Test	Group
Battery	Engine need not be running	1
Starting system	Engine need not be running	2
Primary electrical system	Engine need not be running	3
Secondary electrical system	Engine need not be running	4
Fuel system	Engine need not be running	5
Engine compression	Engine need not be running	6
Engine vacuum	Engine must be running	7
Secondary electrical system	Engine must be running	8
Valve train	Engine must be running	9
Exhaust system	Engine must be running	10
Cooling system	Engine must be running	11
Engine lubrication	Engine must be running	12

Index to Problems

Problem: Symptom	Begin at Specific Diagnosis, Number ____
Engine Won't Start:	
Starter doesn't turn	1.1, 2.1
Starter turns, engine doesn't	2.1
Starter turns engine very slowly	1.1, 2.4
Starter turns engine normally	3.1, 4.1
Starter turns engine very quickly	6.1
Engine fires intermittently	4.1
Engine fires consistently	5.1, 6.1
Engine Runs Poorly:	
Hard starting	3.1, 4.1, 5.1, 8.1
Rough idle	4.1, 5.1, 8.1
Stalling	3.1, 4.1, 5.1, 8.1
Engine dies at high speeds	4.1, 5.1
Hesitation (on acceleration from standing stop)	5.1, 8.1
Poor pickup	4.1, 5.1, 8.1
Lack of power	3.1, 4.1, 5.1, 8.1
Backfire through the carburetor	4.1, 8.1, 9.1
Backfire through the exhaust	4.1, 8.1, 9.1
Blue exhaust gases	6.1, 7.1
Black exhaust gases	5.1
Running on (after the ignition is shut off)	3.1, 8.1
Susceptible to moisture	4.1
Engine misfires under load	4.1, 7.1, 8.4, 9.1
Engine misfires at speed	4.1, 8.4
Engine misfires at idle	3.1, 4.1, 5.1, 7.1, 8.4

Sample Section

Test and Procedure	Results and Indications	Proceed to
4.1—Check for spark: Hold each spark plug wire approximately ¼" from ground with gloves or a heavy, dry rag. Crank the engine and observe the spark.	If no spark is evident:	4.2
	If spark is good in some cases:	4.3
	If spark is good in all cases:	4.6

Specific Diagnosis

This section is arranged so that following each test, instructions are given to proceed to another, until a problem is diagnosed.

Section 1—Battery

Test and Procedure	Results and Indications	Proceed to
1.1—Inspect the battery visually for case condition (corrosion, cracks) and water level. 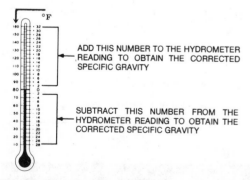 DIRT ON TOP OF BATTERY / PLUGGED VENT / CORROSION / LOOSE CABLE OR POSTS / CRACKS / LOW WATER LEVEL **Inspect the battery case**	If case is cracked, replace battery:	**1.4**
	If the case is intact, remove corrosion with a solution of baking soda and water (**CAUTION**: *do not get the solution into the battery*), and fill with water:	**1.2**
1.2—Check the battery cable connections: Insert a screwdriver between the battery post and the cable clamp. Turn the headlights on high beam, and observe them as the screwdriver is gently twisted to ensure good metal to metal contact. TESTING BATTERY CABLE CONNECTIONS USING A SCREWDRIVER	If the lights brighten, remove and clean the clamp and post; coat the post with petroleum jelly, install and tighten the clamp:	**1.4**
	If no improvement is noted:	**1.3**
1.3—Test the state of charge of the battery using an individual cell tester or hydrometer.	If indicated, charge the battery. **NOTE:** *If no obvious reason exists for the low state of charge (i.e., battery age, prolonged storage), proceed to:*	**1.4**

°F
ADD THIS NUMBER TO THE HYDROMETER READING TO OBTAIN THE CORRECTED SPECIFIC GRAVITY

SUBTRACT THIS NUMBER FROM THE HYDROMETER READING TO OBTAIN THE CORRECTED SPECIFIC GRAVITY

Specific Gravity (@ 80° F.)

Minimum	Battery Charge
1.260	100% Charged
1.230	75% Charged
1.200	50% Charged
1.170	25% Charged
1.140	Very Little Power Left
1.110	Completely Discharged

The effects of temperature on battery specific gravity (left) and amount of battery charge in relation to specific gravity (right)

1.4—Visually inspect battery cables for cracking, bad connection to ground, or bad connection to starter.	If necessary, tighten connections or replace the cables:	**2.1**

Section 2—Starting System
See Chapter 3 for service procedures

Test and Procedure	Results and Indications	Proceed to
Note: Tests in Group 2 are performed with coil high tension lead disconnected to prevent accidental starting.		
2.1—Test the starter motor and solenoid: Connect a jumper from the battery post of the solenoid (or relay) to the starter post of the solenoid (or relay).	If starter turns the engine normally:	**2.2**
	If the starter buzzes, or turns the engine very slowly:	**2.4**
	If no response, replace the solenoid (or relay).	**3.1**
	If the starter turns, but the engine doesn't, ensure that the flywheel ring gear is intact. If the gear is undamaged, replace the starter drive.	**3.1**
2.2—Determine whether ignition override switches are functioning properly (clutch start switch, neutral safety switch), by connecting a jumper across the switch(es), and turning the ignition switch to "start".	If starter operates, adjust or replace switch:	**3.1**
	If the starter doesn't operate:	**2.3**
2.3—Check the ignition switch "start" position: Connect a 12V test lamp or voltmeter between the starter post of the solenoid (or relay) and ground. Turn the ignition switch to the "start" position, and jiggle the key.	If the lamp doesn't light or the meter needle doesn't move when the switch is turned, check the ignition switch for loose connections, cracked insulation, or broken wires. Repair or replace as necessary:	**3.1**
	If the lamp flickers or needle moves when the key is jiggled, replace the ignition switch.	**3.3**

Checking the ignition switch "start" position

STARTER RELAY
(IF EQUIPPED)

Test and Procedure	Results and Indications	Proceed to
2.4—Remove and bench test the starter, according to specifications in the engine electrical section.	If the starter does not meet specifications, repair or replace as needed:	**3.1**
	If the starter is operating properly:	**2.5**
2.5—Determine whether the engine can turn freely: Remove the spark plugs, and check for water in the cylinders. Check for water on the dipstick, or oil in the radiator. Attempt to turn the engine using an 18" flex drive and socket on the crankshaft pulley nut or bolt.	If the engine will turn freely only with the spark plugs out, and hydrostatic lock (water in the cylinders) is ruled out, check valve timing:	**9.2**
	If engine will not turn freely, and it is known that the clutch and transmission are free, the engine must be disassembled for further evaluation:	**Chapter 3**

Section 3—Primary Electrical System

Test and Procedure	Results and Indications	Proceed to
3.1—Check the ignition switch "on" position: Connect a jumper wire between the distributor side of the coil and ground, and a 12V test lamp between the switch side of the coil and ground. Remove the high tension lead from the coil. Turn the ignition switch on and jiggle the key.	If the lamp lights:	3.2
	If the lamp flickers when the key is jiggled, replace the ignition switch:	3.3
	If the lamp doesn't light, check for loose or open connections. If none are found, remove the ignition switch and check for continuity. If the switch is faulty, replace it:	3.3

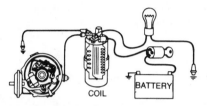

Checking the ignition switch "on" position

3.2—Check the ballast resistor or resistance wire for an open circuit, using an ohmmeter. See Chapter 3 for specific tests.	Replace the resistor or resistance wire if the resistance is zero. **NOTE:** *Some ignition systems have no ballast resistor.*	3.3

 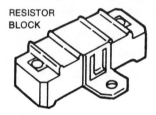

RESISTOR BLOCK

CALIBRATED RESISTANCE LEAD

Two types of resistors

3.3—On point-type ignition systems, visually inspect the breaker points for burning, pitting or excessive wear. Gray coloring of the point contact surfaces is normal. Rotate the crankshaft until the contact heel rests on a high point of the distributor cam and adjust the point gap to specifications. On electronic ignition models, remove the distributor cap and visually inspect the armature. Ensure that the armature pin is in place, and that the armature is on tight and rotates when the engine is cranked. Make sure there are no cracks, chips or rounded edges on the armature.	If the breaker points are intact, clean the contact surfaces with fine emery cloth, and adjust the point gap to specifications. If the points are worn, replace them. On electronic systems, replace any parts which appear defective. If condition persists:	3.4

Test and Procedure	Results and Indications	Proceed to
3.4—On point-type ignition systems, connect a dwell-meter between the distributor primary lead and ground. Crank the engine and observe the point dwell angle. On electronic ignition systems, conduct a stator (magnetic pickup assembly) test. See Chapter 3.	On point-type systems, adjust the dwell angle if necessary. **NOTE:** *Increasing the point gap decreases the dwell angle and vice-versa.* If the dwell meter shows little or no reading; On electronic ignition systems, if the stator is bad, replace the stator. If the stator is good, proceed to the other tests in Chapter 3.	**3.6** **3.5**

WIDE GAP   NARROW GAP

CLOSE   OPEN

SMALL DWELL

LARGE DWELL

NORMAL DWELL

INSUFFICIENT DWELL

EXCESSIVE DWELL

Dwell is a function of point gap

3.5—On the point-type ignition systems, check the condenser for short: connect an ohmeter across the condenser body and the pigtail lead.	If any reading other than infinite is noted, replace the condenser	**3.6**

OHMMETER

Checking the condenser for short

3.6—Test the coil primary resistance: On point-type ignition systems, connect an ohmmeter across the coil primary terminals, and read the resistance on the low scale. Note whether an external ballast resistor or resistance wire is used. On electronic ignition systems, test the coil primary resistance as in Chapter 3.	Point-type ignition coils utilizing ballast resistors or resistance wires should have approximately 1.0 ohms resistance. Coils with internal resistors should have approximately 4.0 ohms resistance. If values far from the above are noted, replace the coil.	**4.1**

OHMMETER

Check the coil primary resistance

Section 4—Secondary Electrical System
See Chapters 2–3 for service procedures

Test and Procedure	Results and Indications	Proceed to
4.1—Check for spark: Hold each spark plug wire approximately ¼" from ground with gloves or a heavy, dry rag. Crank the engine, and observe the spark.	If no spark is evident:	**4.2**
	If spark is good in some cylinders:	**4.3**
	If spark is good in all cylinders:	**4.6**

Check for spark at the plugs

4.2—Check for spark at the coil high tension lead: Remove the coil high tension lead from the distributor and position it approximately ¼" from ground. Crank the engine and observe spark. **CAUTION:** *This test should not be performed on engines equipped with electronic ignition.*	If the spark is good and consistent:	**4.3**
	If the spark is good but intermittent, test the primary electrical system starting at 3.3:	**3.3**
	If the spark is weak or non-existent, replace the coil high tension lead, clean and tighten all connections and retest. If no improvement is noted:	**4.4**
4.3—Visually inspect the distributor cap and rotor for burned or corroded contacts, cracks, carbon tracks, or moisture. Also check the fit of the rotor on the distributor shaft (where applicable).	If moisture is present, dry thoroughly, and retest per 4.1:	**4.1**
	If burned or excessively corroded contacts, cracks, or carbon tracks are noted, replace the defective part(s) and retest per 4.1:	**4.1**
	If the rotor and cap appear intact, or are only slightly corroded, clean the contacts thoroughly (including the cap towers and spark plug wire ends) and retest per 4.1:	
	If the spark is good in all cases:	**4.6**
	If the spark is poor in all cases:	**4.5**

Inspect the distributor cap and rotor

Test and Procedure	Results and Indications	Proceed to

4.4—Check the coil secondary resistance: On point-type systems connect an ohmmeter across the distributor side of the coil and the coil tower. Read the resistance on the high scale of the ohmmeter. On electronic ignition systems, see Chapter 3 for specific tests.

The resistance of a satisfactory coil should be between 4,000 and 10,000 ohms. If resistance is considerably higher (i.e., 40,000 ohms) replace the coil and retest per 4.1. **NOTE:** *This does not apply to high performance coils.*

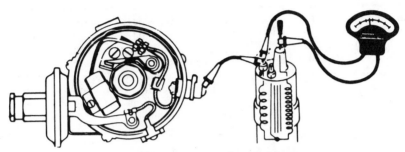
Testing the coil secondary resistance

4.5—Visually inspect the spark plug wires for cracking or brittleness. Ensure that no two wires are positioned so as to cause induction firing (adjacent and parallel). Remove each wire, one by one, and check resistance with an ohmmeter.

Replace any cracked or brittle wires. If any of the wires are defective, replace the entire set. Replace any wires with excessive resistance (over $8000\,\Omega$ per foot for suppression wire), and separate any wires that might cause induction firing.

4.6

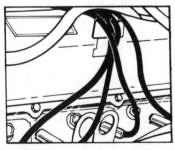
Misfiring can be the result of spark plug leads to adjacent, consecutively firing cylinders running parallel and too close together

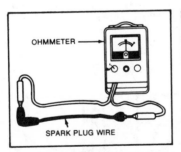
On point-type ignition systems, check the spark plug wires as shown. On electronic ignitions, do not remove the wire from the distributor cap terminal; instead, test through the cap

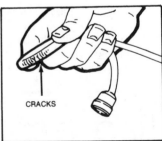
Spark plug wires can be checked visually by bending them in a loop over your finger. This will reveal any cracks, burned or broken insulation. Any wire with cracked insulation should be replaced

4.6—Remove the spark plugs, noting the cylinders from which they were removed, and evaluate according to the color photos in the middle of this book.

See following.

See following.

Test and Procedure	Results and Indications	Proceed to
4.7—Examine the location of all the plugs.	The following diagrams illustrate some of the conditions that the location of plugs will reveal.	**4.8**

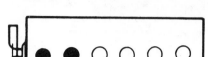

Two adjacent plugs are fouled in a 6-cylinder engine, 4-cylinder engine or either bank of a V-8. This is probably due to a blown head gasket between the two cylinders

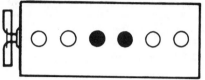

The two center plugs in a 6-cylinder engine are fouled. Raw fuel may be "boiled" out of the carburetor into the intake manifold after the engine is shut-off. Stop-start driving can also foul the center plugs, due to overly rich mixture. Proper float level, a new float needle and seat or use of an insulating spacer may help this problem

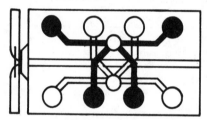

An unbalanced carburetor is indicated. Following the fuel flow on this particular design shows that the cylinders fed by the right-hand barrel are fouled from overly rich mixture, while the cylinders fed by the left-hand barrel are normal

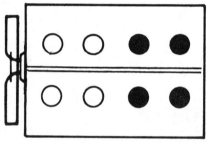

If the four rear plugs are overheated, a cooling system problem is suggested. A thorough cleaning of the cooling system may restore coolant circulation and cure the problem

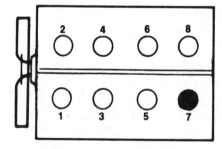

Finding one plug overheated may indicate an intake manifold leak near the affected cylinder. If the overheated plug is the second of two adjacent, consecutively firing plugs, it could be the result of ignition cross-firing. Separating the leads to these two plugs will eliminate cross-fire

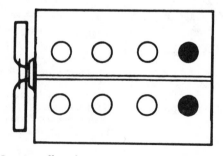

Occasionally, the two rear plugs in large, lightly used V-8's will become oil fouled. High oil consumption and smoky exhaust may also be noticed. It is probably due to plugged oil drain holes in the rear of the cylinder head, causing oil to be sucked in around the valve stems. This usually occurs in the rear cylinders first, because the engine slants that way

Test and Procedure	Results and Indications	Proceed to
4.8—Determine the static ignition timing. Using the crankshaft pulley timing marks as a guide, locate top dead center on the compression stroke of the number one cylinder.	The rotor should be pointing toward the No. 1 tower in the distributor cap, and, on electronic ignitions, the armature spoke for that cylinder should be lined up with the stator.	**4.8**
4.9—Check coil polarity: Connect a voltmeter negative lead to the coil high tension lead, and the positive lead to ground (**NOTE:** *Reverse the hook-up for positive ground systems*). Crank the engine momentarily. **Checking coil polarity**	If the voltmeter reads up-scale, the polarity is correct: If the voltmeter reads down-scale, reverse the coil polarity (switch the primary leads):	**5.1** **5.1**

Section 5—Fuel System
See Chapter 4 for service procedures

Test and Procedure	Results and Indications	Proceed to
5.1—Determine that the air filter is functioning efficiently: Hold paper elements up to a strong light, and attempt to see light through the filter.	Clean permanent air filters in solvent (or manufacturer's recommendation), and allow to dry. Replace paper elements through which light cannot be seen:	**5.2**
5.2—Determine whether a flooding condition exists: Flooding is identified by a strong gasoline odor, and excessive gasoline present in the throttle bore(s) of the carburetor.	If flooding is not evident: If flooding is evident, permit the gasoline to dry for a few moments and restart. If flooding doesn't recur: If flooding is persistent:	**5.3** **5.7** **5.5**

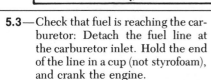

If the engine floods repeatedly, check the choke butterfly flap

Test and Procedure	Results and Indications	Proceed to
5.3—Check that fuel is reaching the carburetor: Detach the fuel line at the carburetor inlet. Hold the end of the line in a cup (not styrofoam), and crank the engine.	If fuel flows smoothly: If fuel doesn't flow (**NOTE:** *Make sure that there is fuel in the tank*), or flows erratically:	**5.7** **5.4**

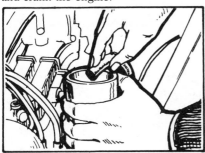

Check the fuel pump by disconnecting the output line (fuel pump-to-carburetor) at the carburetor and operating the starter briefly

Test and Procedure	Results and Indications	Proceed to
5.4—Test the fuel pump: Disconnect all fuel lines from the fuel pump. Hold a finger over the input fitting, crank the engine (with electric pump, turn the ignition or pump on); and feel for suction.	If suction is evident, blow out the fuel line to the tank with low pressure compressed air until bubbling is heard from the fuel filler neck. Also blow out the carburetor fuel line (both ends disconnected):	5.7
	If no suction is evident, replace or repair the fuel pump: NOTE: *Repeated oil fouling of the spark plugs, or a no-start condition, could be the result of a ruptured vacuum booster pump diaphragm, through which oil or gasoline is being drawn into the intake manifold (where applicable).*	5.7
5.5—Occasionally, small specks of dirt will clog the small jets and orifices in the carburetor. With the engine cold, hold a flat piece of wood or similar material over the carburetor, where possible, and crank the engine.	If the engine starts, but runs roughly the engine is probably not run enough. If the engine won't start:	5.9
5.6—Check the needle and seat: Tap the carburetor in the area of the needle and seat.	If flooding stops, a gasoline additive (e.g., Gumout) will often cure the problem:	5.7
	If flooding continues, check the fuel pump for excessive pressure at the carburetor (according to specifications). If the pressure is normal, the needle and seat must be removed and checked, and/or the float level adjusted:	5.7
5.7—Test the accelerator pump by looking into the throttle bores while operating the throttle.	If the accelerator pump appears to be operating normally:	5.8
	If the accelerator pump is not operating, the pump must be reconditioned. Where possible, service the pump with the carburetor(s) installed on the engine. If necessary, remove the carburetor. Prior to removal:	5.8
5.8—Determine whether the carburetor main fuel system is functioning: Spray a commercial starting fluid into the carburetor while attempting to start the engine.	If the engine starts, runs for a few seconds, and dies:	5.9
	If the engine doesn't start:	6.1

Check for gas at the carburetor by looking down the carburetor throat while someone moves the accelerator

Test and Procedure	Results and Indications	Proceed to
5.9—Uncommon fuel system malfunctions: See below:	If the problem is solved: If the problem remains, remove and recondition the carburetor.	6.1

Condition	Indication	Test	Prevailing Weather Conditions	Remedy
Vapor lock	Engine will not restart shortly after running.	Cool the components of the fuel system until the engine starts. Vapor lock can be cured faster by draping a wet cloth over a mechanical fuel pump.	Hot to very hot	Ensure that the exhaust manifold heat control valve is operating. Check with the vehicle manufacturer for the recommended solution to vapor lock on the model in question.
Carburetor icing	Engine will not idle, stalls at low speeds.	Visually inspect the throttle plate area of the throttle bores for frost.	High humidity, 32–40° F.	Ensure that the exhaust manifold heat control valve is operating, and that the intake manifold heat riser is not blocked.
Water in the fuel	Engine sputters and stalls; may not start.	Pump a small amount of fuel into a glass jar. Allow to stand, and inspect for droplets or a layer of water.	High humidity, extreme temperature changes.	For droplets, use one or two cans of commercial gas line anti-freeze. For a layer of water, the tank must be drained, and the fuel lines blown out with compressed air.

Section 6—Engine Compression
See Chapter 3 for service procedures

6.1—Test engine compression: Remove all spark plugs. Block the throttle wide open. Insert a compression gauge into a spark plug port, crank the engine to obtain the maximum reading, and record.	If compression is within limits on all cylinders:	7.1
	If gauge reading is extremely low on all cylinders:	6.2
	If gauge reading is low on one or two cylinders: (If gauge readings are identical and low on two or more adjacent cylinders, the head gasket must be replaced.)	6.2

Checking compression

6.2—Test engine compression (wet): Squirt approximately 30 cc. of engine oil into each cylinder, and retest per 6.1.	If the readings improve, worn or cracked rings or broken pistons are indicated:	See Chapter 3
	If the readings do not improve, burned or excessively carboned valves or a jumped timing chain are indicated: NOTE: *A jumped timing chain is often indicated by difficult cranking.*	7.1

Section 7—Engine Vacuum
See Chapter 3 for service procedures

Test and Procedure	Results and Indications	Proceed to
7.1—Attach a vacuum gauge to the intake manifold beyond the throttle plate. Start the engine, and observe the action of the needle over the range of engine speeds.	See below.	See below

INDICATION: normal engine in good condition

Proceed to: 8.1

Normal engine
Gauge reading: steady, from 17–22 in./Hg.

INDICATION: sticking valves or ignition miss

Proceed to: 9.1, 8.3

Sticking valves
Gauge reading: intermittent fluctuation at idle

INDICATION: late ignition or valve timing, low compression, stuck throttle valve, leaking carburetor or manifold gasket

Proceed to: 6.1

Incorrect valve timing
Gauge reading: low (10–15 in./Hg) but steady

INDICATION: improper carburetor adjustment or minor intake leak.

Proceed to: 7.2

Carburetor requires adjustment
Gauge reading: drifting needle

INDICATION: ignition miss, blown cylinder head gasket, leaking valve or weak valve spring

Proceed to: 8.3, 6.1

Blown head gasket
Gauge reading: needle fluctuates as engine speed increases

INDICATION: burnt valve or faulty valve clearance. Needle will fall when defective valve operates

Proceed to: 9.1

Burnt or leaking valves
Gauge reading: steady needle, but drops regularly

INDICATION: choked muffler, excessive back pressure in system

Proceed to: 10.1

Clogged exhaust system
Gauge reading: gradual drop in reading at idle

INDICATION: worn valve guides

Proceed to: 9.1

Worn valve guides
Gauge reading: needle vibrates excessively at idle, but steadies as engine speed increases

White pointer = steady gauge hand   Black pointer = fluctuating gauge hand

Test and Procedure	Results and Indications	Proceed to
7.2—Attach a vacuum gauge per 7.1, and test for an intake manifold leak. Squirt a small amount of oil around the intake manifold gaskets, carburetor gaskets, plugs and fittings. Observe the action of the vacuum gauge.	If the reading improves, replace the indicated gasket, or seal the indicated fitting or plug: If the reading remains low:	8.1 7.3
7.3—Test all vacuum hoses and accessories for leaks as described in 7.2. Also check the carburetor body (dashpots, automatic choke mechanism, throttle shafts) for leaks in the same manner.	If the reading improves, service or replace the offending part(s): If the reading remains low:	8.1 6.1

Section 8—Secondary Electrical System
See Chapter 2 for service procedures

Test and Procedure	Results and Indications	Proceed to
8.1—Remove the distributor cap and check to make sure that the rotor turns when the engine is cranked. Visually inspect the distributor components.	Clean, tighten or replace any components which appear defective.	8.2
8.2—Connect a timing light (per manufacturer's recommendation) and check the dynamic ignition timing. Disconnect and plug the vacuum hose(s) to the distributor if specified, start the engine, and observe the timing marks at the specified engine speed.	If the timing is not correct, adjust to specifications by rotating the distributor in the engine: (Advance timing by rotating distributor opposite normal direction of rotor rotation, retard timing by rotating distributor in same direction as rotor rotation.)	8.3
8.3—Check the operation of the distributor advance mechanism(s): To test the mechanical advance, disconnect the vacuum lines from the distributor advance unit and observe the timing marks with a timing light as the engine speed is increased from idle. If the mark moves smoothly, without hesitation, it may be assumed that the mechanical advance is functioning properly. To test vacuum advance and/or retard systems, alternately crimp and release the vacuum line, and observe the timing mark for movement. If movement is noted, the system is operating.	If the systems are functioning: If the systems are not functioning, remove the distributor, and test on a distributor tester:	8.4 8.4
8.4—Locate an ignition miss: With the engine running, remove each spark plug wire, one at a time, until one is found that doesn't cause the engine to roughen and slow down.	When the missing cylinder is identified:	4.1

Section 9—Valve Train
See Chapter 3 for service procedures

Test and Procedure	Results and Indications	Proceed to
9.1—Evaluate the valve train: Remove the valve cover, and ensure that the valves are adjusted to specifications. A mechanic's stethoscope may be used to aid in the diagnosis of the valve train. By pushing the probe on or near push rods or rockers, valve noise often can be isolated. A timing light also may be used to diagnose valve problems. Connect the light according to manufacturer's recommendations, and start the engine. Vary the firing moment of the light by increasing the engine speed (and therefore the ignition advance), and moving the trigger from cylinder to cylinder. Observe the movement of each valve.	Sticking valves or erratic valve train motion can be observed with the timing light. The cylinder head must be disassembled for repairs.	**See Chapter 3**
9.2—Check the valve timing: Locate top dead center of the No. 1 piston, and install a degree wheel or tape on the crankshaft pulley or damper with zero corresponding to an index mark on the engine. Rotate the crankshaft in its direction of rotation, and observe the opening of the No. 1 cylinder intake valve. The opening should correspond with the correct mark on the degree wheel according to specifications.	If the timing is not correct, the timing cover must be removed for further investigation.	**See Chapter 3**

Section 10—Exhaust System

Test and Procedure	Results and Indications	Proceed to
10.1—Determine whether the exhaust manifold heat control valve is operating: Operate the valve by hand to determine whether it is free to move. If the valve is free, run the engine to operating temperature and observe the action of the valve, to ensure that it is opening.	If the valve sticks, spray it with a suitable solvent, open and close the valve to free it, and retest. If the valve functions properly: If the valve does not free, or does not operate, replace the valve:	10.2 10.2
10.2—Ensure that there are no exhaust restrictions: Visually inspect the exhaust system for kinks, dents, or crushing. Also note that gases are flowing freely from the tailpipe at all engine speeds, indicating no restriction in the muffler or resonator.	Replace any damaged portion of the system:	11.1

Section 11—Cooling System
See Chapter 3 for service procedures

Test and Procedure	Results and Indications	Proceed to
11.1—Visually inspect the fan belt for glazing, cracks, and fraying, and replace if necessary. Tighten the belt so that the longest span has approximately ½″ play at its midpoint under thumb pressure (see Chapter 1).	Replace or tighten the fan belt as necessary:	**11.2**

Checking belt tension

Test and Procedure	Results and Indications	Proceed to
11.2—Check the fluid level of the cooling system.	If full or slightly low, fill as necessary:	**11.5**
	If extremely low:	**11.3**
11.3—Visually inspect the external portions of the cooling system (radiator, radiator hoses, thermostat elbow, water pump seals, heater hoses, etc.) for leaks. If none are found, pressurize the cooling system to 14–15 psi.	If cooling system holds the pressure:	**11.5**
	If cooling system loses pressure rapidly, reinspect external parts of the system for leaks under pressure. If none are found, check dipstick for coolant in crankcase. If no coolant is present, but pressure loss continues:	**11.4**
	If coolant is evident in crankcase, remove cylinder head(s), and check gasket(s). If gaskets are intact, block and cylinder head(s) should be checked for cracks or holes.	
	If the gasket(s) is blown, replace, and purge the crankcase of coolant:	**12.6**
	NOTE: *Occasionally, due to atmospheric and driving conditions, condensation of water can occur in the crankcase. This causes the oil to appear milky white. To remedy, run the engine until hot, and change the oil and oil filter.*	
11.4—Check for combustion leaks into the cooling system: Pressurize the cooling system as above. Start the engine, and observe the pressure gauge. If the needle fluctuates, remove each spark plug wire, one at a time, noting which cylinder(s) reduce or eliminate the fluctuation.	Cylinders which reduce or eliminate the fluctuation, when the spark plug wire is removed, are leaking into the cooling system. Replace the head gasket on the affected cylinder bank(s).	

Pressurizing the cooling system

Test and Procedure	Results and Indications	Proceed to
11.5—Check the radiator pressure cap: Attach a radiator pressure tester to the radiator cap (wet the seal prior to installation). Quickly pump up the pressure, noting the point at which the cap releases.	If the cap releases within ± 1 psi of the specified rating, it is operating properly:	**11.6**
	If the cap releases at more than ± 1 psi of the specified rating, it should be replaced:	**11.6**

Checking radiator pressure cap

Test and Procedure	Results and Indications	Proceed to
11.6—Test the thermostat: Start the engine cold, remove the radiator cap, and insert a thermometer into the radiator. Allow the engine to idle. After a short while, there will be a sudden, rapid increase in coolant temperature. The temperature at which this sharp rise stops is the thermostat opening temperature.	If the thermostat opens at or about the specified temperature:	**11.7**
	If the temperature doesn't increase: (If the temperature increases slowly and gradually, replace the thermostat.)	**11.7**
11.7—Check the water pump: Remove the thermostat elbow and the thermostat, disconnect the coil high tension lead (to prevent starting), and crank the engine momentarily.	If coolant flows, replace the thermostat and retest per 11.6:	**11.6**
	If coolant doesn't flow, reverse flush the cooling system to alleviate any blockage that might exist. If system is not blocked, and coolant will not flow, replace the water pump.	

Section 12—Lubrication
See Chapter 3 for service procedures

Test and Procedure ·	Results and Indications	Proceed to
12.1—Check the oil pressure gauge or warning light: If the gauge shows low pressure, or the light is on for no obvious reason, remove the oil pressure sender. Install an accurate oil pressure gauge and run the engine momentarily.	If oil pressure builds normally, run engine for a few moments to determine that it is functioning normally, and replace the sender.	—
	If the pressure remains low:	**12.2**
	If the pressure surges:	**12.3**
	If the oil pressure is zero:	**12.3**
12.2—Visually inspect the oil: If the oil is watery or very thin, milky, or foamy, replace the oil and oil filter.	If the oil is normal:	**12.3**
	If after replacing oil the pressure remains low:	**12.3**
	If after replacing oil the pressure becomes normal:	—

Test and Procedure	Results and Indications	Proceed to
12.3—Inspect the oil pressure relief valve and spring, to ensure that it is not sticking or stuck. Remove and thoroughly clean the valve, spring, and the valve body.	If the oil pressure improves: If no improvement is noted:	— **12.4**
12.4—Check to ensure that the oil pump is not cavitating (sucking air instead of oil): See that the crankcase is neither over nor underfull, and that the pickup in the sump is in the proper position and free from sludge.	Fill or drain the crankcase to the proper capacity, and clean the pickup screen in solvent if necessary. If no improvement is noted:	**12.5**
12.5—Inspect the oil pump drive and the oil pump:	If the pump drive or the oil pump appear to be defective, service as necessary and retest per 12.1: If the pump drive and pump appear to be operating normally, the engine should be disassembled to determine where blockage exists:	**12.1** **See Chapter 3**
12.6—Purge the engine of ethylene glycol coolant: Completely drain the crankcase and the oil filter. Obtain a commercial butyl cellosolve base solvent, designated for this purpose, and follow the instructions precisely. Following this, install a new oil filter and refill the crankcase with the proper weight oil. The next oil and filter change should follow shortly thereafter (1000 miles).		

TROUBLESHOOTING EMISSION CONTROL SYSTEMS

See Chapter 4 for procedures applicable to individual emission control systems used on specific combinations of engine/transmission/model.

TROUBLESHOOTING THE CARBURETOR

See Chapter 4 for service procedures

Carburetor problems cannot be effectively isolated unless all other engine systems (particularly ignition and emission) are functioning properly and the engine is properly tuned.

Condition	*Possible Cause*
Engine cranks, but does not start	1. Improper starting procedure 2. No fuel in tank 3. Clogged fuel line or filter 4. Defective fuel pump 5. Choke valve not closing properly 6. Engine flooded 7. Choke valve not unloading 8. Throttle linkage not making full travel 9. Stuck needle or float 10. Leaking float needle or seat 11. Improper float adjustment
Engine stalls	1. Improperly adjusted idle speed or mixture **Engine hot** 2. Improperly adjusted dashpot 3. Defective or improperly adjusted solenoid 4. Incorrect fuel level in fuel bowl 5. Fuel pump pressure too high 6. Leaking float needle seat 7. Secondary throttle valve stuck open 8. Air or fuel leaks 9. Idle air bleeds plugged or missing 10. Idle passages plugged **Engine Cold** 11. Incorrectly adjusted choke 12. Improperly adjusted fast idle speed 13. Air leaks 14. Plugged idle or idle air passages 15. Stuck choke valve or binding linkage 16. Stuck secondary throttle valves 17. Engine flooding—high fuel level 18. Leaking or misaligned float
Engine hesitates on acceleration	1. Clogged fuel filter 2. Leaking fuel pump diaphragm 3. Low fuel pump pressure 4. Secondary throttle valves stuck, bent or misadjusted 5. Sticking or binding air valve 6. Defective accelerator pump 7. Vacuum leaks 8. Clogged air filter 9. Incorrect choke adjustment (engine cold)
Engine feels sluggish or flat on acceleration	1. Improperly adjusted idle speed or mixture 2. Clogged fuel filter 3. Defective accelerator pump 4. Dirty, plugged or incorrect main metering jets 5. Bent or sticking main metering rods 6. Sticking throttle valves 7. Stuck heat riser 8. Binding or stuck air valve 9. Dirty, plugged or incorrect secondary jets 10. Bent or sticking secondary metering rods. 11. Throttle body or manifold heat passages plugged 12. Improperly adjusted choke or choke vacuum break.
Carburetor floods	1. Defective fuel pump. Pressure too high. 2. Stuck choke valve 3. Dirty, worn or damaged float or needle valve/seat 4. Incorrect float/fuel level 5. Leaking float bowl

Condition	Possible Cause
Engine idles roughly and stalls	1. Incorrect idle speed 2. Clogged fuel filter 3. Dirt in fuel system or carburetor 4. Loose carburetor screws or attaching bolts 5. Broken carburetor gaskets 6. Air leaks 7. Dirty carburetor 8. Worn idle mixture needles 9. Throttle valves stuck open 10. Incorrectly adjusted float or fuel level 11. Clogged air filter
Engine runs unevenly or surges	1. Defective fuel pump 2. Dirty or clogged fuel filter 3. Plugged, loose or incorrect main metering jets or rods 4. Air leaks 5. Bent or sticking main metering rods 6. Stuck power piston 7. Incorrect float adjustment 8. Incorrect idle speed or mixture 9. Dirty or plugged idle system passages 10. Hard, brittle or broken gaskets 11. Loose attaching or mounting screws 12. Stuck or misaligned secondary throttle valves
Poor fuel economy	1. Poor driving habits 2. Stuck choke valve 3. Binding choke linkage 4. Stuck heat riser 5. Incorrect idle mixture 6. Defective accelerator pump 7. Air leaks 8. Plugged, loose or incorrect main metering jets 9. Improperly adjusted float or fuel level 10. Bent, misaligned or fuel-clogged float 11. Leaking float needle seat 12. Fuel leak 13. Accelerator pump discharge ball not seating properly 14. Incorrect main jets
Engine lacks high speed performance or power	1. Incorrect throttle linkage adjustment 2. Stuck or binding power piston 3. Defective accelerator pump 4. Air leaks 5. Incorrect float setting or fuel level 6. Dirty, plugged, worn or incorrect main metering jets or rods 7. Binding or sticking air valve 8. Brittle or cracked gaskets 9. Bent, incorrect or improperly adjusted secondary metering rods 10. Clogged fuel filter 11. Clogged air filter 12. Defective fuel pump

TROUBLESHOOTING FUEL INJECTION PROBLEMS

Each fuel injection system has its own unique components and test procedures, for which it is impossible to generalize. Refer to Chapter 4 of this Repair & Tune-Up Guide for specific test and repair procedures, if the vehicle is equipped with fuel injection.

TROUBLESHOOTING ELECTRICAL PROBLEMS
See Chapter 5 for service procedures

For any electrical system to operate, it must make a complete circuit. This simply means that the power flow from the battery must make a complete circle. When an electrical component is operating, power flows from the battery to the component, passes through the component causing it to perform its function (lighting a light bulb), and then returns to the battery through the ground of the circuit. This ground is usually (but not always) the metal part of the car or truck on which the electrical component is mounted.

Perhaps the easiest way to visualize this is to think of connecting a light bulb with two wires attached to it to the battery. If one of the two wires attached to the light bulb were attached to the negative post of the battery and the other were attached to the positive post of the battery, you would have a complete circuit. Current from the battery would flow to the light bulb, causing it to light, and return to the negative post of the battery.

The normal automotive circuit differs from this simple example in two ways. First, instead of having a return wire from the bulb to the battery, the light bulb returns the current to the battery through the chassis of the vehicle. Since the negative battery cable is attached to the chassis and the chassis is made of electrically conductive metal, the chassis of the vehicle can serve as a ground wire to complete the circuit. Secondly, most automotive circuits contain switches to turn components on and off as required.

Every complete circuit from a power source must include a component which is using the power from the power source. If you were to disconnect the light bulb from the wires and touch the two wires together (don't do this) the power supply wire to the component would be grounded before the normal ground connection for the circuit.

Because grounding a wire from a power source makes a complete circuit—less the required component to use the power—this phenomenon is called a short circuit. Common causes are: broken insulation (exposing the metal wire to a metal part of the car or truck), or a shorted switch.

Some electrical components which require a large amount of current to operate also have a relay in their circuit. Since these circuits carry a large amount of current, the thickness of the wire in the circuit (gauge size) is also greater. If this large wire were connected from the component to the control switch on the instrument panel, and then back to the component, a voltage drop would occur in the circuit. To prevent this potential drop in voltage, an electromagnetic switch (relay) is used. The large wires in the circuit are connected from the battery to one side of the relay, and from the opposite side of the relay to the component. The relay is normally open, preventing current from passing through the circuit. An additional, smaller wire is connected from the relay to the control switch for the circuit. When the control switch is turned on, it grounds the smaller wire from the relay and completes the circuit. This closes the relay and allows current to flow from the battery to the component. The horn, headlight, and starter circuits are three which use relays.

It is possible for larger surges of current to pass through the electrical system of your car or truck. If this surge of current were to reach an electrical component, it could burn it out. To prevent this, fuses, circuit breakers or fusible links are connected into the current supply wires of most of the major electrical systems. When an electrical current of excessive power passes through the component's fuse, the fuse blows out and breaks the circuit, saving the component from destruction.

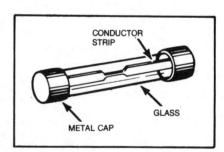

CONDUCTOR STRIP

GLASS

METAL CAP

Typical automotive fuse

A circuit breaker is basically a self-repairing fuse. The circuit breaker opens the circuit the same way a fuse does. However, when either the short is removed from the circuit or the surge subsides, the circuit breaker resets itself and does not have to be replaced as a fuse does.

A fuse link is a wire that acts as a fuse. It is normally connected between the starter relay and the main wiring harness. This connection is usually under the hood. The fuse link (if installed) protects all the

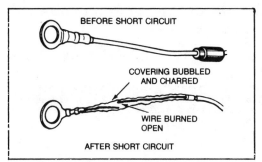

Most fusible links show a charred, melted insulation when they burn out

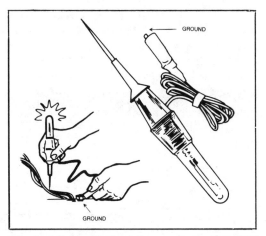

The test light will show the presence of current when touched to a hot wire and grounded at the other end

chassis electrical components, and is the probable cause of trouble when none of the electrical components function, unless the battery is disconnected or dead.

Electrical problems generally fall into one of three areas:

1. The component that is not functioning is not receiving current.

2. The component itself is not functioning.

3. The component is not properly grounded.

The electrical system can be checked with a test light and a jumper wire. A test light is a device that looks like a pointed screwdriver with a wire attached to it and has a light bulb in its handle. A jumper wire is a piece of insulated wire with an alligator clip attached to each end.

If a component is not working, you must follow a systematic plan to determine which of the three causes is the villain.

1. Turn on the switch that controls the inoperable component.

2. Disconnect the power supply wire from the component.

3. Attach the ground wire on the test light to a good metal ground.

4. Touch the probe end of the test light to the end of the power supply wire that was disconnected from the component. If the component is receiving current, the test light will go on.

NOTE: *Some components work only when the ignition switch is turned on.*

If the test light does not go on, then the problem is in the circuit between the battery and the component. This includes all the switches, fuses, and relays in the system. Follow the wire that runs back to the battery. The problem is an open circuit between the

battery and the component. If the fuse is blown and, when replaced, immediately blows again, there is a short circuit in the system which must be located and repaired. If there is a switch in the system, bypass it with a jumper wire. This is done by connecting one end of the jumper wire to the power supply wire into the switch and the other end of the jumper wire to the wire coming out of the switch. If the test light lights with the jumper wire installed, the switch or whatever was bypassed is defective.

NOTE: *Never substitute the jumper wire for the component, since it is required to use the power from the power source.*

5. If the bulb in the test light goes on, then the current is getting to the component that is not working. This eliminates the first of the three possible causes. Connect the power supply wire and connect a jumper wire from the component to a good metal ground. Do this with the switch which controls the component turned on, and also the ignition switch turned on if it is required for the component to work. If the component works with the jumper wire installed, then it has a bad ground. This is usually caused by the metal area on which the component mounts to the chassis being coated with some type of foreign matter.

6. If neither test located the source of the trouble, then the component itself is defective. Remember that for any electrical system to work, all connections must be clean and tight.

Troubleshooting Basic Turn Signal and Flasher Problems

See Chapter 5 for service procedures

Most problems in the turn signals or flasher system can be reduced to defective flashers or bulbs, which are easily replaced. Occasionally, the turn signal switch will prove defective.

F = Front   R = Rear   ● = Lights off   ○ = Lights on

Condition		Possible Cause
Turn signals light, but do not flash	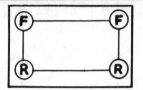	Defective flasher
No turn signals light on either side	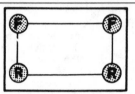	Blown fuse. Replace if defective. Defective flasher. Check by substitution. Open circuit, short circuit or poor ground.
Both turn signals on one side don't work	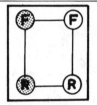	Bad bulbs. Bad ground in both (or either) housings.
One turn signal light on one side doesn't work	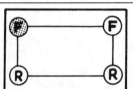	Defective bulb. Corrosion in socket. Clean contacts. Poor ground at socket.
Turn signal flashes too fast or too slowly	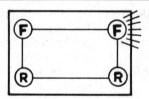	Check any bulb on the side flashing too fast. A heavy-duty bulb is probably installed in place of a regular bulb. Check the bulb flashing too slowly. A standard bulb was probably installed in place of a heavy-duty bulb. Loose connections or corrosion at the bulb socket.
Indicator lights don't work in either direction		Check if the turn signals are working. Check the dash indicator lights. Check the flasher by substitution.
One indicator light doesn't light		On systems with one dash indicator: See if the lights work on the same side. Often the filaments have been reversed in systems combining stoplights with taillights and turn signals. Check the flasher by substitution. On systems with two indicators: Check the bulbs on the same side. Check the indicator light bulb. Check the flasher by substitution.

Troubleshooting Lighting Problems
See Chapter 5 for service procedures

Condition	Possible Cause
One or more lights don't work, but others do	1. Defective bulb(s) 2. Blown fuse(s) 3. Dirty fuse clips or light sockets 4. Poor ground circuit
Lights burn out quickly	1. Incorrect voltage regulator setting or defective regulator 2. Poor battery/alternator connections
Lights go dim	1. Low/discharged battery 2. Alternator not charging 3. Corroded sockets or connections 4. Low voltage output
Lights flicker	1. Loose connection 2. Poor ground. (Run ground wire from light housing to frame) 3. Circuit breaker operating (short circuit)
Lights "flare"—Some flare is normal on acceleration—If excessive, see "Lights Burn Out Quickly"	High voltage setting
Lights glare—approaching drivers are blinded	1. Lights adjusted too high 2. Rear springs or shocks sagging 3. Rear tires soft

Troubleshooting Dash Gauge Problems
Most problems can be traced to a defective sending unit or faulty wiring. Occasionally, the gauge itself is at fault. See Chapter 5 for service procedures.

Condition	Possible Cause
COOLANT TEMPERATURE GAUGE	
Gauge reads erratically or not at all	1. Loose or dirty connections 2. Defective sending unit. 3. Defective gauge. To test a bi-metal gauge, remove the wire from the sending unit. Ground the wire for an instant. If the gauge registers, replace the sending unit. To test a magnetic gauge, disconnect the wire at the sending unit. With ignition ON gauge should register COLD. Ground the wire; gauge should register HOT.
AMMETER GAUGE—TURN HEADLIGHTS ON (DO NOT START ENGINE). NOTE REACTION	
Ammeter shows charge Ammeter shows discharge Ammeter does not move	1. Connections reversed on gauge 2. Ammeter is OK 3. Loose connections or faulty wiring 4. Defective gauge

Condition	Possible Cause

OIL PRESSURE GAUGE

Condition	Possible Cause
Gauge does not register or is inaccurate	1. On mechanical gauge, Bourdon tube may be bent or kinked. 2. Low oil pressure. Remove sending unit. Idle the engine briefly. If no oil flows from sending unit hole, problem is in engine. 3. Defective gauge. Remove the wire from the sending unit and ground it for an instant with the ignition ON. A good gauge will go to the top of the scale. 4. Defective wiring. Check the wiring to the gauge. If it's OK and the gauge doesn't register when grounded, replace the gauge. 5. Defective sending unit.

ALL GAUGES

Condition	Possible Cause
All gauges do not operate All gauges read low or erratically All gauges pegged	1. Blown fuse 2. Defective instrument regulator 3. Defective or dirty instrument voltage regulator 4. Loss of ground between instrument voltage regulator and frame 5. Defective instrument regulator

WARNING LIGHTS

Condition	Possible Cause
Light(s) do not come on when ignition is ON, but engine is not started Light comes on with engine running	1. Defective bulb 2. Defective wire 3. Defective sending unit. Disconnect the wire from the sending unit and ground it. Replace the sending unit if the light comes on with the ignition ON. 4. Problem in individual system 5. Defective sending unit

Troubleshooting Clutch Problems

It is false economy to replace individual clutch components. The pressure plate, clutch plate and throwout bearing should be replaced as a set, and the flywheel face inspected, whenever the clutch is overhauled. See Chapter 6 for service procedures.

Condition	Possible Cause
Clutch chatter	1. Grease on driven plate (disc) facing 2. Binding clutch linkage or cable 3. Loose, damaged facings on driven plate (disc) 4. Engine mounts loose 5. Incorrect height adjustment of pressure plate release levers 6. Clutch housing or housing to transmission adapter misalignment 7. Loose driven plate hub
Clutch grabbing	1. Oil, grease on driven plate (disc) facing 2. Broken pressure plate 3. Warped or binding driven plate. Driven plate binding on clutch shaft
Clutch slips	1. Lack of lubrication in clutch linkage or cable (linkage or cable binds, causes incomplete engagement) 2. Incorrect pedal, or linkage adjustment 3. Broken pressure plate springs 4. Weak pressure plate springs 5. Grease on driven plate facings (disc)

Troubleshooting Clutch Problems (cont.)

Condition	Possible Cause
Incomplete clutch release	1. Incorrect pedal or linkage adjustment or linkage or cable binding 2. Incorrect height adjustment on pressure plate release levers 3. Loose, broken facings on driven plate (disc) 4. Bent, dished, warped driven plate caused by overheating
Grinding, whirring grating noise when pedal is depressed	1. Worn or defective throwout bearing 2. Starter drive teeth contacting flywheel ring gear teeth. Look for milled or polished teeth on ring gear.
Squeal, howl, trumpeting noise when pedal is being released (occurs during first inch to inch and one-half of pedal travel)	Pilot bushing worn or lack of lubricant. If bushing appears OK, polish bushing with emery cloth, soak lube wick in oil, lube bushing with oil, apply film of chassis grease to clutch shaft pilot hub, reassemble. NOTE: Bushing wear may be due to misalignment of clutch housing or housing to transmission adapter
Vibration or clutch pedal pulsation with clutch disengaged (pedal fully depressed)	1. Worn or defective engine transmission mounts 2. Flywheel run out. (Flywheel run out at face not to exceed 0.005″) 3. Damaged or defective clutch components

Troubleshooting Manual Transmission Problems
See Chapter 6 for service procedures

Condition	Possible Cause
Transmission jumps out of gear	1. Misalignment of transmission case or clutch housing. 2. Worn pilot bearing in crankshaft. 3. Bent transmission shaft. 4. Worn high speed sliding gear. 5. Worn teeth or end-play in clutch shaft. 6. Insufficient spring tension on shifter rail plunger. 7. Bent or loose shifter fork. 8. Gears not engaging completely. 9. Loose or worn bearings on clutch shaft or mainshaft. 10. Worn gear teeth. 11. Worn or damaged detent balls.
Transmission sticks in gear	1. Clutch not releasing fully. 2. Burred or battered teeth on clutch shaft, or sliding sleeve. 3. Burred or battered transmission mainshaft. 4. Frozen synchronizing clutch. 5. Stuck shifter rail plunger. 6. Gearshift lever twisting and binding shifter rail. 7. Battered teeth on high speed sliding gear or on sleeve. 8. Improper lubrication, or lack of lubrication. 9. Corroded transmission parts. 10. Defective mainshaft pilot bearing. 11. Locked gear bearings will give same effect as stuck in gear.
Transmission gears will not synchronize	1. Binding pilot bearing on mainshaft, will synchronize in high gear only. 2. Clutch not releasing fully. 3. Detent spring weak or broken. 4. Weak or broken springs under balls in sliding gear sleeve. 5. Binding bearing on clutch shaft, or binding countershaft. 6. Binding pilot bearing in crankshaft. 7. Badly worn gear teeth. 8. Improper lubrication. 9. Constant mesh gear not turning freely on transmission mainshaft. Will synchronize in that gear only.

Condition	Possible Cause
Gears spinning when shifting into gear from neutral	1. Clutch not releasing fully. 2. In some cases an extremely light lubricant in transmission will cause gears to continue to spin for a short time after clutch is released. 3. Binding pilot bearing in crankshaft.
Transmission noisy in all gears	1. Insufficient lubricant, or improper lubricant. 2. Worn countergear bearings. 3. Worn or damaged main drive gear or countergear. 4. Damaged main drive gear or mainshaft bearings. 5. Worn or damaged countergear anti-lash plate.
Transmission noisy in neutral only	1. Damaged main drive gear bearing. 2. Damaged or loose mainshaft pilot bearing. 3. Worn or damaged countergear anti-lash plate. 4. Worn countergear bearings.
Transmission noisy in one gear only	1. Damaged or worn constant mesh gears. 2. Worn or damaged countergear bearings. 3. Damaged or worn synchronizer.
Transmission noisy in reverse only	1. Worn or damaged reverse idler gear or idler bushing. 2. Worn or damaged mainshaft reverse gear. 3. Worn or damaged reverse countergear. 4. Damaged shift mechanism.

TROUBLESHOOTING AUTOMATIC TRANSMISSION PROBLEMS

Keeping alert to changes in the operating characteristics of the transmission (changing shift points, noises, etc.) can prevent small problems from becoming large ones. If the problem cannot be traced to loose bolts, fluid level, misadjusted linkage, clogged filters or similar problems, you should probably seek professional service.

Transmission Fluid Indications

The appearance and odor of the transmission fluid can give valuable clues to the overall condition of the transmission. Always note the appearance of the fluid when you check the fluid level or change the fluid. Rub a small amount of fluid between your fingers to feel for grit and smell the fluid on the dipstick.

If the fluid appears:	It indicates:
Clear and red colored	Normal operation
Discolored (extremely dark red or brownish) or smells burned	Band or clutch pack failure, usually caused by an overheated transmission. Hauling very heavy loads with insufficient power or failure to change the fluid often result in overheating. Do not confuse this appearance with newer fluids that have a darker red color and a strong odor (though not a burned odor).
Foamy or aerated (light in color and full of bubbles)	1. The level is too high (gear train is churning oil) 2. An internal air leak (air is mixing with the fluid). Have the transmission checked professionally.
Solid residue in the fluid	Defective bands, clutch pack or bearings. Bits of band material or metal abrasives are clinging to the dipstick. Have the transmission checked professionally.
Varnish coating on the dipstick	The transmission fluid is overheating

TROUBLESHOOTING DRIVE AXLE PROBLEMS

First, determine when the noise is most noticeable.

Drive Noise: Produced under vehicle acceleration.

Coast Noise: Produced while coasting with a closed throttle.

Float Noise: Occurs while maintaining constant speed (just enough to keep speed constant) on a level road.

External Noise Elimination

It is advisable to make a thorough road test to determine whether the noise originates in the rear axle or whether it originates from the tires, engine, transmission, wheel bearings or road surface. Noise originating from other places cannot be corrected by servicing the rear axle.

ROAD NOISE

Brick or rough surfaced concrete roads produce noises that seem to come from the rear axle. Road noise is usually identical in Drive or Coast and driving on a different type of road will tell whether the road is the problem.

TIRE NOISE

Tire noise can be mistaken as rear axle noise, even though the tires on the front are at fault. Snow tread and mud tread tires or tires worn unevenly will frequently cause vibrations which seem to originate elsewhere; *temporarily, and for test purposes only,* inflate the tires to 40–50 lbs. This will significantly alter the noise produced by the tires, but will not alter noise from the rear axle. Noises from the rear axle will normally cease at speeds below 30 mph on coast, while tire noise will continue at lower tone as speed is decreased. The rear axle noise will usually change from drive conditions to coast conditions, while tire noise will not. Do not forget to lower the tire pressure to normal after the test is complete.

ENGINE/TRANSMISSION NOISE

Determine at what speed the noise is most pronounced, then stop in a quiet place. With the transmission in Neutral, run the engine through speeds corresponding to road speeds where the noise was noticed. Noises produced with the vehicle standing still are coming from the engine or transmission.

FRONT WHEEL BEARINGS

Front wheel bearing noises, sometimes confused with rear axle noises, will not change when comparing drive and coast conditions. While holding the speed steady, lightly apply the footbrake. This will often cause wheel bearing noise to lessen, as some of the weight is taken off the bearing. Front wheel bearings are easily checked by jacking up the wheels and spinning the wheels. Shaking the wheels will also determine if the wheel bearings are excessively loose.

REAR AXLE NOISES

Eliminating other possible sources can narrow the cause to the rear axle, which normally produces noise from worn gears or bearings. Gear noises tend to peak in a narrow speed range, while bearing noises will usually vary in pitch with engine speeds.

Noise Diagnosis

The Noise Is:	Most Probably Produced By:
1. Identical under Drive or Coast	Road surface, tires or front wheel bearings
2. Different depending on road surface	Road surface or tires
3. Lower as speed is lowered	Tires
4. Similar when standing or moving	Engine or transmission
5. A vibration	Unbalanced tires, rear wheel bearing, unbalanced driveshaft or worn U-joint
6. A knock or click about every two tire revolutions	Rear wheel bearing
7. Most pronounced on turns	Damaged differential gears
8. A steady low-pitched whirring or scraping, starting at low speeds	Damaged or worn pinion bearing
9. A chattering vibration on turns	Wrong differential lubricant or worn clutch plates (limited slip rear axle)
10. Noticed only in Drive, Coast or Float conditions	Worn ring gear and/or pinion gear

Troubleshooting Steering & Suspension Problems

Condition	Possible Cause
Hard steering (wheel is hard to turn)	1. Improper tire pressure 2. Loose or glazed pump drive belt 3. Low or incorrect fluid 4. Loose, bent or poorly lubricated front end parts 5. Improper front end alignment (excessive caster) 6. Bind in steering column or linkage 7. Kinked hydraulic hose 8. Air in hydraulic system 9. Low pump output or leaks in system 10. Obstruction in lines 11. Pump valves sticking or out of adjustment 12. Incorrect wheel alignment
Loose steering (too much play in steering wheel)	1. Loose wheel bearings 2. Faulty shocks 3. Worn linkage or suspension components 4. Loose steering gear mounting or linkage points 5. Steering mechanism worn or improperly adjusted 6. Valve spool improperly adjusted 7. Worn ball joints, tie-rod ends, etc.
Veers or wanders (pulls to one side with hands off steering wheel)	1. Improper tire pressure 2. Improper front end alignment 3. Dragging or improperly adjusted brakes 4. Bent frame 5. Improper rear end alignment 6. Faulty shocks or springs 7. Loose or bent front end components 8. Play in Pitman arm 9. Steering gear mountings loose 10. Loose wheel bearings 11. Binding Pitman arm 12. Spool valve sticking or improperly adjusted 13. Worn ball joints
Wheel oscillation or vibration transmitted through steering wheel	1. Low or uneven tire pressure 2. Loose wheel bearings 3. Improper front end alignment 4. Bent spindle 5. Worn, bent or broken front end components 6. Tires out of round or out of balance 7. Excessive lateral runout in disc brake rotor 8. Loose or bent shock absorber or strut
Noises (see also "Troubleshooting Drive Axle Problems")	1. Loose belts 2. Low fluid, air in system 3. Foreign matter in system 4. Improper lubrication 5. Interference or chafing in linkage 6. Steering gear mountings loose 7. Incorrect adjustment or wear in gear box 8. Faulty valves or wear in pump 9. Kinked hydraulic lines 10. Worn wheel bearings
Poor return of steering	1. Over-inflated tires 2. Improperly aligned front end (excessive caster) 3. Binding in steering column 4. No lubrication in front end 5. Steering gear adjusted too tight
Uneven tire wear (see "How To Read Tire Wear")	1. Incorrect tire pressure 2. Improperly aligned front end 3. Tires out-of-balance 4. Bent or worn suspension parts

HOW TO READ TIRE WEAR

The way your tires wear is a good indicator of other parts of the suspension. Abnormal wear patterns are often caused by the need for simple tire maintenance, or for front end alignment.

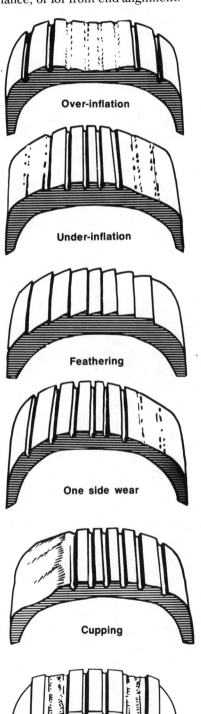

Excessive wear at the center of the tread indicates that the air pressure in the tire is consistently too high. The tire is riding on the center of the tread and wearing it prematurely. Occasionally, this wear pattern can result from outrageously wide tires on narrow rims. The cure for this is to replace either the tires or the wheels.

Over-inflation

This type of wear usually results from consistent under-inflation. When a tire is under-inflated, there is too much contact with the road by the outer treads, which wear prematurely. When this type of wear occurs, and the tire pressure is known to be consistently correct, a bent or worn steering component or the need for wheel alignment could be indicated.

Under-inflation

Feathering is a condition when the edge of each tread rib develops a slightly rounded edge on one side and a sharp edge on the other. By running your hand over the tire, you can usually feel the sharper edges before you'll be able to see them. The most common causes of feathering are incorrect toe-in setting or deteriorated bushings in the front suspension.

Feathering

When an inner or outer rib wears faster than the rest of the tire, the need for wheel alignment is indicated. There is excessive camber in the front suspension, causing the wheel to lean too much putting excessive load on one side of the tire. Misalignment could also be due to sagging springs, worn ball joints, or worn control arm bushings. Be sure the vehicle is loaded the way it's normally driven when you have the wheels aligned.

One side wear

Cups or scalloped dips appearing around the edge of the tread almost always indicate worn (sometimes bent) suspension parts. Adjustment of wheel alignment alone will seldom cure the problem. Any worn component that connects the wheel to the suspension can cause this type of wear. Occasionally, wheels that are out of balance will wear like this, but wheel imbalance usually shows up as bald spots between the outside edges and center of the tread.

Cupping

Second-rib wear is usually found only in radial tires, and appears where the steel belts end in relation to the tread. It can be kept to a minimum by paying careful attention to tire pressure and frequently rotating the tires. This is often considered normal wear but excessive amounts indicate that the tires are too wide for the wheels.

Second-rib wear

Troubleshooting Disc Brake Problems

Condition	Possible Cause
Noise—groan—brake noise emanating when slowly releasing brakes (creep-groan)	Not detrimental to function of disc brakes—no corrective action required. (This noise may be eliminated by slightly increasing or decreasing brake pedal efforts.)
Rattle—brake noise or rattle emanating at low speeds on rough roads, (front wheels only).	1. Shoe anti-rattle spring missing or not properly positioned. 2. Excessive clearance between shoe and caliper. 3. Soft or broken caliper seals. 4. Deformed or misaligned disc. 5. Loose caliper.
Scraping	1. Mounting bolts too long. 2. Loose wheel bearings. 3. Bent, loose, or misaligned splash shield.
Front brakes heat up during driving and fail to release	1. Operator riding brake pedal. 2. Stop light switch improperly adjusted. 3. Sticking pedal linkage. 4. Frozen or seized piston. 5. Residual pressure valve in master cylinder. 6. Power brake malfunction. 7. Proportioning valve malfunction.
Leaky brake caliper	1. Damaged or worn caliper piston seal. 2. Scores or corrosion on surface of cylinder bore.
Grabbing or uneven brake action—Brakes pull to one side	1. Causes listed under "Brakes Pull". 2. Power brake malfunction. 3. Low fluid level in master cylinder. 4. Air in hydraulic system. 5. Brake fluid, oil or grease on linings. 6. Unmatched linings. 7. Distorted brake pads. 8. Frozen or seized pistons. 9. Incorrect tire pressure. 10. Front end out of alignment. 11. Broken rear spring. 12. Brake caliper pistons sticking. 13. Restricted hose or line. 14. Caliper not in proper alignment to braking disc. 15. Stuck or malfunctioning metering valve. 16. Soft or broken caliper seals. 17. Loose caliper.
Brake pedal can be depressed without braking effect	1. Air in hydraulic system or improper bleeding procedure. 2. Leak past primary cup in master cylinder. 3. Leak in system. 4. Rear brakes out of adjustment. 5. Bleeder screw open.
Excessive pedal travel	1. Air, leak, or insufficient fluid in system or caliper. 2. Warped or excessively tapered shoe and lining assembly. 3. Excessive disc runout. 4. Rear brake adjustment required. 5. Loose wheel bearing adjustment. 6. Damaged caliper piston seal. 7. Improper brake fluid (boil). 8. Power brake malfunction. 9. Weak or soft hoses.

Troubleshooting Disc Brake Problems (cont.)

Condition	Possible Cause
Brake roughness or chatter (pedal pumping)	1. Excessive thickness variation of braking disc. 2. Excessive lateral runout of braking disc. 3. Rear brake drums out-of-round. 4. Excessive front bearing clearance.
Excessive pedal effort	1. Brake fluid, oil or grease on linings. 2. Incorrect lining. 3. Frozen or seized pistons. 4. Power brake malfunction. 5. Kinked or collapsed hose or line. 6. Stuck metering valve. 7. Scored caliper or master cylinder bore. 8. Seized caliper pistons.
Brake pedal fades (pedal travel increases with foot on brake)	1. Rough master cylinder or caliper bore. 2. Loose or broken hydraulic lines/connections. 3. Air in hydraulic system. 4. Fluid level low. 5. Weak or soft hoses. 6. Inferior quality brake shoes or fluid. 7. Worn master cylinder piston cups or seals.

Troubleshooting Drum Brakes

Condition	Possible Cause
Pedal goes to floor	1. Fluid low in reservoir. 2. Air in hydraulic system. 3. Improperly adjusted brake. 4. Leaking wheel cylinders. 5. Loose or broken brake lines. 6. Leaking or worn master cylinder. 7. Excessively worn brake lining.
Spongy brake pedal	1. Air in hydraulic system. 2. Improper brake fluid (low boiling point). 3. Excessively worn or cracked brake drums. 4. Broken pedal pivot bushing.
Brakes pulling	1. Contaminated lining. 2. Front end out of alignment. 3. Incorrect brake adjustment. 4. Unmatched brake lining. 5. Brake drums out of round. 6. Brake shoes distorted. 7. Restricted brake hose or line. 8. Broken rear spring. 9. Worn brake linings. 10. Uneven lining wear. 11. Glazed brake lining. 12. Excessive brake lining dust. 13. Heat spotted brake drums. 14. Weak brake return springs. 15. Faulty automatic adjusters. 16. Low or incorrect tire pressure.

Condition	Possible Cause
Squealing brakes	1. Glazed brake lining. 2. Saturated brake lining. 3. Weak or broken brake shoe retaining spring. 4. Broken or weak brake shoe return spring. 5. Incorrect brake lining. 6. Distorted brake shoes. 7. Bent support plate. 8. Dust in brakes or scored brake drums. 9. Linings worn below limit. 10. Uneven brake lining wear. 11. Heat spotted brake drums.
Chirping brakes	1. Out of round drum or eccentric axle flange pilot.
Dragging brakes	1. Incorrect wheel or parking brake adjustment. 2. Parking brakes engaged or improperly adjusted. 3. Weak or broken brake shoe return spring. 4. Brake pedal binding. 5. Master cylinder cup sticking. 6. Obstructed master cylinder relief port. 7. Saturated brake lining. 8. Bent or out of round brake drum. 9. Contaminated or improper brake fluid. 10. Sticking wheel cylinder pistons. 11. Driver riding brake pedal. 12. Defective proportioning valve. 13. Insufficient brake shoe lubricant.
Hard pedal	1. Brake booster inoperative. 2. Incorrect brake lining. 3. Restricted brake line or hose. 4. Frozen brake pedal linkage. 5. Stuck wheel cylinder. 6. Binding pedal linkage. 7. Faulty proportioning valve.
Wheel locks	1. Contaminated brake lining. 2. Loose or torn brake lining. 3. Wheel cylinder cups sticking. 4. Incorrect wheel bearing adjustment. 5. Faulty proportioning valve.
Brakes fade (high speed)	1. Incorrect lining. 2. Overheated brake drums. 3. Incorrect brake fluid (low boiling temperature). 4. Saturated brake lining. 5. Leak in hydraulic system. 6. Faulty automatic adjusters.
Pedal pulsates	1. Bent or out of round brake drum.
Brake chatter and shoe knock	1. Out of round brake drum. 2. Loose support plate. 3. Bent support plate. 4. Distorted brake shoes. 5. Machine grooves in contact face of brake drum (Shoe Knock). 6. Contaminated brake lining. 7. Missing or loose components. 8. Incorrect lining material. 9. Out-of-round brake drums. 10. Heat spotted or scored brake drums. 11. Out-of-balance wheels.

Troubleshooting Drum Brakes (cont.)

Condition	Possible Cause
Brakes do not self adjust	1. Adjuster screw frozen in thread. 2. Adjuster screw corroded at thrust washer. 3. Adjuster lever does not engage star wheel. 4. Adjuster installed on wrong wheel.
Brake light glows	1. Leak in the hydraulic system. 2. Air in the system. 3. Improperly adjusted master cylinder pushrod. 4. Uneven lining wear. 5. Failure to center combination valve or proportioning valve.

Appendix

General Conversion Table

Multiply by	To convert	To	
2.54	Inches	Centimeters	.3937
30.48	Feet	Centimeters	.0328
.914	Yards	Meters	1.094
1.609	Miles	Kilometers	.621
6.45	Square inches	Square cm.	.155
.836	Square yards	Square meters	1.196
16.39	Cubic inches	Cubic cm.	.061
28.3	Cubic feet	Liters	.0353
.4536	Pounds	Kilograms	2.2045
3.785	Gallons	Liters	.264
.068	Lbs./sq. in. (psi)	Atmospheres	14.7
.138	Foot pounds	Kg. m.	7.23
1.014	H.P. (DIN)	H.P. (SAE)	.9861
—	To obtain	From	Multiply by

Note: 1 cm. equals 10 mm.; 1 mm. equals .0394".

Conversion—Common Fractions to Decimals and Millimeters

Common Fractions	Decimal Fractions	Millimeters (approx.)	Common Fractions	Decimal Fractions	Millimeters (approx.)	Common Fractions	Decimal Fractions	Millimeters (approx.)
1/128	.008	0.20	11/32	.344	8.73	43/64	.672	17.07
1/64	.016	0.40	23/64	.359	9.13	11/16	.688	17.46
1/32	.031	0.79	3/8	.375	9.53	45/64	.703	17.86
3/64	.047	1.19	25/64	.391	9.92	23/32	.719	18.26
1/16	.063	1.59	13/32	.406	10.32	47/64	.734	18.65
5/64	.078	1.98	27/64	.422	10.72	3/4	.750	19.05
3/32	.094	2.38	7/16	.438	11.11	49/64	.766	19.45
7/64	.109	2.78	29/64	.453	11.51	25/32	.781	19.84
1/8	.125	3.18	15/32	.469	11.91	51/64	.797	20.24
9/64	.141	3.57	31/64	.484	12.30	13/16	.813	20.64
5/32	.156	3.97	1/2	.500	12.70	53/64	.828	21.03
11/64	.172	4.37	33/64	.516	13.10	27/32	.844	21.43
3/16	.188	4.76	17/32	.531	13.49	55/64	.859	21.83
13/64	.203	5.16	35/64	.547	13.89	7/8	.875	22.23
7/32	.219	5.56	9/16	.563	14.29	57/64	.891	22.62
15/64	.234	5.95	37/64	.578	14.68	29/32	.906	23.02
1/4	.250	6.35	19/32	.594	15.08	59/64	.922	23.42
17/64	.266	6.75	39/64	.609	15.48	15/16	.938	23.81
9/32	.281	7.14	5/8	.625	15.88	61/64	.953	24.21
19/64	.297	7.54	41/64	.641	16.27	31/32	.969	24.61
5/16	.313	7.94	21/32	.656	16.67	63/64	.984	25.00
21/64	.328	8.33						

Conversion—Millimeters to Decimal Inches

mm	*inches*	*mm*	*inches*	*mm*	*inches*	*mm*	*inches*	*mm*	*inches*
1	.039 370	31	1.220 470	61	2.401 570	91	3.582 670	210	8.267 700
2	.078 740	32	1.259 840	62	2.440 940	92	3.622 040	220	8.661 400
3	.118 110	33	1.299 210	63	2.480 310	93	3.661 410	230	9.055 100
4	.157 480	34	1.338 580	64	2.519 680	94	3.700 780	240	9.448 800
5	.196 850	35	1.377 949	65	2.559 050	95	3.740 150	250	9.842 500
6	.236 220	36	1.417 319	66	2.598 420	96	3.779 520	260	10.236 200
7	.275 590	37	1.456 689	67	2.637 790	97	3.818 890	270	10.629 900
8	.314 960	38	1.496 050	68	2.677 160	98	3.858 260	280	11.032 600
9	.354 330	39	1.535 430	69	2.716 530	99	3.897 630	290	11.417 300
10	.393 700	40	1.574 800	70	2.755 900	100	3.937 000	300	11.811 000
11	.433 070	41	1.614 170	71	2.795 270	105	4.133 848	310	12.204 700
12	.472 440	42	1.653 540	72	2.834 640	110	4.330 700	320	12.598 400
13	.511 810	43	1.692 910	73	2.874 010	115	4.527 550	330	12.992 100
14	.551 180	44	1.732 280	74	2.913 380	120	4.724 400	340	13.385 800
15	.590 550	45	1.771 650	75	2.952 750	125	4.921 250	350	13.779 500
16	.629 920	46	1.811 020	76	2.992 120	130	5.118 100	360	14.173 200
17	.669 290	47	1.850 390	77	3.031 490	135	5.314 950	370	14.566 900
18	.708 660	48	1.889 760	78	3.070 860	140	5.511 800	380	14.960 600
19	.748 030	49	1.929 130	79	3.110 230	145	5.708 650	390	15.354 300
20	.787 400	50	1.968 500	80	3.149 600	150	5.905 500	400	15.748 000
21	.826 770	51	2.007 870	81	3.188 970	155	6.102 350	500	19.685 000
22	.866 140	52	2.047 240	82	3.228 340	160	6.299 200	600	23.622 000
23	.905 510	53	2.086 610	83	3.267 710	165	6.496 050	700	27.559 000
24	.944 880	54	2.125 980	84	3.307 080	170	6.692 900	800	31.496 000
25	.984 250	55	2.165 350	85	3.346 450	175	6.889 750	900	35.433 000
26	1.023 620	56	2.204 720	86	3.385 820	180	7.086 600	1000	39.370 000
27	1.062 990	57	2.244 090	87	3.425 190	185	7.283 450	2000	78.740 000
28	1.102 360	58	2.283 460	88	3.464 560	190	7.480 300	3000	118.110 000
29	1.141 730	59	2.322 830	89	3.503 903	195	7.677 150	4000	157.480 000
30	1.181 100	60	2.362 200	90	3.543 300	200	7.874 000	5000	196.850 000

To change decimal millimeters to decimal inches, position the decimal point where desired on either side of the millimeter measurement shown and reset the inches decimal by the same number of digits in the same direction. For example, to convert 0.001 mm to decimal inches, reset the decimal behind the 1 mm (shown on the chart) to 0.001; change the decimal inch equivalent (0.039″ shown) to 0.000039″.

Tap Drill Sizes

National Fine or S.A.E.

Screw & Tap Size	*Threads Per Inch*	*Use Drill Number*
No. 5	44	37
No. 6	40	33
No. 8	36	29
No. 10	32	21
No. 12	28	15
1/4	28	3
5/16	24	1
3/8	24	Q
7/16	20	W
1/2	20	29/64
9/16	18	33/64
5/8	18	37/64
3/4	16	11/16
7/8	14	13/16
1 1/8	12	1 3/64
1 1/4	12	1 11/64
1 1/2	12	1 27/64

Tap Drill Sizes

National Coarse or U.S.S.

Screw & Tap Size	*Threads Per Inch*	*Use Drill Number*
No. 5	40	39
No. 6	32	36
No. 8	32	29
No. 10	24	25
No. 12	24	17
1/4	20	8
5/16	18	F
3/8	16	5/16
7/16	14	U
1/2	13	27/64
9/16	12	31/64
5/8	11	17/32
3/4	10	21/32
7/8	9	49/64
1	8	7/8
1 1/8	7	63/64
1 1/4	7	1 7/64
1 1/2	6	1 11/32

Decimal Equivalent Size of the Number Drills

Drill No.	Decimal Equivalent	Drill No.	Decimal Equivalent	Drill No.	Decimal Equivalent
80	.0135	53	.0595	26	.1470
79	.0145	52	.0635	25	.1495
78	.0160	51	.0670	24	.1520
77	.0180	50	.0700	23	.1540
76	.0200	49	.0730	22	.1570
75	.0210	48	.0760	21	.1590
74	.0225	47	.0785	20	.1610
73	.0240	46	.0810	19	.1660
72	.0250	45	.0820	18	.1695
71	.0260	44	.0860	17	.1730
70	.0280	43	.0890	16	.1770
69	.0292	42	.0935	15	.1800
68	.0310	41	.0960	14	.1820
67	.0320	40	.0980	13	.1850
66	.0330	39	.0995	12	.1890
65	.0350	38	.1015	11	.1910
64	.0360	37	.1040	10	.1935
63	.0370	36	.1065	9	.1960
62	.0380	35	.1100	8	.1990
61	.0390	34	.1110	7	.2010
60	.0400	33	.1130	6	.2040
59	.0410	32	.1160	5	.2055
58	.0420	31	.1200	4	.2090
57	.0430	30	.1285	3	.2130
56	.0465	29	.1360	2	.2210
55	.0520	28	.1405	1	.2280
54	.0550	27	.1440		

Decimal Equivalent Size of the Letter Drills

Letter Drill	Decimal Equivalent	Letter Drill	Decimal Equivalent	Letter Drill	Decimal Equivalent
A	.234	J	.277	S	.348
B	.238	K	.281	T	.358
C	.242	L	.290	U	.368
D	.246	M	.295	V	.377
E	.250	N	.302	W	.386
F	.257	O	.316	X	.397
G	.261	P	.323	Y	.404
H	.266	Q	.332	Z	.413
I	.272	R	.339		

Anti-Freeze Chart

Temperatures Shown in Degrees Fahrenheit +32 is Freezing

Cooling System Capacity Quarts	Quarts of ETHYLENE GLYCOL Needed for Protection to Temperatures Shown Below													
	1	2	3	4	5	6	7	8	9	10	11	12	13	14
10	+24°	+16°	+ 4°	−12°	−34°	−62°								
11	+25	+18	+ 8	− 6	−23	−47								
12	+26	+19	+10	0	−15	−34	−57°							
13	+27	+21	+13	+ 3	− 9	−25	−45							
14			+15	+ 6	− 5	−18	−34							
15			+16	+ 8	0	−12	−26							
16		+17	+10	+ 2	− 8	−19	−34	−52°						
17		+18	+12	+ 5	− 4	−14	−27	−42						
18		+19	+14	+ 7	0	−10	−21	−34	−50°					
19		+20	+15	+ 9	+ 2	− 7	−16	−28	−42					
20			+16	+10	+ 4	− 3	−12	−22	−34	−48°				
21			+17	+12	+ 6	0	− 9	−17	−28	−41				
22			+18	+13	+ 8	+ 2	− 6	−14	−23	−34	−47°			
23			+19	+14	+ 9	+ 4	− 3	−10	−19	−29	−40			
24			+19	+15	+10	+ 5	0	− 8	−15	−23	−34	−46°		
25			+20	+16	+12	+ 7	+ 1	− 5	−12	−20	−29	−40	−50°	
26					+17	+13	+ 8	+ 3	− 3	− 9	−16	−25	−34	−44
27					+18	+14	+ 9	+ 5	− 1	− 7	−13	−21	−29	−39
28					+18	+15	+10	+ 6	+ 1	− 5	−11	−18	−25	−34
29					+19	+16	+12	+ 7	+ 2	− 3	− 8	−15	−22	−29
30					+20	+17	+13	+ 8	+ 4	− 1	− 6	−12	−18	−25

For capacities over 30 quarts divide true capacity by 3. Find quarts Anti-Freeze for the ⅓ and multiply by 3 for quarts to add.

For capacities under 10 quarts multiply true capacity by 3. Find quarts Anti-Freeze for the tripled volume and divide by 3 for quarts to add.

To Increase the Freezing Protection of Anti-Freeze Solutions Already Installed

Cooling System Capacity Quarts	Number of Quarts of ETHYLENE GLYCOL Anti-Freeze Required to Increase Protection													
	From +20° F. to					From +10° F. to					From 0° F. to			
	0°	−10°	−20°	−30°	−40°	0°	−10°	−20°	−30°	−40°	−10°	−20°	−30°	−40°
10	1¾	2¼	3	3½	3¾	¾	1½	2¼	2¾	3¼	¾	1½	2	2½
12	2	2¾	3½	4	4½	1	1¾	2½	3¼	3¾	1	1¾	2½	3¼
14	2¼	3¼	4	4¾	5½	1¼	2	3	3¾	4½	1	2	3	3½
16	2½	3½	4½	5¼	6	1¼	2½	3½	4¼	5¼	1¼	2¼	3¼	4
18	3	4	5	6	7	1½	2¾	4	5	5¾	1½	2½	3¾	4¾
20	3¼	4½	5¾	6¾	7½	1¾	3	4¼	5½	6½	1½	2¾	4¼	5¼
22	3½	5	6¼	7¼	8¼	1¾	3¼	4¾	6	7¼	1¾	3¼	4½	5½
24	4	5½	7	8	9	2	3½	5	6½	7½	1¾	3½	5	6
26	4¼	6	7½	8¾	10	2	4	5½	7	8¼	2	3¾	5½	6¾
28	4½	6¼	8	9½	10½	2¼	4¼	6	7½	9	2	4	5¾	7¼
30	5	6¾	8½	10	11½	2½	4½	6½	8	9½	2¼	4¼	6¼	7¾

Test radiator solution with proper hydrometer. Determine from the table the number of quarts of solution to be drawn off from a full cooling system and replace with undiluted anti-freeze, to give the desired increased protection. For example, to increase protection of a 22-quart cooling system containing Ethylene Glycol (permanent type) anti-freeze, from +20° F. to −20° F. will require the replacement of 6¼ quarts of solution with undiluted anti-freeze.

Index

A

Air cleaner, 4
Air conditioning, 17
Alternator, 68
Antifreeze, 315
Automatic transmission
    Adjustment, 203
    Removal and Installation, 206
Axle shaft bearings and seals, 216

B

Battery
    Jump starting, 27
    Maintenance, 11, 73
Belt tension adjustment
Body, 255
Brakes
    Adjustment, 236
    Bleeding, 241
    Caliper, 243
    Fluid level, 20
    Fluid recommendations, 20
        Disc, 242
        Drum, 246
    Master cylinder, 238
    Parking brake, 254
    Pressure differential valve, 241

C

Camber, 226
Camshaft and bearings, 103
Capacities, 36
Carburetor
    Adjustment, 53, 156-164
    Overhaul, 147
    Replacement, 147
Caster, 226
Charging system, 68
Chassis lubrication, 30
Circuit breakers, 193
Clutch
    Adjustment, 202
    Replacement, 201
Condenser, 47
Connecting rod and bearings, 104
Cooling system, 16
Crankcase ventilation (PCV), 8
Crankshaft, 120
Cylinder head
    Reconditioning, 113
    Removal and installation, 91-95
    Torque sequence, 92-95

D

Distributor
    Removal and installation, 63
    Breaker points, 47

Doors, 255
Drag link, 224
Drive axle, 213
Driveshaft, 210
Dwell angle, 48
Dwell meter, 48

E

Electrical
    Chassis, 176
    Engine, 57
Electronic ignition, 58
Emission controls, 132
Engine
    Camshaft, 103
    Cylinder head torque sequence, 92-95
    Design, 73
    Exhaust manifold, 99
    Front cover, 101
    Identification, 11
    Intake manifold, 96
    Oil recommendations, 28
    Pistons and rings, 124
    Rebuilding, 110
    Removal and installation, 84
    Rocker arm (or shaft), 95, 119
    Specifications, 75
    Timing chain, 102
    Timing gears, 102
    Tune-up
Evaporative canister, 141
Exhaust manifold, 99

F

Firing order, 46
Fluid level checks
    Battery, 11
    Coolant, 20
    Engine oil, 19
    Master cylinder, 20
    Power steering pump, 21
    Rear axle, 20
    Steering gear, 20
    Transmission, 19
Fluid recommendations, 28
Front suspension
    King pins, 223
    Spindles, 223
    Springs, 218
    Wheel alignment, 226
Front wheel bearing, 21
Fuel pump, 26, 145
Fuel system, 145
Fuses and flashers, 192
Fusible links, 193